Absolute Beginner's Guide to

Creating
Web Pages

Todd Stauffer

201 West 103rd Street,
Indianapolis, Indiana 46290

Absolute Beginner's Guide to Creating Web Pages

International Standard Book Number: 0-7897-2732-3

Library of Congress Catalog Card Number: 2002100458

Printed in the United States of America

First Printing: April 2002

04 04 03 02   4 3 2 1

Trademarks

Warning and Disclaimer

Associate Publisher
Dean Miller

Acquisitions Editor
Dean Miller

Development Editor
Sean Medlock

Managing Editor
Thomas Hayes

Project Editor
Tricia Liebig

Copy Editors
Candice Hightower
Sossity Smith

Indexer
Mandie Frank

Proofreader
Juli Cook

Technical Editor
Lindy Humphreys

Team Coordinator
Cindy Teeters

Interior Designer
Kevin Spear

Cover Designer
Trina Wurst

Page Layout
Brad Lenser

Contents at a Glance

Table of Contents

About the Author

Todd Stauffer is the author or co-author of more than 25 computing books, including *HTML Web Publishing 6-in-1*, *HTML by Example* with Ann Navarro, and *Creating Your Own AOL Web Page* with Andy Shafran. Stauffer has written for a number of magazines, including *Publish* magazine, *Silicon Alley Reporter*, *Working Woman*, and *MacAddict*.

Todd has worked as an advertising writer, technical writer, and magazine editor, all in consumer-oriented computing. Outside of computing, he's also a humor columnist and a travel/automotive writer. You can reach him via his Web site, at `http://www.mac-upgrade.com`.

Acknowledgments

I'd like to thank Todd Green and Dean Miller, who gave me the opportunity to write this book, helped develop the outline, managed submissions, and acted as understanding taskmasters throughout the process. Thanks also to Tricia Liebig, Sean Medlock, and Lindy Humphreys for their hard work on the manuscript.

Sections of this book are updated and adapted from my earlier work, *HTML Web Publishing 6-in-1*, published in 1997 by Que. I'd like to thank the editorial team who worked on that book, including Jane Brownlow, Mark Cierzniak, Kate Givens, and Henry Wolin. The material from that book that survives in this one (a lot has changed in Web publishing, but not everything) was developed and managed by those great folks.

As always, thanks to Neil Salkind and the entire staff of the Studio B agency for keeping me clothed and fed and to Donna Ladd for keeping me going strong.

Tell Us What You Think!

As the reader of this book, *you* are our most important critic and commentator. We value your opinion and want to know what we're doing right, what we could do better, what areas you'd like to see us publish in, and any other words of wisdom you're willing to pass our way.

As an Associate Publisher for Que, I welcome your comments. You can fax, e-mail, or write me directly to let me know what you did or didn't like about this book—as well as what we can do to make our books stronger.

Please note that I cannot help you with technical problems related to the topic of this book, and that due to the high volume of mail I receive, I might not be able to reply to every message.

When you write, please be sure to include this book's title and author as well as your name and phone or fax number. I will carefully review your comments and share them with the author and editors who worked on the book.

Fax: 317-581-4666

E-mail: feedback@quepublishing.com

Mail: Associate Publisher
           Que Publishing
           201 West 103rd Street
           Indianapolis, IN 46290 USA

INTRODUCTION

The Internet has come a long way. In fact, even if you're only a few months past 10 years old, you've seen the Internet and the World Wide Web grow up to affect nearly every aspect of global culture—education, commerce, politics, and entertainment. It's been a fast change and one that affects most of us either personally, professionally or both.

One of the results has been the need for Web publishing skills for many knowledge workers, educators, and professionals. Hobbyists, club members, and parents can benefit as well from knowing a little something about Web publishing. In fact, Web publishing may one day be the "typing" of the future—nearly anyone with a secondary education will need a firm grasp on the basics.

For now, it's an important bullet point on many résumés as well as the key to many plum assignments, both paid and unpaid. If you're ready to put together and manage your own Web site, then it's time to get a book on the subject and start learning. The *Absolute Beginner's Guide to Creating a Web Page* is the perfect place to start.

Is This the Book for You?

You can divide the study of Web publishing into two approaches—those that focus on the underlying *code-level* technologies and those that teach the broad strokes of Web publishing via graphical Web editors. This book is a friendly guide to the first of these approaches, showing you how to dig into the HTML and XHTML standards to build Web pages, manage Web sites, and augment them with further levels of complexity—style sheets and scripting among them. At the end of this book, you'll understand many of the more complex issues involved in Web publishing, even if you don't have a single Web page to your name.

Let me stress, however, that this book is not for everyone. The *Absolute Beginner's Guide to Creating a Web Page* is designed to take you from basic computer literacy—you understand how to create files and type in Windows, the Macintosh OS, or a variant of Unix—and help you build, manage, and maintain your first Web pages and Web sites. You'll do this by building, chapter by chapter, an understanding of the authoring codes (for creating Web pages), the graphical and multimedia technologies, and eventually the scripting and programming basics necessary for a full interactive and interesting Web site.

If you're interested in Web publishing skills for use in your company, organization, or education, you should find this book a great place to start. All the principles are outlined, terms are defined, and fundamentals are explained. And that's done without the "cutesy" approach that some other beginner series can devolve into.

But I also want to be honest about the approach. If your goal is a "Web Page in a day," this book isn't for you. Likewise, if you plan to begin your foray into Web publishing using a particular graphical tool, such as Macromedia Dreamweaver, I'd suggest a book that specifically discusses that tool.

I believe that the approach in the *Absolute Beginner's Guide to Creating a Web Page* is the best one, because it's still very important to understand the underlying code of today's Web pages to truly soak up a new skill. Although graphical tools can help (and, in fact, I'll cover a few of them in Chapter 20, "Graphical Editors"), anyone who wants to really understand Web pages and put together entire Web sites should consider the code-level approach that is found in these pages. Fortunately, learning XHTML, style sheets, JavaScript, and even Dynamic HTML really isn't all that tough—in my opinion, a pricey Web editor can sometimes just get in your way!

How This Book Is Organized

This book is very much a tutorial, particularly in the first 19 chapters. It moves linearly from an introduction and overview of the basic Web publishing concepts, through the fundamentals of creating a Web page, and on to more complex topics. Here's a breakdown:

Part I: Creating Web Pages—In this first section you're introduced to the concepts and terms you'll see throughout the book, including the Internet, the Web, HTML, XHTML, style sheets, JavaScript, and many more. Chapter 2, "A Crash-Course in Web Design," offers a primer on Web design fundamentals and Chapter 3, "What You Need to Get Started," covers the tools you'll need before setting out on your Web authoring adventure (text editors and applications to manipulate graphics). This section ends in Chapter 4, "Creating Your First Page," with the creation of a sample Web page and a template for future pages.

Part II: Design and Conquer—In this second section you learn most of the basics of creating Web pages using XHTML. You begin with basic text and paragraph formatting, including headings, text styles, and special types of paragraph blocks, including bulleted and numbered lists. Chapter 6, "Visual Stimulus—Adding Graphics," introduces you to Web images, including how to add them to pages and what file formats you can use. Chapter 7, "Building Hypertext Links," is all about creating hyperlinks—the technology at the heart of the Web—including links that point to external Web pages and those that point to parts of the current document. Chapter 8, "Basics Tables," introduces you to XHTML tables, which can be used, as discussed in Chapter 9, "Advanced Table Elements and Table Design," for formatting entire pages. Chapter 10, "Get Splashy: Style Sheets, Fonts, and Special Characters," discusses style sheets: the "modern" way to change the appearance of text, alter margins, and otherwise control the look of your Web pages. Chapter 11, "Advanced Web Images and Imagemaps," finishes out the section with an in-depth look at Web images, including how to optimize them for use in your pages.

Part III: Building Your Site—Part III moves on to some of the Web-building technologies that can be applied to an entire Web site—a collection of individual pages that work together. Chapter 12, "Creating Sites with HTML Frames," begins with XHTML Frames, which enable you to split a Web browser window into different frames so that more than one Web page can be displayed at once. Frames are a great way to quickly create an "interface" for viewing many different Web documents. Chapter 13, "Adding Multimedia and Java Content," discusses multimedia content—movies, animations, and audio—along with Java technology, which actually enables you to place small computer programs on a Web page with which your users can interact. Chapter 14, "Site-Wide Styles: Design, Accessibility, and Internationalization," finishes this section with a look at how you can use the style sheet specifications to select and alter the look of all the documents that comprise your Web site.

Part IV: Interacting with Your Users—In this section you learn some of the technologies you can use on the Web to receive input from your users and respond to that input. Chapter 15, "Adding HTML Forms," begins with a primer on XHTML forms, which enable you to add entry boxes, checkboxes, menus, and other controls to your Web documents. Chapter 16, "CGIs and Data Gathering," introduces you to CGI programming, which is often used in conjunction with XHTML forms to respond to user input via forms. Chapter 17, "Introduction to JavaScript," and Chapter 18, "JavaScript and User Input," focus on JavaScript, a popular scripting language that you can use to automate portions of your Web page. Chapter 19, "Adding Dynamic HTML," covers some topics that are often called "dynamic HTML" or DHTML, because they combine JavaScript and style sheets to make the appearance of Web pages seem to change in response to choices that the user makes.

Part V: Web Publishing Tools—The last part of the book focuses on software and services you can use to extend your Web publishing experience. Chapter 20, "Graphical Editors," covers some popular graphical Web-authoring packages, such as Macromedia Dreamweaver and Microsoft FrontPage. Chapter 21, "Forums, Chats, and Other Add-Ons," focuses on enhancements for your Web server—specifically, scripts and other programs you can use to add page counters, interactive forums, and chat rooms. Chapter 22, "Web Publishing Services," ends with a look at some different Web server solutions, including free Web servers and companies that offer e-commerce solutions.

In addition to these sections, this book also includes an appendix that features a quick reference to many of the elements in the XHTML specification and the CSS style sheet standards.

Conventions Used in This Book

As you're reading you'll notice that a few different elements are used within the body of the text to break things up and to offer some additional information. Those items include

Notes are designed to define terms or give you additional important or interesting information about a particular topic. You should read the notes you come across, as they generally add something important to the text.

A tip is usually a suggestion or shortcut that's along the same lines as the body text, but a little off topic. If you find the tip useful, you can make use of it in your Web authoring; otherwise, it should be safe to ignore.

You'll also find sidebars in some chapters that go off on an interesting tangent, generally to simply offer more information than you really *need* on a given topic. If you want to ignore sidebars, you should be able to without trouble.

As you read the text, you'll come across some typographic conventions as well. When certain elements and attributes, particularly those that are special parts of the XHTML specification, are mentioned in the text, they'll appear in a `different font`, from the regular body text. Items that you're meant to type, on the other hand, will often appear in `bold`. And code listings that require more than one line will be:

```
separated from the text.
And will often appear in small chunks between the paragraphs
that explain that code.
```

For More Information

To ask a question, report an error, or for more information on the this book, visit `http://www.mac-upgrade.com/abgcwp/` on the Web. There you'll find updates from me, Q&As (if I receive any questions), and links to my e-mail address and online forums for asking questions or making comments.

Thank you for considering this book and I wish you the best of luck—and skill—in your Web publishing projects!

CREATING WEB PAGES

FUNDAMENTALS OF WEB PUBLISHING

The Internet has quickly become so completely integrated into our lives that there's no assessing the full nature of its value. Along with e-mail and other technologies, the World Wide Web is a huge part of the Internet phenomenon. However, those Web pages don't get there by themselves. Knowing something about Web publishing is important for most anyone, particularly those of us with something to create, discuss, share, or sell. If you've ever thought that you'd like to create a Web page, build a Web site, or just know a little something about how this all works, you're ready to learn more about Web publishing.

This chapter discusses the following:

- A brief history of the Internet and the World Wide Web
- The basics of how the Web works, including the protocols and acronyms you see throughout this book
- The present and future of HTML and XHTML, including what exactly you need to learn
- The fact that HTML isn't as difficult as programming and, in fact, is surprisingly easy to learn
- Although HTML isn't programming, Web publishing does offer other levels of complexity, which are discussed here and in later sections of this book

A Two-Minute History of the Internet

The Internet began as the ARPANet, a computer networking project funded by the U.S. government's Advanced Research Projects Agency in the late 1960s to create a computer network that could enable continued communications during war or natural disasters. What was most original about the ARPANet was the approach it took—the network was decentralized, enabling packets of data to find their way from node to node to reach a destination. This meant that data could take more than one path to its final destination, making the network more resistant to problems.

In the early 1980s, TCP/IP (Transmission Control Protocol/Internet Protocol) was created and became the dominant system for swapping packets on the ARPANet. At about this same time, it became clear that TCP/IP would be used to interconnect various other smaller networks of computers, making it possible to share data on a national or even global scale. The term "Internet" was first used to suggest this larger sort of network.

In late 1989, the ARPANet project was disbanded, but by that point universities and scientific organizations had taken over the Internet. In the early 1990s, corporations began to use the Internet for e-mail communication, but a ban on commercial traffic by the National Science Foundation kept the Internet from being a medium for commerce. That ban was lifted in 1991, making the Internet more widely available to individuals, corporations, and institutions outside the government and higher learning, as well as for totally commercial uses such as direct sales and advertising.

In 1991, Tim Berners-Lee of the CERN, in Switzerland, used a NeXt computer to cobble together the code for what would soon become the World Wide Web. By 1993, Mosaic, a graphic Web browser application, had been released. In 1994, Marc Andreesen, one of the original programmers of Mosaic at the University of Illinois National Center for Supercomputing Applications, moved to California and started the Netscape Corporation with venture capitalist and businessman Jim Clark.

Soon after releasing commercial versions of its Web browser for personal computers, Netscape introduced the Netscape Commerce Server. This was a Web server application that not only enabled an organization to post Web sites and send Web pages to browsers running on personal computers, but also to accept credit card numbers over *secure* connections, where the data that's transferred is encrypted so that it can't be read by anyone but the sender and receiver. Throughout the 1990s, the Internet saw intense growth both as a communications medium and as a mechanism for commerce.

Many upgrades and millions of users later, the Internet and the World Wide Web remain an important part of the communications infrastructure for most of the world. The Internet and the Web are increasingly available via non-PC tools such as mobile phones and handheld computers. Television, radio, and print media often refer consumers to the Internet for more information. In times of crisis, the Internet can be the first method by which you reach someone or learn new information.

However, as important as the Internet is to huge governments and global corporations, it's still accessible to the average person, enabling you to create your own Web sites and participate whether your goal is commercial, educational, or more informal. All it takes is a little knowledge and some basic computing tools. Let's start with the knowledge.

It's easy to confuse the Internet and the Web, but they *are* different. The Internet is the global network of wires, servers, and protocols that enables millions of computers to communicate with one another. The Web is a *service* that's made available over the Internet. It's just one means of accessing information and communicating via the Internet, along with e-mail, Internet chat, file transfer, and others.

How the Web Works

The World Wide Web isn't a particular place on the Internet, nor is it a particular computer or something that you can "log into." Instead, the best way to describe the Web is as a *service* on the Internet. Using certain protocols, computers that are designated as *Web server* computers—because they're connected to the Internet and run Web server software—can respond to requests from *client* computers running *Web browser* software.

All a computer needs to be a *Web server* is an Internet connection and Web server software. In fact, such software is built into most modern operating systems—Windows, the Mac OS, and Unix all offer Web servers, sometimes as simpler "Web Sharing" solutions. The Web server sits on the Internet, waiting for *Web browser* applications (Netscape, Internet Explorer, and their ilk) to contact them and ask for documents. The server then responds by sending the document to the address specified by the Web browser.

Every computer on the Internet has an address. When a request comes into a Web server computer from a particular address, it responds by sending the requested file back to that address. When the browser application receives that file, it reacts accordingly, generally by displaying the file as a Web page, image, or multimedia element within the browser's own window. In other cases, the browser might recognize that it can't handle the file, so it hands it off to a *helper* application or saves the file in a designated place on the client computer's hard disk.

During a typical Web surfing session, this back-and-forth communication happens repeatedly for each page—not only do the words need to be downloaded, but so does every image and multimedia feed (sounds, digital movies, and so on). This is possible because both computers are connected to the Internet. They both recognize a protocol for transmitting and receiving commands, and the client computer can recognize the language that's used to re-create and display the Web page in the Web browser application. So, we're dealing with three different protocols or languages here.

The first of these protocols is TCP/IP. This is how computers are connected to one another on the Internet. Each computer is given an address, which is then used to identify the computer and enable it to send commands and data from one place to another. If you have a computer that you plan to use on the Internet, you need to establish a TCP/IP connection for that computer, whether it's via a telephone modem, cable modem, DSL connection, or some other means, such as a corporate or institutional network-based connection.

After you have that TCP/IP connection up and running, launch a Web browser application, which uses the Hypertext Transfer Protocol (HTTP) to trade commands and communication. Then, the Web server sends Hypertext Markup Language (HTML) documents to your Web browser, which displays them to you. Let's look at these protocols—HTTP and HTML—more closely.

What Is HTTP?

The Hypertext Transfer Protocol (HTTP) is the underlying protocol that makes it possible for Web browsers and Web servers to communicate. A fairly simple protocol, it isn't terribly interesting to most Web designers because it's used exclusively by the Web browser and Web server computers to communicate. So, you don't necessarily need to know the intimate details of how HTTP works in order to be a Web author. But the basics don't hurt.

The Web browser requests a connection, via an HTTP command, with the Web server computer. If the Web server computer is able to grant the request, the Web browser then requests particular files that it believes are available on that Web server computer. If the files are available, the Web server computer sends them to the Web browser, which can then display the files if it's capable of doing so.

Note that HTTP isn't the only protocol that's in use on the Internet. There are also protocols designed for transferring files (File Transport Protocol, or FTP) or transferring e-mail messages (Post Office Protocol, Simple Mail Transport Protocol), among others. In fact, there are even variations on HTTP, such as Secure HTTP (SHTTP), which uses an encrypted, or coded, communication between the Web browser and server to transmit and receive secure information, such as Web commerce information and credit card numbers.

But the protocol tends to work behind the scenes. Indeed, the only place where you really need to worry about the protocol you're using is when you're creating hyperlinks, as discussed a little later in this section. (You also dig a little deeper into HTTP when you're creating HTML forms, discussed in Chapters 15, "Adding HTML Forms" and 16, "CGIs and Data Gathering.")

Although newer versions of HTTP are under development, the most common version is HTTP 1.1, which differs from the original in that it enables a connection between a browser and server to stay open longer, resulting in slightly better performance.

What Is HTML?

The Hypertext Markup Language (HTML) is a series of standard codes and conventions designed to create pages and emphasize text for display in programs such as Web browsers. Using HTML, you can create a Web page that includes formatted text and commands that cause the Web browser to load and display images or other multimedia elements (movies, sounds, and animations) on that page.

A Web page is defined as a single HTML document, regardless of its length. When viewing a single Web page in your browser, you may not have to scroll the page at all, or you may have to scroll through many screens. In either case, you're viewing just one Web page.

HTML's name gives you a hint as to what it is—it's a *markup language*, which distinguishes it, primarily, from a programming language. In general terms, HTML is a set of instructions that tells a Web browser how certain text and images should be displayed on the page. In most cases, this is done using commands that dictate the organization of a document. For example, an HTML document might include a command, like the following, that tells the browser that certain text is to be regarded as a heading in the document:

`<h1>Welcome to My Page</h1>`

The `<h1>` and `</h1>` surrounding the heading text are called *tags,* and they make up the `<h1>` *element,* which tells a Web browser that the text between the tags is a "level one" heading. The browser then knows to treat this text differently than regular paragraph text, or text that is supposed to be a bulleted list.

Likewise, an HTML document can include a command that tells the Web browser to load an image file and place it on the page:

```
<img src="image.jpg"/>
```

This code tells the Web browser to load an image called image.jpg and place it on the Web page.

Even the images and multimedia you see on a Web page are part of the markup of HTML. Whereas in a Word document images are embedded as part of the document, an HTML document points to the location of image files, which must be individually available alongside it. Every HTML document is nothing more than a plain text document and no images or multimedia are a part of that HTML document.

So, when a Web browser reads an HTML document, it also reads instructions for loading and positioning any images or multimedia files that you've decided to include. Among those instructions, an HTML document almost invariably includes instructions for creating a *hyperlink*—a link to other HTML documents.

Hypertext and Hyperlinks

One of the keys to HTML—and, by extension, a key to the way the Web works—is its support of *hypertext* links. Using special commands in HTML, a Web author can change certain text to make it "clickable." When the user clicks hypertext, as shown in Figure 1.1, that user's Web browser generally responds by loading a new Web page. (I say "generally" because sometimes clicking hypertext will cause a helper application such as RealAudio or Telnet to appear, or it may cause a file to be downloaded to your hard disk.)

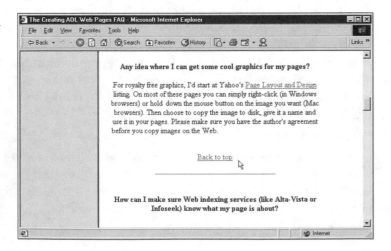

However, not all links are necessarily text—images can also be clickable. In that case, it's more appropriate to call the link a *hyperlink* instead of hypertext, but it's not terribly important. The terms are basically interchangeable.

What's more important is recognizing what a big part hyperlinks play in Web publishing and the World Wide Web. Nearly every page on the Web is in some way linked to every other page. On a smaller scale, hyperlinks make it important for you to consider the organization of your site. They also make it possible for your Web page to take part in a larger world of related pages.

How is it possible to link to all these pages? Using HTML markup, you simply create a link that points the Web browser to another address on the Web. Every page on the Web (and most other Internet resources) has a special address that uniquely identifies it, enabling the Web browser to specifically request that page. Those addresses are called Uniform Resource Locators (URLs).

 Note   This book is much easier to read if you say "URL" like the name "Earl" instead of "You-are-ell."

Uniform Resource Locators

Most Internet services have some sort of addressing scheme so you can find a particular resource easily. For each service, the format of these addresses tends to be a bit different.

For example, you would send an e-mail message to my America Online account using the address `tstauffer@aol.com` in an e-mail application. On the other hand, to access the AOL public FTP site (where you might download the AOL software application), you would enter the following address in your FTP application: `ftp.aol.com`.

Web browsers are capable of accessing many different types of Internet services, and the Web is about accessing individual documents. So, the URL is a combination of addresses, such as `ftp.aol.com`, and some additional elements that allow you to specify the type of Internet service and the particular document you'd like to retrieve. That way, URLs can be used to access, by address, most any document or service that's accessible via a Web browser. An URL follows the format:

`protocol://internet_address/path/filename.ext`

or

`protocol:internet_address`

Here's an example of an URL to access a Web document:

`http://www.microsoft.com/windows/index.html`

Look at this address carefully. According to the format for an URL, http:// is the protocol and www.microsoft.com is the address of Microsoft's Web server computer. That's followed by a slash (/) to suggest that a path statement is coming next.

The path statement tells you that you're looking at the document index.html, located in the directory windows.

> **Note**
>
> If you're familiar with DOS, Windows, or Unix, you probably recognize path statements straight away. If you use the Mac OS, you simply need to realize that a path statement offers directions to a specific file on the server computer's hard drive. A Web browser needs to know in exactly which directories and subdirectories (folders and subfolders) a file can be found, so a path statement is a standard part of any URL.

The two basic advantages to URLs are:

- First, they enable you to indicate explicitly the type of Internet service involved. HTTP, for example, indicates the Hypertext Transfer Protocol. However, a URL could easily include a different protocol. You'll look at this part of the URL in a moment.

- Second, the URL system of addressing gives every single document, program, and file on the Internet its own unique address.

The Different Protocols for URLs

HTTP is the protocol most often used by Web browsers to access HTML pages. Table 1.1 shows some of the other protocols that can be part of an URL.

TABLE 1.1 Possible Protocols for an URL

Protocol	Enables Access to...
http://	HTTP (Web) servers
https://	Some secure HTTP (Web) servers
file://	HTML documents on your hard drive
ftp://	FTP servers and files
gopher://	Gopher menus and documents
news://	A Usenet newsgroup server
news:	A particular Usenet newsgroup
mailto:	An e-mail message addressed to a particular e-mail address
telnet:	A Remote Telnet (login) server

By entering one of these protocols, followed by an Internet server address and a path statement, you can access nearly any document, directory, file, or program available on the Internet or on your own hard drive. As you can see in Table 1.1, URLs extend beyond Web servers to other types of Internet protocols. FTP servers are used specifically for transferring files (as opposed to viewing those files). Gopher servers were the (largely defunct) precursors of Web servers that made plain-text documents available for retrieval. A Telnet server is used for remote login connections, where you enter a username and password, and then use command-line syntax to accomplish things on the server computer. Most Web browsers can display FTP site listings and Gopher menus, and some can send e-mail messages, but most require a helper application for Telnet access.

Note

The `mailto:`, `news:`, and `telnet:` protocols have slightly different requirements for creating an URL. `mailto:` is followed by a simple e-mail address, `news:` is followed by just the newsgroup name, and `telnet:` is followed by just a server address (no path statement).

HTML Versus XHTML

As you've seen, HTML is a markup language designed to combine text, multimedia, and hyperlinks to create a Web page. HTML is also a moving target, though, because several different versions have been introduced since it first appeared in the early 1990s. Although each version has built upon the last, and most Web browsers are designed to be "backward-compatible" with previous versions, it's important to know something about current and future versions of HTML.

Who Sets HTML Standards?

The World Wide Web Consortium (`http://www.w3.org`) is responsible for creating the specifications that other companies adhere to (for the most part) when creating such things as Web browser applications and devices for viewing Web pages. The W3C is an industry group, founded by Tim Berners-Lee, that includes most of the major players in the corporate world of Web development (such as Microsoft, Netscape, AOL, and AT&T).

One of the tasks the W3C undertakes is maintaining the HTML specification. Because technology is always changing, the W3C constantly works on new versions of the HTML standard. Every so often, it publishes *working drafts* that attempt to codify the advances in technology and capabilities of HTML and the Web, while keeping in mind the needs of the majority of Web browsers and users. (For instance, the

W3C might reject or alter an element that one of the browser companies invents because it only works in visual Web browsers, leaving out users of text-based browsers or browsers for the visually impaired.)

After a working draft has been published and is bandied about by peers and the public for a while, it becomes final and is published as the official *recommendation*. Then, Web browsers and authoring tools implement the parts of the *recommendation* that they haven't already (by the time the specification is official, most companies have rolled in the majority of the new elements discussed at the recommendation stage) and then release new versions of their products. While browser companies aren't forced to follow the specification set by the W3C, failing to do so means the pages created by Web authors may be incompatible in different browser versions. So, most of the browser companies attempt to keep up with the standards.

The HTML specification has gone through this updating process many times, through various versions, from an HTML 1.0 standard to the most recent HTML 4.01 standard (finished in 1999). Since then, HTML development has been focused on making HTML's core elements compatible with XML (eXtensible Markup Language), a newer standard that is designed to be a foundation for many other markup languages. XML can be used to create and define markup languages that are specific to certain applications, industries, and so on. Because of the power of XML, one of the W3C's recent goals has been to *recast*, or rewrite, HTML in XML so that the standards are compatible. At the same time, it's done everything it could to keep the new HTML as similar to the old HTML as possible, so as not to introduce too many compatibility problems.

Why a New Standard?

The result of this recasting of HTML is called XHTML. While it may seem that changing the name to XHTML would mean it's a really big deal, the truth is the current version, XHTML 1.0, is only slightly different than its predecessor, HTML 4.01. XHTML does have a few differences, but mostly it's just a bit more strict than HTML has been in the past, requiring that authors be more diligent in the way they implement their Web pages. Overall, though, it's easy enough to grasp.

Why the new standard? Essentially, as more Web browsers support XML, XHTML will become only one module of many different XML-based markup languages that can be understood and displayed by browsers and other applications. That makes it possible, for example, to create a math-specific markup language to display complex mathematical formulae in pages rendered by XML-compliant applications.

Strict adherence to the XHTML standard will also make the future a bit easier to cope with. Already many different types of devices and applications are used to access the Web, from phones and handheld computers to devices used by the physically challenged. XHTML is designed to take all those browsers into account. The better your code conforms to the standard, the better it will render in a variety of circumstances.

Which Should You Use?

It may seem obvious that you should use the latest standard, XHTML 1.0, but it actually isn't *quite* that simple. The problem is, even within the XHTML 1.0 standard, there are two basic approaches: a *strict* approach and a *transitional* approach. While using strict XHTML would seem ideal, doing so can have an unintended drawback—it can fail to work in older Web browser applications. Although the vast majority of computer users upgrade their Web browsers fairly regularly, there are still quite a few older computers out there, with older browsers that may not recognize all the changes XHTML requires.

So, you have to decide if you'll work with strict XHTML or transitional XHTML. In fact, you have to declare one or the other within your Web document, as discussed in Chapter 4, "Creating Your First Page." Throughout this book, you'll focus on the strict XHTML commands and settings. However, under some circumstances I'll also show you the transitional options, when they differ. That way, you can opt to use a transitional approach to XHTML, which simply includes more of the older commands and properties, while knowing the difference between the two.

Note

Neither the strict approach nor the transitional approach is right or wrong. Eventually (we're talking years), the strict approach will be more completely supported by Web browsers and recommended more stringently, so that non-graphical Web browsers and other devices can access your data. For the immediate future, however, using the transitional elements and properties is perfectly acceptable.

HTML Is Not Programming

You might be a little intimidated by all these acronyms, abbreviations, and specifications-speak. Don't be. Heck, I had to look most of that stuff up as I was writing this, just to make sure I was up-to-date! In most cases, HTML and XHTML concepts are surprisingly simple after you have the basic sense of the way the markup works.

It may be comforting to keep repeating to yourself that HTML isn't anywhere near as complex as programming. Whereas *programming* is the process of creating scripts or applications using complicated computer languages such as C++ or Java, creating Web pages is generally referred to as *authoring*. That's because most of what you're doing is simply entering text, and then adding codes in and around that text to organize it on the page. From there, you add elements that cause images or multimedia to appear on the page, or elements that make the page look better. That's what a good portion of this book deals with and it's all you need to know to put together informative, organized Web pages.

Beyond basic XHTML markup, two other Web publishing concepts are discussed in this book. The first concept is *style sheets*, which make Web pages look pretty (or at least different), with a variety of sizes, fonts, colors, and so on. The second concept is *scripting*, which actually *is* programming, but on a smaller scale and used in tandem with XHTML markup and style sheets.

Markup Fundamentals

While scripting and style sheets can get a little involved, the markup itself is pretty straightforward. Essentially, you type text on a page, and then you add elements to the page to organize it. HTML and XHTML have only two basic types of elements— empty elements and non-empty elements.

Empty elements do something on their own—they add a line to the page, add an image to the page, or cause a multimedia file to be loaded and displayed. One example is a simple element that's used to create a horizontal line on the page:

```
<hr />
```

Non-empty elements, also called *containers*, are used to do something to the text that they surround. For example, if you wanted to strongly emphasize certain text on the page, you could do so with strong tags surrounding the text:

```
This is a <strong>very</strong> important point.
```

Notice the slash. In both HTML and XHTML, the slash is used to indicate the closing tag of a non-empty element, such as the strong element. In XHTML, it's also important to put that closing slash in an empty element, such as the horizontal rule tag shown earlier. In older HTML implementations, the trailing slash wasn't necessary.

Note The trailing slash in an empty element is often added with a space for readability, such as **<hr />**. The space isn't required, though, so **<hr/>** would be valid, as well.

HTML and XHTML must be much more complicated than this, right? Otherwise, it's tough to justify the other hundreds of pages in this book. Well, they *are* a bit more complicated, but not so much in theory as in practice. A good deal of getting to know HTML or XHTML is understanding the element *attributes*, which are simply used to fine-tune the way a particular element appears or acts on the page. For example, consider the basic tag for placing an image on the Web page:

```
<img src="image.jpg" />
```

The `<img />` portion of the tag is really the complete image element, although it wouldn't be of much use without the `src` (source) attribute that tells the image element what file to locate. Beyond that attribute are others, such as the `alt` (alternative text) attribute that offers text that can be displayed when the image can't be, or the `align` (alignment) attribute that can be used to align the image, as in the following:

```
<img src="image.jpg" alt="Welcome to the site" align="top">
```

Now you see how elements can get more complicated—they tend to offer a lot of options.

If you're familiar with previous versions of HTML, these lines of code may look slightly different from what you've seen. The examples in this book conform to the syntax guidelines for XHTML coding, which include the following:

- XML is case-sensitive, so all elements should be lowercase, such as `<p>`, `</p>`, and `<br />`.

- All elements must have closing tags or trailing slashes, even if they are empty elements, such as `<hr />`.

- All attributes must have quotes around them, such as `<img src="file.jpg" align="left">`;.

Even if you aren't used to the HTML of the past, know that XHTML is easy to read and learn, thanks to these new conventions.

Decorating with Style Sheets

Basic markup elements are the first level of complexity in HTML and XHTML. The second level of complexity, particularly with XHTML, comes from the need to use and understand style sheets. *Style sheets* are how Web pages get some of their personality and, well, style. You'll use style sheets to change the fonts, colors, sizes, and placement and positioning of text and other elements on the Web page.

This is an important distinction. When you're using typical XHTML markup to create a Web page, you're not really altering or determining the exact *appearance* of the text—at least, not in terms of the font faces, sizes, and other such attributes. Instead, XHTML markup is used to categorize and arrange text.

In the past, HTML and HTML extensions (elements supported by browsers, but not endorsed by the W3C) have made it possible to directly alter the appearance of text or other items on the page, using elements such as the `<font>` element or attributes such as `color` and various others. Although many such pages (including some I've developed) continue to use those conventions, the transition to XHTML requires that these elements be avoided in favor of style sheets.

When using style sheets, instead of directly altering text or other items on the page, portions of the page are labeled and then compared against a style sheet that the Web browser can use to style the page. The Web browser can also opt *not* to style the page, as in the case of the more limited browsers built into mobile phones and handheld computers. In that case, the style sheets separate the XHTML code from the styling of the page, making it possible for more devices to access the page and organize it correctly, while using as much of the style information as it can.

For instance, a text-only browser built into a mobile phone may be able to display certain text as a heading and other text as a hyperlink, but may not be able to specify Arial as the font family and 14-point as the font size. When you place those style-specific commands in a style sheet, the text-only browser is free to ignore them, while still displaying the page and its organizational elements.

Note Up to Chapter 10, "Get Splashy: Style Sheets, Fonts, and Special Characters," we'll be discussing primarily organizational XHTML markup. In Chapter 10, you'll see how style sheets fit into the mix, as well as more discussion on the difference between style sheets, which are recommended, and direct style markup, which isn't.

Adding Scripts to the Mix

The third level of complexity for the Web author is scripting. Today's browsers support standard scripting languages, which enable you to do quite a bit to make your Web page less static and more exciting and interactive to the user. The possibilities range from something as simple as a *rollover* effect (when the user points at text in the browser window, it changes the color, size, or some other attribute of the text, as shown in Figure 1.2) to complex applications that can be accessed via a Web browser.

Note You might notice that Figure 1.2 is a Mac screenshot. Web authoring isn't platform-specific, so you'll see both Mac and Windows screenshots throughout the text. In fact, if you have access to Windows, Macintosh, Unix, or other operating systems, it's always a good idea to view your pages on as many platforms as possible to make sure they look good to all your potential visitors.

Scripting is indeed programming, but you'll find that it isn't terribly difficult to grasp, particularly when you understand the fundamental concepts behind programming logic. The scripting language JavaScript (and its relatives ECMAScript and JScript) is a straightforward scripting language that enables you to get started quickly with useful scripts.

FIGURE 1.2

The rollover effect is achieved through a combination of XHTML, style sheets, and scripting.

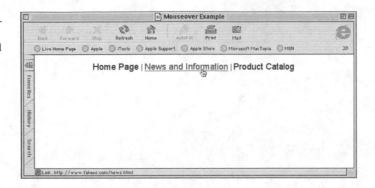

Scripting also works with both XHTML and style sheets to add interactivity to your pages, bringing things together in Dynamic HTML or DHTML. Although XHTML has replaced DHTML as everyone's favorite Web-related acronym, you'll see that creating dynamic pages can be useful and entertaining as well.

Summary

This chapter covered a bit of the background that you need to understand before jumping into Web publishing. It started with a brief history of the Internet, and then it discussed the World Wide Web, including its protocols, its languages, and its addressing scheme, the URL. HTML and XHTML were defined and discussed, and you learned that XHTML is the future of Web development and will be the specification taught in this book. XHTML comes in both strict and transitional varieties, with the transitional version allowing older elements and compatibility with older browsers. Throughout this book, the emphasis will be on strict XHTML, but transitional elements and markup will be discussed, too.

The chapter concluded with a discussion of the different levels of complexity involved in Web publishing, from the relatively simple—creating and organizing Web pages—to the somewhat more complex—styling the pages and adding scripts and other dynamic elements.

In Chapter 2, "A Crash-Course in Web Design," you'll be introduced to the fundamentals of Web design, including how to organize your page, how to plan pages and sites that work well, and how to use XHTML standards to their fullest to build robust and compatible sites.

A CRASH-COURSE IN WEB DESIGN

Chapter 1, "Fundamentals of Web Publishing," hinted at some of the issues we'll discuss in this chapter, particularly style sheets and their role in HTML markup. There's a definite tug-of-war in the world of Web design, where two different approaches—a visual approach and an organizational approach—have clashed with earlier HTML specifications. XHTML clarifies this considerably, separating organizational and visual design and making it a little easier to develop Web pages that look good while communicating effectively in a wide variety of applications. What that approach means to you, and why you might care, is what you'll read about in this chapter.

This chapter discusses the following:

- The fundamentals of organizing and presenting your page
- What good sites look like and how to plan a site so that it works well
- HTML trends and considerations, including accessibility, internationalization, and browser compatibility

The Fundamentals of Page Design

Planning for the Web takes a number of forms, from planning individual pages to planning an entire site made up of pages that you've decided to group together on the Web. Let's begin with a look at the individual page—how a page should look, and how to avoid some common mistakes as you're beginning to create pages. In this section, we'll look at some fundamental tenets of page design for the Web:

- The theory behind XHTML and style sheets
- Organizing the page according to the logic of HTML and XHTML
- Separating content on the page from the design of the page
- The use of images, multimedia, and interactivity to further your Web design goals

At the end of this section, we'll take a look at some sample Web pages and consider their design advantages.

Web Design Theory

HTML was created to help disseminate scientific and academic information over what started off as a government and higher-education project—the Internet. Over time, HTML became the language of many different Web-based tasks, including education, entertainment, and commerce. HTML wasn't really conceived for those tasks, however, particularly when it came to creating highly visual pages. So, developers of Web browsers, such as Netscape and Internet Explorer, added their own non-standard HTML-like commands and cleverly tweaked the HTML specification to create some tricky and attractive-looking pages.

While that was okay with Web designers and Web browser developers, it didn't always sit right with the W3C, which is in charge of maintaining and codifying the Web's standards. Perhaps even more importantly, it didn't fit well with XML, the next generation of markup languages that the entire computing world has shown an interest in.

In the past few years, HTML has been recast as XHTML and returned to its roots of organizing and disseminating information instead of beautifying it. Making pages look good is left to a technology called *style sheets*, as was touched on in Chapter 1. In other words, XHTML once again separates the organization of the page from its appearance, as HTML did originally. So what does this mean for Web authors?

In a nutshell, it means you'll want to consider the *function* of your Web design before you consider its *form*. While it may seem appropriate to figure out what the page will look like before wondering what it will say, that's a notion you'll need to alter slightly. XHTML's primary focus is organizing and communicating information, so that's the best way to approach learning and using XHTML.

However, that's not to say that pages can't be attractive and entertaining. They can be both of those things. But XHTML offers methods that are more correct for accomplishing those entertaining, attractive pages. These methods will also make your page accessible to browsers designed for the physically challenged, non-graphical browsers for handheld devices or mobile phones, or even browsers designed to access the Web using audio only, such as phone-based browsers. With a well-organized, XHTML-compliant page, you should be able to do all of this in a way that's satisfying to your designer's eye.

Organizing Your Page

It's difficult to separate your overall Web site from each individual page—you'll need to consider your Web site's organization before you can finish each page and make it part of the whole. We'll discuss some of that in upcoming sections.

Having said that, there are some basics you should consider for each page you create. Web pages can vary dramatically in the way they organize material, from a basic page with paragraphs and headings to a more complex page that uses a newsletter-style approach. Of course, some pages may have no discernible organization, which is to be avoided whenever possible.

Here are some quick tips:

- **Keep it simple**—While plenty of exciting Web technologies are available— images, sounds, video, and animation—you should only use them if they further the goals of your page's content.

- **Create content-driven designs**—Your page should be primarily designed to focus your user's attention on the content and communicate that content as quickly as possible. This means using subheads, emphasized text, and hyperlinks to help your reader quickly understand the information you're trying to present.

- **Chunk-ify**—Using headings, bulleted lists, and other markup elements, you can take a long page of text and break it into chunks of information that are easier for your visitor to digest. Adding images and dividing lines also make the page easier to read.

- **Balance page length**—Another issue when designing a page is knowing when to quit and move on to another page. Web pages that scroll on forever will often lose the reader's attention, and the page may end up taking a long time to download. On the other hand, pages that are too short can also be annoying to the readers because they have to keep clicking to the next page to keep reading.

To summarize, it's important to remember that your visitors are likely looking for useful pages that offer them important or entertaining information. At the same time, most people don't enjoy reading long passages on a computer screen, so you'll want to break things up along organizational lines with headings, emphasized text, images, and other such elements (see Figure 2.1). Finally, remember that not all your visitors are even using a visual browser. If you stick to conventional organization and XHTML recommendations, you can create an appealing page that always works well on handheld computers and assistive browsers.

FIGURE 2.1

On the left, a solid page of text; on the right, a page broken up with headings and lists.

Before you begin creating pages within your site, you should consider how best to present your material. One way to do that is to consider how traditional publications, such as books, newspapers, and magazines, organize information. For instance, this book attempts to keep your interest by organizing pages logically, using subheadings within topics, and breaking things up with images. You can do the same things with a Web site, with the added advantages of hyperlinks and multimedia.

A newsletter or newspaper uses headings, subheads, and sidebars to communicate information, as well as images that are positioned with text wrapping around them. Again, you can accomplish a similar look using XHTML to organize the page for best viewing (see Figure 2.2). Quite a few Web sites use the newsletter approach, including most daily newspapers. For instance, the New York Times (http://www.nytimes.com/) uses such an approach, with hyperlinks that lead you deeper into each story.

You can even model your Web site after a mail-order catalog. If you're selling products or real estate, you might want to create pages that include pictures, descriptions, prices, and so on. Like a mail-order catalog, you'll want all the pages to be consistent, attractive, and easy for the reader to use. You can do this with a combination of basic XHTML elements, images, and an attention to detail.

FIGURE 2.2

With the
newsletter
approach, using
XHTML table
elements, the
page is broken
up into columns
and rows.

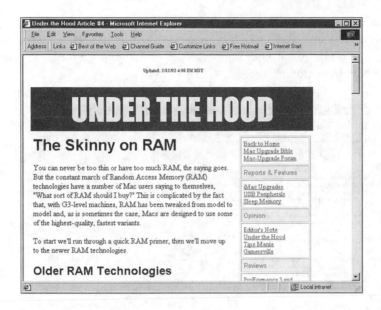

Images and Multimedia

Beyond the basics of dividing your pages into chunks of information, you can also
use images and multimedia on the Web. While these items shouldn't be used indis-
criminately, they can make your Web site much more interesting and useful to the
reader.

You'll use two basic types of images—those you create yourself, and existing photos.
Images you create yourself can be anything from logos and banner images to
charts, graphs, or cartoons that you use to get your point across. Photos can be
taken with a digital camera, captured from videotape or DV camcorders, or scanned
with a scanner. Whatever the approach, images can go a long way toward keeping
your readers interested while communicating key information quickly.

USA Today offers a lesson to Web authors—why write out something that can be
communicated effectively in a table or chart? If you have such information, you can
often create a chart or graph in a program such as Excel, and then export it as a
Web-compatible image.

When you *export* an image, you're simply saving it in a new file format. While most
Web browsers can't display native Excel charts, they can display images saved in the GIF
and JPEG file formats. So, you'll export your chart as a compatible image, using a special command in the application (often it's File, Export).

Then, add the image to your Web page and you've instantly made things a bit easier to understand and a touch more convenient for the reader, who can take in the information more quickly. (Figure 2.3 shows a Web page that uses a graphic to communicate information.)

FIGURE 2.3

Using an image can improve a page's appearance and readability by breaking up the text a bit.

Images are great for catalog sites, classifieds, and even press releases that you create for your company or organization. In fact, the only way you can go wrong is to either use images that don't communicate the right information or use too many images on one page. Avoid extraneous images, which can slow down your page's download in the visitor's Web browser, and you'll be on the right track.

With multimedia, the possibilities are even more exciting, but the problems are manifold. While adding a video, audio clip, or animated short to your page may be fun and entertaining, most multimedia still takes a long time to reach the user's browser.

There's another problem with some multimedia, which will be expanded on in Chapter 13, "Adding Multimedia and Java Content." To view many multimedia elements, your reader will need additional software. If your reader doesn't have that software, they'll have to go through the additional step of downloading it.

That means you should only use multimedia when it's absolutely necessary to communicate something useful, or when you make it available as an option. You can allow users with high-bandwidth connections to view the multimedia, without slow-ing down those using modems or other lower-bandwidth Internet connections.

Bandwidth refers to the amount of data that can be retrieved or sent via a particular Internet connection at one time. High-bandwidth connections are available in many businesses and homes via DSL, cable modems, and other technologies. However, it's still a growing market, with the majority of users using dial-up modems or other slower con-nections.

As you'll see in Chapter 13, there are quite a few decisions you need to make when it comes to using multimedia in your pages, but it's definitely an interesting and exciting option for Web authors. At the same time, multimedia can be a huge stum-bling block for slower Web connections, so it's something to be added with care.

Interactivity and Scripting

You'll find that your Web pages can be used to interact with the user, creating a two-way dialog instead of simply publishing items and making them available for pas-sive consumption. Web pages can be used to receive feedback from users, accept purchase orders, and even enable users to communicate with one another. One way to manage all this is to use XHTML form elements that add menus, buttons, and switches to your Web page. These form elements are similar to parts of other appli-cations you'll find on your computer (dialog boxes for settings, for instance), but can be used on a Web page to accept input of some kind from your visitors (see Figure 2.4).

FIGURE 2.4
Form elements are used to interact with the user.

You can also use a combination of interactive elements (such as menus, buttons, or other application-like selectors) to enable users to navigate your Web site. This adds a level of complexity to your Web authoring, but it can make your Web site easier to use. You can even use some special commands that react to the user pointing at a particular part of the page, for instance, making the page almost seem alive with activity.

However, the extent of interactivity you choose still hinges on the basic questions of Web design. Do the buttons, menus, and active elements communicate additional information? Do they help the user navigate the page (or Web site) more effectively? And do they add more to the experience than they detract? If they don't, a simpler page design may be the better answer.

What Good Pages Look Like

So what does a good Web page look like? Some of my favorite pages are simple in their presentation, with a focus on the content instead of on images or multimedia. This focus makes it possible for a page to be viewed on any number of Web browsers and other items.

For a representative of this category, you need to look no further than the W3C itself, where the HTML and related specifications are debated and codified. Although the site can be dense with information, it's broken up with boxes, headings, hyperlinks, and paragraphs (see Figure 2.5).

FIGURE 2.5

The W3C's site offers some insight into text-heavy, well-organized pages. (The page shown is http://www.w3.org/MarkUp/.)

Most Web sites aren't designed to communicate material that's quite as heavy (and, well, dense) as the Web publishing standards, so you'll likely encounter sites that are a bit more lively. ClNet's sites tend to do a good job of this, offering straightforward navigation and very clean presentation of story headlines, summaries, and datelines. Just by glancing at the site, you get a good idea of what material is available and how it's organized. Figure 2.6 shows `http://www.news.com/`, the main technology news site at ClNet.

FIGURE 2.6

Note that ClNet's news page does have images, but they're used somewhat sparsely to enhance the text, not overwhelm it.

Planning a Site

You've now seen some of the elements that define a good Web page. But in most cases, what you'll create as a Web author won't be a single page, but an entire site. If that's the case, you'll want to do a little planning before you get too deep into the creative process. How you implement your Web site will affect a number of things, including how you design individual pages, how you save those pages on a Web server, and even how the pages are decorated and beautified—particularly if you rely on style sheets for your site.

In this section, let's look at some of the considerations you need to make when planning your site:

- Thinking about the audience for your Web site and how that will affect the design
- Your options for designing and implementing Web sites
- The elements and ideas that make a good site

Considering Your Audience

Perhaps the most important factor in site design is considering your audience, not only for the topics you'll be covering, but also for the technology and capabilities they're likely to have. You should also consider how voluntary their participation in your site is, and how much they'll put up with before deciding to leave.

Most Internet ventures—such as Webzines, catalogs, and online applications—need to be incredibly well designed, not only visually, but from a site-wide organizational point of view. That's because the audience for these sites is not necessarily a captive one—a user may opt to leave your site very quickly, for any number of reasons. The way to convince your users to stay on your site (aside from compelling content or wonderful prices) is with a straightforward design that doesn't get in the way. You should also do everything you can to make the user comfortable, while doing nothing that makes them wait, confuses them, or irritates them.

Sound like a tall order? Generally, you can satisfy these things by considering a few basic criteria:

- **Organize your site**—Make it easy for your visitors to find the information they're seeking. For example, if you want users to contact you via the Web, postal mail, or phone, you should have a link that clearly states Contact Information, Address and Phone Info, or something similar. If you put this important information in a section called Other Info or About Our Organization, it may be a bit tougher for the user to find. How you organize your site can dictate other things, such as how difficult it is to use and update.

- **Focus on navigation**—Hand-in-hand with site organization is site navigation. Put more simply, you need to create hyperlinks to other pages on your Web site that make sense to the user, and ideally that are always in the same place. Navigation should also be simple to grasp and easy on the eyes.

- **Stay within technical boundaries**—Don't require your users to have a particular multimedia technology for basic navigation or information gathering. For instance, if you require all your visitors to view a Macromedia Flash animation to see important information on your site, you're cutting out a large chunk of your audience, particularly if your site isn't specifically targeted at high-tech issues or applications. Although a site devoted to movie trailers might require QuickTime, you shouldn't require it on your astronomy discussion site without good reason and/or alternatives.

- **Remember your target and goals**—If you're aiming your site at a particular group or demographic, you should consider their level of computing expertise and the technology they're likely to use. The more general-interest your site is, the less complicated and more clearly designed it should be. If you're creating a site for Internet gaming, it's probably okay to design the site with bells, whistles, and links everywhere. If you're creating a site about strategy board games, however, you may want a simpler site for newer Internet users who may not have the latest technology.

One of the best sites when it comes to usability, organization, and universal usefulness is Yahoo!. It's a low-requirements site that still offers good organization along with some bells and whistles (see Figure 2.7).

FIGURE 2.7

Yahoo!'s pages organize a great deal of content and are targeted at all sorts of browsers.

Organizing the Site

Once you have a sense of your audience, the next consideration is how to organize your site. How you do this is up to you, but we can discuss some general guidelines.

For a simple site, the organization will probably be clear. If you have, say, five different pages, you can probably store all of them in the main directory on your Web server, and you can place hyperlinks to each of them on each of the other pages on your site. Let's say you have a real-estate site that includes five pages: the index page, a page of homes for sale, a page about the area, a page about mortgage rates at local banks, and a page about you, the agent. Such a site is easy to organize because you can include links to every one of those pages at the top of all the other pages (see Figure 2.8).

FIGURE 2.8
With this simple approach to organizing your site, you can link to every page.

But what if that same page had links to individual pages that discussed each house? There might be 10–15 houses available at a given time, so you couldn't possibly put a link to each house at the top of every page. Instead, links to those houses might only show up on a special index page for linking to the house pages.

Now you've made the organization a bit more complex, as it's beginning to look like the chart shown in Figure 2.9.

FIGURE 2.9
As the organization becomes more complex, so can the interface for users.

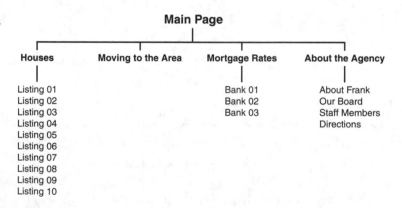

At this point, you'll need to start making decisions. On one hand, each of the individual house-description pages could have links to all the other house-description pages—but that will become tedious to update. Or, each of the house-description pages could have direct hyperlinks to the contact and mortgage information pages— although that might be confusing to the user.

Another solution would be to take the Yahoo! approach and make the path to the current page apparent on the page itself, as shown in Figure 2.10. In fact, note that the page shown is using a hybrid approach—the current path to the page is shown, as well as convenient links at the top of the page. These options, if consistently presented on every page on the site, can make navigation as easy as can be for the user.

FIGURE 2.10

At the top are standard links for main sections of the site; on the page itself, links make the path apparent.

As the site grows even more complicated and the pyramid of pages grows, you'll have to continue to refine this approach. But this is a solid approach, used by sites as large as Yahoo! and About.com. It's worth considering on your own pages.

Design Ease and Consistency

I've harped on consistency quite a bit already, and for good reason—giving your pages a consistent look helps define them as a cohesive Web site, and a consistent approach to the site's interface makes it easy to navigate. If you don't have these things, you risk alienating the user.

Beyond the organization of your site, there are two areas where consistency pays off. First, the interface that's used to navigate the pages should be consistent. For most sites, that means having basic, text-based navigation hyperlinks that appear on every page, even if some pages also use images or multimedia for navigation.

Second, a consistent look is something that's even easier to manage when you use style sheets with your XHTML pages. Style sheets, discussed in Chapter 10, "Get Splashy: Style Sheets, Fonts, and Special Characters," and Chapter 14, "Site-Wide

Styles: Design, Accessibility, and Internationalization," allow you to define the font family, text color, and many different attributes of text, paragraphs, and other elements on your page. They're a strength when it comes to consistency because you can define a single style sheet for an entire Web site. This is a simple way to choose the look of all your pages at once, while adhering to XHTML standards and making your pages available in a variety of situations and mediums. As you're creating pages and designing sites over the next few chapters, keep in mind that you'll be able to give your sites a unique look using style sheets, which are discussed in Chapter 10.

HTML Trends and Issues

I've mentioned that one of the reasons for creating XHTML was to enable compliant Web sites to better support a disparate audience of Web browsing applications and devices. That's one of the trends that XHTML development has been moving toward. Combined with broader support for style sheets in Web browsers, the newer standards make it easy for Web sites to communicate with many different types of devices, and look good on them, too. That includes assistive browsers, handheld computers, and even browsers designed to speak content aloud and accept voice commands from the user.

Beyond simply adhering to these standards, you'll find that making your Web pages broadly available will require you to take advantage of all the tools at your disposal. In a sense, creating accessible and widely useful Web sites is a mindset, because it means taking advantage of some additional attributes and doing a little extra work to support browsers other than Internet Explorer and Netscape. Let's take a quick look at some of these issues.

Accessibility

The latest XHTML standards give you a number of ways to offer support for Web browsers that assist site-impaired and other special-needs users. For instance, an image element can include alternative text that can be displayed instead of the image. (This is discussed further in Chapter 6, "Visual Stimulus—Adding Graphics.") This text can be used on non-graphical browsers to explain what the images show. In certain cases, you can even create a hyperlink to a longer, text-only description of the image that might be useful for blind visitors with Web browsers that speak text aloud or make text available in Braille.

Other elements offer assistive features as well. For instance, the elements used to create HTML forms pages—those that enable you to choose from menu items, radio buttons, and entry boxes—now offer increased assistive features. This makes it easier for visitors with assistive browsers to use your sites.

The most important factor in making your pages available to a wide audience, however, is to design them as simply and logically as possible. That means using headings, paragraphs, bulleted lists, and other elements with more emphasis on the content of the page than on its look. For instance, even pages that use simple XHTML table elements for design purposes can be difficult to interpret on nongraphical Web browsers. A more simply organized page, using headings and paragraph text, can be viewed on a variety of Web-enabled devices.

Internationalization

XHTML offers some elements and attributes that make it a little easier to publish flexible pages for a worldwide audience. For instance, a number of elements can accept the `lang` attribute, which enables you to specify the language being used for a particular element. This language attribute can be reinterpreted by the browser, or displayed differently if desired. This attribute, along with the `<q>` element (which can be used to display quoted text in different international formats), is discussed in Chapter 5, "Formatting Your Text."

Another aspect of internationalization is the use of automatic translation software to make your page readable in other languages. In general, this software is most effective on the simplest pages. If you'd like others to be able to translate and read your pages, you should endeavor to use the clearest language possible. Stick to the simplest words and grammar, and avoid colloquialisms, metaphors, and cliches. (For instance, "He's a bear on the ballfield" won't translate out of English all that well, while "He is a good player" will.) You might even offer special simplified pages for the cleanest international translations, if you feel it's appropriate. Some sites that offer these translation capabilities include

- **Google.com**—See `http://www.google.com/help/faq_translation.html` for details.
- **AltaVista.com**—Offers the BabelFish service at `http://babelfish.altavista.com/`.
- **FreeTranslation.com**—Another site that will translate nearly any page is at `http://www.freetranslation.com/default.htm?tab=web`.

Browser Compatibility

Finally, browser compatibility has been a constant challenge and sometimes a source of frustration. Different browsers will sometimes interpret commands differently, or may offer their own elements in place of those that are part of the XHTML standard. While this problem has gotten better as browsers have incorporated more of the official standards, sometimes you still need to add two different elements that do the same thing to support different browsers. You should also make a habit of testing your pages in different browsers to see the differences. Using style sheets and other tricks can eliminate some of the problems, but it's an issue to keep an eye on. It'll be discussed throughout the book.

Summary

In this chapter you were introduced to the basic principles of Web page and site design, including some of the fundamental tenets. The simpler your page and the simpler the system for navigating your Web site, the more accessible your Web site will be to readers. This includes organizing each individual page, organizing entire sites, and considering how your design approach can affect all your users, including those who are using non-graphical browsers or who want to translate your page into spoken text, Braille, or another written language. You also saw some examples of good sites and got some suggestions for other sites to emulate.

In the next chapter, you'll be introduced to the tools you need to create Web documents, and you'll see how to publish those documents on the Web.

WHAT YOU NEED TO GET STARTED

Web publishing doesn't require expensive or complicated tools. In fact, you'll find that you can get away with using just a simple text editor, like those that come with Windows, Unix, or the Mac OS. In addition, you can find useful downloadable shareware applications to help you with HTML, graphic images, and multimedia. Beyond the basic tools, you also need to look into Internet services if you plan to make your Web pages available on the Internet.

This chapter discusses the following:

- The different types of editors for creating Web pages
- Tools for graphics, animation, and scripting
- How Web server space works
- Obtaining Web server space and uploading files to that space

The Basic Tools

As discussed in Chapter 1, "Fundamentals of Web Publishing," HTML documents are nothing more than plain-text documents with markup commands that instruct a Web browser to arrange and format text in certain ways. Other commands are used to add images, hypertext, and multimedia to the page, but those commands are still plain-text commands that are interpreted by the Web browser.

The plain-text nature of HTML documents means that all you really need to hand-code HTML is a text editor application. It can be something as simple and friendly as Windows Notepad (see Figure 3.1) or the Mac's SimpleText editor. You have similar choices in other operating systems—vi or emacs in any Unix and Unix-like OS, and TextEdit in Mac OS X.

FIGURE 3.1

HTML pages can be edited in simple text editors such as Windows Notepad.

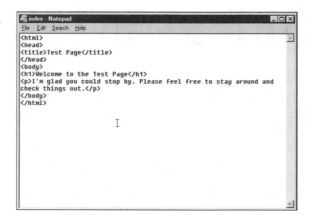

The main issue to remember is that your documents need to be saved as plain-text or ASCII documents, so your text editing application must be capable of saving such documents (as opposed to, say, Microsoft Word format or Rich Text Format). You can use a word processing application to create your HTML documents, as long as you save the documents as plain-text.

Note

ASCII stands for *American Standard Code for Information Interchange*, a standard method for representing English letters and numbers in computing. The most universal format for text documents on computing platforms, it's the basis of many files being read by different sorts of computers, such as HTML documents.

If you do opt to use a word processor (which I don't really recommend), note that many of them have the specific option of saving files as HTML documents. Generally, you *don't* want to do that because the word processor translates the page, as typed, into HTML, adding markup to maintain the appearance of the document in your word processor. In other words, it ignores the HTML markup that you've entered yourself and adds markup so that the page appears with the tags intact when displayed in a browser (see Figure 3.2).

FIGURE 3.2

If you use a word processor for your pages, save them as text, not as HTML. Otherwise, your element tags appear when the page is viewed in a Web browser.

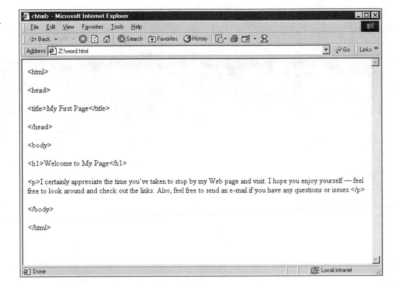

Instead, you should save the document as plain-text, text, or ASCII text, but with the filename extension `.htm` or `.html` (more on that later).

Ideally, though, you'd use either a text editor—which can be very basic or rather specialized—or an HTML editor that enables you to edit the HTML *source code* (the text and markup) directly. Let's look at each possibility.

Note Where do you find these programs? Throughout the next few sections, you'll see the Web sites associated with the individual editors that are recommended. But if you'd like to do a little surfing on your own, try `www.download.com/`, which offers links to the vast majority of shareware, freeware, and demonstration applications available for all the different computing platforms.

Text Editors

As noted, you can opt to use the simple text editors included with your operating system. In Microsoft Windows, it's Notepad; in the Mac OS it's SimpleText or TextEdit. Unix and Linux systems offer a number of text editors, from basic to sophisticated.

If you'd like to move up to the next level, however, you'll find that a good program-mer's text editor may be helpful in creating and organizing your HTML code. Popular editors for Microsoft Windows include TextPad (www.textpad.com), UltraEdit (www.ultraedit.com, shown in Figure 3.3) and EditPlus (www.editplus.com), among many others. The Macintosh has fewer text editors, although BBEdit and BBEdit Lite (www.barebones.com) are very highly regarded, for both Mac OS 9 and Mac OS X. (Mac OS X also includes Unix-style text editors via its Terminal application.)

FIGURE 3.3

In UltraEdit you can manage multiple text files, see HTML codes in special colors, and access a quick reference panel of HTML ele-ments.

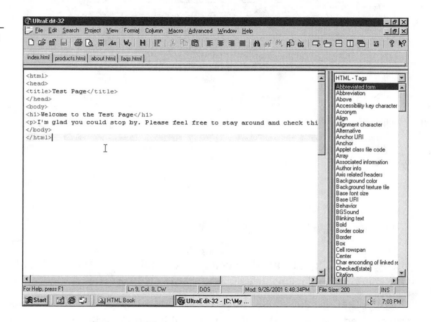

Most text editors you come across are designed to work well for HTML authoring, as well as other types of markup and programming. You'll find that some of them automatically recognize markup as such, turning them into different colors for easy viewing. Others may offer a toolbar button for displaying an HTML document in a Web browser (to test how it looks and whether hyperlinks are working correctly), a spell-checking feature, or other interesting options. Experiment a bit to find a text editor that really works well for you.

HTML Editors

The other type of editor you might consider downloading or purchasing is one that's specifically designed for HTML documents. These editors come in two basic flavors—*source code editors* and *WYSIWYG editors*. WYSIWYG, which stands for "What You See

Is What You Get," means you're editing the Web page as it will look in a Web browser. In this case, you're not marking up text and adding HTML commands and elements, but rather typing text, importing images, and moving items around on the page, much as you'd do in a word processing or desktop publishing program.

Because this book focuses on editing XHTML source code (the raw text and markup elements), WYSIWYG editors are not discussed until Chapter 20, "Graphical Editors." You'll find that a WYSIWYG editor is a great tool to have on hand for prototyping and editing Web sites. That said, it's important to learn the raw XHTML first, particularly if you aspire to do Web publishing professionally, because no WYSIWYG editor is perfect. They can't always adhere to the latest standards, they aren't all capable of more complex tasks (such as scripting or interactive elements), and sometimes you need to "dig into the code" to get them to work exactly as you'd like them to. If you want to go beyond a text editor, you might look into one that's specifically designed to help you edit HTML source code. For Microsoft Windows, some recommended editors include HotDog Professional and HotDog PageWiz (www. sausagetools.com), HandyHTML (www.silveragesoftware.com), and CoffeeCup HTML Editor (www.coffeecup.com). For Macintosh, popular options include PageSpinner (www. optima-system.com) and WebDesign (www.ragesw.com). The latter is shown in Figure 3.4.

FIGURE 3.4

WebDesign is a Mac HTML editor that makes it easy to edit HTML source code.

If you need to watch out for anything with HTML editors, it's that they're up-to-date and support the level of HTML (or XHTML) that you want to use for your authoring. For the purposes of this book, you should use an editor that supports HTML 4.01 Transitional or XHTML 1.0 Transitional, if it's an option. (If you're trying to create strict documents, you can use XHTML 1.0 Strict if the editor supports it). Older HTML editors may support an older standard, or may recommend elements or markup that don't conform to the newer standard. You can probably still use them; just be aware of the differences.

Note
Some editors can support different compatibility modes, so you may find an option in the preferences to format pages as strict, transitional, XHTML 1.0, or HTML 4.01. In other cases, the editor may only support one specification, so it's good to know which one.

Other Tools You'll Want

Beyond editors to help you create your HTML documents, the Web author's arsenal isn't complete without some other tools. In particular, you definitely need a good image editing application on hand to help you convert and tweak the images that you plan to use on your Web pages. As you dig deeper into Web authoring, you may also find you'd like to work with other applications that enable you to create animated content and multimedia content, as well as other tools that simply make being a Web author easier.

Graphics Editors

If you plan to put images on your Web pages—and I bet you do—you need a decent application for translating, cropping, resizing, and otherwise tweaking your images. Of course, your options include some wonderful and expensive commercial applications, such as Adobe Photoshop and Macromedia Fireworks. If you don't have such applications, however, you might opt instead for downloadable shareware options. Two of the most popular for Microsoft Windows are Paint Shop Pro (www.jasc.com/) and LView Pro (www.lview.com/). For Macintosh, the standard-bearer is GraphicConverter (www.lemkesoft.com/). For Linux and other open source operating systems, it's the Gnu Image Manipulation Program or GIMP (www.gimp.org).

Whichever graphics application you opt to use, you want to be able to perform at least a few basic tasks:

- Creating images using shapes and text.
- Cropping and resizing images.

- Changing the number of colors used to render the image.
- Saving images in JPEG, GIF, or PNG formats.
- Working with the special features of the various graphics file formats, such as transparent GIFs and progressive JPEGs.

These things are discussed in much more detail in Chapters 6, "Visual Stimulus—Adding Graphics," and 11, "Advanced Web Images and Imagemaps." For now, bear in mind that you might want to shop around (either on the Web or in the computer store) for a graphics editing application.

Animation Tools

Web animation comes in a few different forms. One way to animate images on a Web page is to use the animated GIF specification, which is less interactive (it doesn't respond to user input such as mouse clicks) but common for animated images such as online advertisements.

You'll find a few animated GIF applications available as freeware or shareware, although some animation tools—particularly those designed for creating Web advertisements—tend to be a bit more expensive than shareware image-editing applications. Try Ulead GIF Animator (www.ulead.com) and Animagic GIF Animator (www.rtlsoft.com/animagic/index.html) for Microsoft Windows. For Macintosh, try GifBuilder (homepage.mac.com/piguet/gif.html) or VSE Animation Maker (vse-online.com/animation-maker/index.html).

Up one step from animated GIFs are Macromedia Flash animations. Flash is very popular, in part because it allows for interactivity. Viewers of a Flash animation can click controls to make choices within the animation, altering what they see next. This is popular with car manufacturers, Web application businesses, and many others who want to show products or ideas in a multimedia presentation.

Aside from Macromedia's own Flash application (www.macromedia.com/flash/), which retails for several hundred dollars, other Flash tools include CoffeeCup Firestarter (www.coffeecup.com/) for Microsoft Windows and ez-Motion (www.beatware.com/) for Macintosh. Chapter 13, "Adding Multimedia and Java Content," discusses Flash in more detail.

Multimedia Tools

Editors and image applications are the basic tools in the Web author's arsenal, but you may want to go beyond those basics if your focus is on multimedia content. You may find yourself creating movies using QuickTime, Windows Media, or other multimedia formats. Or, you may find yourself creating and editing sound files for your Web site—anything from basic background sounds using the MIDI standard (for computer-synthesized playback of songs) to the MP3 standard for CD-like recorded audio playback.

If that's the case, you want to shop around for applications that enable you to create and edit such media. Before venturing too far afield, however, be aware that such tools may come bundled with Microsoft Windows and the Macintosh OS, depending on the version of the operating system with which you're working. Microsoft Windows Me and later versions include Windows Movie Maker, which enables you to edit video recorded on a *DV-compatible* camcorder. You can then turn that video into Windows Media or a similar format that can be displayed via the Web. Similarly, many Macintosh models include iMovie, which offers simple editing of DV video and exporting to the QuickTime movie format. QuickTime Pro is available for both Windows and Macintosh users, offering some simple tools for editing and translating movie files into QuickTime format for display on the Web.

Note   *DV* stands for *Digital Video*, a file format for video images that are recorded using DV-compatible camcorders (often on MiniDV cassettes). The video is easy to edit using a computer application such as Movie Maker or Apple's iMovie. DV is quickly becoming a popular competitor for VHS camcorders.

Likewise, many different applications are available for editing and translating sound files into one of many Web-compatible sound formats. Such applications include Sound Forge XP (www.sonicfoundry.com) for Microsoft Windows and Sound Studio (www.felttip.com/) for Macintosh. iTunes, included with most Macs, is also capable of creating MP3 and other sound files, and the QuickTime Pro player can be used to translate between different sound formats.

Scripting Resources

Some of the Web editors discussed earlier can also be helpful with popular scripting languages such as JavaScript and JScript. At the same time, you may want to seek out utility applications that can help you with JavaScript, or even cut-and-paste JavaScripts that you can use when creating your pages. A few such applications for Microsoft Windows are iCoder (www.eport.webhoster.co.uk/iCoder/), JavaScript Tools (www.sausagetools.com/), and JavaScript Developer (www.liquidsoftware.cjb.net/).

Finding a Web Server

Before you can display your HTML pages on the Web, you need access to a Web server. This may already be taken care of for you, especially if you are creating pages and posting them within your organization or corporation. When you want to update the site, you just need to know how and where to send your HTML and related files, or you might need to know how to copy them over the network to your Web server.

Otherwise, if you're working within a smaller organization or on your own, you need to make some arrangements for obtaining Web server space and figuring out how to get your files online.

What Is a Web Server?

A Web server is simply a computer that runs software designed to send out HTML pages and other file formats (such as multimedia files). The server should have a relatively high-speed connection to the Internet (faster than typical modem connections, for example) and should be powerful enough to deal with a number of simultaneous connections.

Generally, Web server software requires a fairly robust operating system (like Unix, Linux, Windows NT/2000, or Mac OS X). However, software is available for other versions of Microsoft Windows, and earlier Macintosh OS versions are popular for smaller (and reasonably worry-free) Web sites.

Dealing with an ISP

For any sort of connection to the Internet, you probably need to work with an Internet service provider (ISP). ISPs offer dial-up and special high-speed connections to the Internet, as well as Web servers and other types of Internet servers for your use.

Tip

You can access lists of ISPs around the country (and the world) at `thelist.com` or `www.yahoo.com/Business_and_Economy/Companies/Internet_Services/Web_Presence` `_Providers/`. You might also check with your current ISP for Web deals, because many popular online services offer free or cheap Web space.

For the typical smaller Web site, you want a *hosted* account, sometimes called a *shared hosting* account. This simply means that you share space on one of the ISP's Web server computers with others who have hosted accounts. Generally, this gives you an URL that begins with the name of the ISP's host computer, but points to a special directory for your HTML pages. For example:

`http://www.isp.com/username/index.html`.

For this type of service, prices range from free (particularly if you already use other services from that ISP) to $25 or so, depending on the amount of storage space you have and how many megabytes of downloaded *traffic* your site is allowed to handle. The more traffic, the more expensive your site is.

At the next level, you might decide that you'd prefer to have your own *domain name*. This means your Web site is accessible at an URL similar to `http://www.yoursitename.com`, such as `http://www.fakecorp.com`. Clearly, this is desirable for organizations and businesses, although you may opt to register a domain name for your own personal or avocational use as well.

Domain names always have domain name extensions, such as `.com`, `.net` and, `.org`, which are used to differentiate otherwise identically named sites. For instance, `w3.com` and `w3.org` are two different Web sites. The number of domain name extensions has multiplied recently, with possibilities such as `.biz` and `.info`.

In general, ISPs help you register a domain name when you're establishing new service, but that isn't completely necessary. You can register domain names on your own via a number of different services, such as Register.com (`www.register.com/`) and Network Solutions (`www.networksolutions.com/`). Prices for domain registration can vary, although most name brand services charge $25–$35 per year for a domain name.

You'll often find that your favorite domain names are already registered. On many of the registration service sites, you can perform a *WhoIs* lookup to see whether a domain name is registered, and to whom. Paying for a domain name that you really want, particularly if someone is "squatting" the address and not using it is still common (although perhaps not as glamorous).

After you have a domain name registered, your ISP can set up a Domain Name Service (DNS) record that tells other DNS servers around the world to point to a particular server computer whenever that domain name is requested. So, `www.fakecorp.com` points to the server that the ISP has provided for your Web pages, and others are able to access your pages easily.

DO YOU ALREADY HAVE SERVER SPACE?

If you use an ISP for your Internet access, there's a decent chance that you already have Web server space available to you. Most of the major national and international ISPs (such as ATT WorldNet, America Online, and Prodigy.net) offer free Web space with most of their account types.

If your ISP offers free space, all you need to do is find out how much space you get and how to take advantage of it. You may also want to look into any options your ISP offers for registering domain names. In most cases, having your own domain name associated with the Web server space costs extra. See Chapter 22, "Web Publishing Services," for more on free and commercial Web server options.

What Software Does Your Server Run?

For HTML documents, images, and most multimedia feeds, the software that your ISP uses for its Web server computers is largely irrelevant. However, when you get into more advanced tasks—or when you decide you want to take advantage of inter-activity options and add-ons—the type of software your ISP uses can become much more important. So, these are a few questions you might consider asking a customer service representative at your ISP (or a prospective one):

■ *Can I run CGI scripts? If so, which languages?* Although most basic Web sites don't deal in CGI scripts, you may need them if you want to add interactivity to your site in the guise of HTML forms, bulletin-board forum software, or database access. Note that in some cases a particular language version may be required (such as Perl 5 instead of Perl 4), so knowing the version numbers can be helpful. (See Chapters 16, "CGIs and Data Gathering," and 21, "Forums, Chats, and Other Add-Ons," for more information.)

Perl is a scripting language that's commonly used for programs that are stored on Web servers and used to interact with Web browsers.

■ *Which extensions and server side includes are available?* Depending on the Web server software and any extensions that are installed, you may be able to add special commands to your HTML documents that make it possible to display the current time, hit counter, and quite a few other options that are specific to particular Web server applications (see Chapter 21).

Every time a user loads a page on your site, it's called a *hit*. The *hit counter* is one way to keep track of how many visitors a page on your site has received.

■ *How are statistics reported?* With some ISPs, you may be able to access a spe-cial URL that shows you how many people have visited your Web site, along with other information from them (such as which pages referred them to your site). In other cases, statistics are stored in a special file that you need to download to your computer and then process with a statistical analysis pro-gram (generally available as a free download).

Asking these questions—particularly when you're a bit more familiar with the answers you want to hear—may help you decide on an ISP to use for your Web serving. See later chapters, particularly Chapter 21, for more details.

Accessing Your Web Server Space

After you've decided on an ISP, you're ready to create your HTML pages and upload them to the server. To do all this correctly, though, you probably need to ask a few questions:

■ *What is my site's default URL?* This should be the ISP's host address and a directory for your username. For example, if your username is jsmith, the default URL for your site might be www.fakeco.net/jsmith/, members.fakeco.net/jsmith/, or something similar. Different ISPs organize this in different ways, so you need to make sure you get this right.

Note | With most Web server programs, the default page that is first loaded is named index.html or index.htm. So that's the name you use for the first page you'd like to present to users when they access your Web site.

■ *How do I upload files to my site's directory?* You should get instructions for accessing your Web site's directory on the Web server using an FTP application. This is discussed in more detail in the section "Updating Your Web Site," later in this chapter.

■ *What limitations are there on the names I can give my files?* The Web server's operating system may not be instantly obvious to you. If this is the case, you want to ask if there is a certain filename length or a certain format for naming files that you need to follow.

Tip | When in doubt, use the DOS 8.3 filename convention in the style filename.ext, where the filename can be no more than eight letters and .ext is a three-letter extension, such as .htm.

■ *Can I create subdirectories within my main Web site directory?* Most Web servers give you this ability, but some don't.

With those questions answered, you are able to upload and access your Web pages easily.

Organizing a Web Site's Files

You may recall from Chapter 1 that a URL is composed of a protocol, a server address, and a path to a particular document. All of those components are important. When you're creating and organizing your Web site's files, however, the most important is the path statement. If you have a system for how you store files when you're creating them on your computer (*locally*), you'll have less trouble later when you store your files on a Web server computer.

Although a Web site can be arranged in a number of different ways, you should keep in mind some rules of thumb. For the most part, you should organize your Web site files to make it easy to update your pages in the future. If you have to move all your files around every time you change something on a single page, you are also forced to change all the hypertext links on many other pages—and that can be incredibly time-consuming. Early on in the process, you should consider how your site's files will be organized. This is true even if you're only planning one page or a few pages. Organizing the images and multimedia feeds that go along with those pages is still important.

Types of File Organization

These are different types of organization for Web sites:

■ *Single-directory sites:* Smaller sites, with just a few HTML pages and images, can often get by with a single directory on the Web server. All your graphics and HTML pages go in this one directory. One of the biggest advantages of this system is that links to local files and graphics require no special path statements. The disadvantage is that this sort of system can be unwieldy as your site grows, making it more difficult to update in the future.

■ *Directories by function:* One way to organize more complicated sites is to put each section of related Web pages in the same directory. For example, in your main directory you might only store the index page and its associated graphics. For a business site you'd have subdirectories for sections called About, Products, Support, and so on. In each of these subdirectories, you'd include all the related HTML files and the image files for those pages.

■ *Directory by file type:* Some people prefer to create subdirectories according to the type of file, as opposed to the content of the page. Your main directory may have only the index page of your site. Other subdirectories might be called Images, Pages, Downloads, and so on. The main advantage of organizing this way is that files generally have to be replaced only once. If you use a graphic on a number of different pages, for example, you can replace it once in the Images subdirectory and all the HTML pages that access the graphic use the new one.

■ *Hybrid:* The best way to organize a large site is to use a hybrid of the two preceding methods. Creating separate subdirectories for nonrecurring items (such
as individual Web pages in each category) while creating other subdirectories
for items used multiple times (such as graphics) enables you to get at all the
files in an efficient way. A hybrid file organization is shown in Figure 3.5.

FIGURE 3.5

In this hybrid
site (displayed
in Windows
Explorer), differ-
ent functions
are organized
into different
folders, but a
single image
folder is also
used for all
images.

The other thing to remember when determining how you're going to organize your
Web directories is that the directories themselves become part of the URL when you
create them and store files using them on the Web server. So, if you go with the
hybrid approach, your URLs might make more sense to the user. For example:

`www.fakecorp.com/products/mousetrap.html`

This is as opposed to a straight "functional" organization, which would result in an
URL like this:

`www.fakecorp.com/webpages/mousetrap.html`

In this case, the products directory tells the user what he will see and how the Web
site is organized.

Creating the Hierarchy

Once you've selected a system, the next step is to create local folders that mirror the
directories you're using on your Web server. If you create a folder called `images`
where you plan to store image files, you'll need that folder in the same *relative* location on your local hard disk and on the Web server computer.

Note In some operating systems they're called *folders*, and in others they're called *directories*. It's just two names for items that are functionally equivalent. You'll often hear *folders* used when referring to local hard disks (particularly in Windows and Mac OS) and *directories* used when referring to the server computer (which is often running Unix or a Unix-like OS).

For each Web site, create a folder somewhere on your computer. The name of it isn't important, since it will be the equivalent to the nameless root directory (/) on your Web server. For instance, if you're creating a new personal site, start by naming a folder `mysite`. That's where your main `index.html` page will be stored. Inside that folder, add other subfolders that you plan to use as part of your organizational hierarchy, such as `images` or `products`, depending on the approach you're taking. Remember that these folders need to be the same names you plan to use for subdirectories on your Web server. In fact, a good rule of thumb is to use all lowercase letters for them, in both places, just to avoid any problems with case-sensitive servers.

This organizational structure will do two things for you. First, it keeps you from accidentally placing files in the wrong directories when you're uploading them to your Web site. Second, it makes it easier to create *relative URLs*, which is a topic you'll dig into in Chapter 7, "Building Hypertext Links."

Naming Your Files

You've already seen that file extensions are an important part of all the filenames you use for your Web site. Because other Web browsers may rely on a file's extension to know what sort of document or file it is, you need to include the appropriate extensions with all your Web site files.

Your Web site almost always begins with a file called `index.html` or `index.htm`. Most Web server software programs load this page automatically if the URL of your site is accessed without a specific path and file reference. For example, typing `http://www.fakecorp.com/` will probably result in the page `http://www.fakecorp.com/index.html` being loaded into your browser. Your Web site's first page (whether it's a "front door" page or the first page of your site) should be designed with this in mind.

The thing to consider when naming your files is how you plan to organize your site. If you're using a single-directory organization, your filenames should be as unique as possible, and graphics and other files should probably have names that relate to their associated Web pages. For instance:

```
about_company.html

about_header.jpg

about_ceo_photo.jpg
```

These names help you determine which files are associated with which HTML pages when you go to update those files. If you have more structure to your site (for instance, if you've created an `about` directory on the Web server), names such as `company.html` might be more appropriate because the ultimate URL path you're creating would be `about/company.html`.

Updating Your Web Site

If you organize your site well, updating it is simply a matter of replacing an out-dated file with a new file using the same filename.

You need to check with your company's system administrator or your ISP's technical staff to figure out exactly how you update files. (When you sign up for service, most ISPs will tell you how to do this or provide you with documentation that explains the process.) With an ISP, you can usually use an FTP program to put new files in your directory organization on the Web site, as shown in Figure 3.6. (Some HTML editors include the built-in ability to upload pages via FTP.) The process is simple:

1. Your Web space provider requires you to enter a username and password to gain access to the Web server. In most cases, you point your FTP program to the Web server itself (for example, `www.isp.com`), although sometimes you'll log into a computer with an address that starts with `ftp`. If your Web site has its own domain name, you might need to sign into that, such as

   `www.fakecorp.com` or `ftp.fakecorp.com`.

FIGURE 3.6

An FTP client program is being used to transfer Web site files from my local hard drive (bottom) to the Web server computer (top).

2. If the server recognizes your username and password, you'll be connected to the server. Most likely, you'll be in your personal Web site's main directory. (If not, you need to use the `cd` command or otherwise change directories in your FTP program.)

3. You can add files using the `put` command in your FTP program. If you're uploading new files, remember to place them in the same relative locations that you used on your local hard disk. (Put the image files in the `image` directory on the server, and so on.) You may need to create the directories on the server the first time you log in.

4. To replace an existing file, you use the `put` command again, this time uploading the replacement file with the same name as the file you want to replace (including the upper- or lowercase letters). This will overwrite the file, so consider whether you want a backup of the older file before you replace it. You won't be able to recover the older version unless you've created a backup of it.

As you can see in Figure 3.6, it's a good idea to maintain a folder or directory on your own hard drive that is as identical as possible to the Web site and its directory structure. That way FTP updates are easy, as is testing to ensure that your filenames and local hyperlinks have been built correctly.

Summary

In this chapter, you took a look at some of the tools that you need—and some others you might simply want—to create Web pages. You also got some suggestions for other tools, including those that help with images, animation, and multimedia files. Next, the chapter discussed obtaining Web server space from an ISP, including some of the important questions you need to ask. The chapter ended with a discussion of how your Web site's files and directories should be organized, and how you go about updating your Web site as you create and edit HTML and other Web files.

In Chapter 4, "Creating Your First Page," you'll create your first Web page, as well as a template that includes the main structural elements that you'll need on every XHTML document you create.

CREATING YOUR FIRST PAGE

*I*n this chapter, you begin creating HTML documents by piecing together the required skeleton of XHTML elements into a basic template. After you've created that template, you move on to the basics of entering text for your page. After that, you learn how to save your document, test it by viewing it in a browser window, and validate it to make sure your code adheres to set standards.

This chapter discusses the following:

- Creating an HTML template
- Structuring Web documents properly
- Typing text into paragraphs
- Saving, testing, and validating the page

Build Your HTML Template

As you saw in Chapter 3, "What You Need to Get Started," all you need to create HTML documents is a basic text editor. HTML pages, although they include the .htm or .html file extensions, are simply ASCII text files. Any program that generates ASCII text files works fine as an HTML editor—even a word processor such as WordPerfect or Microsoft Word, as long as you save correctly.

After you have that program, you're ready to create a basic template for your HTML documents. This is the skeleton of the HTML page that you use for building content-filled pages, using the markup elements discussed later in the book. The skeleton includes the *document* elements, which are simply the markup elements that define the file you're creating as a Web page.

Add Document Elements

The first XHTML elements you learn about are the document elements. These are the tags that are required for every HTML document you create. They define the different parts of the document.

Note

Don't let me confuse you by switching back and forth between *XHTML* and *HTML*. When I'm referring directly to the elements, I'll call them *XHTML elements*, because that's the specific standard we're going to adhere to throughout this book. When I'm referring generically to HTML as a concept or to Web documents and applications, I'll call them *HTML documents* or *HTML editors*.

Like a magazine article, an HTML document has two distinct parts—a head and a body. The head of the HTML document is where you enter the title of the page.

To create the head portion of your HTML document, type the following into your text editor:

```
<head>

</head>
```

This section tells the Web browser what special information should be made available about this page, and what it should call the document in the title bar of the browser window.

Now that you've got a head, you need a body, right? The body is where you do most of your work; entering text, headlines, graphics, and all your other Web goodies. To add the body element, start after the </head> tag and enter the following:

```
<body>

</body>
```

Between these two tags, you enter the rest of the text and graphics for your Web page.

Now, wrapped around the `<head>` and `<body>` elements, you'll add an element that's designed to tell that world that it's dealing with an HTML document: the `<html>` element. Above the first `<head>` tag, enter this:

```
<html>
```

After the `</body>` tag, type the following:

```
</html>
```

Even though your document is saved in plain ASCII text, a Web browser will know that the page is really supposed to be an HTML document.

But wait... this isn't just any old HTML document. It's an XHTML document! Because you're using XHTML, you need to be a little more specific with that first `<html>` tag:

```
<html xmlns="http://www.w3.org/1999/xhtml">
```

This attribute for the `<html>` element is `xmlns`, and it stands for *XML namespace*. It's required for XHTML-compatible documents, particularly those that strictly conform to the XHTML 1.0 standard.

So, the end result of all these elements would look like

```
<html xmlns="http://www.w3.org/1999/xhtml">
<head>
</head>
<body>
</body>
</html>
```

Now you have a nearly complete Web document, at least as far as your Web browser is concerned.

The DTD

Before any HTML document—and particularly one adhering to the XHTML standard—is truly complete, you need to add something called the DTD, or *document type definition*, to the top of the page. It's a dirty little secret that most of today's Web browser applications will read a page that doesn't have a DTD and display it without problems. However, this definition will become more and more important in the future. What is it? It's a quick element at the top of the page that enables everyone to know which languages and standards you're using for that page. As XML becomes more important on the Web, and as a wider variety of applications and devices are used to access the Web, this definition will become a requirement.

You should put a DTD at the top of every HTML document you create. Fortunately, they're simple to add. All you have to do is pick the right one.

If you're working with a page that already exists, or that has been generated by a typical WYSIWYG HTML editor, you probably want to update it with the following DTD:

```
<!DOCTYPE html

    PUBLIC "\//W3C//DTD XHTML 1.0 Transitional//EN"

    "DTD/xhtml1-transitional.dtd">
```

This is the XHTML Transitional DTD, which simply tells the Web browser that you're using the XHTML 1.0 Transitional specification for your pages. The PUBLIC attribute is followed by the specific DTD name, including the language used, which is English (EN). Note that even if you're using another language for the text on your page, the language of XHTML is always EN.

The next line of the DOCTYPE is the URL of that particular DTD file that's maintained by the W3C. This line is optional, but there's no harm in including it.

As you'll see in later chapters, the XHTML Transitional DTD enables you to use elements that directly affect the look and feel (fonts, colors, and so on) of text on the page. As noted in Chapter 1, "Fundamentals of Web Publishing," HTML isn't really designed to do this, so the XHTML Strict DTD doesn't support such codes.

Specifically, the XHTML Transitional DTD causes a Web browser to run in a backward-compatibility mode. This enables a number of non-standard elements, such as those created by the browser companies instead of the W3C, to *render*, or display in the browser, without generating errors. The other option is to have the browser run in strict mode, which requires the XHMTL Strict DTD:

```
<!DOCTYPE html

    PUBLIC "\//W3C//DTD XHTML 1.0 Strict//EN"

    "DTD/xhtml1-strict.dtd">
```

You use this definition if you don't plan to use any browser-specific codes, and you plan to use style sheets to change the appearance of elements on your page. For most of the pages you create using this book, the XHTML Strict DTD should work well.

Note Why use one or the other? As you work through the book, you'll see that using the XHTML Strict DTD will require you to use style sheets to change the appearance and layout of the text on your page, while the XHTML elements will only be used for organizing the page. With the XHTML Transitional DTD in force, you can use some special HTML elements and attributes to change the appearance of text, lists, tables, and other elements. The XHTML Transitional DTD is simply a little more lax about allowing older elements, which is why I recommend adding it to existing HTML documents that you're updating.

Also note that you don't need to space the DOCTYPE element (which is the only element in XHTML that can be uppercase), as shown in the prior examples. You can place the attributes for the DOCTYPE element on the same line if desired, as in the following:

```
<!DOCTYPE html PUBLIC "\//W3C//DTD XHTML 1.0 Strict//EN" "DTD/
➥xhtml1-strict.dtd">
```

The comment Element

One other element needs to be discussed before you put together your template. The comment element is a bit different from other elements. It contains text, but it doesn't have an opening or closing tag. Instead, the text for your comment is enclosed in a single tag that begins with <!-- and ends with -->. The text inside the tag is ignored by the Web browser.

Hiding the text enables you to create a private message to remind you of something, or to help those who view the raw HTML document to understand what you're doing. That's why it's called the comment element. For example:

```
<!--This is a comment that won't display in a browser-->
```

Generally, you use the comment element for your own benefit—perhaps to mark a point in a particular HTML document where you need to remember to update some text, or to explain a particularly confusing part of your page to others who may need to update it in the future. Because it's fairly easy for anyone to view your raw HTML document, you might also use the comment element to create a copyright message or give information about yourself.

It might seem like a good idea to place comment tags around other HTML elements you'd like to hide temporarily, but it's better to delete obsolete links and elements when you don't want to use them. Some browsers may inadvertently display certain elements even if they are hidden using the comment element.

Create an HTML Template

Now it's time to take what you know and create a template. By saving this template as a text file, you have a quick way to create new HTML files. Simply load the template and select File, Save As to save it as your new Web page.

1. Start by entering the following in a blank text file:

```
<!DOCTYPE html PUBLIC "\//W3C//DTD XHTML 1.0 Strict//EN"
"DTD/xhtml1-strict.dtd">
<html xmlns="http://www.w3.org/1999/xhtml">
<head>
<title>Enter Title Here</title>
<!--Designed By Lucy Smith-->
<!--Last updated 10/12-->
</head>
<body>

</body>
</html>
```

2. Next, save this as an ASCII text file called `template.html` (or `template.htm` if you're using DOS or an early version of Windows).

Now, whenever you're ready to create a new HTML document, simply load `template.html` into your text editor and select File, Save As to rename it to something more meaningful, such as `index.html` or `products.html`. You can then alter the page by adding text, links, and other markup elements.

The Document Head

As the name implies, the *head section* of any HTML document precedes the main information (or the body). The head section is defined by the `<head>` element, which is a container element. Text contained between these `<head>` and `</head>` tags tells the browser application general information about the file and is not displayed as part of the document text itself.

The `<head>` element can hold a number of other elements, including the following:

- `<title>`—The document's name
- `<base>`—The original URL of the document
- `<meta>`—Additional information about the page

Only the `<title>` element is required. The rest are optional and often do not appear in basic HTML documents. However, it's important to know how all these elements work because they can help you produce a richer, more sophisticated Web site.

Your Web Page's Title

The `<title>` element is used to give your page a name. Most graphical Web browsers display the title in the browser window's title bar. Likewise, the title is often used when the page is saved using a Web browser's bookmark or Favorites feature. The title is not the name of the file itself (such as `index.html`) but instead a few descriptive words, such as Customer Support Page or FakeCorp's Site Map.

The title element should be added inside the `<head>` element, as follows:

```
<head>
<title>FakeCorp's Bargain Page</title>
</head>
```

You should make your title informative, but keep it relatively short. A long title can look odd at the top of a browser window and may be truncated when added to a visitor's bookmark or Favorites list. Your page's title may also be used in search engines and other places as a link to your page, so it's worth some consideration. Here are some simple suggestions to help you create a better title:

- *Avoid generic titles*—Say exactly what your site does, what the page is about, and why it's interesting. Remember that any page title might be used as a bookmark or entry in a search engine such as Google or AlltheWeb.com.

- *Avoid catchy slogans*—Remember that your title should indicate the nature of the service or the purpose of the page. Just giving a company's name or motto doesn't always help, particularly if the title of many or all of your pages is the same. Instead, work your organization's name into an informative title, such as FakeCorp's Customer Support or About FakeCorp's Executive Team.

- *Use no more than 60 characters*—The XHTML specification does not limit the length of the `<title>` element. However, before you give your Web pages endlessly descriptive names, keep in mind that the space where the title is displayed (either the viewer's title bar or window label) is limited. Keep your title short.

The `<base>` Element

File paths and URLs can get a little complicated, and they tend to be a stumbling block for new Web page designers. The `<base>` element can be used to make this process a bit more palatable. Essentially, the `<base>` element is used to set the root level of all a page's relative URLs. It's a bit involved, so we'll save the specifics for Chapter 7, "Building Hypertext Links." It's mentioned here because it goes in the head of your document.

The `<meta>` Element

The `<meta>` element is used to add *metadata*, which simply means data about data. In this case, the element is used to add information about your Web page that other people or computers can use. One very common use for the `<meta>` element is to provide keywords and a description of your content to Web search engines such as Yahoo! and Excite. This makes your page easier to find for people who have similar interests.

When *search robots* encounter your page, they'll look for two fairly common `<meta>` elements:

```
<meta name="description" content="Products offered by FakeCorp">
<meta name="keywords" content="hair, perm, highlights, comb, dryer">
```

Note Often called **bots**, search robots are small programs designed to comb the Web for interesting pages to catalog. Some of them are designed to read and store the description and keywords you enter for your page.

The first `<meta>` element in the preceding example is used by robots to describe your site in its listing in a Web directory. For the `content` attribute, descriptions should be between 50 and 200 words, depending on the search robot (shorter is probably best). Another example might be as follows:

```
<meta name="description" content="Virtual writer's group
➥for New York, including job listings, tips, advice and
➥discussion.">
```

The other `<meta>` element is for keywords that you want the search robot to associate with your site. If a user enters these keywords at a major search engine, it's more likely to present your page as one of the results. The following is an example, using the New York writers' group page from the preceding example:

```
<meta name="keywords" content="writers, writer, free-lance,
➥ for hire, articles, submissions, postings, want ads">
```

These aren't the only uses for the `<meta>` element; just some very common ones. The `<meta>` element must include the `content` attribute and either the `name` or `http-equiv` attribute, but never both. In fact, the `name` attribute accepts generic values, which may or may not be useful to a browser. For instance, you could add your name and a copyright for your page:

```
<META name="author" content="Rich Guy">
<META name="copyright" content="&copy; 2002 FakeCorp, Inc.">
```

In general, it's used to convey hidden information to the Web browser (when used with `name`) or to access HTTP server properties (when used with `http-equiv`).

> `<meta>` can be used with the `http-equiv` attribute to automatically load new Web pages, as discussed in Chapter 7.

The Body Section

The body section of all HTML documents is defined by the `<body>` container element. It has an opening tag, `<body>`, to show where the body starts, and a closing tag, `</body>`, to indicate where the body ends. Inside the body is where you'll put everything that your visitors will actually see in the browser window—text, hyperlinks, headings, images, form elements, tables, and all other XHTML markup.

The sample XHTML in Listing 4.1 shows where the body fits into the overall Web page structure. Note that it's embedded inside the `<html>` and `</html>` opening and closing tags, which means it's a substructure of `<html>` itself. Almost everything else in your document is contained in the body and thus fits inside the `<body>` and `</body>` tags.

LISTING 4.1   Sample HTML Body Element

```
<!DOCTYPE html PUBLIC "\//W3C//DTD XHTML 1.0 Strict//EN" "DTD/xhtml1-strict.dtd">
<html xmlns="http://www.w3.org/1999/xhtml">
<head>
<title>FakeCorp Web Deals</title>
</head>
<body>
<h1>FakeCorp's Web Deals</h1>
...actual content of page
</body>
</html>
```

Figure 4.1 shows Listing 4.1 as displayed in a Web browser (including some Web content that appears inside the `<body>` element, but isn't shown in the listing).

FIGURE 4.1

Text, headings, and pretty much everything else you see on a page goes between the *<body>* and *</body>* tags in your HTML document.

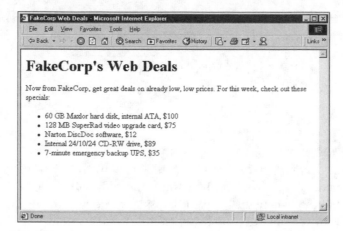

WELL-FORMED CODE

As you'll see in this chapter and throughout the book, an important part of the process of creating XHTML-compatible documents is using *well-formed code*. The term *well-formed* means that the documents you author conform to some basic rules that are part of the basic XHTML standard. If you've worked with HTML in the past, you might notice that things are getting a bit more strict under XHTML.

For instance, well-formed XHTML tags are all lowercase (<body> instead of <BODY>), and they should all have closing tags. In the past, some container elements, such as the paragraph element, would let you get away with using only one of the tags. For empty elements, you close the tag by adding a slash (/) before the final bracket (>).

Other rules apply, as you'll see in later chapters. For instance, older HTML specifications allowed for empty attributes, such as NOSHADE, but XHTML requires an attribute to have a value, such as noshade="noshade".

Entering Paragraph Text

Most of the text you type between the <body> and </body> tags is enclosed in another important container element: the <p> (paragraph) element. This element is used to show a Web browser which text in your document constitutes a paragraph.

You might think that a paragraph element would be superfluous. In most text editors, you can simply press the Return or Enter key on your keyboard to create a new paragraph in the document. For HTML documents, though, that doesn't work. In most cases, Web browsers are designed to ignore more than one space between words, so they'll ignore any returns that you add to your HTML document while you're creating it.

To give the appearance of paragraphs, you have to use the paragraph container element. It uses the following format:

```
<p>Here is the text for my paragraph. It doesn't matter how long it is,
how many spaces are between the words or when I decide to hit the return
key. It will create a new paragraph only when I end the tag and begin with
another one.
</p>


<p> Here's the next paragraph. </p>
```

The paragraph element tells the Web browser that all the text between the `<p>` and `</p>` tags is in a single paragraph. When you start another paragraph, the Web browser drops down a line between the two paragraphs.

> Note
>
> In earlier HTML implementations, the `<p>` element could be used as an empty element. You could simply place a `<p>` tag at the beginning or end of a paragraph of text. This isn't *well-formed code*, however. It doesn't work under the XHTML Strict DTD, which requires that all container elements have a closing tag. To be on the safe side, use both tags to enclose all of your paragraphs.

This is another example that has some extra spaces. Remember, spaces and returns almost never affect the way the text is displayed onscreen. In a paragraph container, the browser ignores more than one space and any returns:

```
<p>Thanks for shopping at FakeCorp.</p>
```

And:

```
<p>

Thanks

for shopping at

FakeCorp.

</p>
```

These look exactly the same when displayed in a Web browser, as shown in Figure 4.2.

FIGURE 4.2
Notice that
pressing the
Return key when
entering text has
no effect on how
it's rendered.

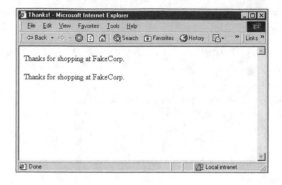

The `<br />` Element

You've learned how to create entire paragraphs. But what if you want to specify
where a particular line is going to end? Let's say you want to enter an address into a
Web document, as follows:

```
<p>
Donald Johnson
12345 Main Street
Yourtown, NY 10001
</p>
```

This looks about right when you type it into your text editor. However, when it's displayed in a Web browser, it looks like the top part of Figure 4.3.

You already know what the problem is: Web browsers ignore extra spaces and
returns. But if you put each of those lines within its own paragraph containers, you
end up with an extra space between each line. That looks wrong too, as shown at
the bottom of Figure 4.3.

FIGURE 4.3
Pressing Return
or Enter and
using `<p>` con-
tainers doesn't
add simple line
returns in HTML
documents.

The answer to this conundrum is the empty element <br />, which forces a line return in your Web document. (The "br" in the tag stands for "break.") Properly formatted, the address would look like this:

```
<p>
Donald Johnson<br />
12345 Main Street<br />
Yourtown, NY 10001<br />
</p>
```

This looks just right in a Web browser, as shown in Figure 4.4.

FIGURE 4.4

Here's the listing with <br /> elements at the end of each line of text.

Note

Although some versions of Netscape's browser recognize more than one <br /> tag and create additional line breaks, the HTML standard doesn't recognize more than one <br /> tag in a row. One accepted way to add space in an HTML document is the <pre> container, as discussed in Chapter 5, "Formatting Your Text." The most appropriate way to add space on your page is via style sheets, as discussed in Chapter 10, "Get Splashy: Style Sheets, Fonts, and Special Characters."

Saving, Testing, and Validating

As you're working on a new page, it's important to go through a three-step process to make sure the page is saved properly, works well in a Web browser, and conforms to HTML standards.

Saving Your Page

If you're working from an HTML template, you've probably saved your page with a meaningful name because that's recommended immediately after you load the `template.html` document. (If not, you may have accidentally added text and markup to your `template.html` document.) If you don't have your HTML document saved with a meaningful name, select File, Save As to save the file.

When you're saving the file, remember that it should be in the same *relative* position where it will be after it's uploaded to a Web server. This can be a bit difficult to grasp at first, but it's closely related to the discussion of directories and site structure in Chapter 3, "What You Need to Get Started." If you're saving the file `products.html` in your products folder on your hard drive, it should be bound for the products directory on your Web server. Otherwise, moving files around can mess up their links to images and hyperlinks, as you'll see in Chapters 6, "Visual Stimulus—Adding Graphics," and 7, "Building Hypertext Links."

Testing Your Page

You need to use a Web browser to check on the appearance of your Web page as you create it. Almost any Web browser can load local pages from your hard drive, just as they can load HTML pages across the Web. Check the menu of your Web browser for a command such as File, Open File. Then use the Open dialog box to locate the HTML document and load it into your browser, as shown in Figure 4.5.

FIGURE 4.5

Select a file and click Open to load an HTML document from your hard drive and display it in the browser window.

To test an HTML document in your Web browser:

1. Select File, Save to save any changes you've made to the HTML document in your text editor.

2. Switch to your Web browser application, and then choose File, Open File to open the file in your browser.

3. The document should appear in your Web browser. Check it for problems, typos, and other issues.

4. Switch back to your text editor and make any changes that are necessary, or continue working on the page. When you're done, select File, Save again.

5. If the page is already open in your Web browser, you should be able to click the Reload button to see the changes you just made and saved in the HTML document.

Validating the Page

Finally, after you've saved and tested your page, you're ready to validate it. Although validation isn't a requirement, it's a good idea. In essence, an automated testing application determines whether your page meets the W3C's guidelines for compatibility with HTML (or XHTML, in many cases). If your page validates, you know it completely conforms to the standard and that you don't have any *syntax errors* that could affect the display of your markup. If the page doesn't validate, either you're dealing with a typo or you've used an element that isn't valid in the HTML or XHTML specification you're testing against. Most validators will give you an error report so that you can fix the error.

Note

A Web page doesn't *need* to pass a validator in order to work correctly in Web browsers. Indeed, many pages on the Web today wouldn't pass a validator. But adhering to the standards is growing more and more important, particularly with XHTML. If your page passes, it's likely to be displayed correctly in the broadest range of browsers.

So how do you test? You have a few choices. The most obvious choice is HTML Tidy, whose source code is maintained by Dave Raggett of the W3C. The code is available in numerous formats, including a validation program that runs at the Windows command line. Many other versions of the software have been written and ported, including Windows, Mac, and Unix graphical applications and editors. See `http://www.w3.org/People/Raggett/tidy/` for a list of these other versions. Note that some popular HTML editors also support HTML Tidy add-ons and plug-ins, such as support within NoteTab for Windows and BBEdit plug-ins for Macintosh.

Likewise, you can use a third-party validator application that you download to your computer. CSE HTML Validator Lite (`http://www.htmlvalidator.com/lite/`) is one such application for Windows that has the added advantage of being freeware. A Real Validator (`http://www.arealvalidator.com/`) is a Windows shareware option.

Finally, you can use a validator that checks HTML over the Web. In this case, you need to have uploaded your page to a Web server already, and you need to know the URL of the page that you want to validate. Then, you visit the validator's Web page and enter the URL. A number of such validators exist, but you only need to concern yourself with the W3C's, which is the most authoritative. You can find it at `http://validator.w3.org/`.

Note   The W3C also offers a validator for style sheet coding (CSS, or cascading style sheets) at `http://jigsaw.w3.org/css-validator/`.

Summary

In this chapter you learned how to create an HTML template, including the fundamentals of the DTD and the main page elements. You then learned how to add to that basic template by filling out the head of the document, as well as typing text into paragraphs within the body of the document. Then you learned how to save, test, and validate your pages.

In Chapter 5, you'll learn the elements used for organizing and formatting text on the page, including headings, block-level elements, and lists.

PART II

DESIGN AND CONQUER

FORMATTING YOUR TEXT

At this point, you're familiar with the HTML template, you've typed some text into paragraphs, and you've successfully saved and validated the work you've done so far. In this chapter, you learn quite a bit about styling and organizing text as you type it into the body of your HTML document.

This chapter discusses the following:

- Adding headings and horizontal lines to organize the page and make it easier for the reader to understand
- Styling the text you're typing into your Web page
- Using different container elements to format entire paragraphs of text
- Adding bulleted and numbered lists to your Web page

Organize the Page

After you've placed some basic paragraphs on your page, you may be ready to break them up a bit. You can do that with two different elements discussed in this section: headings and horizontal lines. Headings are very important to a well-organized page, particularly one that offers a lot of text. Horizontal lines can be helpful, too, in defining sections of a Web document visually.

Add Headings

Heading elements are containers, and unlike many other XHTML elements, they double as paragraph elements. Ranging from level 1 to level 6, headings enable you to create different levels of emphasized headlines to organize your Web page. This is an example:

```
<h1>Level one headers are the largest for headlines</h1>

<h2>Level two is a little smaller for major subheads</h2>

<h3>Level three is again smaller, for minor subheads</h3>

<p>This is regular text.</p>

<h4>Level four is about the same size as regular text, but emphasized</h4>

<h5>Level five: again emphasized, but smaller than regular text</h5>

<h6>Level six is generally the smallest heading</h6>
```

See Figure 5.1 for the results.

FIGURE 5.1

The different levels of headings you can use.

Ideally, headings should be used in descending order, and you shouldn't skip a number—that is, an <h3> shouldn't be the next heading to follow an <h1> without an <h2> between them. In practice, some Web authors will use a particular heading size to make text appear smaller or larger as desired. This is not well-formed code, though, because different browsers can render small headings in different ways. The better plan is to use style sheets to choose font sizes, as discussed in Chapter 10, "Get Splashy: Style Sheets, Fonts, and Special Characters."

You cannot include a heading element on the same line as regular text, even if you close the heading element and continue with unaltered text. A heading element has the same effect as a <p> element, in that it creates a new line after its "off" tag. Consider the following:

```
<h1>This is a heading</h1> And this is plain text.
```

This will look nearly the same in a browser as

```
<h1>This is also a heading</h1>

<p>And this is paragraph text.</p>
```

In both cases, the Web browser places the header text and text that follows on different lines, with the header text appearing larger and the plain text appearing at "normal" size. (Also note that the first example is not well-formed code. The second half of the line should be enclosed in a paragraph element.)

Horizontal Lines

Want to divide paragraphs with more than just spaces? The <hr /> element places a line across the width of the Web browser's window. If the reader changes the size of the window, the line resizes to match. The <hr /> element is an empty element, so it does not require a closing tag. (The "hr" stands for "horizontal rule," which simply means a horizontal line.)

A horizontal rule inserts a paragraph break before and after the rule. The <hr /> element can be added anywhere in a document, although it always appears on its own line.

```
<hr />

<h2>Review: Burrito Factory</h2>

<p>This week we report on two great lunches at the Burrito Factory, a
wonderful little restaurant with locations on the Upper West Side and in
the West Village.</p>
```

The <hr /> element can also accept some attributes that change its appearance, but these attributes should be used only if you're working within the confines of the XHTML Transitional DTD. These attributes are not strict XHTML. (If you do want to stay strict, you should use style sheet commands instead of these attributes, as discussed in Chapter 10.) They give you control over the weight of the line, its length, and the location of the horizontal rule within the browser's window. You can also drop the etched look of the line in favor of a solid black rule. Table 5.1 lists the <hr /> parameters and what they do.

TABLE 5.1   Style Attributes for <hr />

Attribute	Description
size	Sets thickness of the horizontal line
width	Sets width in pixels or a percentage of the viewer window's width
align	Enables the line to be justified left, center, or right within the viewer window
noshade	Changes the appearance of the horizontal line to be solid black with no etched effect

Note The term *pixel* refers to a *picture element* on a computer display or, in Web terms, a single *dot*. If you make something 5 pixels wide, that's wider than 2 pixels, although the exact width would vary depending on the resolution of the user's display. The <hr /> element is 1 pixel wide by default.

You can add any of these attributes by typing them into the <hr /> element before adding the closing bracket (/>). An example is

```
<hr size="4" width="50%" align="center" noshade="noshade" />
```

Styling Your Text

When you're ready to move beyond simple paragraphs of plain text, your next step is to begin styling that text. All it takes is a little more markup, in the form of tags that you place on either side of the text you're typing onto the page. Beyond that, you need to put a little bit of thought into which type of style elements you're going to use—*physical styles* or *logical styles*.

Physical styles are those that specifically tell the browser how the text should be emphasized or changed. Boldface, for example, is a physical style. Logical styles, on the other hand, simply suggest to the browser that the marked-up text should be emphasized in some way. The elements <em> (for "emphasize") and <strong> (for "stronger emphasis") are logical elements.

It might seem that the logical elements are redundant, but they really aren't—in fact, they're preferred. That's because not all Web browsers can display particular physical styles, such as boldface. If a cellphone-based browser can't display boldface, it ignores your `<b>` element. If you use a logical element instead, however, the phone may be able to emphasize the text onscreen in another way. For instance, the `<strong>` element generally makes text appear bold in a graphical browser. In a non-graphical browser, however, the `<strong>` element could be rendered differently—perhaps underlined or highlighted. But that same non-graphical browser would probably ignore the `<b>` element.

In general, you should at least consider using a logical style before automatically typing a physical style, even though the physical styles may seem more familiar. That way, your meaning and emphasis can reach a broader community of readers and visitors.

Physical Style Elements

If you've used almost any word processor, you instantly recognize the physical style elements. Physical styles emphasize your Web page's plain text with boldface, italic, and underlining. These elements are absolute, which means that every Web browser should display these physical style elements in exactly the same manner.

Although some browsers may not be able to display logical text styles the way you expect them to be displayed, there is no way for a browser to misinterpret a physical style. Bold is bold. Italic is italic. If the browser can't display a physical style, it almost invariably ignores it.

Table 5.2 contains some descriptions of physical styles.

TABLE 5.2   Physical Styles and Their Meanings

Element	What It Does...
`<b>, </b>`	Boldface
`<i>, </i>`	Italic
`<tt>, </tt>`	Monospaced typewriter font
`<u>, </u>`	Underlined
`<big>, </big>`	Makes text bigger
`<small>, </small>`	Makes text smaller
`<sub>, </sub>`	Subscript
`<sup>, </sup>`	Superscript

Adding a physical style element to your Web page is simple. The key is selecting the text that is contained by the style tags. The contained text is what is styled in the Web browser:

1. Enter text into your HTML document.

2. Place the cursor at the beginning of the text you'd like to style. Type the opening tag for the style element you'd like to apply to this text.

3. Move the cursor to the end of the text you want to style.

4. Type the closing tag for the style you're applying to this text. This is an example of some physical style elements added to the example Web page:

```
<p><tt>Site News:</tt> We've changed around the posting schedule for
<i>new</i> restaurant reviews. They'll now be posted on
<b>Wednesdays</b>, by popular demand, so that everyone has ample
chance to get out on <u>Thursday and Friday</u> to try them
out.<sup>*</sup></p>

<p><sup>*</sup>This promise is subject to our sleeping schedule and
whether or not the restaurant is open earlier in the week!</p>
```

Figure 5.2 shows how these physical styles are rendered in a Web browser.

FIGURE 5.2

Generally
browsers don't
vary in how
they display
physical styles.

Note Placing markup tags right next to the text they represent is important, as in `Tuesday` `and <b>Thursday</b>` as opposed to `Tuesday and<b> Thursday</b>`. This ensures proper spacing in the browser. In the second example, some browsers (or other agents) may render the line with `andThursday` running together.

Logical Style Elements

In Chapter 4, "Creating Your First Page," you learned that the paragraph element doesn't just create space between blocks of text—it actually defines the enclosed text as an element called a "paragraph." That's an important distinction, because it means a paragraph is actually a logical element in HTML. The paragraph element doesn't define a fixed amount of line spacing in point size, or a particular margin. Instead, it leaves the exact determination of what a paragraph is (within certain limits) up to the Web browser application.

In HTML, *logical styles* work similarly. A logical style is one that can be rendered by the Web browser in any way that it chooses. Although most browsers tend to render paragraph text in a familiar way (single-spaced with a blank line between the paragraph and the next container), paragraphs could be rendered in other ways—all green text with a flush-right margin, for example—if the browser programmer or user decided this was necessary. The same holds true for text that's surrounded by a logical style container element. The browser makes the text bold, italic, highlighted, green, spoken louder (in a text-to-speech browser), or whatever is appropriate for that particular browser application.

Each logical style element has an opening tag and a closing tag that form a container for the inserted text. Table 5.3 describes these logical styles.

TABLE 5.3 Logical Styles and Their Meanings

Element	The Enclosed Text Is...
`<em>, </em>`	Emphasis
`<strong>, </strong>`	Stronger emphasis
`<cite>, </cite>`	A citation or a reference to an outside source
`<code>, </code>`	Computer programming code
`<dfn>, </dfn>`	The primary or defining instance of the term
`<samp>, </samp>`	Sample output, often rendered in a way similar to code
`<kbd>, </kbd>`	Representing text typed at the keyboard
`<var>, </var>`	A variable or value
`<q>, </q>`	Quoted text
`<abbr>, </abbr>`	An abbreviation
`<acronym>, </acronym>`	An acronym

In a graphical browser, `<em>` usually italicizes text and `<strong>` usually makes it boldface. But in other browsers, `<em>` might do something different, such as underline the text with a solid line, while `<strong>` might cause the text to be highlighted. In a text-to-speech browser, `<em>` text might be louder than paragraph text and `<strong>` text louder than both. The basic idea is that `<strong>` is just a bit more emphatic—visually or otherwise—than `<em>`.

The other styles in Table 5.3 tend to be used for particular purposes, mostly related to scientific or technical documentation. Again, a browser designed for such documentation could be very creative in how it displays those elements. In most browsers, they'll be italicized, monospaced, or won't have special styling at all.

Internet Explorer for Macintosh enables you to use a personal style sheet to view pages any way you like. Select Web Content in the Preferences dialog box, and then enable the Use My Stylesheet command. (You need to locate a stylesheet document, as discussed in Chapter 10.) Netscape and IE for Windows enable you to choose colors and fonts. Opera (`http://www.opera.com`), which is available for a variety of operating systems, offers extensive control over how elements appear in your browser window.

Listing 5.1 shows an example similar to the one shown in Figure 5.2, but it uses logical styles instead of physical ones. The results are pictured in Figure 5.3.

LISTING 5.1 Logical Styles

```
<p><em>All users</em> need to remember to log out of their terminal accounts
<strong>before leaving</strong> the computer lab. To <dfn>log out</dfn>, type
<kbd>logout</kbd> or <kbd>exit</kbd> at the prompt. When you see the result <samp>Thank
you. Goodbye.</samp> on screen, you'll know that it's safe to turn off the terminal
display. Please do so using the button on the front of the display.</p>
```

FIGURE 5.3

In a typical browser, logical styles are rendered in a way that's similar to physical styles.

The `<q>` element is used to place language-specific quotation marks around text within paragraphs or similar container elements. In current browsers, this usually just adds quotation marks around the text. In future browsers, it may offer curly quotes, for example. In other cases, it can be used for alternative display and/or for responses by assistive browsers, such as a change in inflection for a computer-voiced browser page. This is an example:

```
<p><q lang="en">I'm not really sure what you mean,</q> Jack said.</p>
```

The `lang` attribute is optional and accepts two-letter abbreviations for different language types, such as "fr" for French and "es" for Spanish (Español).

The last two logical style elements, `<abbr>` and `<acronym>`, are a little different. In essence, they're used to provide additional information about truncated words. The Web browser may or may not opt to render this additional information for the reader, but it can be helpful. Both elements can accept two attributes: `lang` (for language) and `title`. The `title` attribute is used to hold the actual definition of the abbreviation or acronym. Theses are some examples:

```
<abbr lang="en" title="United States of America">U.S.A.</abbr>

<acronym title="situation normal all fouled up">snafu</a>

<acronym lang="fr" title="Association Canadienne pour la Recherche en
➥Economie de la Sante">ACRES</a>
```

Ideally, if a browser recognizes an abbreviation or acronym, that browser somehow expands the definition of the abbreviation or acronym when prompted. For example, Internet Explorer displays the definitions in a small pop-up window when it's pointed to, as shown in Figure 5.4.

FIGURE 5.4

In IE for Windows, the text in the title attribute is displayed when you mouse over a word that's contained by `<abbr>` or `<acronym>`.

Tip

You might notice that this is an easy way to make text pop up around items that aren't actually abbreviations or acronyms, but simply words (or phrases) for which you'd like to see little pop-up windows appear (with definitions or help, for instance) when the mouse is pointing at them.

Paragraph Style Elements

Chapter 4 discussed the paragraph element, which is used for most of the text that you put on your Web pages. However, `<p>`, `</p>` isn't the only paragraph container element. Other elements can also be used in place of the paragraph element to contain blocks of text in different ways.

The `<pre>` Element

The *preformatted text* element, represented by the tags `<pre>` and `</pre>`, is a little different from the paragraph element in that it recognizes every space and hard return that you type between the tags. Unlike the paragraph element, you don't need to add `<br />` or other tags to render line returns. Between `<pre>` tags, the lines tend to look exactly like what you type. The following example is illustrated in Figure 5.5:

```
<pre>
Missed the Saturday dance,
    Heard they crowded the floor.
I couldn't bear it without you,
    I don't get around much anymore.
</pre>
```

FIGURE 5.5

With *pre* tags, your spacing and returns are honored.

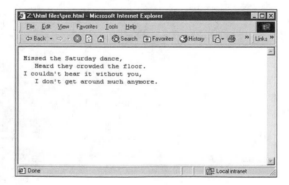

Preformatted text is excellent for items like programming code examples that you want to indent and format appropriately. The <pre> element also enables you to align text for table creation by padding it with spaces. However, because those tables appear in monospaced font, you may prefer to spend the extra time constructing the standard HTML tables, discussed in Chapter 8, "Basics Tables."

Note

Actually, you can use style sheets to change the font of text inside a <pre> element, which makes it more attractive for uses like the preceding poem. However, this doesn't help much with <pre> tables, discussed in the next section, because such tables rely on the monospaced font to make columns line up correctly.

Using <pre> for Tables

One use for <pre> is to create a primitive table. The key to making this work correctly is alignment. If you simply enter text between the two <pre> tags, you can use the space bar to line up each column, and what appears in the browser should be very similar to what you type. For instance:

```
<pre>
Year       Event
1965       I was born
1966       First novel completed
</pre>
```

Realize, however, that if you use XHTML elements within the <pre> element, you'll need to compensate for the space taken up by their tags. For instance:

```
<pre>
Year       Event
1965       I was born
<b>1966</b>       <i>First</i> novel completed
</pre>
```

Because the tags in the third line don't exist on the final page, the spacing will be correct, even though it looks misaligned when typed.

Tip

In fact, in <pre> tables you should probably avoid emphasis styles (both logical and physical). It is nearly impossible to align columns correctly in every browser when one row is bold and other rows (or columns) are plain text. Different browsers make bold text a fraction wider than regular text, so the row or column becomes increasingly mis-aligned. Even if it looks good in your browser, chances are it doesn't work in all of them.

To create a simple table:

1. Open your template and enter the following (or a similar table) between the `<body>` tags. You may need to play with the spacing a bit to line everything up:

```
<h1>Average Hourly Rate, Per Region</h1>

<pre>

Region     Handywork   Creative    Business   Advertising

NorthWest    $40         $50         $75         $100

NorthEast    $35         $45         $70         $95

SouthEast    $30         $40         $65         $90

SouthWest    $25         $35         $55         $75

</pre>
```

2. Save the HTML document, and then use the Open File command in your browser to proof it. Keep playing with it until it looks right.

Note Even within the `<pre>` container element, tabs are not recognized by browsers. If you're using a text editor or word processor, fight the urge to use the Tab key to align `<pre>` elements. Use the spacebar instead. (Some HTML editors add spaces when you press the Tab key, which would work okay.)

The `<blockquote>` Element

Historically, the `<blockquote>` container element has been used more for its physical attributes than for its logical ones. Generally, the `<blockquote>` element indents each of the margins of the paragraph it contains, making it look different from other paragraphs on the page. Although that remains the case even in XHTML, it shouldn't be your primary motive for using `<blockquote>`. The following is a listing that uses `<blockquote>` simply for its indenting qualities:

```
<h1>Site News!</h1>

<blockquote>The site is up and running, including some
<strong>introductory reviews</strong>, <em>a feature on baking at
home</em> and <tt>Quick Bites</tt> -- a column focused on getting quick,
healthy meals around town. Also, don't forget to check out the
<em>Discussion Forums</em> and please consider signing up for a
subscription to the <strong>Just In...</strong> newsletter, featuring
updates and new restaurants as soon as we post them.</blockquote>
```

Figure 5.6 shows what this looks like in a browser.

FIGURE 5.6

The
`<blockquote>`
element in
action.

Now, although this isn't illegal by any means, it'd be better to use a paragraph element, and then rely on style sheets to change the width of the margins. According to the W3C, the `<blockquote>` element should be used for presenting quoted material, such as

`<p>From the Gettysburg Address:</p>`

`<blockquote>Four score and seven years ago, our forefathers brought forth on this continent a new nation, conceived in liberty and dedicated to the proposition that all men are created equal.</blockquote>`

This example is a more correct use of the `<blockquote>` element (and it's shown in Figure 5.7). That said, it's okay to use `<blockquote>` to simply indent text, as long as you realize that some browsers may (and are allowed to) interpret the paragraph slightly differently.

FIGURE 5.7

The
`<blockquote>`
element used
appropriately.

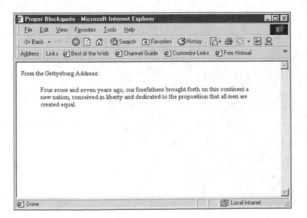

For the record, the `<blockquote>` element renders as regular body text font, the same style featured throughout the rest of your HTML document. It doesn't recognize additional spaces and returns that you enter as you type in the HTML document. As with `<p>`, the text in a `<blockquote>` container is spaced uniformly.

The `<blockquote>` element can also accept the `cite` attribute, which enables you to include the URL for a particular quotation. You can use this to show a source that you've used (if it's online), as in

```
<blockquote cite="http://eserver.org/history/gettysburg-address.txt">Four
score and seven years ago, our forefathers brought forth on this continent
a new nation, conceived in liberty and dedicated to the proposition that
all men are created equal.</blockquote>
```

Although few popular browsers do much with the `cite` attribute, in the future it may become more common for browsers to provide a link or other behavior in response to this attribute.

The `<address>` Element

The `<address>` container element is used to create paragraph-like text that's specially formatted to stand out as information about the author of the page. In most browsers, the `<address>` element is displayed as an italicized paragraph. But, as with any logical style, browsers are free to display `<address>` text any way they want to.

An example of `<address>` might be

```
<address>Page created and maintained by Ed Smiley</address>
```

Traditionally, the `<address>` element is used toward the end of a Web page to give information like

- When the page was last updated.
- Who should be contacted concerning the page (usually the Webmaster's e-mail address).
- What the URL for this page is.
- Phone numbers or physical addresses for the company or association.

Most of these elements aren't vital to your page's contents, but they're nice additions to consider. An example of a full address might be

```
<address>
This page last updated 6/12 at 9:08pm.<br />
Contact edsmiley@fakecorp.com with corrections or problems.<br />
FakeCorp<br/>
1732 93rd Street<br />
```

```
New York, NY 10025<br />
212-555-1200<br />
</address>
```

Notice the use of `<br />` to insert line breaks within an `<address>` element. This address is shown in Figure 5.8.

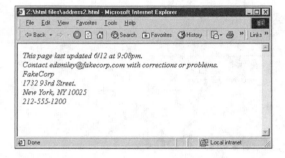

Marking Changes: `<ins>` and `<del>`

`<ins>` and `<del>` are elements that are particularly interesting in more formal business and academic settings. Ideally they're interim tags, to be used while you're working with an HTML document and before it's final.

You can use the `<del>` element to surround text that you feel should be deleted, and then use the `<ins>` element around text that should be inserted in its place. (They can also be used individually, if you're simply deleting or inserting text.) This is most useful when more than one person is working on the same HTML document and you want to see the changes. If you're familiar with the Track Changes feature in Microsoft Word, that's basically what you're doing with these elements.

Both elements can accept the `datetime`, `cite`, or `title` attributes, which you can use to better explain what you're doing. The `datetime` attribute is used to show the date and time of the insertion or deletion, using a somewhat clunky, but functional, approach:
`2001-12-05T09:00:00-05:00`

This stands for 9:00 a.m. EST on 12/5/2001. Note that the `-05:00` represents distance from mean (Zulu) time, so for PST, you'd use `-08:00` and so on. The `cite` attribute is used to reference an URL that includes an explanation of the insertion or deletion. The `title` attribute can be used to explain it within the tag. This is an example:

```
<p>It's important for the <ins datetime="2001-12-05T09:00:00-05:00"
title="Changed after the board's vote on this matter">Board of
Directors</ins><del>Office of the President</del> to have an opportunity to
make its case to the shareholders.</p>
```

This is shown in Figure 5.9.

The <ins> and <del> elements can also be used around blocks of XHTML markup, like entire <p> container elements of text.

Using Lists on Your Web Page

List elements, just as with paragraphs and preformatted text, are XHTML container elements that can accept other markup within their boundaries. XHTML lists require at least two elements, one that defines the type of list and one to contain each item within the list. Those contained items can be words, sentences, paragraphs, or other XHTML elements, such as images.

Most XHTML lists follow this format:

```
<list type>
<li>First item in list</li>
<li>Second item in list</li>
<li>Third item</li>
</list type>
```

Each of the <li> elements is an item, and each item begins on a new line. How that line begins depends on whether the list is ordered or unordered.

Ordered and Unordered Lists

It might be better to think of ordered and unordered lists as numbered and bulleted lists, respectively, especially when discussing their use in HTML documents. For numbered/ordered lists, the element is <ol>, and for bulleted/unordered lists, the element is <ul>.

For either of these lists, a list item is designated with the element <li>. In the case of ordered lists, the <li> tag inserts a number; for unordered lists, it inserts a bullet point.

This is an ordered list:

```
<ol>
<li>Item number one.</li>
<li>Item number two.</li>
<li>Item number three.</li>
</ol>
```

And this is an unordered list:

```
<ul>
<li>First item.</li>
<li>Second item.</li>
<li>Third item.</li>
</ul>
```

To see how these look in a browser, see Figure 5.10.

FIGURE 5.10

Ordered (numbered) and unordered (bulleted) lists.

Aside from other XHTML markup, you can include other lists within lists, as long as they're carefully *nested* within one another. For example:

```
<ol>
<li>item 1</li>
<li>item 2</li>
<li><ul>
<li>item 3.1</li>
<li>item 3.2</li>
</ul></li>
<li>item 4</li>
</ol>
```

The rule is simple—you need to end the list that's nested within the original list before you can end the original list. In fact, you need to end the list item in which that nested list resides before you can move on.

Ordered List Attributes

You have the option of changing the way lists act and appear on the page. However, it's worth noting that these are transitional attributes, not compliant with the XHTML Strict DTD, so have the XHTML Transitional DTD specified if you're going to use them. The better approach is to use style sheets, as discussed in Chapter 10.

Most graphical browsers recognize some additional attributes for ordered list items, including start, value, and type. Likewise, unordered lists can accept the type attribute, which enables you to change the appearance of the bullet. Table 5.4 covers the attributes for ordered lists.

TABLE 5.4   Attributes for Ordered List Items

Tag	Display List Value As...
`<ol type="A">`	Uppercase letters
`<ol type="a">`	Lowercase letters
`<ol type="I">`	Uppercase Roman numerals
`<ol type="i">`	Lowercase Roman numerals
`<ol type="1">`	Numbers

In addition, the start attribute can be used to change the starting value for that list. For example, you could have a numbered list start at the value 10 by beginning it with this tag:

```
<ol start="10">
```

You can also use the value attribute to change the value of an individual list item. For example, this is how to change the numbering within the list:

```
<ol>
<li>Item #1</li>
<li>Item #2</li>
<li value="1">Item #1</li>
<li>Item #2</li>
</ol>
```

Bullet List Attributes

This example is also transitional, so you should use a style sheet if you're trying to keep to the XHTML Strict DTD. If you're not, you can change the appearance of bullets in unordered lists with the `type` attribute. The bullet styles are as follows:

- *Solid circle*—`<ul type="disc">`
- *Solid square*—`<ul type="square">`
- *Open circle*—`<ul type="circle">`

Note that not all Web browsers can render these bullet styles, and not all do it correctly when they try. You might get squares for all these bullets, for example.

Definition Lists

The final list element is the definition list, which is designed to allow for two levels of list items: the defined term and its definition.

The elements for this list are the main list container element `<dl>` (definition list) and two list item container elements, `<dt>` (definition term) and `<dd>` (definition). The `<dt>` element is designed to fit on a single line of your Web page, although it wraps to the beginning of the next line if necessary. The `<dd>` element accepts a full paragraph of text. In most visual browsers, the definition text is continuously indented beneath the `<dt>` term. For example:

```
<dl>
<dt><b>genus</b> <i>(n.)</i></dt>
<dd>A group or type marked by common characteristics.</dd>
<dt><b>geocentric</b> <i>(adj.)</i></dt>
<dd>Of, related to or coming from the center of the earth.</dd>
<dt><b>geography</b> <i>(n.)</i></dt>
<dd>The study of the earth, its topography and its natural or manufactured
features.</dd>
</dl>
```

Notice that standard XHTML markup is permissible within the boundaries of a definition list, and that using bold and italics for the defined terms adds a dictionary-like quality. This is shown in Figure 5.11.

FIGURE 5.11

A typical
definition list.

Not all browsers display definition lists in the same way, so adding spaces to `<dt>` items to get them to line up with the `<dd>` text is often a waste of time.

Just because definition lists allow for two different types of list items, you don't need to use both. Using just the `<dt>` element in your list, for example, results in a list not unlike an unordered list—except that nearly all browsers display it without bullets. For example:

```
<dl>
<dt>Uptown - above 60th Street
<dt>Midtown - 14th to 60th Street
<dt>Downtown - below 14th Street
</DL>
```

And, although the `<dd>` element isn't as useful, it could be used on its own to indent paragraphs repeatedly within the definition list structure.

Summary

In this chapter, you learned about quite of few of the basic XHTML elements that are used to change the organization of text on your Web pages. The chapter began with a look at the heading elements, and then it explained the physical and logical elements that are used to emphasize and stylize text. You then saw the various elements used to alter the organization and appearance of paragraphs, followed by the elements used to create lists on the page.

In Chapter 6, you'll learn how to create images for your Web documents and add them using the `<img />` element and its attributes.

VISUAL STIMULUS— ADDING GRAPHICS

*T*he vast majority of Web pages you encounter have images that either enhance the appearance of the Web pages, add to their usability, or communicate information. Generally, these images are easy to create and easy to add to your Web document. All you need are the correct tools and the knowledge of a few additional XHTML elements. It's important to realize that your images are not visible to all of your Web users, however, so you'll want to compensate for non-graphical browsers. Fortunately, attributes that substitute text when images can't be displayed are built-in, as are other options for customizing the appearance of images on your pages.

This chapter discusses the following:

- Creating or translating images for use on the Web
- Placing an image in your HTML document
- Attributes for altering an image and offering alternative text
- Aligning an image on the page

Images on the Web

When you're talking about images on the Web (and in computing in general), what you're really talking about is a particular type of computer file. Such files can be any sort of visual element—a drawing, something placed on a digital scanner, a photo from a digital camera, even an image of text created in a graphics application—but that element is always in a particular file format.

This means that a text editor like Windows Notepad or Mac's SimpleText won't be able to read an image properly. Instead, you'd need to use an image-browsing application, an image-editing application, or a Web browser. Ultimately, it's the file format that differentiates the image document from a text document and, by extension, from an HTML document.

It's a simple matter to add images to your Web pages—all it takes is the `<img />` element. Realize, however, that you're not adding the images to your HTML document. You place a *pointer* in your HTML document, which tells a Web browser how to find and load the image from its location either on your Web server or on the Internet. The image file and HTML document need to exist separately (see Figure 6.1).

FIGURE 6.1

The image on this page is the result of an instruction in the HTML document to locate the image file and place it in the browser window.

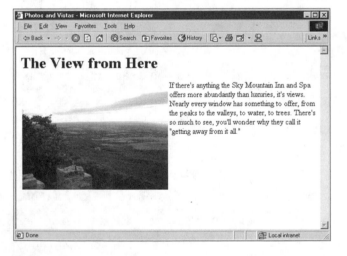

This issue of "where the image file is" can be a bit confusing, so let me clarify. Just as with any HTML document, an image file is referenced using a unique URL. This URL can point to an image file that's in the same folder or directory as the HTML document, one in a different directory on the same disk or Web server, or one that's somewhere else on the Internet. But the important issue is that you're using an URL. You'll see how exactly to do that later, in the section "The `<img />` Element." First, though, let's go through a quick primer on graphic file formats and how to create and/or translate images for the Web.

What Images Can You Use?

As mentioned, images are special files in particular formats that are recognized by Web browsers and other applications. On the Web, these file formats include JPEG, GIF, and PNG. But images can come in many other formats as well, such as PCX, TIFF, PICT, and so on.

For the sake of compatibility, however, only those first three formats are appropriate for use on your Web pages. If you have files in other formats, you'll want to translate them. Here's a look at the image formats that are Web-compatible:

- **JPEG (Joint Photographic Experts Group, pronounced "J-Peg")—** This format is generally used for photographs because it looks best at millions of colors. If you have an image that's been scanned using a scanner or taken with a digital still camera, it's possible that the image is already in JPEG format.

- **GIF (Graphics Interchange Format, pronounced "Jiff" or "Giff")—** This file type is best used for images that are computer-created—particularly text and mouse-drawn graphics that require fewer colors. GIF files are highly compressed, so they take less time to travel over the Internet—an important consideration. GIF also supports transparency within the image (so that images can appear to be sitting directly on the Web page's background) and animation.

- **PNG (Portable Network Graphics, pronounced "Ping")—**This format was actually created as a replacement for GIF, in part because GIF uses a patented compression scheme whereas PNG is free of patents. PNG also supports transparency and animation.

So, if you're creating an image in a drawing or photo-editing application, you'll likely choose PNG or GIF, particularly if it isn't a photographic-quality image. If the image is a photograph in another format, you'll likely use an image program to translate it into JPEG format, as discussed later in this chapter.

You should avoid copying or translating images for your own use if you don't have the rights to do so. Web browsers and other applications will allow you to copy images from other Web sites, and you may have access to other images that you'd like to use on your Web pages. Many images, such as logos and photographs (among many others), are copyrighted and owned by individuals or corporations. Your best bet is to use only images that you create, not just translate or alter. Of course, I'm not an attorney, so consult one if you have a particular legal question.

What Images *Should* You Use?

When you're choosing or creating the images for your Web page, you should focus on two basic issues. The images should be there for a good reason (not just to make the page look pretty) and should download quickly to the user's browser.

The photos, charts, and graphs that you use will likely improve both the appearance of your page and its ability to communicate with the reader. Text alone won't always hold a reader's attention, so images can be used to break up the text, summarize key points, or simply make the page more attractive.

Clear images communicate their function almost instantly. In fact, *icons*—which are simply small images similar to the folders and documents that appear in Microsoft Windows or the Macintosh OS—are often a clever way to get a point across graphically, while keeping your images small and to a minimum.

The images that communicate best may not even seem to be images at all—instead, they may be text. You'll find it's often convenient to create images that are largely text, if only to put more visually appealing text on your page. Figure 6.2, for instance, shows title text that looks a little more stylish than an HTML heading.

FIGURE 6.2

Images on a page can include stylized text.

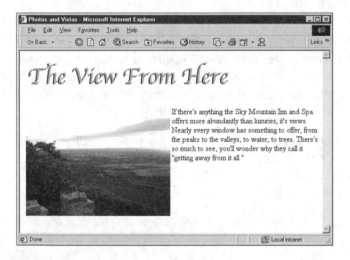

Although adding Web images to your pages is a fairly painless process, creating those images can be a bit tougher. The trick with Web images is to keep them interesting, entertaining, and useful, yet small and unobtrusive. It takes a bit of getting used to, but the best Web designers understand that having a balance is the most important element for successful images. Here are a few basic rules:

■ Images and drawn graphics should have a clear purpose on your page. Having images just for the sake of having pictures on the page should be kept to a minimum. Most Web surfers are looking for information or services, not cool images.

- Image files should be small and load quickly. By the same token, your Web page should load quickly, too—which means it can't be overwhelmed with images.

- Take advantage of technology to improve your images. Make sure you choose the correct image format for your graphic, and use your image-editing application to trim the image and make it as small as possible while still being useful. You should also consult Chapter 11, "Advanced Web Images and Imagemaps," to learn more about advanced issues that can make your images more highly compressed and efficient.

There are two measurements of image size on Web pages: the amount of the screen that an image takes up, and the storage space the image's file requires on the server computer. So, when we say you should have small images, it isn't only that the image shouldn't take up much space on the page. More importantly, it should be small in actual *file size*, which makes the image download to a user's Web browser more quickly.

How do you make files smaller? Some applications have special tools that help you shrink your images' file sizes. But mostly it's a question of choosing the correct image format (JPEG for photos, GIF or PNG for drawn or painted graphics and text), using the fewest number of colors possible, and cropping or trimming the images so that you only use as much space as necessary. For other hints and ideas, see Chapter 11.

Creating and Translating Web Images

Once you've considered the implications of using images on the Web, you can set yourself to the task of creating and/or translating images. You'll need a image-editing application (discussed in Chapter 3, "What You Need to Get Started"), and you'll need either some existing images or some ideas for creating new images. In this section, we'll discuss two different applications—Paint Shop Pro for Microsoft Windows and GraphicConverter for Macintosh.

Using Paint Shop Pro

Paint Shop Pro for Windows is the most popular shareware option for image editing, particularly among Web designers. And there's good reason—the basic tasks are simple.

If you already have an image you're working with, you should load that image into Paint Shop Pro by selecting File, Open. The image can be anything—a photograph, a drawing you've created in another application, or even an image that you've created in Paint Shop Pro. Once the image is loaded, you're ready to crop it and prepare it for the Web.

Cropping the Image

Cropping an image simply means selecting the portion of the original image that you'd like to use as the final image on your Web page. In many cases, it's a good idea to crop an image to the bare minimum you'd like to use. This is partly so that the image will fit well on your page, but also so that it's as small as possible while still communicating important information. With images that you create in other programs, you may also find it useful to crop each image so that less of its background will appear on the Web page.

In Paint Shop Pro, with the image loaded, select the Crop tool and drag an outline around the area that you'd like to keep. You do this by pointing at the top-left corner of the area, and then clicking and holding the mouse button while you drag to the bottom-right corner of the portion you'd like to keep. Release the mouse button and the area should be surrounded by a box (see Figure 6.3).

FIGURE 6.3

Selecting an area for cropping in Paint Shop Pro.

Crop tool —

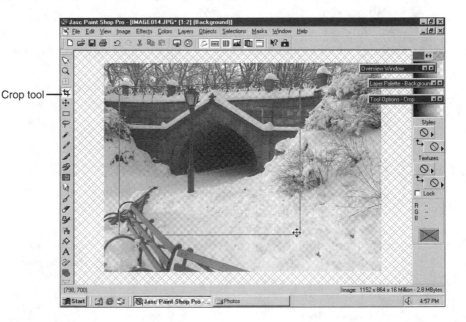

With the selection made, choose Image, Crop from the menu or double-click inside the box that you've drawn. The image is cropped to the portion inside the box. Choose File, Save to save the changes, or choose File, Save As to give the cropped image a new name, thus keeping the original image as well.

Resizing an Image

Often you'll find that even once you've cropped a high-resolution photo to the desired size, you've still got something that's a little too big to fit comfortably and effectively on your Web page. The solution is to resize the image, which is fairly simple to do in Paint Shop Pro.

With the image open in a document window, select Image, Resize. In the Pixel size section of the Resize dialog box, you can enter a new size, in pixels. Note that when you change the width, the height changes automatically. That's because the Maintain Aspect Ratio option is turned on at the bottom of the Resize dialog box. This ensures that a resized image won't be stretched or compressed in a way that makes it look distorted. (If you *want* distortion, turn this option off.)

If you'd prefer, you can click the radio button next to Percentage of Original and enter a new width or height. That way you can quickly change the size of the image without worrying about an exact size in pixels.

When you've made your changes, click OK and the image will change in size.

ALL ABOUT PIXELS

What's all this about pixels? Pixels are *picture elements*, which is a fancy way to say "dots." Images on your screen are composed of a certain number of dots. The more dots, the larger the image will appear.

Your computer display is set within your operating system to display a fixed number of pixels—usually 1,024×768, or sometimes 800×600. (It may have a different setting, usually dependent on the size of the display.) Images from digital cameras can be "megapixel" images—1,024×768 at the lowest, with some of them pushing 2,048×1,536 or higher. Clearly, that's more pixels than you need for a Web image. The solution is to crop the images and/or resize them.

You may come across one other measurement, called *pixels per inch (ppi)*. Different items have different pixel resolutions, which is why pixels can be so darned confusing. If you're asked by an application, images for a Web page generally don't need to be more than 72 ppi. As you'll see in Chapter 11, you can change the ppi of images to make them take up less storage space and travel over the Internet more quickly.

Adding Text

To add text to an image (or to create an image that's exclusively text), you simply click the Text button (it looks like a capital "A") and then click in the image window to begin adding text. When you click, the Text Entry dialog box will appear.

Enter the text you'd like to add to the image in the Enter Text Here entry box. Then use the commands elsewhere in the dialog box to fine-tune the appearance of the text, including font, size, style, alignment, and even kerning (space between characters) and leading (space between lines). When you're done, click OK.

> **Note**
>
> One option enables you to *anti-alias* the text, which means to smooth the appearance of the text onscreen. This is a great idea for most Web images because the text looks more polished and professional.

After you click OK, your text becomes an object in the image, as shown in Figure 6.4. If you'd like to move the text, you can do that by pointing at the very middle of the text until you see the mouse pointer change into a four-way arrow. Now click and hold the mouse button, and then move the mouse around and you'll drag the text around on the image. When you get to its new home, release the mouse button.

FIGURE 6.4

Adding text in Paint Shop Pro.

Text tool

> **Tip**
>
> If you point at one of the corners of the text area, and then click the mouse and drag, you can change the size of the image, actually stretching it in different directions. This is an interesting way to get some "tall text" or "fat text" effects.

Saving or Translating the Image File

When you're ready to save an image for the Web, you'll want to select File, Save As, so that you can choose the appropriate image file format. In the Save As dialog box, enter a name for the image in the File name entry box. I recommend you avoid using spaces in the filename because they're a little tougher to deal with on the Web.

Now you'll see the Save as Type menu, which you can use to choose the file type. For photographic images, choose JPEG—JFIF (JFIF Compliant) as the type. For images you've created in Paint Shop Pro, choose either CompuServe Graphics Interchange or Portable Network Graphics. With that selection made, you can click Save to save your new image in its Web-compliant format.

| Note | You can do a lot more when saving images, including tricks to make them take up less space as files. See Chapter 11 for more details. |

Using GraphicConverter

GraphicConverter is the most popular shareware graphics solution for Macintosh, with both Mac OS 9 (and earlier) and Mac OS X versions available. To load your image into GraphicConverter, select File, Open. Once it's loaded, you'll be able to crop, resize, and save or translate it.

Cropping (Trimming) the Image

To crop an image in GraphicConverter, click the Selection tool in the toolbar (it looks like a dotted rectangle) and move the mouse pointer over to the image. Now draw a box around the portion of the image that you'd like to keep. You do this by pointing at the top-left corner of the area you'd like to keep, and then clicking and holding the mouse button while you drag to the bottom-right corner of the portion you'd like to keep. Release the mouse button and the area should be surrounded by a dotted line (see Figure 6.5).

To crop out the rest of the image and keep the outlined portion, choose Edit, Trim Selection. You'll see a new, smaller version of the image. Choose File, Save to immediately save the change. (If you'd like to give the cropped image a new name so that the original remains intact, choose File, Save As, as discussed later in the section "Saving or Translating the Image File.")

Selection tool

FIGURE 6.5

Selecting an area
for cropping in
GraphicConverter.

Resizing an Image

To resize an image in GraphicConverter, open the image in a document window and select Picture, Size, Scale from the menu. In the Scale dialog box, enter a new value in either the Width or Height entry box. The other value will change automatically as long as the Keep Proportions option is checked. Note that you can alter the units for the measurement you're changing by selecting Pixel or Percent from the pop-up menu that appears next to both the Width and Height entries.

When you're done making adjustments, click the OK button.

Note | Typically, you won't want a photo to be more than a few hundred pixels wide by a few hundred pixels tall. In most cases, a 300×200 image will take up about 25% of the user's display. For more on pixels, see the "All About Pixels" sidebar earlier in this chapter.

Adding Text

To add text to an image (or to create an image that's exclusively text), you simply click the Text button (it looks like a capital "A") and then click in the image window to create a text area. You can use the mouse to drag the sides of the text area to make it larger. Then, simply start typing the text you want to add to the image (see Figure 6.6).

FIGURE 6.6

Adding text in GraphicConverter.

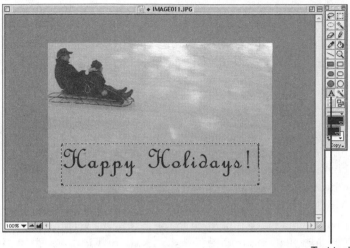

Text tool

If you'd like to move the text area, place the mouse pointer over it until the pointer turns into a hand. Now click and hold the mouse button, and you'll see the hand turn into a fist. Move the mouse around to drag the text around on the image. When you get to its new home, release the mouse button.

If you'd like to change the style of the text, you can do so while the text area is still highlighted. (If it isn't, first click the Selection tool, and then click the text area again). Simply double-click the Text tool and a dialog box will appear in which you can change the font, size, alignment, and style of the text. When you're done, click the OK button.

Note

Anti-alias means to smooth the appearance of text onscreen. This is a great idea for most Web images, as anti-aliasing text tends to make it look more polished and professional.

Saving or Translating the Image File

Once you have the image open and ready to save or translate, choose File, Save As. In the Save dialog box, enter a name for the image in the Name entry box. I recommend names without spaces because they're easier to add to your HTML documents. Next, select a format from the Format menu—JPEG/JFIF for photographic images, GIF or PNG for images you've created in GraphicConverter. (When you choose the format, a three-letter filename extension is appended automatically.) Click Save.

When you choose JPEG/JFIF, a dialog box appears. In that dialog box, you can choose the quality level of the image. The lower the quality, the smaller the file size of the image. You can also choose to use either QuickTime or JPEG 6.0 as the compression library—choose JPEG 6.0. Click OK to finish saving the image as a JPEG.

The `<img />` Element

When you want to insert a graphic file on a Web page, you actually do so with an URL. This URL is the specific location on the Internet where the graphic file is located. It can be on the same Web host computer that your HTML document is on, or it can be on a host somewhere else on the Internet.

The most basic `<img />` element can be used to create an *inline image*, which appears exactly where you place it relative to the text in the HTML document. The other kind of images, floating images, are discussed later in the section "Left- and Right-Aligning Images." The basic difference between the two types is that inline images aren't aligned against a margin—they're anchored in the text of the page. Floating images can be made to stick to the left or right margin.

To add an inline image to your page, you'll use the `<img />` element. This element acts as a placeholder in your text where the browser will put the graphic. The basic image element has the following syntax:

```
<img src="image_URL" />
```

The src attribute means *source* and refers to the location of the image (it's on some hard drive somewhere in the world). The actual URL for the image file replaces the words *image_URL*.

The *image_URL* can be a full URL with full machine name (such as `http://www.fakecorp.com/images/product1.jpg`). Alternatively, the URL can refer to the image file's *relative URL*. In this case, you refer to the file's location relative to the directory where the Web page is.

A relative URL is one that doesn't include an entire Internet address, such as `/images/product1.gif`. When you enter an URL in this way, the machine address portion of the URL (as in `www.fakecorp.com`) is assumed to be the same as that of the HTML document that includes the relative URL reference.

The following is sample HTML code for adding an inline graphic to the page (see Figure 6.7):

```
<p><img src="three.gif" />Rudolpho's offers excellent
vegetarian options, including a fabulous array of olive-based
appetizers, delectable breads and great house wines. The
mix-and-match pastas give you an array of choices for sauce
```

and pasta style and the atmosphere is the perfect blend of
sidewalk cafe and intimate conversation nooks. The only
downside -- weak service and a surprisingly woeful dessert tray.
Three stars.</p>

FIGURE 6.7

Notice that the
image appears
on the same line
as the text. It's
an inline image.

Notice that the `<img src />` element is using a relative URL. Actually, it could have just as easily been a complete URL like

```
<img src="http://www.fakecorp.com/three.gif" />
```

Both are similarly useful, but you only need to use a complete URL if the image you're loading resides elsewhere on the Internet. If it's in a subdirectory, something like this will work just fine:

```
<img src="/images/image1.gif" />
```

Note

It's important to avoid linking to files using a direct file URL to your hard drive. (This will sometimes happen when you use less-sophisticated or older HTML editors.) Remember, your computer's hard drive isn't on the Internet—your Web server's hard drive is. So, if you create an image link like `<img src="file:///c|web_site/image.gif">`, your users will not be able to see the image once the page is uploaded to your Web server.

Alternative Text

Not everyone on the Internet has access to Internet Explorer, Netscape, or another graphical browser. In some cases you may be dealing with text-only Web browsers, such as those on cell phones, handheld computers, and "dumb" terminals at college campuses or libraries. In other cases, you may be dealing with sight-impaired users or others whose browsers offer assistive features.

So how can you accommodate these users, even when you use images in your Web pages? HTML provides a simple solution: the `alt` (alternative) attribute. This attribute defines a text string that replaces the image in browsers without graphics support. This text is often displayed in a box to separate it from the surrounding body text. Here's an example:

```
<img src="graph1.gif" alt="Chart shows sales up 25 percent in six months"
➥/>
```

You should consider `alt` a required attribute for well-formed XHTML code, and it offers the most benefit to the widest possible audience. In that spirit, it's also important not to place irrelevant text in the `alt` attribute (like "put text here" or "colorful bullet point"). Many assistive browsers will be forced to waste time by rendering that text in speech or in Braille, for instance. In other words, keep your `alt` text relevant and brief.

If you have a strong desire to explain an image in more detail, you can do so with another attribute: `longdesc`. This attribute enables you to specify an URL which can be linked to and explain the image in more detail, as in

```
<img src="graph1.gif" alt="Chart shows sales up 25 percent in six months"
➥longdesc="http://www.fakecorp.com/charts/chart1.html" />
```

Aligning Text and Images

On their own, Web browsers don't do much to help text and images share space on a Web page. Web browsers treat inline images like characters in the line of text. Often this doesn't look very good, particularly with photographs. Instead, you'd probably prefer an image to look more like an image on a magazine page, with the text wrapped around it.

Fortunately, you can do something about this. `<img />` comes with an attribute called `align`, which determines how text and images interact with one another on a Web page. Specifically, `align` controls how text that's placed on the same line as an image will line itself up along the vertical sides of the image.

The `align` attribute is written as

```
<img align="value" src="image_URL" />
```

The standard (inline) values for the align attribute are shown in Table 6.1.

TABLE 6.1   Standard Values for the `align` Attribute

Value	Effect on Text
`"top"`	Aligns the bottom of the text to top of the image
`"middle"`	Aligns the bottom of the text to the middle of the image
`"bottom"`	Aligns the bottom of the text to the bottom of the image

The bottom value is the default for <img />, so you don't need to specify it if that's what you want to use. When using any of the standard values, Web browsers leave white space around the text on the line, and the text wraps down to the next line beneath the bottom of the image. Figure 6.8 shows how a Web browser handles each of these attribute values.

FIGURE 6.8

The image is aligned to bottom, top, and middle, respectively.

Right- and Left-Aligning Images

The align attribute can accept two other values, left and right, which change the image from an inline image to floating images. They won't appear exactly where you place the <img /> element in the text, but rather on the selected margin near the text that surrounds the <img /> element. In addition, the text will wrap around the image, somewhat like an image on a magazine page, as shown in Figure 6.9. Here's an example:

```
<p><img src="valley.jpg" align="left" />Views. If there's
anything the Sky Mountain Inn and Spa offers more abundantly
than luxuries, it's views. Nearly every window has something
to offer, from the peaks to the valleys, to water, to trees.
There's so much to see, you'll wonder why they call it "getting
away from it all." </p>
```

FIGURE 6.9

The top image is left-aligned; the bottom is right-aligned.

Note Older browsers will recognize two other attributes, `vspace` and `hspace`, which can be used to add space between a floating image and text. These commands are not well-formed code, however. In Chapter 10, "Get Splashy: Style Sheets, Fonts, and Special Characters," you'll see that style sheets can be used to create the same effect.

Width and Height

Two other attributes for `<img />`, `width` and `height`, are worth mentioning. These two attributes are designed to make your Web page appear in the user's browser just a bit more quickly.

By telling the browser the size of the images (in pixels), the browser is able to mock up the layout and lay in the text before it finishes retrieving the images. This makes it appear that your page is loading more quickly in the browser window, and it allows the visitor to read text and click hyperlinks even as the page continues to download. Here's an example of the `width` and `height` attributes in action:

```
<p><img src="mountains.jpg" align="left" width="250" height="100" />
Views. If there's anything the Guest Cottage offers more abundantly
than luxuries, it's views. Nearly every window has something to offer,
from the peaks to the valleys, to water, to trees. There's so much to
see, you'll wonder why they call it "getting away from it all."</p>
```

Need to know the size of an image? In most cases, your image-editing application can help you. Just look for an `Info` command. In Paint Shop Pro, select Image, Image Information. In GraphicConverter, choose Picture, Show Information.

Note that the `width` and `height` attributes can actually be used to change the apparent size of an existing image and force it to conform to the pixel size that you specify. That means you could take an image that's 300 pixels wide and 150 pixels high and force it to appear 150 pixels wide and 75 pixels high simply by specifying those sizes:

```
<img src="bigimage.jpg" width="150" height="75" />
```

This is certainly possible, but it's not a great idea for one reason: file size. The file size of the image remains the same, regardless of the height and width specified. In the preceding example, you're forcing your visitors to download the full image and view it at half size. The better plan would be to crop or scale the image in an image-editing application, and then use that smaller image on your page.

Summary

In this chapter, you learned about the file formats that can be used on the Web, and how to modify and translate other images so that they can be saved in those formats. You also learned how to crop images and create images that include text. Then, you learned how to use the `<img />` element to add images to your Web documents, including many of the attributes associated with `<img />` that are used to align the image against text on the page, add alternative text, and specify the width and height of the image.

In Chapter 7, you'll learn how to add hyperlinks to your pages so that you can link to other Web pages, other Web sites, and even other Internet services.

BUILDING HYPERTEXT LINKS

ypertext was the basic concept that propelled the idea of the Web forward, allowing information and ideas to be linked together in a way that hadn't happened before on the Internet. Combined with most Web browsers' graphical and multimedia capabilities, hypertext links (hyperlinks) make the Web an entirely new medium for communication and publishing.

This chapter discusses the following:

- How hyperlinks work, including relative links versus absolute links and the various HTML elements used for links
- Creating the links and putting them on your Web page
- Linking to parts of the same page and building graphical links
- Creating special links, including links to other Internet services
- Automatic link stuff: changing pages and opening new Web browser windows

How Hyperlinks Work

On the Web, hyperlinks are the basis of all movement and manipulation. Clicking a link on a Web page generally moves you to the related resource by loading that resource in your Web browser or in a helper application. Sometimes that's a new Web page; sometimes it's another Internet service, like an e-mail message or an FTP (file transfer protocol) server. Before the user can click a link, however, it has to be created by the Web author.

You use an XHTML element, the `<a>` anchor element, to create a hyperlink. The anchor requires the `href` attribute, which is used to tell the Web browser which new URL is being referenced by the hyperlink. So, to create a hyperlink, you'll first need to determine the URL for the target page or resource.

The Uniform Resource Locator

Every hyperlink contains a *Uniform Resource Locator*, or *URL*. The URL is the address of the Web page that appears in the Location or Address box near the top of your Web browser when you're surfing the Web. It's also the address that shows up, in many cases, at the bottom of your Web browser's window when you move the cursor over a hyperlink.

As mentioned in Chapter 1, "Fundamentals of Web Publishing," the URL consists of two major items: the protocol and the destination (although they have all types of other names). The protocol tells you what kind of Internet resource you're dealing with. The most common protocol on the Web is http://, which retrieves HTML documents from the Web.

The destination can be a filename, a directory name, or a computer name. An URL such as `http://www.fakecorp.com/products/index.html` tells you exactly where the HTML document is located and what its filename is. If the URL is `ftp://ftp.netscape.com/`, the URL is telling the browser to access a computer named ftp.netscape.com using the File Transfer Protocol.

Relative Versus Absolute URLs

There's another distinction you can make when it comes to URLs for your hyperlinks. If a particular Web page's URL is basically the same as the current page—except, perhaps, for the filename—it's possible to use a *relative* URL to reference that page. Consider the following two pages:

`http://www.olelondonisp.net/drwatson/index.html`

`http://www.olelondonisp.net/drwatson/resume.html`

Both of these URLs are absolute URLs—they could both be used to reference their respective pages (index.html and resume.html) from anywhere on the Internet. But what if you're creating a hyperlink on the first page (index.html) that points to the second page (resume.html)? In that case, you could use a relative URL, because the rest of the information is the same.

It's a little like working with files in folders on your PC or Mac. If you save a file in a particular folder and then decide to open a new file, generally you don't have to go spelunking through your entire hard drive to find that folder again. Many applications will open right to the last-used folder.

A Web browser does the same thing. When it encounters an URL that's nothing more than a path or filename, such as resume.html, the browser will assume that the author meant "Use the current URL and directory, but open a new file." For instance, let's say the current page is stored in this directory:

```
http://www.olelondonisp.net/drwatson/
```

It's assumed that the relative link should simply be tacked onto that URL:

http://www.olelondonisp.net/drwatson/ + resume.html

This results in the following:

```
http://www.olelondonisp.net/drwatson/resume.html
```

So, you could use the following relative URL to refer to the second page from the first page:

```
resume.html
```

This is shown in Figure 7.1. If index.html and resume.html are in the same directory (and on the same Web server computer), everything will work fine.

FIGURE 7.1

The links shown are relative links, which should work fine as long as those pages are in the same directory as the page being edited.

This relativity, if you will, means you can also reach other directories on the server using common notation. For instance, if you want to access an item that's in a sub-directory of the current directory, you could use an URL such as `/pages/house.html` or even `/assistants/roger/resume.html` to access those items. If those are valid subdirecto-ries of the directory where the HTML document currently resides, those items will be accessed.

Similarly, you can use special notation to cause the URL to access a directory that's the parent of the current directory. For instance, suppose you're saving the current HTML document in the `products` directory, which is a subdirectory of the site's main (or root) directory. In that case, you could access the main index page using an URL like this:

`../index.html`

Likewise, you could access a subdirectory of the root directory using an URL like this:

`../service/contact.html`

The two periods at the beginning are standard notation that represents the *parent* of the current directory. They mean "go up one directory level." Figure 7.2 shows you where these files would be located to give you a sense of the hierarchy.

Note Using relative links can be a bit risky because they make it harder for you to move direc-tories and subdirectories around on your site. If you reorganize your site at some point, your relative links may no longer work correctly.

FIGURE 7.2

If the current page is in the products direc-tory, its parent is the root direc-tory of the Web site.

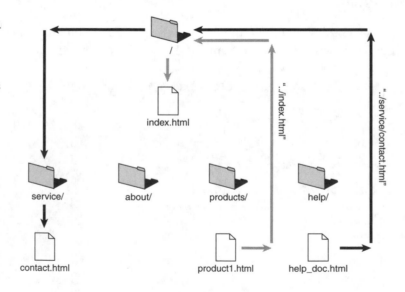

The <base> Element

You've already seen that relative URLs take some of the effort out of creating hyperlinks. But, as noted, relative URLs are always "relative" to the directory where the current HTML document is stored. But what if you'd like some other location to be the URL that gets added to your relative URL to make up the entire address? You can do that with the <base> element.

Take this example:

1. You've created a directory structure that begins at this URL:

   ```
   http://www.fakecorp.com/
   ```

2. Within that directory you've created some subdirectories, like images, about, and products.

3. You create a page called widget.html within a new_products subdirectory of the products directory. The URL to that file would be

   ```
   http://www.fakecorp.com/products/new_products/widget.html
   ```

4. Let's say you want to get to the contact.html page that's inside the about directory. One solution would be to use the two periods introduced earlier, which would result in a relative URL such as

   ```
   ../../about/contact.html
   ```

5. Unfortunately, that's not much more fun than typing an absolute URL, such as http://www.fakecorp.com/about/contact.html. Plus, you're probably a bit more likely to commit a typo. But there is another option. You could use the <base> element to set the base URL to your site's root directory:

   ```
   <head>
   <base href="http://www.fakecorp.com/" />
   </head>
   ```

6. What this means is that all relative URLs will be relative to the base href URL instead of to the document's current location. So, to access that contact page, the URL would now be

   ```
   about/contact.html
   ```

Essentially, adding a <base> element means that the base URL is added together with any relative URLs to create a complete reference. In the example, the base URL http://www.fakecorp.com/ is added to the relative URL about/contact.html to create this absolute URL:

```
http://wwww.fakecorp.com/about/contact.html
```

Notice, though, that the `<base>` element will affect *every* relative URL on the page. You'll need to change any relative URLs that don't take the base URL into account. That said, the `<base>` element doesn't affect absolute URLs at all, so you don't need to worry about them.

Creating Links

Most hypertext links by themselves are added to HTML documents using the anchor element (`<a>`, `</a>`). This element surrounds the text that describes what the link points to. The URL itself must be in quotes, and it uses the `href` (hyperlink reference) attribute. A link in HTML takes the following format:

```
<a href="URL">put your link text here</a>
```

So, if you want to link the text "About our company" with the HTML document called `about.html` that resides in the root directory of the `www.fakecorp.com` machine, the HTML code would look like this:

```
<a href="http://www.fakecorp.com/about.html">About our company</a>
```

Try to make your link text descriptive. Links that say things such as "Click here" or "Follow this link" don't give the users enough information about what they are getting into.

As mentioned earlier in this chapter, absolute URLs aren't the only ones you can use for hyperlinks. If, for instance, `team.html` is in the same directory and on the same machine as the page containing the following HTML code, the URL shown will work fine:

```
<a href="team.html">About our executive team</a>
```

Another interesting aspect of relative links is that they don't change just because you move the files. It's like furniture in your living room. If you moved from one address to another, chances are that the armchair and couch could still be found if you told a friend, "Look in the living room." If you used an absolute reference ("Go to 123 Main and look in the living room"), you'd have to change part of that reference when you moved to a new place.

In the same way, you'd have to change an absolute URL, such as `http://www.oldfakecorp.com/about.html`, if you moved to a new server computer (such as `www.fakecorp.com`). If the URL were relative, however, it would still work fine in the new location.

Make sure you've enclosed *something* inside your anchor—whether it's text or an image element. If you don't put anything in there, you aren't giving your audience much of a target to click.

One thing you *can't* do with a link is nest one link within another—you must close the first anchor element before starting another one. The following example is illegal:

```
Order <a href="product1.html">Product #1 or
<a href="product2.html">Product #2</a> from our store.</a>
```

Instead, the link would need to be something more along these lines:

```
Order <a href="product1.html">Product #1</a> or
<a href="product2.html">Product #2</a> from our store.
```

You can also create links that point to any sort of file that a Web browser can display, such as a text file (.txt) or an image file (.jpg, .gif, .png). In fact, you can link to many types of multimedia files as well, and they'll be handed off to a helper application, if appropriate (see Chapter 13, "Adding Multimedia and Java Content").

Linking on the Same Page

Picture this—you've got a long Web page with different sections, and you want to include a link that takes the user to a different part of the page that is already being displayed. It's easy. You'll first name a portion of your page, and then you'll create an anchor that points to that named portion.

First things first. On some part of your page, you'll use the `<a>` element with the `name` attribute, as in

```
<a name="q1"><h2>Question 1</h2></a>

<p>What is the cause of the root of the problem?</p>
```

For the record, though, this actually isn't well-formed code for XHTML because XML doesn't really support the `name` attribute. Instead, you should use the `id` attribute, which is much more acceptable (as you'll see in later chapters). Furthermore, `id` (in this context) isn't implemented in many earlier Web browsers. So, for the foreseeable future, the solution is actually to include them both:

```
<a name="q1" id="q1"><h2>Question 1<h2></a>
```

And just to be perfectly clear, the name and id specified can be anything alphanumeric that begins with a letter, and it can include dashes, underscores, periods, and colons. So "12" wouldn't be acceptable, while "question:one" or "myitem56" or "r134567" would all be acceptable.

Now, to reference that section with a link, you simply create an anchor tag that points to that name but includes the pound sign (#) as part of the URL:

```
<p>See <a href="#q1">Question 1</a> for more information.</p>
```

It may help to see all this in context. Figure 7.3 shows a sample HTML document that includes a number of named anchors on the same page.

FIGURE 7.3

Here's a page that includes multiple named anchors and links.

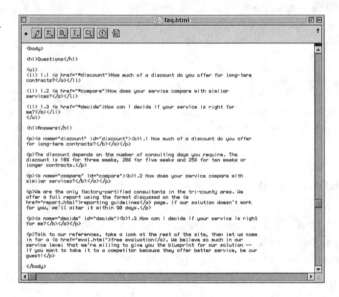

Named anchors can also be referenced when you're linking from other pages, even across the Internet. The named anchor simply becomes part of the URL that defines the page:

```
<p>For more, see <a href="http://www.fakecorp.com/questions.html#q1">
➥Question 1</a> on the Questions page.</p>
```

In this example, the browser locates the page `questions.html`, locates the section of that page named "q1", and displays it in the browser window.

Building Links Using Images

If you'd like users to click an icon or a picture to move on to a new page or part of the current page, you can create a link that uses an image in the place of descriptive text. For instance, if you have an image named "icon.gif" you can use it as a link like so:

```
<a href="moutains.html"><img src="mount1.jpg alt="Read about the mountain
➥range" /></a>
```

This places a highlighted border (most color browsers use blue by default) such as the one shown in Figure 7.4. This tells your user that the image can be followed by clicking it, just like any other hyperlink.

FIGURE 7.4

Images can be either large or small and still be clickable hyperlinks.

 Tip

> If you use alternative (alt) text when an image is also a hyperlink, users of non-graphic browsers will see a textual hyperlink, just as they normally would. Otherwise, they may not see anything and/or won't be able to access the hyperlink.

If you're working in transitional XHTML, you can add another attribute to your `<img>` element that can change the size of the border, in pixels, that appears around the image. The attribute, cleverly named `border`, accepts a number:

```
<a href="about.html"><img src="button_about.gif" alt="About Us" border="0"
➥/></a>
```

While the number can be any integer you desire, using 0 will keep the border from appearing at all on the page. In strict XHTML, this border issue should be handled with a style sheet, as discussed in Chapter 10, "Get Splashy: Style Sheets, Fonts, and Special Characters."

Using Special Links

URLs are so flexible that you can use them to create links to practically anything on the Net. You can create links to e-mail, FTP, Gopher, Usenet newsgroups, and even Telnet sessions. This makes it possible for Web pages to put related information together on the same page. For instance, you could have a link to a Web page that describes a downloadable shareware program, a link to a Usenet newsgroup where that software is discussed, and a link to an FTP server where the program can be downloaded. In other words, your readers no longer have to fire up individual Internet programs to get to the information you want them to see.

This flexibility is part of what has made the Web browser the single most important Internet tool. From your browser, you can do just about everything you can do on the Net, including accessing a variety of resources that technically aren't part of the World Wide Web. And when the browser doesn't support a service, generally it's launched in another application automatically, such as your e-mail application or a multimedia viewer.

As a Web author, you can create links that lead your visitors to those resources. Regardless of the type of service accessed, each hyperlink uses the anchor element. From there, the only things that change are the protocols for the hyperlinks and the type of URL address used.

Creating a `mailto:` Link

Putting an e-mail link in an HTML document is pretty easy. All you need is a valid e-mail address, which is made up of four parts: the account or username, the @ symbol, the machine name, and the domain name.

Here's an example of an e-mail address:

`questions@mac-upgrade.com`

The account name is questions and the domain name is `mac-upgrade.com`. In this example, there is no machine name. However, consider an e-mail address like this:

`robert@mail.fakecorp.com`

In this case, `mail` is a machine name.

After you have a valid e-mail address, you just use `mailto:` as the protocol for it in an anchor element. An example of an e-mail link is as follows:

```
<a href="mailto:questions@mac-upgrade.com">Send questions directly to
➥me.</a>
```

Figure 7.5 shows another example of a `mailto:` link. Many authors like to "sign" their home page by putting an e-mail link at the bottom.

FIGURE 7.5

When users click an e-mail link on your home page, a new message window will appear in their e-mail applications.

Want to specify the subject line? It won't work in all browsers, but the safest way to do this is to use the `title` attribute for the `<a>` anchor:

```
<a href="mailto:orders@fakecorp.com" title="I want the new book!">Order the
➥book</a>
```

Creating a Link to an FTP Site

FTP is mostly used to copy files between computers. Users of FTP have to log on to remote computers, often as guests, and get the files they want.

The only thing you need to put in a link to an FTP site is an Internet address to an FTP server computer. So, if a valid FTP site is `ftp.microsoft.com`, the link would look like the following:

```
<a href="ftp://ftp.microsoft.com/">Microsoft's FTP Site</a>
```

If you're inviting your Web visitors to download a particular file from your site, you should specify the file path for them. This keeps users from trying to find their way through unknown directories.

For example, let's say you have a compressed program (program.zip) in a directory called downloads (downloads/) that you want people to access. A link to it might look something like the following:

```
<a href="ftp://ftp.fakecorp.com/downloads/program.zip">The program (PKZip
➥format)</a>
```

This tells the Web browser to connect with FTP, go directly to the correct directory, and immediately begin downloading the file.

ARE FTP SERVERS IMPORTANT?

If you're building a Web site for a company that has a lot of files to make available to customers or visitors, it's a good idea to put the files on an FTP server and then just include a link to that server on your Web page. This prevents your Web page from becoming cluttered with download links, and FTP servers are more efficient at sending files than HTTP (Web) servers are.

That said, smaller sites don't need to have FTP servers. The HTTP protocol is capable of transmitting binary files—particularly those that are in .exe form or have been compressed using PKZip (.zip) or StuffIt (.sit) compression engines. Then, a simple http:// link to the file will cause the receiving browser to download the file and save it to the user's hard disk. For example:

```
<a href="http://www.fakecorp.com/downloads/program.sit">Click to
➥download</a>
```

This should work fine—the user will be prompted to select a place to store the file on his or her hard disk.

Gopher Servers

Before the Web came into existence, one of the most popular ways of storing and accessing information was through Gopher sites. Gopher is basically a collection of text-based menus that present information in a hierarchical format, as shown in Figure 7.6. As you might imagine, there aren't a ton of these sites left, thanks to the Web's popularity.

FIGURE 7.6

You can point your users directly to a Gopher server with a simple hyperlink.

Gopher is very similar to the Web except that it doesn't have any built-in multimedia capabilities, such as graphics or sound. You can incorporate a link to a Gopher site on your Web page by adding an anchor around the computer's address and putting gopher:// in front of it. A Gopher link would look like the following:

```
<a href="gopher://marvel.loc.gov">The Library of Congress</a>
```

Link to Newsgroups

Usenet newsgroups are the discussion groups of the Internet. Although they're called "news," they're really centered around posting and replying to messages and having discussions. You may want to point people to a newsgroup because your home page relates specifically to what goes on in that group. Or, if you think that the users might have more questions than you can answer, you can include a link to a related newsgroup in hopes of decreasing the amount of e-mail you receive.

While Usenet remains popular, many discussion groups have moved to the Web, where bulletin board software makes the discussions easier to follow and more graphical. See Chapter 21, "Forums, Chats, and Other Add-Ons," for a discussion of bulletin board options for Web sites.

Whatever the case, a link to a Usenet newsgroup is different from most other hypertext tags. To put in a link to a newsgroup, simply enter **news:** followed by the newsgroup name in the anchor. A typical newsgroup link would look like the following:

```
<a href="news:alt.tv.startrek">Discuss Star Trek on Usenet</a>
```

In this case, the user's browser would do one of two things: Access its own news server (if one has been preconfigured) and attempt to locate the message group, or hand the command off to a helper application designed to access Usenet newsgroups.

If, for some reason, you were going to point the user to a particular news server computer instead of a particular newsgroup, you could do that using the double-slash version of the protocol:

```
<a href=news://news.fakecorp.com/>Visit our news server</a>
```

Links to Telnet Servers

A link to a Telnet server allows your user to log directly onto a computer that has a remote access server enabled. In most cases, this is a text-based remote access session, such as those between terminal computers and Unix or mainframe servers. Indeed, no popular browsers support Telnet directly, so the user will likely need a Telnet helper application that will be launched when the link is clicked.

The syntax for a Telnet link is pretty straightforward: You just type **telnet://** followed by the remote computer's address as the URL. A typical Telnet link would look something like the following:

```
<a href="telnet://mac1.fakecorp.com/">Log into the corporate Telnet
➥server</A>
```

You can also create a link that automatically enters the logon name to use for guest accounts. All you have to do is specify the logon name they should use, followed by the @ sign before the machine name. So, if you want a person to access your computer with the logon name of guest, the HTML code would be

```
<a href="telnet://guest@mac1.fakecorp.com/">Log in anonymously.</a>
```

When the browser sees this, it notifies the user of the correct logon name.

Cool Tricks: Targets and Client-Pull

Before we finish this chapter, let's look at two unrelated but interesting things you can do with URLs and links. In one case, you'll augment the anchor element with another special attribute; in another, you'll use a completely different element to load a new Web page.

Open a New Window

We'll discuss targets for hyperlinks more in Chapter 12, "Creating Sites with HTML Frames," where you'll see how targets can be used to change pages in different frames within the Web browser. In this section, though, we're interested in one special case—opening a hyperlink in a new Web browser window.

To do this, you'll use the target attribute to the anchor element. The specific target in question is called "_blank", and it forces the linked page to appear in a new window. Here's an example:

```
<a href="http://www.w3.org/" target="_blank">Click
here for more information on HTML and XHTML.</a>
```

You can specify the target attribute in the <base> element, too, if you'd like all hyperlinks on the page to open in new browser windows. For example, using <base href="http://www.fakecorp.com/" target="_blank" /> in the <head> of your document would accomplish this.

Changing Pages Automatically

Using a process called *client-pull*, the `<meta>` element and its attributes enable you to load another HTML page automatically after a predetermined amount of time. You can also use these tags to reload, or *refresh*, the same HTML document over and over. It's called *client-pull* because the user's Web browser (often called the *client* in Internet-speak) is instructed to automatically load (or *pull*) a new page from the Web server without the user clicking anything or the Web server sending any special commands.

The client-pull concept is based on the `<meta>` element, introduced in Chapter 4, "Creating Your First Page," which is used in the head of your document. For client-pull, the `<meta>` element takes the attributes `http-equiv` and `content`. Client-pull follows this format:

```
<head>
<title>Title of Page</title>
<meta http-equiv="refresh" content="seconds; url="new URL" />
</head>
```

The `http-equiv` attribute always takes the value "refresh" in client-pull; it only loads a new document if the `content` attribute includes an URL. Otherwise, it refreshes (reloads) the current document.

The `content` attribute accepts a number for the amount of time (in seconds) you want the browser to wait before the next page is loaded (or the current page is refreshed). After that number, you type a semi-colon and **url=** followed by a valid URL for the page that should be loaded automatically.

Here's an example that just refreshes the current page after waiting ten seconds:

```
<head>
<title>Page Title</title>
<meta http-equiv="refresh" content="10" />
</head>
```

In this next example, we'll use client-pull to load a new page after waiting 15 seconds:

```
<head>
<title>Page One</title>
<meta http-equiv="refresh" content="15;
url="http://www.fakecorp.com/index2.html" />
</head>
```

Summary

In this chapter, you learned how URLs are built and how they work together with the `<base>` and `<a>` anchor elements to make hyperlinks possible. You saw how to create hyperlinks that lead to outside Web sites, how to link to parts of a particular Web page, and how to use images as hyperlinks. Beyond that, you saw how to create hyperlinks to various types of Internet resources, as well as how to manage some automatic link-related tasks.

In the next chapter, you'll learn the basic XHTML table elements, which allow you to place data visually in rows and columns. You'll also see how to create the table and change its appearance using the `<table>` element and attributes.

BASICS TABLES

You've seen how lists and paragraph elements can be used to organize text logically on the page. The next level of complexity is the *table*, which can be used to divide a section of the Web page into different rows and columns. You can use the table elements to more precisely place rows and columns of data, text, links, and even images. In Chapter 9, "Advanced Table Elements and Table Design," you will see how you can use tables for something even grander—page layout.

This chapter discusses the following:

- The `<table>` element
- Table captions
- Table rows and headings
- Creating table data cells
- Advanced options and attributes for the `<table>` element

Creating a Table

You use the table container element to hold together a group of other elements that define each individual row, and within each row, elements define each *cell*. Indeed, working with XHTML tables is very similar to working with a spreadsheet application. An XHTML table consists of rows and columns. Where a row and a column meet, you find a cell. Each individual cell is designed to be a container of data. XHTML table cells can contain nearly any text and XHTML elements, such as hyperlinks and images.

Tables take the following format:

```
<table>
<caption>Caption text for table</caption>
<tr><th>column head 1</th><th>column head 2</th><th>column head 3</th></tr>
<tr><td>cell1-1 data</td><td>cell1-2 data</td><td>cell1-3 data</td></tr>
<tr><td>cell2-1 data</td><td>cell2-2 data</td><td>cell2-3 data</td></tr>
...additional rows...
</table>
```

The main element is the `<table>` container. Using the optional `<caption>` element, you can add a line that explains the table or gives it a title. Within the `<table>` element, you add container elements for table rows, `<tr>`, and table data, `<td>`. Most tables also use the table heading element, `<th>`, which is useful for the title text for rows and columns.

Note   Although these table elements have been around for many years now, there are some popular Web browsers that can have trouble with them—particularly, browsers in some mobile phones and Personal Digital Assistants (PDAs). If you'd like your pages to be visible to these users, you may opt for simpler layouts (using lists, for example). Or you can offer two pages, one that uses tables and one that uses the `<pre>` element.

The `<table>` Element

You begin any XHTML table with the `<table>` element, which is designed to contain all the elements necessary to create a table. Between the `<table>` and `</table>` tags, you use the `<tr>` table row container element to create each row. Then, each `<td>` container element defines a cell, in which you place that cell's data:

1. To begin a table, enter a set of `<table>`, `</table>` tags in your HTML document.

2. Between the table tags, add a set of `<tr>`, `</tr>` tags for each row you'd like in the table.

3. Now, in the first row definition, add a set of `<th>`, `</th>` table header tags for each column header (and, hence, each column) you'd like to define. Type the text for each column header inside each `<th>` element. (Remember, the `<th>` element is optional. In most graphical browsers, it simply makes the text boldface. Your first row can use the `<td>` element if desired.)

4. In all the remaining rows, add a set of `<td>`, `</td>` tags to define each individual cell. Between each set of `<td>` tags, enter the text and/or XHTML markup for that cell.

At this point, you need to be sure that your table has the same number of columns and/or column headings in each row. If your first row has three `<th>` elements, the second row needs to have three `<td>` elements, the third row needs three, and so forth. (You can skip cells, but we won't cover that until the section "Changing a Cell's Span" later in this chapter.) The table renders incorrectly if you don't define a consistent grid.

Note   Want a blank cell? You can create one using the *non-breaking space* entity code, ` `, within a cell definition. For example, `<td> </td>` should create a blank cell in most browsers.

One example of a basic table using this format is the following:

```
<table border="1">
<caption>Regional Sales Teams</caption>
<tr><th>West</th><th>South</th><th>North</th></tr>
<tr><td>Will H.</td><td>Sally F.</td><td>Jude L.</td></tr>
<tr><td>Harvey D.</td><td>Paul M.</td><td>Dale E.</td></tr>
<tr><td>Ryan C.</td><td>John L.</td><td>Roger E.</td></tr>
</table>
```

Note   Although `<table>` has many attributes, the `border` attribute is perhaps the most basic one. Use the attribute `border="1"` for a one-pixel border around the table (interior lines are also drawn). A larger number can make the border thicker.

So far, this isn't too tough. Once you're familiar with the concept, you can see how tables are similar to other containers, such as XHTML lists and paragraph elements. (In fact, as with list and paragraph elements, an XHTML table automatically begins and ends with space around it, separating it from other XHTML elements that come before or after it.) Figure 8.1 shows how this example might look in a browser.

FIGURE 8.1

This basic
XHTML table is
a great way to
communicate
tabular data.

Captions and Summaries

The <caption> element is a container, inside which you type the name or a description for your table, along with any XHTML markup you'd like to use for that description. For example:

```
<caption><b>Consumer Retail Sales</b>, according to the <i>Wall Street
➥Journal</i></caption>
```

Just about any sort of markup tags are possible inside the <caption> element, although some—like list elements—wouldn't make much sense. You could use hyperlinks within the caption, however, which might be useful for referring the reader to another Web page for more information about the table, or to the source documents you use for data in the table.

If you use the <caption> element, it should come immediately after the opening <table> tag. Note that only one <caption> element is permitted per table.

By default, the caption text appears at the top of your table. If you'd like to force it to appear somewhere else (at the bottom of the table, for example), you can use the attribute align. Note that align isn't supported under the XHTML Strict DTD, but most browsers recognize it if you're using the XHTML Transitional DTD. The values for align include align="top" and align="bottom", which simply mean the caption appears at the top or bottom of the table. (In most browsers, the caption is automatically centered horizontally.) For example:

```
<caption align="bottom">Feed prices since spring, source: USA
➥Today</caption>
```

Each table you create can have a summary, which is a string of text that's used, in most cases, to help users of non-visual or assistive browsers (such as text-to-speech browsers) to recognize the purpose and structure of a table. The summary is added via an attribute to the <table> element, called summary. Place the summary text in quotes following the attribute. The following is an example:

```
<table summary="This table shows that sales in the Western region were 500
➥in spring and 600 in summer; sales in the Northern region were 300 in
spring and 400 in summer and sales in the Southern region were 200 in
spring and 650 in summer.">
<caption><b>Sales (in thousands) for Spring and Summer
Quarters</b></caption>
<tr><th>Quarter</th><th>West</th><th>North</th><th>South</th></tr>
<tr><th>Spring</th><td>500</td><td>300</td><td>200</td></tr>
<tr><th>Summer</th><td>600</td><td>400</td><td>650</td></tr>
</table>
```

Table Rows

The table row element can accept two attributes you may be interested in using, align and valign. These attributes are used to align the cells in that row horizontally and vertically, respectively. This is an example that uses align, shown in Figure 8.2:

```
<table border="1">
<tr align="center"><th>Year of Survery</th><th>Coffee
➥Preferred</th><th>Tea Preferred</th></tr>
<tr align="right"><th>1980</th><td>65%</td><td>35%</td></tr>
<tr align="right"><th>1990</th><td>60%</td><td>40%</td></tr>
<tr align="right"><th>2000</th><td>45%</td><td>55%</td></tr>
</table>
```

FIGURE 8.2

Cells are aligned to their right margins.

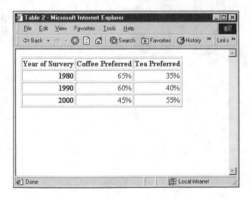

This align attribute can accept "center", "left", and "right" as values. valign can accept the values top, bottom, and center. You'll find this particularly useful when aligning images, as shown here:

```
<table border="1">
<tr valign="top">
```

```
<td><img src="image1.png"></td>
<td><img src="image2.png"></td>
<td><img src="image3.png"></td>
</tr>
</table>
```

Although the cells have to stretch to the height of the tallest image, all of the images in this example are aligned to the top of their respective cells to give the table a more uniform look. Figure 8.3 shows this top alignment, as well as the example with images aligned to `center`.

FIGURE 8.3

In the first table, cells are aligned to top. In the second, they're aligned to center.

Like most XHTML elements, the spaces and returns you add in the middle of table row elements aren't rendered by the browser. So you can feel free to create spaces or returns between the various elements if it helps you when you're authoring the page. In particular, you may find it's helpful to place each cell on its own row as you get into more and more content and markup in each cell.

Table Cell Elements

You've already used the `<th>` and `<td>` elements to include headers and data in your tables. You may have noticed that, essentially, the only difference between the two is that `<th>` emphasizes the text (boldfaces it, in graphical browsers) and `<td>` does not.

Technically, `<th>` is an element that the browser interprets as a header, so it displays text in a way that's distinct from the `<td>` element. In practice, this generally means it's boldface. In theory, however, it could mean the table is rendered very differently, particularly in non-graphical browsers, so you should only use the `<th>` container on cells that truly represent header data.

Note | For best compatibility with assistive browsers, you should use `<th>` for the header data in your table whenever possible, if your columns and rows have headings. That helps assistive browsers organize and communicate the table data.

Aside from accepting nearly any type of XHTML markup tags within them, both tags can accept two attributes that help you align data within the cell. These attributes are `align` and `valign`. For example:

```
<td align="center" valign="bottom">
```

`align` is used to align the data within the cell horizontally, accepting values of `left`, `right`, and `center`. Note that `align` in a `<td>` or `<th>` element is redundant if you've already used the `align` attribute with `<tr>`, unless you're specifically trying to override the row's alignment in a particular cell.

`valign` is used to align the data vertically within cells. Possible values are `top`, `bottom`, and `center`. Sometimes this doesn't actually look much different in a Web browser, especially if all your cells contain approximately the same amount of data. In the case of two cells that are different in the amount or size of the content enclosed, though, the `valign` attribute can make a significant difference in the appearance of the table. Figure 8.4 is an example of the `valign` attribute in action. Note the difference in the alignment of the second two images because the first image stretches the height of the overall row.

FIGURE 8.4

Cells vertically aligned to top, bottom, and center.

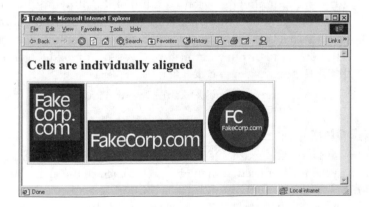

In addition to the alignment attributes, `<th>` supports another interesting attribute—the `scope` attribute. This allows you to specify the range of cells for which the `<th>` element is the header. It can accept the values `row` and `col` to specify that a particular `<th>` element is the header for its row, or its column, respectively. For example:

```
<tr><th scope="row">Processor</th><td>G9-1.6</td><td>G9-1.7</td></tr>
```

Changing a Cell's Span

Sometimes you need two or more cells with common borders (whether they're in the same row or the same column) to act as a single cell. You might fuse two cells together because they include the same information. Or, you might want to enter a single heading one time, and enable it to span over a number of columns.

Whatever the reason, attributes for the `<th>` and `<td>` elements enable you to force one cell to span more than one row or column. Those attributes are `colspan` and `rowspan`. The following is an example:

```
<table border="1">
<caption>PortaBook Specifications</caption>
<tr><th> </th><th>model 100</th><th>model 200</th></tr>
<tr><th>Processor</th><td>G9-1.6</td><td>G9-1.7</td></tr>
<tr><th>Hard disk</th><td>78GB</td><td>90GB</td></tr>
<tr><th>Video card</th><td colspan="2">Rageous 428p</td></tr>
<tr><th>AV Output</th><td rowspan="2">n/a<td>Yes</td></tr>
<tr><th>Docking port</th><td>Optional</td></tr>
</table>
```

Note that `colspan` is causing the entry `Rageous 428p` to span the second two columns of the fourth row—its function is fairly clear. The `rowspan` attribute can be a little more obscure—it's spanning the second column of the fifth and *sixth* rows. That means, in the sixth row, the entry `Optional` actually appears in the third column, even though it seems that only two cells are defined in that row. Remembering not to put a cell there (or realizing your mistake if you get an odd-looking table) goes along with the territory when you decide to use `rowspan`.

Viewed in a browser, the table looks like the one in Figure 8.5.

Cell and Row Colors

As you're working with your tables, you may want to change the background color of some of your rows or even of individual cells. Each of the elements is able to accept a `bgcolor` attribute that can be used for this. The `bgcolor` attribute is not compatible with the XHTML Strict DTD, however, so you only want to use it with the XHTML Transitional DTD.

The bgcolor attribute accepts a color name as its value and works with the <table>,
<tr>, and <td> elements, as shown in this example:

```
<table>
<tr><th>Region</th><th>June</th><th>July</th><th>August</th></tr>
<tr bgcolor="yellow"><th>North</th><td>600,000</td><td>400,000</td>
➥<td>800,000</td></tr>
<tr><th>South</th><td>300,000</td><td>200,000</td><td>400,000</td></tr>
<tr bgcolor="yellow"><th>East</th><td>230,000</td><td>490,000</td>
➥<td>980,000</td></tr>
<tr><th>West</th><td>320,000</td><td>120,000</td><td>490,000</td></tr>
</table>
```

Aside from color names, the bgcolor attribute also accepts three two-digit hex numbers
that represent the RGB (red, green, and blue) values for a particular color. For example,
bgcolor="#FFFFFF" creates a white background. (For more on this, see Chapter 10,
"Get Splashy: Style Sheets, Fonts, and Special Characters.")

As you can see in Figure 8.6, one reason to change the background color of your
tables it to shade alternating rows of data. As accountants and engineers have
known for years, it's easier to communicate information in tables when alternating
colors make the individual rows of data stand out.

Additional Table Attributes

Now that you have created a basic table, you can move on to a more advanced understanding of the `<table>` element itself and its optional attributes. You've already seen some of them, including `align` and `border`, but a few others are worth examining:

- `width`—Sets the relative width of your table as part of the browser window (or an absolute width), usually in pixels. The values can be either percentages, as in `width="50%"`, or an integer representing pixels.

- `border`—Defines the width of the border surrounding the table. The value is a number (integer) in pixels.

- `align`—Not strict XHTML, but it can be handy if you're using the XHTML Transitional DTD. `align` can be used much as it's used for the `<img>` element, enabling you to create a "floating" table that enables text to wrap around it.

- `cellspacing`—Tells the browser how much space to include between the walls of the table and between individual cells. The value is a number (an integer) in pixels.

- `cellpadding`—Tells the browser how much space to use between data elements and the walls of the cell. The value is a number in pixels.

- `rules` and `frames`—Used to determine which lines are drawn between cells (rules) and around the table (frames). This one is exclusive to visual browsers, but it's allowed under the XHTML Strict DTD.

Let's take a look at each attribute briefly.

The width Attribute

By default, a table in XHTML takes up only as much space as needed to display the data in the cells of its longest row. Only when the table has filled the width of the browser window does it begin to wrap the data in its cells to a second line. Expanding the size of the browser window (if the user still has room on his display) rearranges the text in those cells accordingly.

With the width attribute, you can take a little bit more control over how the table looks. The value that width accepts is either an integer representing the number of pixels wide that the table should be, or the percentage of the page that the table should take up. In this second case, the table is still free to grow or shrink when the user changes the size of her Web browser window, but within certain constraints.

For example, a table that takes up 75% of the browser window could be created with the following table definition, which is shown in Figure 8.7:

```
<table width="75%">
<tr><th>Region</th><th>June</th><th>July</th><th>August</th></tr>
<tr bgcolor="yellow"><td>North</td><td>600,000</td><td>400,000</td>
➥<td>800,000</td></tr>
<tr><td>South</td><td>300,000</td><td>200,000</td><td>400,000</td></tr>
<tr bgcolor="yellow"><td>East</td><td>230,000</td><td>490,000</td>
➥<td>980,000</td></tr>
<tr><td>West</td><td>320,000</td><td>120,000</td><td>490,000</td></tr>
</table>
```

FIGURE 8.7

Using the width attribute, you can force tables to different sizes.

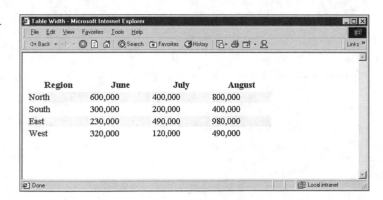

Note that the width attribute forces the table to that width, even if the data doesn't need that much room. For example, a table with a width="100%" attribute takes up the entire width of the browser window, regardless of the amount of data in the cells.

Tip

With absolute values for width, you can also include a suffix that defines the units used, as in px for pixels or in for inches (for example, width="3.5in"). Absolute values for table widths are not recommended, because tables should react to user input (like a user changing his browser window size). That said, it's a fairly common practice to use absolute values, particularly when designing entire pages using tables (as discussed in Chapter 9).

The border and align Attributes

By default, most browsers render a table without lines defining its perimeter and cells. Using the border attribute, you can change this so that a table has lines that separate cells from one other. You can also specify the width of the line that surrounds the table on the outside, in pixels. For example:

```
<table border="8">
```

The align attribute can be used with the <table> element to either center the table on the page or cause the table to become a floating object, with text wrapping around it on the left or right. Although this can be handy for page presentation and layout, it's not compatible with the XHTML Strict DTD and you should only use it if you're working under the XHTML Transitional DTD.

The following is an example of both attributes, the result of which is shown in Figure 8.8:

```
<table border="8" align="center" width="50%">
<caption>Candy Sales Per Student Per Type</caption>

<tr>
<th>Type</th><th>Melissa</th><th>Brian</th><th>Roger</th>
</tr>

<tr>
<th>Chocolate Bars</th><td>50</td><td>25</td><td>50</td>
</tr>

<tr>
<th>Fruit Chews</th><td>50</td><td>45</td><td>30</td>
```

```
</tr>

<tr>
<th>Lollipops</th><td>15</td><td>25</td><td>40</td>
</tr>

</table>
```

FIGURE 8.8

A table with a
thick border,
centered on the
page.

The `cellpadding` and `cellspacing` Attributes

Although the `border` attribute is used to set the pixel width of the lines that enclose cells in your table, the `cellpadding` and `cellspacing` attributes give you fine control over the amount of space used in other parts of the table. The `cellspacing` attribute specifies how much space is between cells, in pixels. As shown in Figure 8.9, including the `cellspacing` attribute also increases the size of the interior border walls, even if the actual `border` attribute is set to a low number. For example:

```
<table border="1" cellspacing="10">
```

However, `cellspacing` is equally effective when you aren't using a border on your table at all:

```
<table cellspacing="10">
```

The `cellpadding` attribute is used to specify the amount of space that should be displayed between a cell's wall and the contents of that cell. (Again, this measurement is in pixels.) The default setting for `cellpadding` (that is, if you don't include the attribute at all) is 1. You can set `cellpadding="0"`, but that causes the items in each cell to bump up against the border. The following example is the second table shown in Figure 8.9:

```
<table border="1" cellpadding="10">
```

FIGURE 8.9

Two tables:
`cellspacing`
with a border
and `cellpadding`
with a border.

Summary

This chapter taught you the basics of creating an XHTML table, from entering the `<table>` element to adding the row (`<tr>`), heading (`<th>`), and data cell (`<td>`) elements. You also learned some of the attributes for cells and rows, including alignment, background colors, and attributes that enable you to span more than one row or more than one column with a single cell. Then, you saw some of the more involved attributes for a `<table>` element, including those that alter the spacing of cells and the borders between them. This has all been primer for Chapter 9, where you'll learn some advanced uses for tables, including formatting entire pages using table elements.

ADVANCED TABLE ELEMENTS AND TABLE DESIGN

*I*n Chapter 8, "Basics Tables," you learned the basics of table design and saw how to create tables that communicate information in rows and columns. Obviously, that's a primary use of the XHTML table elements. In this chapter, you'll be introduced to one of the other common uses of table tags—formatting entire pages. Using the table tags gives you some interesting options for controlling the appearance of your Web page, including the placement of paragraphs, interface controls (such as hyperlinks for different pages in your Web site), and even images. You'll look at many of those possibilities in this chapter.

This chapter discusses the following:

- The basics of designing a Web page with a table
- Creating page sections, setting table widths and heights, and border appearance
- Examples of using table design for different types of pages

Table Design Theory

Since the HTML tables standard appeared on the scene, the sophistication and professionalism of Web pages have improved dramatically. With the control over cells that the standard offers, it's easier to put pictures, text, lists, and links wherever you want them on the page. In this way, you can create an *all-page table*, or a table that is used to control the design of the entire Web page.

You do this by aligning cells, creating spanning cells (or fusing cells together), and adding the appropriate cell padding and spacing, as you saw in Chapter 8. You can add some other tricks as well, including nested tables, which enable you to place one table inside another.

At its most basic, though, using tables for layout simply gives you rows and columns with which to work. As with a page in a newsletter, newspaper, or magazine, you can visually divide your Web page to make it easier to read or to guide the eye to different elements, such as the hyperlinks used to change pages. For example, take this page on a fictional realtor's Web site that's designed to display the particulars of a home that's for sale:

```
<table border="1" cellpadding="5">

<!-- Top control area -->
<tr>
<td colspan="2" align="center">
<a href="index.html">Home Page</a> |
<a href="homes.html">Home for Sale</a> |
<a href="info.html">Homebuyer Information</a> |
<a href="rates.html">Mortgage/Rates Info</a> |
<a href="contact.html">Contact Me</a>

</tr>


<!-- Main body of page -->
<tr>
<td rowspan="2" valign="top">
<h1>Farmhouse Living</h1>
<p>This 3/2 traditional has a full basement (modern
touches like Italian lighting and Berber carpet) for
a media room, home office or an unemployment den for
that English-major college grad of yours. Screened porch
in back overlooks a nice badminton/croquet lawn complete
```

```
with a walking garden on the side and a dog run in the trees.
325 Main Street. $129,000.</p></td>
<td>
<img src="house2.jpg" width=250 alt="Exterior of House" />
</td>
</tr>

<tr>
<td>
<img src="fall1.jpg" width="250" alt="Side Garden" />
</td>
</tr>
</table>
```

Figure 9.1 shows this example as displayed in a browser window.

FIGURE 9.1

Here's a page that uses a simple table to separate elements.

Note

As you create more and more complicated page tables, you'll find it's helpful to use the comment element liberally throughout, if only to remind you what a particular row or cell is meant to do.

Here's a quick walkthrough of what's being done to create this table:

1. It begins with a standard `<table>` opening tag, which includes a border definition and a setting for cell padding.

2. Next, the first row is defined, followed by a single data cell that spans two columns. Within that data cell is the markup, text, and anchors that define the top-of-the-page links used to move between the pages on this Web site.

3. That cell and row are closed, and then the next row is defined. Note that this row will have two different `<td>` elements, meaning it will have two columns. (That's why the previous row's data cell spanned two columns.)

4. In the first cell, text is entered. If more than one paragraph is required, standard `<p>` containers can be used.

5. In the second cell, `<img />` elements will cause images to appear on that side of the table. (Note that the width of the images will dictate the width of this column—and, hence, the width of the other column—as mentioned in Chapter 8.)

6. Finally, the second row is closed and the table is closed.

This page is really a simple layout, but tables allow you to add the navigation toolbar at the top, which is separated out into its own table row. Next, in the second row, the table is divided into two columns, separating the description from the images that appear along the side. (The only other way to do this would be to use floating images [those using an `align="right"` or `align="left"` attribute], which wouldn't align themselves as neatly.)

It's a clean, inviting interface that's easy to work with. But let's back up a little bit and look at exactly how to put together these types of pages.

Using Images in Tables

Using an XHTML table to display images really offers some advantages. It's nice to have such exacting control over the placement of the images. Plus, tables make it easier to align text and images so the user knows how they're related to one another.

For example, another page that our fictional real estate agent might want to post on the Web is a listing of all available homes. Using a table, the home images and descriptions are simple to align:

```
<table border=1 cellspacing=2 cellpadding=2 width="100%">
<tr><td colspan="2"><h1>Current Home Sale Listings</h1></td></tr>
<tr>
<td>
```

```
<p>This 3/2 traditional has a full basement (modern
touches like Italian lighting and Berber carpet) for
a media room, home office or an unemployment den for
that English-major college grad of yours. Screened
porch in back overlooks a nice badminton/croquet lawn
complete with a walking garden on the side and a dog
run in the trees. 325 Main Street. $129,000.</p>
</td>
<td>
<img src="325main.png" alt="Front of 325 Main Street" />
</td>
</tr>
<tr>
<td>
<p>You don't see garden estates at these prices anymore.
Brick fenced entry (with a fancy remote control) opens to
a winding drive up the front lawn to this colonial in the
best Jeffersonian tradition. Inside, you'll find formal
living and dining, a basement game room (perfect for
media or art projects) and a downstairs master suite with
whirlpool tub. This one even has extras like a butler's pantry
(for storing all those family-sized cans of ravioli-os) and a
second, back staircase for creeping quietly down in the middle
of the night to get one more small sliver of homemade pie. And,
best yet, a babbling brook right there on the property.
19 E. Gables Road. $279,000. </p>
</td>
<td>
<img src="brook.png" alt="Babbling brook" /><br />
</td>
</tr>
</table>
```

Figure 9.2 shows this one in action. Note how the table tags make it easy to align images with text.

FIGURE 9.2

Tables can help
you align
images and text
in creative ways.

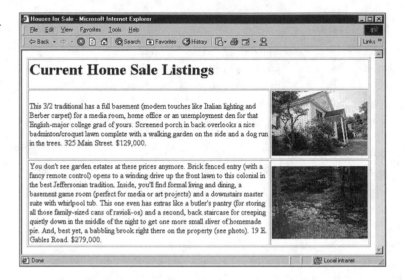

Nesting Tables

Here's another bit of theory to ingest before we move on—I've mentioned that a table cell can accept all sorts of data. As it happens, this includes a second table. When you place one table inside another, you're said to be *nesting* the tables. It can get a little confusing in your raw HTML code, but you'll find that nesting tables is an invaluable solution to a number of layout problems.

For starters, you'll recall from Chapter 8 that a table can have a width. Let's say you want a particular *cell* to have a fixed (or specific) width. You want to create two cells—one that's about 25% of the page and one that's about 75%. The 25% side will be used as a sidebar of sorts, perhaps for navigation. The 75% side will be used for the text you're interested in putting on the page. Figure 9.3 shows a table that fits this description.

One way to do this is to use the `width` attribute for the `<td>`, as in `<td width="75%">`. Sure, that seems easy, but unfortunately, it's not strict XHTML. If you're using the transitional DTD, you could use the `width` attribute.

The other solution is to use a nested table. Because the `<table>` element can legally accept a `width` attribute (in XHTML), you can put a table in one of the cells and thereby define its width. The code in Listing 9.1 matches up with Figure 9.3.

Note

If you add cell padding or cell spacing to your original table, note that those pixels will affect the overall width of the column that includes your nested table. For instance, with 3 pixels of cell padding, a column with a 150-pixel nested table will actually be 156 pixels wide. In other words, to be exact, you may need to do a little math or go without cell padding or cell spacing.

FIGURE 9.3

Here's a table where the width of the cells has been specified.

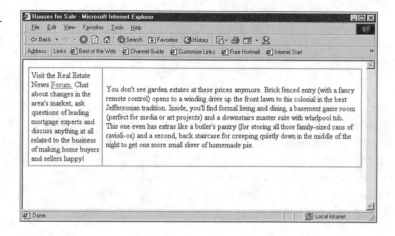

LISTING 9.1   Nesting a Table Within a Table

```
<table width="100%" cellpadding="0"cellspacing="0">
<tr>


<td>
   <table width="150" cellpadding="3">
   <tr>
   <td>markup for left side</td>
   </tr>
   </table>
</td>


<td>
   <table cellpadding="5">
   <tr>
   <td>markup for right side</td>
   </tr>
   </table>
</td>


</tr>
</table>
```

In this case, the nested tables are used simply to create single cells over which you have some formatting control. By setting the left-side table to 150 pixels, you're able to fix its width. The rest of the overall page table will still resize to the browser window, but this left-side table is fixed.

Okay, so you've seen a basic nested table. But what about a table that has even more functionality—for instance, one that's used for formatting *inside* the cell? In place of the left-side table in Listing 9.1, consider what the page might look like with the following table in its place:

```
<table width="150" cellpadding="2" border="1">
<tr bgcolor="yellow"><td>Home Listings</td></tr>
<tr><td>
129k, 3/2, Sumner<br />
139k, 4/2, Ridgewood<br />
142k, 4/2, Highland<br />
159k, 4/2/2, Haven<br />
179k, 5/2.5, Haven<br />
229k, 5/3/2, Laurel<br />
</td></tr>
<tr bgcolor="yellow"><td>Call for more: 645.3567</td></tr>
</table>
```

Figure 9.4 shows this table in action. (Note that I've made each of the listings a hyperlink for Figure 9.4, although I left the anchor elements out of this listing for clarity.) This little nested table replaces the left side with something more interesting: an interface control.

FIGURE 9.4

Here a complete table is nested on the left side.

While you're nesting tables, don't forget the possibilities presented by *floating* tables, which are aligned to the right or left using the `align` attribute with the `<table>` element. Floating tables are great for adding tabular information in a way that's a bit more visually pleasing. Text wraps around the table, while other markup can be used to call attention to the table's contents. For instance, using the code in Listing 9.1, slip a floating table into the right-side nested table, as shown in Listing 9.2.

LISTING 9.2 Add a Floating Table to the Mix

```
<table width="100%" cellpadding="0"cellspacing="0">
<tr>

<td>
   <table width="150" cellpadding="3">
   <tr>
   <td>markup for left side</td>
   </tr>
   </table>
</td>

<td>
   <table cellpadding="5">
   <tr>
   <td>
       <!-- Here's the floating table -->
<table align="right" cellpadding="5" width="200" border="1">
         <tr bgcolor="yellow"><td>19 E. Gable Road</td></tr>
   <tr><td><b>Price:</b> $279,000</td></tr>
   <tr><td><b>Appraisal:</b> $309,000</td></tr>
   <tr><td>Owner is moving to Florida and interested in a
quick sale. Call 645.3567 and ask for Andy</td></tr>
</table>

   <h1>Your Own Mini-Estate</h1>

   <p>You don't see garden estates at these prices anymore.
Brick fenced entry (with a fancy remote control) opens to a
winding drive up the front lawn to this colonial in the best
Jeffersonian tradition. Inside, you'll find formal living and
dining, a basement game room (perfect for media or art
projects) and a downstairs master suite with whirlpool tub.
This one even has extras like a butler's pantry (for storing
```

LISTING 9.2   (continued)

```
all those family-sized cans of ravioli-os) and a second, back
staircase for creeping quietly down in the middle of the night
to get one more small sliver of homemade pie.</p>

    </td>
    </tr>
    </table>
</td>
</tr>
</table>
```

Remember that it's the `align="right"` attribute to the table that makes it a floating table. The result of all this nesting is shown in Figure 9.5.

FIGURE 9.5

You can nest a floating table (on the right) for an interesting effect.

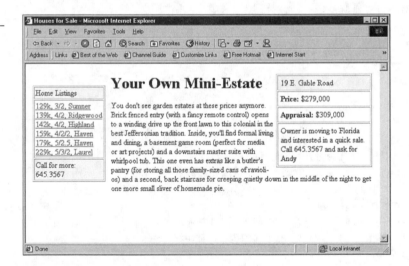

Grouping Columns and Rows

So far, most of the markup you've seen is actually the basic table elements used for larger chunks of text and images—that's most of what table-based layout is about. There are a few more elements to discuss, however, and you'll find that they're important as your tables grow in complexity. These new elements will enable you to group your rows, defining different portions of the table (and hence the page). Other elements enable you to better group and define your columns, as you'll see in this section.

Table Row Groupings

Table row groupings are reasonably straightforward. They're designed to help you group your rows into different sections of the table, just as you group different elements into a head and body in an HTML document. In this case, the elements are `<thead>`, `<tfoot>`, and `<tbody>`. The idea behind these elements is to enable a Web browser or other application to consider the header and footer to be separate from the body, so that, for instance, the body of the table can scroll while the header and footer stay in place. Likewise, a browser can decide that the header and footer information on each page of a multi-page table will appear when printed, just like the header and footer of a typical word processing document.

Each of these elements is a container, and each one is designed specifically to hold certain types of table rows and data. Note also that you still need to use the `<tr>` container element for each row, and that each of these row grouping elements should have at least one row contained within it. Also, if you plan to include a table header and a table footer, there's one oddity—the footer needs to be typed in first, before the body, so that the browser knows it's there. Here's an example:

```
<table border="1">
<thead>
<tr>
<th colspan="2">Customer</th><th rowspan="3">Sales Month:</th>
</tr>
<tr>
<th>September</th><th>October</th><th>November</th>
</thead>
<tfoot>
<tr>
<td colspan="4">Source: New York Gazette-Tribune</td>
</tr>
</tfoot>
<tbody>
<tr>
<td>NonCo, Inc.</td><td>450,000</td><td>350,000</td><td>50,000</td>
</tr>
<tr>
<td>RichCo, LLC</td><td>345,000</td><td>230,000</td><td>12,400</td>
</tr>
<tr>
<td>FakeCorp, Ltd.</td><td>120,000</td><td>543,000</td><td>10,000</td>
</tr>
```

```
...additional rows...
</tbody>
</table>
```

This is a fairly simple example, and one you might not encounter too often. After all, the vast majority of HTML documents you create probably won't be designed to show page after page of scrolling tables of numbers. That's pretty dull for a Web page.

Instead, one place you'll likely want to consider using these row grouping tags is when you're building a full page using table elements, and you'd like a non-scrolling header and footer. (Remember, of course, that the browser isn't required to render them as non-scrolling.) Defining your document in this way—with a banner image in the header, for instance, and navigation links in the footer—gives you some extra flexibility without affecting older browsers that don't recognize the row groupings. Here's one way such a table could be created:

```
<table cellpadding="5">

<thead>

<tr><td colspan="5"><img src="top_banner.png" alt="Flatland Real
➥Estate"/></td></tr>

</thead>


<tfoot>

<tr>

<td><a href="about.html">About</a></td>

<td><a href="listings.html">Land and Homes</a></td>

<td><a href="buyer.html">Buyer's Broker Services</a></td>

<td><a href="seller.html">Sell Your Home</a></td>

<td><a href="mortgage.html">Mortgage Info</a></td>

</tr>

</tfoot>


<tbody>

<tr>

<td colspan="5">

<img src="fall1.jpg" width="250" alt="Side Garden" align="right" />

<h1>Farmhouse Living</h1>

<p>This 3/2 traditional has a full basement (modern touches
like Italian lighting and Berber carpet) for a media room,
home office or an unemployment den for that English-major
college grad of yours. Screened porch in back overlooks a
nice badminton/croquet lawn complete with a walking garden
on the side and a dog run in the trees. 325 Main Street.
```

```
$129,000.</p></td>
</tr>
</tbody>
</table>
```

In many browsers, the header and footer will appear in their proper places independent of the body of the table, as shown in Figure 9.6.

FIGURE 9.6

Using row groupings can augment the look and organization of your all-page table.

Column Groupings

You'll find that column groupings are a touch more complex, if only because they offer a few more options and reasons for being. You may have noticed already that columns seem to be afterthoughts with the XHTML spec, because most of what gets defined are rows and data cells. You can group columns, however, and you can select individual columns (or groups of columns) for certain types of markup, as you'll see.

In this section we're dealing with two different elements, the `<colgroup>` and `<col>` elements. The `<colgroup>` element is used to create groups of columns, to which you can then assign other attributes. (Or, future browsers may recognize groups of columns for some reason, although none of them really do that now.) The `<col>` container can be used on individual columns to assign properties without putting them in a particular group.

With `<colgroup>`, you'll use the span attribute to assign the number of columns in a particular group. For example, take a table that has five columns in it. Here's an example of `<colgroup>` being used to break it into two different groups (see Figure 9.7):

```
<table border="1" cellpadding="5">
<colgroup span="3" align="center"> </colgroup>
<colgroup span="2" align="right" width="100"> </colgroup>
<tr><th>Quantity</th><th>Prod ID</th><th>Description</th>
<th>Unit Price</th><th>Sub-Total</th></tr>
<tr><td>12</td><td>0876547</td><td>#4 wing nuts</td>
<td>$1.00</td><td>$12.00</td></tr>
<tr><td>10</td><td>0876501</td><td>#4 wood screws </td>
<td>$1.50</td><td>$15.00</td></tr>
<tr><td>20</td><td>0887965</td><td>ProBuild Hammer</td>
<td>$9.50</td><td>$190.00</td></tr>
<tr><td>5</td><td>0927125</td><td>Caulking gun</td>
<td>$4.00</td><td>$20.00</td></tr>
<tr><td>10</td><td>1034526</td><td>3-Pk Masking Tape</td>
<td>$2.00</td><td>$20.00</td></tr>
</table>
```

FIGURE 9.7

Using
<colgroup>
to define and
align groups of
columns.

Note that <colgroup> can accept an align attribute and/or a valign attribute, which is applied to each of the columns specified in the span of the element. All the groups are defined first, before the first row definition. (They're defined before the applicable <thead> or <tbody> elements as well.) The <colgroup> element can also include a width attribute, which defines a default width for each of the columns in that group. For instance, <colgroup span="4" width="10"> would set each of those columns to a default width of 10 pixels.

Note

The `<colgroup>` element can accept a special width value, written as `width="0*"` (as can the `<col>` element, discussed next). That tells the browser to determine the default width based on the least amount of space required by the lengthiest entry in that column. If the longest entry requires 50 pixels, for instance, that's what the width of the column will be.

The other element, `<col>`, is used inside a `<colgroup>` element when you'd like to define the characteristics of columns individually *within* their group. In other words, if you have a column that needs a different setting from the one that's specified in the `<colgroup>` element, you can use `<col>`. Here's an example, using the data that was used for Figure 9.7:

```
<table border="1" cellpadding="5">
<colgroup span="3" align="center">
<col width="50" />
<col span="2" width="100" />
</colgroup>
<colgroup span="2" width="150">
<col align="center" />
<col align="right" />
</colgroup>
<tr><th>Quantity</th><th>Prod ID</th><th>Description</th>
<th>Unit Price</th><th>Sub-Total</th></tr>
<tr><td>12</td><td>0876547</td><td>#4 wing nuts</td>
<td>$1.00</td><td>$12.00</td></tr>
<tr><td>10</td><td>0876501</td><td>#4 wood screws</td>
<td>$1.50</td><td>$15.00</td></tr>
<tr><td>20</td><td>0887965</td><td>ProBuild Hammer</td>
<td>$9.50</td><td>$190.00</td></tr>
<tr><td>5</td><td>0927125</td><td>Caulking gun</td>
<td>$4.00</td><td>$20.00</td></tr>
<tr><td>10</td><td>1034526</td><td>3-Pk Masking Tape</td>
<td>$2.00</td><td>$20.00</td></tr>
</table>
```

In this example, we still have two column groups. However, some of the columns are getting a bit more individual attention. In the first group, the first column is getting a different width from the second two columns; in the second group, the two columns have the same width, but different alignment properties. The `<col>` element can handle the same attributes as `<colgroup>`, including span. The only major difference is that `<col>` doesn't define a new group—it only sets attributes for columns. Refer to Figure 9.8 to see how these changes affect the table.

FIGURE 9.8

Using <col> to
set attributes
within the
column groups.
Note the col-
umn width
and alignment
differences
when compared
to Figure 9.7.

As you'll see in Chapter 10, "Get Splashy: Style Sheets, Fonts, and Special Characters,"
<col> isn't completely dissimilar from other elements that are used for style and attribute
markup, such as <span> and <div>. In fact, you'll likely find yourself using <col> with
style sheet markup.

So far, most of what we've seen of <colgroup> and <col> has affected a basic data-
focused table, but these elements can be just as effective with an all-page table that's
used for page layout. You've got some interesting options for managing entire columns
of markup with a few easy elements. Here's an earlier example updated to manage
the columns:

```
<table border="1" cellspacing="2" cellpadding="2" width="100%">
<colgroup>
<col width="500">
<col align="center">
</colgroup>
<tr><td colspan="2"><h1>Current Home Sale Listings</h1></td></tr>
<tr>
<td>
<h1>Farmhouse Living</h1>
<p>This 3/2 traditional has a full basement (modern
touches like Italian lighting and Berber carpet) for
a media room, home office or an unemployment den for
that English-major college grad of yours. Screened porch
in back overlooks a nice badminton/croquet lawn complete
with a walking garden on the side and a dog run in the
trees.</p>
</td>
<td>
<img src="325main.png" alt="Front of 325 Main Street" /><br />
<b>325 Main Street. $129,000</b>
```

```
</td>
</tr>
<tr>
<td>
<h1>Mini Estate</h1>
<p>You don't see garden estates at these prices anymore.
Brick fenced entry (with a fancy remote control) opens to
a winding drive up the front lawn to this colonial in the
best Jeffersonian tradition. Inside, you'll find formal
living and dining, a basement game room (perfect for media
or art projects) and a downstairs master suite with whirlpool
tub (see photo). This one even has extras like a butler's pantry
(for storing all those family-sized cans of ravioli-os) and a
second, back staircase for creeping quietly down in the middle
of the night to get one more small sliver of homemade pie.</p>
</td>
<td>
<img src="brook.png" alt="Babbling brook " /><br />
<b>19 E. Gables Road. $279,000.</b>
</td>
</tr>
</table>
```

Figure 9.9 shows how this looks in a browser.

FIGURE 9.9

Here's an example of `<colgroup>` and `<col>` for a table that's focused more on page layout than tabular data.

Frames and Rules

One last set of attributes can be used both for advanced tabular data and page layout tables. These attributes are `frame` and `rules`. The `frame` attribute is used to determine which lines around the *outside* of a table are rendered when the `border` attribute is used. The `rules` attribute is used to determine which lines are drawn *inside* a table, between cells, when `border` is used.

An example might be

```
<table border="1" frame="hsides" rules="rows">
...table markup...
</table>
```

The result is a table that has only an outline of the table and its columns, as shown in Figure 9.10. (Compare it to Figure 9.9, which shows the full set of border lines.)

FIGURE 9.10

You can use the frame and rules attributes to choose the portions of a table's border that you want to display.

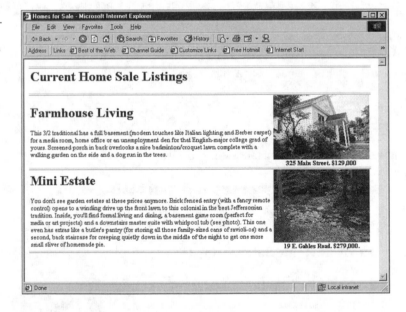

Each attribute offers a number of options. The `frame` attribute, which deals with the four outer sides of the table, is set to show them all by default when the `border` attribute is used. Other values for `frame` are

- `void`—No sides of the table are rendered
- `above`—The top of the table is drawn
- `below`—The bottom is drawn

- ▨ `hsides`—The left and right sides are drawn
- ▨ `vsides`—The top and bottom are drawn
- ▨ `lhs` or `rhs`—Left or right side only, respectively

You can also use the values `box` or `border` to draw all four sides. (This might be necessary in some scripting, for instance, although in regular markup you'd simply omit the `frame` attribute.)

Note
It's worth noting that the `frame` attribute for the `<table>` element has nothing to do with the HTML Frames elements discussed in Chapter 12, "Creating Sites with HTML Frames." In this case, the `frame` attribute is meant to suggest the outline of cells and rows in an XHTML table.

For the lines inside your table, you can vary the value you assign to `rules`. Those potential values include

- ▨ `none`—No lines drawn inside the table
- ▨ `groups`—Lines will only appear between row groups—those defined by `<thead>`, `<tfoot>`, and `<tbody>`—and column groups defined by `<colgroup>` containers
- ▨ `rows`—Lines only appear between rows
- ▨ `cols`—Lines only appear between columns
- ▨ `all`—Lines appear on all sides of every cell, as in the default value

Although these attributes are part of the strict XHTML specification, be aware that you can also accomplish some of these visual changes with style sheets, as discussed in Chapter 10. That probably would be preferable if you're working with late-model visual Web browsers. (Non-visual and older Web browsers will ignore all these attributes anyway.)

Table Design Examples

Now that you've learned a good bit of the theory behind table design and the bulk of the elements and attributes you can use for a table, let's turn our attention to some slightly more complex examples. You'll find that XHTML table elements are useful for a wide variety of page design approaches. Almost anytime you want some control over the placement of paragraphs, images, and other rows or columns of data, a table is the right choice. Let's look at two examples—one that focuses on dividing the page into rows, and one that focuses on creating and managing columns.

A Row-Centric Table

This fairly clean-looking page example is designed for that fictional real estate agent. In this case, you'll notice that the page is rather *row-centric*. By that I mean that most of what you're seeing are a bunch of rows, each one with really only a single column of data. When you need multiple columns, you simply nest another table with as many columns as desired. This is one way to design reasonably simple-looking pages that still use tables for fine control over the layout. (And you can usually keep the rows and columns straight in your head when you think this way.)

Note also that this page sets a border of 0 for the main table, so as to offer white space around most of the elements. As part of the example, the row grouping elements are used, so that a browser that wanted to could render the header (image and links) and footer (contact address information) separately, non-scrolling or on each page of a printout. See Listing 9.3 for the entire document (in strict XHTML), including the declarations that are required for such documents (and were introduced back in Chapter 4, "Creating Your First Page").

LISTING 9.3 A Row-Centric All-Page Table Design

```
<?xml version="1.0" encoding="iso-8859-1"?>
<!DOCTYPE HTML PUBLIC "-//W3C//DTD HTML 4.01//EN"
   "http://www.w3.org/TR/html4/strict.dtd">

<html xmlns="http://www.w3.org/1999/xhtml">
<head>
  <title>Inside the House</title>
</head>
<body bgcolor="#ffffff">

<!-- Start the whole-page table -->
<table border="0" width="100%" cellpadding="10">

<thead>
<!-- Top banner image -->
<tr>
<td align="center"><img src="images/heading.jpg" /></td>
</tr>

<!-- Control center row -- >
<tr>
```

LISTING 9.3 (continued)

```
<td align="center">
<a href="index.html">Main Page</a> |
<a href="house.html"> The House </a> |
<ahref="area.html">Moving to the Area</a> |
<a href="terms.html">Terms of Sale</a> |
<a href="map.html">Directions</a>
</td>
</tr>
</thead>

<tbody>

<!-- Thumbnail images in a nested table -->
<tr>
<td align="center">
<table width="450" border="1" cellspacing="2" cellpadding="5">
  <tr>
    <td width="33%"><img src="images/master.jpg" /></td>
    <td width="33%"><img src="images/kids_bedroom.jpg"  /></td>
    <td width="34%"><img src="images/living_room.jpg" /></td>
  </tr>

  <tr>
    <td width="33%" valign="top">Master Bedroom includes
luxury bath with whirlpool tub</td>
    <td width="33%" valign="top">Second Bedroom features
good light and cool breezes</td>
    <td width="34%" valign="top">Rustic living area includes
stone fireplace with gas logs</td>
  </tr>
</table>

</td>
</tr>

<!-- Main body text and floating table-->

<tr>
```

LISTING 9.3 (continued)

```
<td>
 <h1>Your Own Mini-Estate</h1>

    <table align="right" cellpadding="5" width="200" border="1">
            <tr bgcolor="yellow"><td>19 E. Gable Road</td></tr>
     <tr><td><b>Price:</b> $279,000</td></tr>
     <tr><td><b>Appraisal</b> $309,000</td></tr>
     <tr><td>Owner is moving to Florida and interested
in a quick sale. Call 555.1023 and ask for Rich</td></tr>
     </table>

    <p>You don't see garden estates at these prices anymore.
Brick fenced entry (with a fancy remote control) opens to a
winding drive up the front lawn to this colonial in the best
Jeffersonian tradition. Inside, you'll find formal living and
dining, a basement game room (perfect for media
or art projects) and a downstairs master suite with whirlpool tub.
This one even has extras like a butler's pantry (for storing all
those family-sized cans of ravioli-os) and a second, back staircase
for creeping quietly down in the middle of the night to get one
more small sliver of homemade pie.</p>

</td>
</tr>
</tbody>

<!--Last row, info line -->
<tr>
<td align="center">
<address>For more information or for an appointment,
call 945.555.1023 or send e-mail to
➥<a href="mailto:rich@fakeestate.com">Rich Salesguy</a>
with the subject line "Mini Estate." Thanks!</address>
</td>
</tr>

</body>
</html>
```

The result is shown in Figure 9.11.

FIGURE 9.11

Here's the page as shown in Listing 9.3. Note the nested tables.

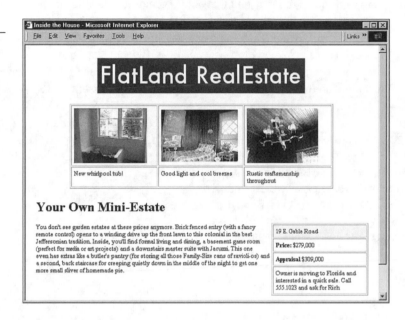

Focusing on Columns

Being row-centric is great for basic tables, but it falls down a little when you decide you'd like to organize your page into multiple columns. A columnar approach is popular for sites that would like to look a lot like a newsletter, or otherwise organize a lot of information in as little space as possible. That's partly why this design approach is popular with portal sites, such as Excite (`http://www.excite.com/`) and Yahoo! (`http://www.yahoo.com`), and with news sites such as the New York Times site (`http://www.nytimes.com/`).

If you'd like to try this design, you'll find it's certainly possible. For the most part, you'll simply have very large data cells, with `<td>` container tags many, many lines apart. It can be a little tough to see this when you look at the raw HTML code, because columns that appear side-by-side in a Web browser must be defined one after the other in your HTML document.

But it won't be that tough, particularly if you use HTML comments liberally to remind you where you are in your all-page table. See Listing 9.4 for a sample of a column-focused page. Figure 9.12 shows what the results look like in a Web browser.

Note In my experience, browsers can be a little independent-minded when it comes to the `align` attribute. You may find that your columns look a little different in different browsers. It's also important to know that `<colgroup>` and `<col>` are relatively recent additions. The solution, in some cases, is to use `<td width="xx">` on cells within your table. Because a column must be as wide as its widest cell, generally you can get away with specifying the width of just your top data cells in each column. I've used that technique in this listing instead of relying on `<colgroup>` and `<col>`.

LISTING 9.4   Here's a Page Specifically Divided into Columns

```
<?xml version="1.0" encoding="iso-8859-1"?>
<!DOCTYPE HTML PUBLIC "-//W3C//DTD HTML 4.01//EN"
    "http://www.w3.org/TR/html4/strict.dtd">

<html xmlns="http://www.w3.org/1999/xhtml">
<head>
<title>Real Estate News!</title>
</head>
<body>
<!-- Begin Page Table -->

<table width=100% border="0" cellpadding="5" cellspacing="0" bgcolor="#eeeeee">

<!-- Begin top rows -->
<thead>
<tr>
<td align="center" colspan="3">Updated: 10/14/02 2:15 PM EDT</td>
</tr>

<tr>
<td align="center" colspan="3"><img src="title.png" alt="Real Estate News" /></td>
</tr>

<tr>
<td align="center" bgcolor="#eeeeee" colspan="3">
<a href="http://www.fakeestate.com/">Home</a> |
<a href="reports/mortgage.html">Mortgage Report</a> |
<a href="column/index.html">Nancy's View</a> |
```

LISTING 9.4   (continued)

```
<a href="recent.html">Archives</a> |
<a href="http://www.fakeestate.com/cgi-bin/forums">Forums</a>
</td>
</tr>

<tr>
<td colspan="3"> </td>
</tr>
</thead>
<!-- End top rows -->



<!-- Begin main row -->
<tbody>
<tr>

<!-- Begin left-side column -->

<td valign="top" bgcolor="#eeeeee" width="150">

<b>Just posted, new message areas!</b><br />
<p> Visit the Real Estate News
<a href="http://www.fakeestate.com/cgi-bin/forum">Forum.</a>
Chat about changes in the area's market, ask questions of
leading mortgage experts and discuss anything at all related
to the business of making home buyers and sellers happy!</p>

<b>Cool Links</b><br />
<p>Check out these other interesting sites for news and views about real estate:</p>

<p>
<a target="_blank" href="http://www.realworldestate.com/">World of RE</a>
</p>

<p>
```

LISTING 9.4   (continued)

```
<a target="_blank" href="http://www.mortgage-planet.com">Mortgage Planet</a>
</p>

<p>
<a target="_blank" href="http://www.realfakedeal.com">Real Deal RE</a>
</p>

<p>
<a target="_blank" href="http://www.fixituppers.com">FixItUppers.com</a>
</p>

</td>

<!-- End left-side column -->


<!-- Begin middle column -->

<td valign="top" bgcolor="#ffffff">

<h1>Closing Costs Head Down</h1>

<p>Thanks to local competition and a soft national economic outlook,
many banks are lowering or rebating key closing costs to move more
traffic to their banks and encourage new and existing home purchases.
In some cases, the advantages are available for individuals interested
in refinancing their homes.</p>

<p><a href="news/10.14.closing.html">Read more...</a></p>


<h1>Insurance Investigation Begins</h1>

<p>The State Attorney General is looking into the practices of two
regional title insurance companies that may have overcharged customers
in the past five years. Spokespeople for both companies say they're
```

LISTING 9.4   (continued)

```
working with the state government to uncover the errors.</p>

<p><a href="http://www.stategov.gov/page/news.html">Visit the state site...</a></p>


<h1>Nancy: Doing the Books</h1>

<p> In this week's column, Nancy takes a look at some of the personal
accounting options you have for tax time and personal budget management.
The end goal? Putting together the perfect portfolio for increasing the
amount a bank is willing to lend you.</p>

<p><a href="columns/10.14.nancy.html">Read Nancy's column...</a>


<!-- End middle column -->

</td>


<!-- Begin right-side column -->

<td width="150" valign="top" bgcolor="#eeeeee">

<img src="images/feature.jpg" width="100" alt="featured home" />

<p><b>Featured Property</b></br>
This week's featured listing is a 4/2/2 with a finished, walk-out basement,
13 acres and it's own swimming hole fed by the Rogers River. If you've ever
wondered what those relaxation books mean by "walking meditation" wait until
you take a stroll on your own riverfront property.</p>

<p><a href="features/10.14.property.html">[4/2/2 Riverfront]</a></p>

<!-- End right side column -->

</tbody>
```

LISTING 9.4   (continued)

```
</td>
</tr>
</table>


</body>
</html>
```

FIGURE 9.12

Here's the page as shown in Listing 9.4, with its column-focused newsletter look.

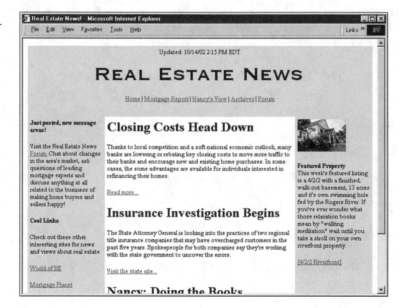

Summary

In this chapter, you learned some of the advanced techniques for using table elements to organize and lay out an entire page. You began with some theory—a look at the techniques involved in adding images to tables, using nested tables and grouping the columns and rows within your table so that they can be labeled and altered. Then, you saw how those techniques can all come together in some example table-based layouts, including one that focused on formatting rows and one that focused on creating columns on the page.

In the next chapter you'll be introduced to style sheets, the modern approach to changing the look and feel of your pages.

GET SPLASHY: STYLE SHEETS, FONTS, AND SPECIAL CHARACTERS

TML, in its most ideal form, is application-neutral. Pages created in HTML (and even more so in XHTML) should render as completely and informatively on a cell phone's display or a palm-held computer as they do in a full-fledged graphical browser application on a Windows or Macintosh computer. As mentioned in previous chapters, this is done by separating the styling of a page from the content and organization of that page. This chapter discusses that styling, and also touches on the less ideal ways that you can style your page—the transitional options.

This chapter covers the following:

- The basics of creating style sheets, including the theory behind them
- The building blocks of style sheets, including `<style>`, `<span>`, and `<div>`, as well as a discussion of linking versus embedding style sheets
- Creating new classes and adding inline style attributes to other HTML elements
- The various properties and styles you can render using style sheets
- Adding special characters and symbols to your document's text

Style Sheets in Theory

Early versions of HTML didn't have much control over the look-and-feel of the page. In the early 1990s, most Web pages were fairly basic-looking. You had a text font (generally Times or similar), a monospaced font (usually one with a typewriter look to it), and many of the basic HTML elements you've seen in this book, such as headings, lists, images, and hyperlinks. Heck, it even took a while before HTML tables appeared in the specification.

As the Web became more popular as a commercial medium, the graphics designers started to get their hands in Web design, and the Web browser companies—particularly Netscape and Microsoft—began to oblige them with proprietary elements that did more to change the look of a page. These elements included `<center>`, `<font>`, and the once-popular and always-maligned `<blink>` element.

Although some of these elements were included in HTML specifications (notably HTML 3.2), they were frowned upon by the HTML gurus, in part because they encouraged graphic-focused coding. For instance, the following markup became a popular approach to creating headings that cut the `<h1>` elements out of the mix:

```
<font face="Arial, Helvetica" size="+2">Welcome to the Site</font><br />
```

Because of this, browsers that don't recognize the `<font>` element (again, a handheld computer comes to mind) not only ignore the `<font>` element, but also they don't communicate the fact that the enclosed text is supposed to be a header. If `<h1>` is used, both the graphical and *non-graphical* browsers can figure out a way to tell the user, "Hey, this is a header."

Note What do I mean by non-graphical browsers? They're browsers that don't display different fonts or font sizes, and in many cases can't support images. This might include Web browsers built into handheld computers (such as Palm or PocketPC devices). Non-graphical browsers can also include assistive browsers that are speech-enabled or communicate in Braille. These browsers can't recognize elements such as `<font>`, but they may have a way to communicate the difference between `<h1>` and `<h2>` elements.

What Are Style Sheets?

Although the `<font>` element and its ilk were (and are) immensely popular for visual browsers, these style-only elements would be ignored by non-graphical browsers, at best, or would be a problem, at worst. So, some solution needed to be reached. That solution is *style sheets*, which enable the Web developer to use the strict XHTML elements, such as `<h1>`, while also being able to style that element, such as

```
<h1 style="font-family: Arial, Helvetica">Welcome to the Site</h1>
```

Everyone is happy—users with graphical browsers see pretty fonts, and users with non-graphical browsers still have an `<h1>` element that enables them to recognize this line as a heading and format it appropriately, even if they're forced to ignore the style attribute.

That's the theory behind the style sheet—you separate the look-and-feel of the page from the organization and content of the page. It's a strong enough theory, in fact, that it's required for strict XHTML—you can only use those older formatting tags if you specify a transitional DTD.

Why Use Style Sheets?

Style sheets are helpful in a few other ways. They can actually be separated from the HTML document entirely. As you'll see in this chapter, the `style` attribute isn't the only way to assign styles. You can set up an entire Web site to know that a `<p>` container (or nearly any other element) should be in a certain font, color, size, or some other visual, aural, or tactile property. So, style sheets can make it easier to set a particular series of style guidelines for your Web site and force all your pages to adhere to it.

Separating style tags from organizational tags maintains another goal of HTML and XHTML—making the code human-readable. Consider the following line:

```
<p><font face="Arial, Helvetica, San Serif" size="+2" color="green">
Thanks for visiting. Please sign the guest book below and let me know if
there's anything else you'd like to see on the site.</font></p>
```

This isn't impossible to read and decipher, but it's even easier to read if you specify in the style sheet definitions that the `<p>` element has a certain font face, size, and color, using a definition at the top of the page like this:

```
<style>
p { font-family: Arial, Helvetica, San Serif; font-size: 16pt; color:
➥green }
</style>
```

Now, for the body of the document, you'll only need to enter this:

```
<p>Thanks for visiting. Please sign the guest book below and let me know
if there's anything else you'd like to see on the site.</p>
```

And, if that happens to be the style you want for your entire page, or your entire Web site, suddenly all `<p>` elements can be defined with those characteristics. Even if that *isn't* the style you want for every single one of your paragraphs, you can still define a style ahead of time and then assign it to a particular element or selection with a minimum of hassle. In other words, style sheets are definitely a timesaver, and they're great for giving your pages a uniform look.

Finally, style sheets are useful in a grander, industry-wide sense because they stop the browser companies from coming up with as many proprietary (and often incompatible) elements. In the mid-1990s, creating proprietary elements became something of a horserace, with Netscape and Internet Explorer diverging on the different ways that you aligned and styled text and other items. With the style sheet approach, there's a set standard for everything and, perhaps surprisingly, there are only a few actual XHTML elements to learn in order to implement style sheets.

Understanding CSS and XHTML

As with XHTML and HTML, the style sheet language we'll be dealing with has a set specification—*CCS2*, or *Cascading Style Sheets 2*. This standard is what's used most often in Web publishing, and it's the standard that most modern visual Web browsers recognize. (Some browsers support only CCS1, but not too much has changed in CCS2, so most of that markup will be recognized.)

The CSS approach is fairly straightforward. You'll find that the specification offers a number of properties, each of which can accept a range of values. Those properties are used as part of the style attribute for a given XHMTL element; that element is then styled by the browser, if possible. Here are a few examples:

```
<h1 style="font-family: Arial, Helvetica, Sans Serif">Your Restaurant
Reviews</h1>
```

```
<p style="font-size: 12pt">Welcome to the section of the site where you
review the restaurants. If you disagree with something we've said, have a
different take on a dish or if you'd like to let everyone know about a
find you've made, do it here!</p>
```

Using style sheets isn't required in XHTML documents—you can simply go without this level of formatting. And if you do decide to format, technically you don't have to use CSS. You could use a different style sheet specification, if you declare it in your Web browser's `<head>` section. That said, most Web browsers are designed to recognize CSS, not other style sheet specifications, so CSS is the best bet.

CSS has been supported in Web browsers since around the 4.0 level of Netscape and Microsoft's applications. At this point, you can be assured that the basic formatting of your page, using style sheets, is recognized by upwards of 90% of the graphical Web browsers out there. In other words, you can leave the `<blink>` and `<font>` elements behind for good!

If you're concerned about CCS2 versus CCS1, don't be. Very little has changed between the two specifications. CSS2 really just builds on the CSS1 specification, particularly in more complex operations—style elements for tables, for non-visual presentation (audio and Braille, for instance), and for some advanced topics such as CSS-based positioning and internationalization. These are discussed in later chapters. The non-visual CSS properties are in Chapter 14, "Site-Wide Styles: Design, Accessibility, and Internationalization," and CSS positioning is discussed in Chapter 19, "Adding Dynamic HTML."

What Style Sheets Replace

Before we dig deeper into style sheets, let's back up and cover some of the older elements and attributes that have remained among the favorite methods for styling a Web page. Many pages (including some of mine!) continue to use the `<font>` element, along with some attributes that are officially discouraged as of XHTML 1.0 (and, in some cases, the HTML 4.0.1 standard that preceded it).

The `<font>` element can accept a number of different attributes, including `face`, `size`, and `color`. The `<font>` element is a container that is placed around the text that it is to affect, as in

`<font face="Arial, Helvetica" size="+2">Welcome to My Site</font>`

For the `face` attribute, you can include a list of font family names. If the first name isn't installed on the user's system, the second name listed will be used, if possible. You can also use the names "Sans Serif" and "Serif" to use the default fonts of those types assigned in the browser. For size, you can specify a size from 1 to 7, or you can tell `font` to render the text in a size that is a certain number larger or smaller than the current size. (For instance, if the `<font>` element appeared within an `<h1>` element, the attribute `size="-2"` would make the font of that `<h1>` element two "sizes" smaller.) The `color` attribute can accept color names (red, green, blue, aqua, yellow...) or hexadecimal values (discussed in the "Understanding Color Values" section later in this chapter).

The `<center>` container element is one popular way to center nearly any markup that appears between the tags—images, text, hyperlinks, and even multimedia objects. `<center>` is easily replaced with the `<div>` element (discussed in the next section), so it shouldn't be missed.

A few other attributes in the past have included the `<blink>` container (causes text to blink on and off), the `<s>` and `<strike>` containers (make text appear as strikethrough text), and the `<u>` container (underlines text).

As has been noted in previous sections, many of the elements we've learned about thus far have been able to accept an `align` attribute in previous HTML specifications. That isn't allowed in strict XHTML, but it's easy enough to fix with style sheets. Likewise, many elements (including the `<body>` element, `<p>` element, and others) that have accepted a `bgcolor` attribute (background color) in the past now rely on style sheets for that option.

Creating Style Sheets

Now that you've seen some of the theory of style sheets, let's move on to the elements and attributes that actually enable you to put style sheets to use. That includes a quick discussion of the different methods you can use to implement styles:

- **The style attribute**—Using the style attribute for various XHTML elements, you can add style to an individual element or container.

- **Defining element styles**—Using special style definitions, you can define elements—such as `<p>`, `<blockquote>`, `<h3>`, and so on—so that they have a particular styling on the entire page, or even throughout your Web site. If you'd like every paragraph to use a particular font, for instance, you can create a style sheet definition that does that.

- **Defining element classes**—Finally, you can create new *classes* that are styled, and elements can be assigned particular classes. If you create a particular class of `<p>` element that is red text, for instance, you can then use that class definition when you're creating a red paragraph on your page. Other paragraphs (or other elements) can be styled differently, if desired.

So, you have all these options. Beyond that, you can also decide how you're going to make those style sheet definitions available. You have two basic choices. First, you can *embed* the style information in each individual Web page. You'll do that either by adding style information in the `<head>` of the document, or by adding style information to any of the individual elements in your page using the `style` attribute.

Second, you can *link* to a style sheet, which enables you to create a central style sheet document and use it for multiple pages. We'll cover all of those eventualities in the upcoming sections.

The `style` Attribute

Let's begin with the most basic way that you can embed styles in your Web document—using the `style` attribute. The `style` attribute is a simple way to tell almost any XHTML element, "Hey, I'd like to apply a style sheet style to you." Most XHTML elements can accept a `style` attribute, which can then be used to style that element.

For instance, you've seen `<p>` and `<h1>` elements accept the `style` attribute earlier in this chapter. But other elements can accept the `style` attribute as well. The following would suppress the underlining of the hyperlink:

```
<a href="index.html" style="text-decoration": none">Click to visit the
➥online store</a>
```

Or the following would change the background color of the selected table cells:

```
<tr><td style="background: yellow">100</td><td>200</td>
<tdstyle="background: yellow">300</td></tr>
```

To add more than one element at a time, simply separate the properties and their values using a semicolon:

```
<p style="align: left; font-style: italic; font-weight: bold;
background: yellow">Here's some bold, italic text on a yellow
background.</p>
```

You'll find that the `style` attribute is a simple way to quickly add a few different style properties within your page. However, it doesn't substitute for creating an overall style definition using the `<style>` element, as discussed next.

The `<style>` Element

The `style` attribute is useful for the occasional property change, but when you're really serious, it's time to think about using the `<style>` element. This element, which is placed in the `<head>` of your document, is where you can embed style definitions that can be used throughout the page. The basic format is this:

```
<head><style type="text/css">
p { font-style: small-caps }
</style>
<style type="text/css">
Element {property: setting}
</style>
</head>
```

It's fairly straightforward. For example, if you'd like to set every paragraph on the page so that its text is in small caps, you'd create the following `<style>` element in the head of the document:

```
<style type="text/css">
p { font-style:italic}
</style>
```

The typed element (such as the "p" in the preceding example) is called the *selector* in CSS-speak, and anything between the brackets is called the *definition*. The overall entry is a *rule*.

Selectors should be familiar to you—they're the letters that make up XHTML elements, such as p, h1, and ul, which you've seen in earlier chapters. When you create a rule, you're assigning a particular style definition to an element of your choosing, as in

```
ul { list-style: disc }
```

The <style> element can have more than one rule. Each rule technically ends with a closing bracket, so you could place more than one rule on a single line. But, it's best to format each definition on its own line, as in

```
<style type="text/css">
p { font-style:italic}
h1 { color: blue }
ul { list-style: disc }
</style>
```

Also, a particular definition can have more than one property within it. Properties are separated by semicolons, but you might consider placing each property on a separate line to make it more readable:

```
<style type="text/css">
p { font-style:italic;
    background: yellow;
    padding-left: 12px
  }
</style>
```

Again, all that spacing isn't required, but you can see that it helps make the rule clearer.

It's worth noting that you can assign the same definition to a number of elements at the same time simply by adding more selectors, separated by commas. For instance:

```
<style type="text/css">
p, h1, h2, h3, blockquote, ul, ol  { font-family: Arial, Helvetica }
</style>
```

This approach enables you to quickly set the font or a similar attribute for a group of elements at once, making them all more uniform on the page.

Finally, part of the point of calling the standard Cascading Style Sheets is to suggest that there's a certain amount of *cascading* (or, more technically, *inheritance*) going on. For instance, if a particular font style is assigned to a <table> element, elements within that table—row and cell definitions—are also assumed to have those characteristics.

The same is true, for instance, for the `<body>` element, which can be used to set some overall defaults for your page, such as font properties, background colors (or images), and so forth. Once these properties are set, all other elements within the `<body>` element will inherit these properties unless they're specifically overridden with either a definition of their own or the `style` attribute. For example, the following style definition would cause the main body font to be a sans-serif font (Arial, Helvetica), but would override that for unordered lists (ul), using Times or Times New Roman instead:

```
<style>
body { font-family: Arial, Helvetica; font-size: 12pt }
ul { font-family: Times New Roman, Times}
</style>
```

Creating Special Classes

Beyond simply redefining the properties of existing XHTML elements, you can go further with style sheets by creating new *classes*. In essence, these classes enable you to assign to a particular style a particular element sometimes, while leaving the original element's definition alone. For instance, consider this code snippet:

```
<head>
<style>
h1.red { color: red }
</style>
</head>
<body>
<h1>This Heading is the Default Color</h1>
<h1 class="red">This Heading is Red</h1>
</body>
```

Using the `h1.red` selector instead of just `h1` means you're not assigning a style that will appear every time you use `<h1>`. Instead, it will only appear when you use the `class` attribute to specify that style rule. You can use this approach in many different ways, not the least of which is to define more than one class for the same element:

```
<style>
p.body { font-family: Times New Roman, Times; font-size: 14pt }
p.footnote { font-family: Arial, Helvetica; font-size: 10pt }
</style>
```

In this case, all you have to do is change the `class` attribute's value for a particular `<p>` element and that element's content will change appearance.

You can also create a class that isn't tied to a particular element, which enables you to add that class to any element in the body of the page that you'd like to style. For example:

```
<style>
.small { font-family: Arial, Helvetica; font-size: 10pt }
</style>
```

This rule could be used to change the formatting of pretty much any container that handles text, such as `<ul class="small">` to `<blockquote class="small">` and so on.

Using the `<span>` Element

When you're working with style sheets, you'll find that a new element, `<span>`, can come in handy. In essence, `<span>` is used to apply style sheet formatting to whatever markup you'd like to use it for. Anything from a single letter to entire paragraphs can be contained by the `<span>` element, which can then be used to apply a certain style or style class to the selection.

Note

The `<span>` element has the same basic scope as the `<em>` element (it's an *inline* element), so it isn't designed to enclose elements such as images and multimedia objects. If you need to apply formatting to large sections of your page, use the `<div>` element (discussed in the next section).

You've got three ways to define and use `<span>`. The first method is to simply use it with the `style` attribute for a quick styling fix, as in

```
<span style="font-variant: small-caps">

This text is in small caps.
</span>
```

Just as you can define the style for almost any other element, you can define the style for span, as in

```
<style>
span { font-family: Arial, Helvetica; font-size: 12pt }
</style>
```

You can then use `<span>` on its own as a simple way to apply some different formatting to a selection, such as

```
<p><span>Coming soon: More interesting content!</span></p>
```

So, that's one way to use <span>, but it's probably not the most interesting way because it limits you to a single style definition. The second way to define <span> is to create classes of the <span> element, the same way you might create a class for a <p> or <ul> element:

```
<head>
<title>Drop and Small Caps</title>
<style>
span.dropcap { font-family: Times New Roman, Times; font-size: 28pt;
➥float: left}
span.smallcaps {font: Arial, Helvetica; font-variant: small-caps }
</style>
</head>
```

With those rules in place, you could use the <span> element with a class attribute to change the appearance of the enclosed markup, as in

```
<p><span class="dropcap">I</span><span class="smallcaps">t was a dark and
➥stormy night.</span>
The clouds rolled in – thundered in – and the bleak black was only
➥occasionally interrupted
by bright flashes of fear.</p>
```

Putting these rules together with such markup, you'd end up with a page that looks similar to Figure 10.1.

FIGURE 10.1

Here you can see the <span> element at work, changing the markup using universal style classes you've created.

The third thing you can do with <span> is use it with a defined standalone class, such as

```
<style>
.dropcap { font-family: Times New Roman, Times; font-size: 24pt; text-
➥align: top }
</style>
```

Using `<span class="dropcap">`, you can apply this styling to a section of text, just as you could use the `class` attribute with another text container tag to apply the drop-cap style.

Using the `<div>` Element

Another style-related element is `<div>`, which is short for "division," and can be used to create sections within your entire Web document. The `<div>` element can be used to apply almost any formatting to nearly any elements that it contains, including tables, images, and multimedia objects. You could think of `<div>` as sort of a user-defined element that's one rung below the `<body>` and `<head>` elements in significance. (In specifications-ese, it's called a *block-level* element, which means it automatically has white space around it, like a `<p>` or `<blockquote>` element.)

The `<div>` element can be used in a way that's similar to `<span>`. Style sheet rules can be defined for it, and then the `class` attribute can be used to apply those styles to the enclosed markup. For instance:

```
<h1>Dining Out</h1>
<div style="background-color: yellow">
<p>Some tips for a better business dining experience:</p>
<ul>
<li>Call ahead and check to see if the restaurant takes reservations.</li>
<li>For six or more people, request special accommodations, such as
➥seating in a quiet area, banquet room or near a window with a view.</li>
<li>If you call early enough (before dinner) you can also ask for a quick
rundown of their house and recommended wine selections. Then, look them up
and have an idea if they're good recommendations.</li>
<li>Know whether the restaurant offers vegetarian, kosher, diabetic or
➥other dietary considerations, particularly if you aren't familiar with
➥all of your diners.</li>
<li>Consider any other special needs in your party (wheelchair access,
➥special seating) and request or discuss those items ahead of time.</li>
<li>Discreetly hand your credit card to the head waiter when you're first
➥seated, or otherwise let him or her know that you'll be taking the check.
This can avoid tussles at the end of the meal.</li>
<li>Tip well, including bartenders and bar wait staff if you wait for your
table in the bar or lounge area.</li>
</ul>
</div>
```

As you can see from this listing and from Figure 10.2, the `<div>` element can be used around multiple types of container elements, such as `<p>` and `<ul>` containers. The `<div>` element is designed to do just this—to create artificial divisions for styling and alignment purposes.

FIGURE 10.2

Using the `<div>` tag enables you to span multiple elements with a style definition.

Tip

`<div>` can accept an `align` attribute that is recognized in many browsers, even those that predate style sheet support. Use `<div align="center">`, `</div>` to center all markup—paragraphs, tables, images—contained in the `<div>` element. (This is preferable to the `<center>` element, which is not a recommended part of the HTML or XHTML specification.)

As with other elements, including `<span>`, the `<div>` element can be defined with a style rule, it can be assigned classes directly, or it can work with independent class rules.

Linking Versus Embedding

There's one other issue before we move on to the various styles that are available for use—and it's a fairly important issue. It turns out that you have two different methods for style sheet definitions available to you. So far, you've seen many examples of the first option—embedded style sheet definitions, using the `<style>` container within the head of the document. This is particularly useful if your style sheet only applies to the page in which it's embedded.

Of course, many of us don't design Web sites that way. Our Web sites will often have common elements and styles on many, most, or all the pages. In that case, you may find it more convenient to create a more universal style sheet, and then link to it from within each document.

This linking approach offers two advantages. First, the obvious advantage is that you don't have to add the `<style>` container to the top of each page that you create. Second, using a single document for your style sheet definitions means you can quickly and easily alter the look-and-feel of your entire Web site with a simple change to the style sheet document. Plus, it's easier to manage a large Web site, even one developed by different Web authors and designers, if they are all expected to link to a predetermined style sheet.

Of course, even with linked style sheets, you can override a given style with a `<span>` or `<div>` element or by using the `style` attribute within an element. Likewise, you can still use the `<style>` element on individual pages to add to the style sheet document or to override portions of the linked style sheet document.

So, how do you link? First, you need to create the style sheet document. It should be plain ASCII text, just like an HTML document. Save the file with a `.css` extension, such as `styles.css`. The file can include rules that define element styles and rules that define classes. Within the style sheet, you can also use a special comment tag if you choose—text between `/*` and `*/` is ignored, as in

```
/* Begin rules for headings */
h1 {
 font-family: Arial, Helvetica;
 font-size: 24pt;
 font-weight: bold;
 word-spacing: 2pt;
 }
```

Once the file is created and saved, you can link to that file using the `<link />` element, which is placed in the head of your document:

```
<head>
<title>Main Page</title>
<link rel="stylesheet" href="http://www.fakecorp.com/styles.css">
</head>
```

Note that the URL to which you link can be a relative URL, but it would vary depending on where in your site's hierarchy you've saved the style sheet file. If you use the `<base>` element on your pages, you can use a relative URL that builds on the `<base>` element, as discussed in Chapter 7, "Building Hypertext Links."

Note

Want to play around with linked styles a bit? Visit `http://www.w3.org/StyleSheets/Core/` to learn about some styles that the W3C has created, which you can use on your own page. Any typical HTML document with a simple `<link />` element pointed to one of the W3C's stylesheets will be recast with new fonts, styles, and effects. It's a cool way to see how powerful style sheet linking is.

Properties and Styles

Now that you've seen the different ways to add styles to your pages, let's take a look at the variety of styles that you can add using CSS1 and CSS2. This section doesn't cover them all; only the most popular. However, you can visit `http://www.zvon.org/xxl/css1Reference/Output/index.html` for an excellent reference to the CSS1 specification. (It also has links to a CSS2 reference.) The official CSS2 specification is at `http://www.w3.org/TR/CSS2/`.

In the following sections, I'll touch on some of the styles for text, fonts, backgrounds, and links, and for working with borders, margins, and padding.

Text Styles

The text styles in the CSS definition are those that enable you to determine how text will be rendered, positioned, and aligned on the page. These styles can be used with nearly any XHTML element, giving you control over how text and inline images appear in your document. Table 10.1 shows many of these text styles.

TABLE 10.1 CSS Text-Style Properties

Property	Value	Example(s)
word-spacing	Number and units	1pt, 4em, 1in
letter-spacing	Number and units	3pt, 0.1em, +1
line-height	Number and units	14pt
text-decoration	Value	underline, line-through, box, blink
text-transform	Value	capitalize, lowercase, uppercase, none
text-indent	Number and units or percentage	1in, 5%, 3em
vertical-align	Value or percentage	baseline, sup, sub, top, middle, 50%
text-align	Value	left, right, center, justify

The properties `word-spacing`, `letter-spacing`, `line-height`, and `text-indent` accept length values, which include a number and the units of length. An example of this would be extra point-size spacing:

```
p.wide { letter-spacing: 2pt }
```

When creating CSS-compliant rules, length (among many other values) includes both a number and the measurement unit. The number can be either positive or negative; there should be no space between the number and the unit. Unit measurements you can use include px (pixels), in (inches), mm (millimeters), cm (centimeters), pt (points), em (the height of the current font), and ex (the height of the current font's letter "x").

`text-decoration` is used to change the appearance of text in your document, and it includes the values listed in Table 10.1. The value `none` is also possible.

The `vertical-align` and `text-align` properties give Web designers much-desired control over centering and justifying text in a document. Vertical alignment is best used with elements that appear inside another element. For instance, this style definition creates a class of the `<em>` element that can be used as a superscript:

```
em.super { vertical-align: super }
```

So, adding this class within another paragraph creates text that is superscript compared to the surrounding text:

```
<p>The only thing we have to fear is fear itself. <em class="super">F.D.R,
➥public speech, 1933</em>.</p>
```

Font Properties

While the `<font>` element is frowned upon, that doesn't mean there isn't an entire Web out there with defined fonts and snazzy-looking paragraphs! One way to get in on the action is to define fonts—including font family, size, weight, color, and more—using style sheet properties to create rules. With fonts in particular, remember inheritance. You can specify font properties for the `<body>`, for instance, and then override that specification for elements or classes that need to be different from the main body. Table 10.2 offers some of the font-related CSS styles and shows how they can be used.

TABLE 10.2   CSS-Defined Style Properties

Property	Value	Example(s)
font-family	Name of font	Helvetica, Serif, Symbol
font-size	Number/percentage	12pt, +1, 120%
font-weight	Number/strength	normal, bold, bolder, 100, 900

TABLE 10.2   (continued)

Property	Value	Example(s)
font-style	Name of style	italic, oblique, normal
font-variant	Name of style	normal, small-caps
font	Combination	12pt Serif
color	Word/hex number	red, green, blue, #FF00FF

Here's a quick rundown of all these style sheet properties:

The `font-family` property allows you to choose the name of the font that you'd like text to appear in. With any `font` property, you want to be as general with font family names (such as Helvetica or Courier) as possible because the user's browser will have to decide what that font name's closest counterpart is on the user's system. So, avoid names like "Helvetica Oblique" or "Courier Heavy 12."

In fact, `font-family` allows you to specify alternative font names for different computer systems, like this:

```
<style type="text/css">
  p.standard { font-family: Helvetica, Arial, sans-serif }
</style>
```

Note   Font family names with spaces should be put in quotes, like `"Century Schoolbook"`, when found in a style definition rule. When they're used with the `style` attribute, you can use single quotes, as in `style="font-family: 'Century Schoolbook', serif"` because the `style` attribute itself requires double quotes.

The `font-family` property can also accept one of five generic font names: `serif`, `sans-serif`, `cursive`, `fantasy`, and `mono-space`. If you stick with these generic names (or at least include them in your list of values), you'll always have at least some measure of predictability in your visual browser.

`font-size` can be a percentage, point size, or word size, such as `larger` or `smaller`. `font-weight` refers to the boldness of the font, with possible values like `bolder`, `lighter`, or numerical values from 100–900. (Normal is 400.) `font-style` values determine the italic nature of the font. Possible values are `italic`, `oblique`, and `normal`.

The `font-variant` property is simply used to set the font to either `normal` or `small-caps`.

The `font` property is basically a shorthand reference for the four that appear preceding it in the table. You can simply use any of the related values for the catch-all `font` property, effectively describing its entire appearance in one definition. The `font` property's implementation can be problematic in different browsers, so it's recommended that you define font properties separately (particularly `font-family` and `font-size`) for cross-platform compatibility.

Background and Color Properties

Style sheets can be used to give unprecedented control over what appears in the background of your Web page. Not only can you specify a color or an image for the background, but you can also decide how the image will be repeated, whether it acts like a "watermark," and other characteristics.

Although background properties are popularly applied to the <body> tag (so that they affect the entire document), background properties can actually be assigned to nearly any XHTML element, from inline elements (<em> or <span>) to block elements such as <p> or <h1>. This makes it possible to set highlighting colors around individual words or background colors for blocks of text in paragraphs, lists, and elsewhere. Table 10.3 discusses the background properties.

TABLE 10.3   CSS Background Properties

Property	Value	Example(s)
background-color	Color name of RGB value	white, #0000FF
background-image	url( )	url(image.gif), url(http://www.fakcorp.net/bgnd.jpg)
background-repeat	Word value	repeat, repeat-x, repeat-y, no-repeat
background-attachment	word value	scroll, fixed
background-position	Direction or percentage	top, left center, 20%, 65%
background	Combination	white url(image.gif) repeat-x fixed

The possible values for color include black, red, maroon, white, green, olive, lime, aqua, teal, blue, navy, yellow, brown, gray, silver, orange, purple, and fuchsia. If you opt to use a red-green-blue (RGB) value for your colors, you can do that in one of two ways. You can either use a three-digit hexadecimal number in the form #0F0F0F, or you can specify a 256-color value for each of red, green, blue, as in "color: rgb(255,255,0)".

Note

Hexadecimal numbers are in base 16 instead of base 10, meaning they have a "ones" place and a "sixteens" place. Because we only have ten numerals, including 0, the letters A-F are used to represent the values 10–15. So, the base 10 value of the number FF would be (15*16)+15 or 255, while the hexadecimal number 10 has a base 10 value of 16.

As for the background colors, you may find them interesting but largely unnecessary. That's because you can use the `background` property as a shorthand reference to all (or any) of the other properties:

```
<style type="text/css">
  body { background: url(http://www.fakecorp.com/images/back.gif)
white repeat-x fixed }
</style>
```

If you need or want to use the precise `background` property, here are some quick explanations of the less obvious ones:

- `background-repeat`—This property uses one of four codes (shown in Table 10.3) to determine how a background image will be repeated to *tile* itself over the entire browser window area. `repeat-x` sets it to repeat horizontally; `repeat-y` sets it to repeat only vertically.

- `background-attachment`—Determines whether or not the background image will scroll along with the rest of the Web document (scroll), or if the page scrolls over the background as it stays in place (fixed).

- `background-position`—Accepts direction names or percentages to determine the position of the top-left corner of the background image.

Alignment and Block Appearance Properties

XHTML elements that include white space around them tend to be called *block* elements because in effect, they create a box of text (and other markup) that can then be considered an object on the page. (Just to confuse matters, the CSS specification refers to blocks as *boxes*, so this section really talks about *box* properties.) And because the box is an object, there are certain ways you can alter its alignment and appearance, including setting margins, padding the box, adding a border, and so on. While you saw some of these properties for tables in Chapter 9, "Advanced Table Elements and Table Design," it's interesting to note that with style sheets, you can apply them to any block-level element.

The CSS style sheet definition creates a number of properties specifically designed to help you control the appearance of these boxes. Table 10.4 shows you the box properties.

TABLE 10.4 CSS Box Appearance Properties

Property	Value	Example(s)
margin	Length or percentage	1in, 5% 10%, 12pt 10pt 12pt 10pt
padding	Length or percentage	1in, 5% 10%, 12pt 10pt 12pt 10pt
border	Width/style/color	medium dashed red, 2in grooved, blue
width	Length/percentage	.5in, 10%
height	Length/percentage	10em, 12pt
float	Direction	left, right, none
clear	Direction	none, left, right, both

The margin and padding properties work in very similar ways, with the number of values included in the definition determining which sides of the page are being affected:

■ A single value, such as {margin: 5pt}, means that margin is applied to the top, right, bottom, and left sides of the page.

■ Two values, such as {padding: .5in .4in}, means the initial value is applied to the top and bottom, while the second value applies to the right and left.

■ Three values, such as {padding: .5in .4in .3in}, means the first number applies to the top, the second to the right and left, and the third to the bottom.

■ Four values, such as {margin: 5em 4em 6em 9em}, means the numbers apply to the top, right, bottom, and left, respectively.

The difference between the two properties is that margin applies extra space outside the borders of the current element, while padding applies spaces between the edges of the element's box and the text it encloses.

Note that both of these properties can also be broken out into directional versions, such as "margin-left: 12px" or "padding-bottom: 1in", which is useful when you need to specify only one side for margin or padding.

The border property is a shortcut property, like background. In border's case, it can accept values for the width, style, and color of the border of a particular element. The width can be thin, medium, thick, or a length; the color can be any color name or set of hexadecimal pairs; and the style values include none, dotted, dashed, solid, double, groove, ridge, inset, outset. For example:

p.redborder {border: red dashed 20px}

The border property is a shortcut for many different properties, including a series of border-size properties (border-left-size, border-right-size, and so on) and border-width properties (border-bottom-width, border-left-width, and so on). Even as a short-cut property, you can include directions, such as "border-left: 12px blue dotted" and so on.

The width and height properties can be used to specify the width or height of any block element, using either a length or percentage. (The value "auto" can also be used in individual cases to override a setting and change the width and height to normal.)

The float property can be used to allow text to flow around an element. This works the same way that align="left" and align="right" do for the <img /> element, except that the float property works for any element:

```
h2.wrap { float: left }
```

And finally, the clear property can be used to determine whether or not an element will allow other elements to float to one side of it (that is, whether or not the element will wrap around other elements). If clear has a value of left, the element is moved below any floating element to its left; if the value is right, the element is moved below any images floating to the right. For instance, with the style rules:

```
<style type="text/css">
  img.right { float: right }
  h2.no_wrap { clear: right }
</style>
```

Adding this markup would create a page that looks like Figure 10.3:

```
<h2>3 Bedroom Traditional</h2>

<img class="right" src="house1.jpg">

<p>This 3/2 traditional has a full basement (modern touches like Italian
lighting and Berber carpet) for a media room, home office or an
unemployment den for that English-major college grad of yours. 325 Main
Street. $129,000.</p>

<h2 class="no_wrap">Mini Mansion</h2>

<p> This one even has extras like a butler's pantry and a second, back
staircase for creeping quietly down in the middle of the night to get one
more small sliver of homemade pie. And, best yet, a babbling brook right
there on the property.

19 E. Gables Road. $279,000.</p>
```

FIGURE 10.3
With clear, the second <h2> heading refuses to wrap next to the floating image, beginning below the image instead. (Note the extra white space above the "Mini Mansion" heading.)

Styles for Links and Objects

Changing the style of your hyperlinks may be some of the easiest fun you can have with style sheet properties. Not only can you choose the colors that your links appear in, but you can use style sheets to change the appearance of a link when someone points the mouse at it—a popular way to make pages appear a bit more active. This is done using something called *pseudo classes*—specifically, those designed for links and similar objects.

The pseudo classes are shown in Table 10.5.

TABLE 10.5 Pseudo Classes

Property	Explanation
:link	Properties of the hyperlink before it's clicked
:visited	Properties of the hyperlink after it's clicked
:hover	Properties of the link or object while the mouse pointer is over it
:focus	Properties of the link or object while text is being entered or it's selected by the keyboard
:active	Properties of the link or object while it's being selected (that is, while the mouse button is down or the Enter key is pressed)

These classes can be defined in style sheet rules with `color`, `font`, and `background` properties, as in

```
<style type="text/css">
a:link { color: red; background: white }
a:visited { color: pink; background: white }
```

```
a:hover { color: blue; background: yellow }
a:active { color: orange; background: yellow }
</style>
```

When defined in this way, the styles are automatically assigned to `<a>` elements used throughout the page.

First Letter and First Line

Two other pseudo classes might grab your attention. The `:first-letter` and `:first-line` classes can be used to create drop caps, small-cap introductions, or similar effects. For instance:

```
<style type="text/css">
p.drop:first-letter {
    font-family: Times, "Times New Roman";
    font-size: 450%;
    float: left;
    margin-right: 5px;
    }
</style>
```

This would create a drop-cap at the beginning of each paragraph, with the attribute `class="drop"` as part of the `<p>` element. The same sort of thing would work for `first-line`.

Special Table Styles

Many of the text and box styles discussed so far can be used on markup that appears inside tables. But what about using styles with the table elements themselves, particularly `<table>`, `<td>`, and `<tr>`? All of these elements can be used with the background, color, and box style properties discussed earlier in this chapter.

With table rows especially, you may find it useful to define style rules that can be used for background colors, alignment, and more. For example:

```
<style>
tr.yellow { background-color: yellow }
</style>
```

This definition creates a class of `<tr>` that can be used to create rows that have a yellow background. Other background and box properties could also be used with the `<tr>` element or with individual `<td>` elements.

While it's clear that the `<tr>` element can accept many style properties to style each row, what about defining styles for columns? If you use the `<colgroup>` or `<col />` elements discussed in Chapter 9, you can assign style properties to them. For instance, you could give a particular column a background color. First, define the style:

```
<style>
col.yellow { background-color: yellow }
</style>
```

Then, using the `<col />` element, you can assign a particular column the style class that you've created:

```
<table>
<colgroup>
<col />
<col class="yellow" align="right" />
</colgroup>
<tr><td>January</td><td>$100.50</td></tr>
<tr><td>February</td><td>$50.95</td></tr>
<tr><td>March</td><td>$1000.55</td></tr>
</table>
```

Because the second `<col />` element is the one that has been assigned a style class, the second column will appear with a background color.

You may want to change the border and margin characteristics of your table, which you can do with the `border` and `margin` properties discussed earlier in the section "Alignment and Block Appearance Properties." You'll find that you can alter both the `<table>` and individual `<tr>` elements with those styles, as well as the `<col />` element. For instance:

```
<table style="border: solid red">
```

This opening tag begins a table with a solid red border around it. Whether or not the table has interior lines would rely on the `border` property with individual `<col />` and `<tr>` elements. (Note also that the current versions of most Web browsers differ in their implementation of table borders. You might want to stick with the table `border`, `frame`, and `rules` attributes discussed in Chapter 9 for a while longer.)

In my experience, Listing 10.1 generates a red border around all cells in Internet Explorer 5 (and higher), but only a red border around the entire table in Netscape 6. Ideally, it would create a border around all cells.

LISTING 10.1   Using Border Properties with HTML Table Elements

```
<!DOCTYPE html PUBLIC "-//W3C//DTD XHTML 1.0 Strict//EN"
    "http://www.w3.org/TR/xhtml1/DTD/xhtml1-strict.dtd">

<html xmlns="http://www.w3.org/1999/xhtml">

<head>
<style>
.redborder { border: solid red }
</style>

</head>

<body>

<table class="redborder">
<colgroup>
<col  class="redborder"/>
<col class="redborder" />
</colgroup>
<tr class="redborder"><td>January</td><td>$100.50</td></tr>
<tr class="redborder"><td>February</td><td>$50.95</td></tr>
<tr class="redborder"><td>March</td><td>$1000.55</td></tr>
</table>

</body>
</html>
```

Special Characters

In previous chapters, you've seen ways to add special quotation marks (using the `<q>` element), and I touched briefly on the use of the non-breaking space (` `). There are many other special characters you can add to your HTML document, although how to add them may not be readily apparent.

What do you do if you need to render a character that can't be typed into a plain-text document? Or what about special characters, such as < and >, that XHTML uses as part of its own syntax? You add them using special *entities* that look much like the non-breaking space already discussed. This can be used to solve one thorny problem—how to actually display XHTML elements in an HTML document. For example, consider these two lines:

```
Students should remember to use the <b> and </b> elements.
Students should remember to use the &lt;b&gt; and &lt;/b&gt; elements.
```

In a browser, the first line will make the word and appear boldface. In the second line, the entities `&lt;` and `&gt;` are used to represent the less-than and greater-than signs, respectively, so that they aren't interpreted as XHTML by the browser. Instead, when the browser displays the second line, it will look like the first line does on this page.

All entities begin with an ampersand and end with a semicolon. Some use letters between those two symbols, while others use numbers. Table 10.5 shows some of the other named entities you can use in your pages.

Note Although the table displays entity names, all of those entities can also be referenced by number. For instance, a non-breaking space can be rendered as ` ` as well as using ` `. See the Web resources discussed later in this chapter for the numbers that correspond to these entity names.

TABLE 10.5 Named ISO Entities for HTML Documents

Entity Name	What It Represents
	Non-breaking space
&lt;	Less-than sign (<)
&gt;	Greater than sign (>)
&frasl;	Forward slash (/)
&amp;	Ampersand (&)
&copy;	Copyright symbol
&trade;	Trademark symbol
&reg;	Registered trademark symbol
&para;	Paragraph symbol
&lsquo;	Left single quotation mark
&rsquo;	Right single quotation mark
&ldquo;	Left double quotation mark
&rdquo;	Right double quotation mark
&yen;	Yen currency symbol
&euro;	Euro currency symbol

TABLE 10.5   (continued)

Entity Name	What It Represents
&pound;	English Pound currency symbol
&cent;	Cent currency symbol
&ndash;	En dash (–)
&mdash;	Em dash (—)
&iexl;	Inverted exclamation point
&iquest;	Inverted question mark

Aside from these entities, there are many others, including special language characters. For instance, to represent ñ, which is the letter n and a tilde, you can use ñ in your document. For an uppercase Ñ, you would use Ñ in your text. Entities work similarly for other language characters, such as ö for ö (an o with an *umlaut*) or é for é (an e with an *acute* accent).

Other types of diacritical marks are supported, along with codes for Greek letters, mathematical characters, and many other special marks and symbols. For easy-to-follow references, see http://www.w3schools.com/html/html_entitiesref.asp or http://hotwired.lycos.com/webmonkey/reference/special_characters/. For a comprehensive look at the definitions of these entities, see http://www.w3.org/TR/REC-html40/sgml/entities.html.

Summary

In this chapter you learned the theory behind style sheets, why they're recommended, and how they can be implemented on your pages. You learned what the Cascading Style Sheets specification is, as well as some of the XHTML elements, such as <span> and <div>, that work hand-in-hand with style sheet concepts. The second portion of this chapter was devoted to the myriad styles that can be used to dress up your pages, including text, font, background, and block properties. You learned some of the special pseudo classes, which can be used for special effects in style sheet-enhanced pages. And you learned some special ways that style sheet properties can be applied to HTML tables. Finally, you were introduced to the entity codes you can use in HTML documents to represent special characters.

In Chapter 11, "Advanced Web Images and Imagemaps," you'll learn a little more about Web images, including how to optimize them for quick downloading and how to turn them into clickable imagemaps.

ADVANCED WEB IMAGES AND IMAGEMAPS

hapter 6, "Visual Stimulus—Adding Graphics," discussed the basics of creating Web images and putting them on the page, but there's a lot more to cover. Creating and translating images that work well on the Web is an art and a science. You want images that look good, but you want the image files to be small so that they transfer very quickly over the Internet. You can do much more with images than simply create them and post them on the Web. You can animate them, in certain cases, and you can use certain XHTML elements to turn images into clickable *imagemaps*, in which different parts of the image can be used as hyperlinks to different URLs.

This chapter discusses the following:

- Making your images better, smaller, and faster
- Creating and using animated image sequences
- Creating clickable imagemaps for Web site navigation

Making Your Images Better

In Chapter 6, you learned the basics of choosing your image format, saving images, and translating them. You also saw how to crop and resize images; two steps that can help reduce their file size. In this section, let's dig in and a take a look at some of the more advanced options you find in our two graphics editors of choice: Paint Shop Pro for Windows and GraphicConverter from Macintosh. (Getting these applications is also discussed in Chapter 6.)

The issues covered include optimizing your images by tweaking settings in the graphics application. You then see the myriad of options that you're likely to encounter when saving or translating images, and how those options can affect the final images you decide to put on the page.

Optimizing Web Images

Aside from cropping and resizing your images, probably the most important considerations are to use as few colors as possible (in most cases) and to lower the resolution of the images to the appropriate dots per inch (dpi) for onscreen display.

Color Depth

Using fewer colors is generally appropriate for GIF and PNG format images. JPEG images, if they're photographic, almost always require millions of colors. (You can translate JPEG to 256 colors, but photos look pretty bad at that setting.) *Colors* means the palette of colors available to the image. If you use fewer colors in the palette, it's likely that the image is smaller in file size because very similar colors are made the same. The size of the palette is called the *color depth*.

In Paint Shop Pro, you can change the color depth of an image by opening the image and choosing Colors, Decrease Color Depth from the menu. You're then presented with some choices in the Decrease Color Depth dialog box, shown in Figure 11.1.

FIGURE 11.1

The Decrease Color Depth dialog box.

In this dialog box, you likely want to choose the Standard/Web-safe palette in the first column of options, because the Web is the destination for this image. The Web-safe palette is recognized by Web browsers as the most accurate across different platforms.

Next, you choose a reduction method, which you can experiment with if desired. The Nearest Color method is the most self-explanatory—when it's tossing out a particular color that's not supported by the smaller palette, it chooses the color that's closest. The other two are different approaches that diffuse colors and *dither*, or vary a pattern of dots, to get slightly different resulting colors.

Tip

After a color change has been put into place, you can choose Edit, Undo Decrease Colors to undo that change, so you can return the image to its original palette and experiment with other changes.

In GraphicConverter, choose Picture, Colors. In the menu that appears, choose the Change to… option that you'd like to try—that selection is the number of colors used in the image. Note that you can also use the Picture, Colors, Minimize Color Table option to use the smallest palette of colors possible.

Remember, if you're dealing with color photographs, lowering the color palette often doesn't work, partly because JPG works only with millions of colors or 256 colors, and partly because photos just look bad when you take out color information. If you're creating images from scratch in GIF or PNG, however, lowering the color palette should be helpful. In fact, generally you can start with a lower color palette (say, 256 colors or the Web-safe 216-color palette) when you first create a new image document. In both Paint Shop Pro and GraphicConverter, you can choose a color depth in the New dialog box.

Resolution

Although you don't often change the color depth of scanned or digital camera images, you may often want to change their resolution. Many images that are captured via scanner or camera use more resolution information than is necessary for them to be displayed onscreen. In general, images for the Web only need to be 72 dots per inch (dpi, sometimes also pixels per inch, or ppi), instead of the 200 dpi or higher that is often used for scanned images destined for a printer.

To change the resolution in Paint Shop Pro, select Image, Resize. Turn on the Actual/Print Size radio button, and then change Resolution to 72 ppi. Click OK. Now you likely need to resize the image, because changing the resolution in Paint Shop Pro makes it larger. Choose Image, Resize again, and then turn on the Pixel Size radio button. Enter the pixel size you want for either the width or the height. If the

Maintain Aspect Ratio option is checked (as it should be), the other measurement changes automatically. Click OK, and your image is now the correct size and the correct resolution for the screen.

In GraphicConverter, select Picture, Resolution. In the Resolution dialog box, enter 72 in each of the fields, leave the Convert picture option checked, and then click OK. The image is converted to the new resolution.

Image Compression and Progressive Encoding

When you save your Web images, you still aren't finished making decisions, particularly if you're dealing with JPEG images and (to a lesser extent) PNG format documents. That's because you've got some additional choices to make in the Save dialog box of your image-editing application.

Compression

When saving JPEG images, usually you can choose a quality setting. The lower the quality, the more *compressed* the image file is, and the smaller its file is. It's a direct trade-off, but one you might consider if you find that, even after cropping, sizing, and changing the resolution of an image, you're still stuck with an image file that's too big.

In Paint Shop Pro, you can change the compression setting when saving a JPEG image. First, choose File, Save As. If the image isn't already in JPEG format, choose JPEG-JFIF Compliant from the Save As Type menu. Now click the Options button. In the Options dialog box, note the Compression Factor slider. The more you drag that slider to the right, the higher the compression and the lower the quality. Make your selection, click OK, and then save the file.

Paint Shop Pro has a neat feature, the Optimizer, which can help you make JPEGs that are small in file size but still good-looking. Click Run Optimizer in the Options dialog box and the Optimizer appears. (Note that it also has a wizard option, which can walk you through the optimization process.)

In GraphicConverter, you also set compression options when saving. Choose File, Save As, and make sure JPEG/JFIF is selected in the Format menu. Now click the Options button. In the JPEG/JFIF dialog box, use the Quality slider to choose the balance point between compression and quality. Note that with the Calculate File Size option turned on, you can see the approximate size of the file that you are saving (see Figure 11.2).

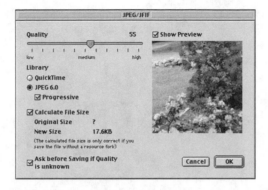

Saving Progressive Images

In the options for saving JPEG, GIF, or PNG images in an image editing program, generally you'll find a setting that enables you to make the image *progressive*, or *interlaced*. What this means is simple—the image can appear in a browser window as it downloads, instead of appearing only after the entire image has been received by the client computer. This makes your Web page appear in the browser a bit more quickly, while giving the user a sense of what the image will look like before it has completely appeared.

Both Paint Shop Pro and GraphicConverter make a progressive option available in the same option dialog box you access to set compression for a JPEG image. (GraphicConverter's is shown in Figure 11.2.) PNG and GIF images can also be progressive (with GIFs, the option is generally called interlaced), so look in the Options dialog box when saving them.

Image Transparency

Although image transparency doesn't really make an image download any faster or appear any more quickly in a Web browser window, it's still an interesting effect to play with. Transparency is supported in the GIF and PNG formats, enabling you to select *one* color within the image and make it transparent so that any background images or colors show through it.

This is most useful for creating images that appear to "float" on the page. Or, with the right shading and photographic qualities, a portion of the image might actually appear to be sitting on the Web browser's background, as shown in Figure 11.3.

The transparent color you choose needn't be the background color—you can make other parts of the image transparent, if you have a reason to. Only one color can be transparent, however, so you might need to plan ahead when creating the image. If your background is two-tone, you need to change that before you can make the whole thing transparent.

FIGURE 11.3

The image's background is transparent, so the rest of the image appears to be sitting on the page.

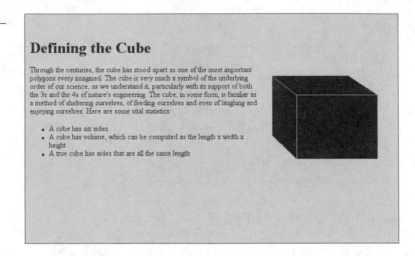

In Paint Shop Pro, you can make a color transparent by selecting Colors, Set Palette Transparency. You might then be told that the image needs to be converted before transparency can be added. This is particularly true if the image started as a high-color photograph. (See the "Color Depth" section earlier in this chapter for details.)

After you have the image in the correct format, you see the Set Palette Transparency dialog box (see Figure 11.4). You can choose no transparency, set it to the current background color (which you often do), or set it to a particular color. If you'd like to choose a particular color, you don't have to enter its number by hand (unless you happen to know the number). Instead, you can simply move the mouse pointer to the image and click the color you want to turn transparent—its number appears in the dialog box. When that's done, click the OK button.

FIGURE 11.4

In Paint Shop Pro, you can click the image to select the transparent color.

In Paint Shop Pro itself, the portion that is now transparent turns a pinkish color. That color will be transparent after the image is saved as a GIF or PNG and displayed in a Web browser.

In GraphicConverter, transparency is even a bit easier. With the image on the screen, simply click the transparency tool in the toolbar—it looks like a magic wand with the letter "T" as part of the icon. Now drag the pointer to the color in the image that you want to turn transparent and click the mouse button. Immediately, that color turns gray, indicating that it's transparent. You can click another color to change the selection, or you can save the image as a PNG or GIF and it's ready to be displayed.

Creating Animated Images

The GIF format (specifically, GIF89a) supports a certain level of animation, akin to a flipbook animation you might have sketched into the corner of your grade school textbooks. By creating a series of images that are quickly displayed one after another on the screen, you can use these image formats to create the appearance of animation. If you've spent some time browsing the Web, no doubt you've seen this animation, generally in the form of Web advertisements.

Creating your own animations requires nothing more than some dedication and an animation application. Although many animation applications are pricey options from big-name graphics companies such as Macromedia and Adobe, others are available as shareware. In fact, most distributions of Paint Shop Pro include Animation Shop, which is a good option for Microsoft Windows users. For Macintosh, you might consider GifBuilder (`http://homepage.mac.com/piguet/gif.html`), which is freeware, or VSE Animation Maker (`http://www.vse-online.com/`), which is shareware.

To create an animated GIF, generally you need to begin by either creating a series of GIF images (in Paint Shop Pro or GraphicConverter, for example) or creating image frames within the animation tool. Then those frames are put together in sequence and saved as an animated GIF. You can then add the GIF to your pages with a standard `<img />` element. The following is a quick look at the process in different applications.

Note   Animation can be time-consuming because you need to create a series of GIF images or frames, usually by painting them. You'll find that the more sophisticated applications enable you to set the duration or frames, and to automatically add transitions and effects that make fewer painted frames appear more "animated" and interesting. But such animation applications tend to be pricey.

Jasc Animation Shop

Animation Shop makes GIF animation fairly easy to accomplish. You begin by creating a new project (File, New), and then either drawing frames on the screen or importing them using the Animation, Insert Frames, From File option. Animation Shop can also be used (via the File, Open command) to open and work with animations in the popular FLI and FLC animation formats.

If you're creating a banner advertisement, try the Banner Wizard (File, Banner Wizard). It walks you through the process of creating a fairly simple banner advertisement, complete with transitions.

After you've created the project, you see each frame in the window. (You need to scroll to see more than the first few frames.) Using the tools in the toolbar, you can add text, draw, paint, and otherwise make changes to each frame. To add more frames, choose Animation, Insert Frames, Empty, and then use the dialog box to specify the number of frames that you'd like. Remember, each frame represents another progressive change in the animation, so you may need to create a few frames if your animation is complicated.

After you've created your frames, you can select a frame and then select Effects, Insert Image Transition to add a transition effect. Or choose Effect, Insert Image Effect if you'd simply like to add a special effect to that frame. You've got a few different effects to choose from.

To test your handiwork, choose View, Animation. Now you see the VCR-like controls spring to life, enabling you to play your animation to test it. If it's moving too quickly, you may need to change the duration of some or all the frames. You can do that by selecting Animation, Frame Properties and changing the settings in the dialog box. To determine whether or not the animation will *loop* and to choose a transparency color (if desired), choose Animation, Animation Properties.

Looping means the animation will play again once it's completed. In some cases, you can choose to have an animation loop one time, a fixed number of times, or continuously.

To save your animation, choose File, Save. With CompuServe Graphics Interchange selected in the Save As Type menu, you can name the image and click Save to save it as a GIF. Then you simply add it to your page as you would any GIF image.

VSE Animation Maker

Animation Maker isn't as full-featured as Animation Shop, but it's relatively inexpensive. With Animation Maker, you can create individual frames using paint and text tools, or you can import a series of images (PICT images are supported) using the Frame, Open PICT and Insert command.

Animation Maker doesn't have built-in transitions, but you can double-click a frame in the Frames window to change the percentage of time it spends on the screen, give it a name, and see its size. To control the overall speed of your animation, you choose Set, Speed, and then select how many frames per second (or seconds per frame) you want the animation to be. To test the animation, click the Play arrow in the main window or select Set, Play Animation.

If you'd like to create an animation that loops continuously, choose Set, Settings, and then, in the Loop section, decide if the animation should loop infinitely or just a set number of times. You can also specify a comment in this dialog box.

When you're done creating the animation, choose File, Save As, GIF. In the Save GIF file dialog box, you can turn checkboxes on and off to make selections about the comments and delay times. Then you can select a transparent color, if desired, and finally click Save to view a Save As dialog box so that you can name the file. When saved, you can add the GIF to your Web page using a standard `<img />` element.

Using Imagemaps

One other use for images on Web pages that hasn't been touched on yet is the *imagemap*. Put simply, an imagemap enables you to define different portions of an image as hyperlinks that point to different URLs. The sections of such an image are often called *hot zones*, and they're defined using the imagemap specifications.

You have two different imagemap approaches to consider: client-side and server-side. *Server-side* imagemaps are the older type. In essence, they rely on the server computer (specifically, a *map server*) to recognize and deal with the clicks that a user makes. Most graphical Web browsers now support the client-side approach, which simply means that the browser itself can recognize where the user clicks and launches the specified URL. This section focuses on client-side maps because they are the dominant type. Server-side maps are discussed briefly at the end of this chapter.

Creating a Client-Side Imagemap

To begin creating a client-side map you need an appropriate graphic. You can create one in an image-editing application, or you can use an existing photo or image and overlay it with hot zones.

These hot zones are defined by x,y coordinates, where 0,0 is the top-left corner of the image. Using these coordinates and telling the browser what shape the hotzone should be makes it fairly simple to create a clickable image. The only real catch is figuring out what the various coordinates should be. One way to do this is to use your image-editing application. You can find the x, y coordinates in both Paint Shop Pro (in the bottom-left corner of the image window) and GraphicConverter (in the top-right corner of the image window, using the Picture, Show Position command). You can point to various parts of your image to learn the coordinates, and then jot them down for use in the imagemap.

You can also work with a map-editing program, such as MapEdit (`http://www.boutell.com/mapedit/`), which is available for both Windows and Macintosh. Using MapEdit, you can create hot zones (the clickable shapes that work as hyperlinks) that you'd like to use for your map. In fact, MapEdit actually saves the client-side imagemap information to your HTML document, enabling you to skip some of the steps in the rest of this chapter. (You probably want to read them anyway, just to see what's going on.)

You may find that other map-editing applications create a *map definition file*. This is the file that's generally used for a server-side imagemap, but it contains the coordinate information that you can use for a client-side map.

Then, to add the client-side map to your page, you use a new attribute to the `<img />` element, called `usemap`, along with an entirely new element, the `<map>` container element. Inside the `<map>` element, you use `<area />` elements to specify the coordinates and URLs for each of the hot zones.

Adding `usemap` to `<img>`

To create a client-side imagemap, you need to add the new attribute `usemap`, as follows:

```
<img src="map_image.gif" usemap="#map_name" />
```

Notice that the point of `usemap` is to specify a named link for the map definition information that you'd like to use. Elsewhere in the document, you enter the map definition itself in a `<map name="map_name">` element that has the same name specified in the `usemap` attribute. An example of the `<img />` element might be

```
<img src="main_banner.gif" usemap="#banner_map" alt="Top banner for
➥navigation" />
```

This element goes in the HTML document at the point where the image for the imagemap will appear. This `<img />` element displays the image and tells the browser that this is a client-side imagemap. Before you have a complete imagemap, however, you need to create the definition that the browser uses for that map.

The `<map>` and `<area>` Elements

The `<map>` container is used to create each of the hot zones that are used as hyperlinks in your imagemap. Each zone is created using an `<area />` element, which defines the shape, coordinates, and URL associated with that hotzone:

```
<map name="map_name">
<area shape="shape_type" coords="coordinates" href="URL" alt="text" />
<area shape="shape_type" coords="coordinates" href="URL" alt="text" />
...
</map>
```

> The `<map>` element can be anywhere in the document. Often, it's easiest to put it at the top of the body section, so you can get to it quickly. It doesn't display anything in the browser window, so its placement won't affect other elements.

If your map-editing application created a map definition file, you'll find that most of the information required for your `<map>` definition is in that file. If not, the coordinates you approximated in your graphics editing application should suffice. Based on those numbers, you can come up with `<area>` elements that define each of the hot zones in your imagemap.

First, though, you need to know something about the shapes that are supported. The shapes for client-side hot zones differ a bit from those for server-side maps, which is important to know if you're using an imagemap editor to determine coordinates. Only three basic shapes are accepted by the `shape` attribute, and then the numbers are given to the `coords` attribute. The three basic shapes are as follows:

- `rect`—The rectangle requires the coordinates for the top-left corner and the bottom-right corner. For example, 0,0, 10,10 places the left and top lines of the rectangle at 0,0 and the right and bottom lines at 10,10.

- `circle`—A circular hot zone requires three different coordinates: center-x, center-y, and a radius. An example might be 100,100,20, which would represent a circle with a center at 100,100 on the page, and a radius of 20 pixels.

■ polygon—The third shape, a polygon, enables you to specify a shape with any number of sides. Each vertex requires a pair of points as its definition. The coordinates 100,100,200,200,0,200 would create a three-sided polygon (a tri-angle) with its top at 100,100, its bottom right at 200,200, and its bottom left at 200,0.

The href attribute is used to assign an URL to each hot zone. If no URL is desired, the attribute nohref="nohref" can be used to define a particular hot zone that doesn't reference a URL.

Tip

The simpler your imagemap is, the better. For the most part, today's imagemaps use rectangular hot zones because rectangles are easy to define, they're button-like, and there isn't much novelty left in the idea of complicated clickable images. You may find a good reason to use the other shapes, particularly when you're creating clickable photos or educational sites. For basic navigation, though, rectangles are easy.

For example, consider a bar that you might put at the top of your site as a graphical navigation option:

```
<body>
<img src="banner.gif" usemap="#banner_map" alt="navigation banner"
➥border="0" />


<h1>The Movie Site</h1>


<p>Welcome to the Movie Site, the number one place on the Internet for
information about movies, stars, directors and more.</p>


<map name="banner_map">
<area shape="rect" coords="45,45,115,70" href="films.html" alt="Film
➥Details" />
<area shape="rect" coords="150,45,220,70" href="actors.html" alt="Actor
➥Bios" />
<area shape="rect" coords="260, 45, 330, 70" href="directors.html"
➥alt="Director Filmographies" />
<area shape="rect" coords="370, 45, 440, 70" href="producers.html"
➥alt="Producer Info" />
<area shape="rect" coords="480, 45, 550, 70" href="reviews.html" alt="User
➥Reviews" />
<area shape="rect" coords="0, 0, 585, 75" href="help.html" alt="To Help"
➥/>
</map>
</body>
```

Figure 11.5 shows this image.

FIGURE 11.5
An imagemap that might be used for navigation.

Notice in the previous example that the last `area` element has coordinates that cover the entire image. According to the client-side specification, the area that's defined *first* takes precedence when two areas overlap. So, if someone clicks in one of the first four hot zones, they'll be taken to the appropriate URL. If they miss a hot zone, though, they'll be taken to a document called `help.html`, where you can tell them how to use the map correctly.

If you elect not to create your own default hot zone, client-side maps automatically ignore clicks that fall outside your other hot zones.

Working with Server-Side Maps

Most likely, you don't need to work with server-side imagemaps. For years now, the HMTL standard and Web browsers have supported client-side maps, which are more efficient and effective. At this point, they're really only useful when very old Web browsers are used to access the map.

If you do need to work with a server-side map, it certainly isn't difficult. All you have to do is add the `ismap="ismap"` attribute to your `<img />` element, and then wrap the `<img />` element in an anchor element that points to an imagemap definition file that's stored on the server. When the server detects that an imagemap definition file is being requested, it automatically launches the imagemap server, which then handles all the hot zone requests. For example:

```
<a href="/maps/topbanner.map">
<img src="topbanner.gif" ismap="ismap" alt="Banner image" />
</a>
```

You need to ask your ISP or administrator how and where to store imagemap definition files, as it can vary somewhat depending on the Web server application and platform. You need to create the map definition file by using a map editor application such as MapEdit, mentioned earlier. That map definition file is the one that you store on the server and access via the anchor element.

Summary

This chapter began by discussing some of the advanced techniques you can use to make the image files on your Web pages smaller, faster, and more efficient. You also saw how to create transparent colors within images, and how to animate GIF format images. Then you saw how to create imagemaps, which enable you to create clickable hot zones on your images, hyperlinking to different URLs.

In Chapter 12, "Creating Sites with HTML Frames," you'll see how to create a Web interface using the <frameset> element, which divides a single browser window so that multiple HTML documents can be displayed at once.

BUILDING YOUR SITE

CREATING SITES WITH HTML FRAMES

For a long time, Web authors wanted to display many similar documents via their Web sites, offering common controls (in the form of hyperlinks or imagemaps) that quickly allowed the viewer to move through the pages.

Using the standard approach of individual Web pages, you would be forced to replicate these links or controls on every page. With the advent of the HTML Frames specification, however, it was possible to split the browser window to allow more than one Web page to appear at a time. Suddenly, with the ability to split the window into frames, Web authors had a whole different option for designing their sites. This continues into the XHTML standard. Frames aren't always recommended, however, as you'll see in this chapter.

This chapter discusses the following:

- What frames are, and how to decide if you should use them
- Adding frames to your site, including the frameset elements and the target attribute
- Advanced frames issues, including special targets and inline frames

The Great Frames Debate

For a while, the problem with HTML frames was that many browsers couldn't view them. The frames specification was added after HTML 3.2 standard, which was created around 1997. (At that time, frames were already popular, but only with Netscape users.) Frames have been formalized in the HTML 4.0 standard, and most browsers have handled frames well. Interestingly, frames still remain just a bit controversial. Before we get to that, though, let's understand what frames are.

What Frames Are

The HTML frames specification enables you to display two or more pages in the same Web browser window at the same time. Those pages have separate URLs, separate scroll bars (if necessary), and otherwise act pretty much independently. Figure 12.1 shows a site that's using a frames interface.

FIGURE 12.1

A Web page that's using frames to make multiple documents easily accessible.

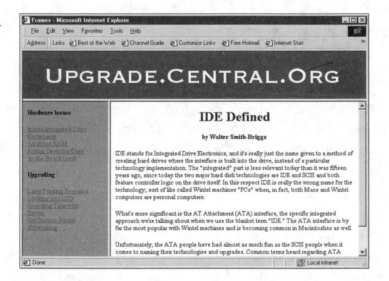

Splitting the page into frames is done by replacing the <body> element in your Web page with an element called <frameset>. The <frameset> container is designed to hold individual <frame /> elements, which then define the frames on the page and determine which URLs are loaded in the frames as default pages.

Once you've created those frames, the individual pages within the frames can include hyperlinks that specify which frame another URL should be loaded into. For instance, you could have a frame that you've determined is the "main viewer" frame where your documents will appear. (In Figure 12.1, this is the frame where the IDE Defined article appears.)

On the document used as an index, you can include hyperlinks that load different pages in that main viewer window, giving you an effect that's a little like a remote control changing channels on a television screen. In Figure 12.1, the document that contains the links All About RAM and Prying Open the Case is such an index. It's not the same HTML document as the article that appears in the main viewer. What's more, each of the hyperlinks in that index document uses a `target` attribute to specify that its URL will be loaded in the main viewer frame. So, clicking a link on the left side changes the article that appears on the right side.

Note also that the frames often have their own scroll bars and, in many cases, moveable dividers. While viewing a page that uses frames, you can often click and drag on the divider to change the size of the frame.

What's Wrong with Frames?

So far, frames sound cool, don't they? It seems odd that they'd be controversial, but there are some reasons why they are. First, using frames will sometimes make it more difficult for the viewer to discover the full URL to a particular page, because a frameset can be used to view many different pages at once. When you load a new document in one frame on the page (for instance, in that "main viewer" frame), the user may have trouble accessing that frame's page again directly via URL. (It's usually possible, but not as easy as using a bookmark or favorite.) Instead of showing that page's URL in its address bar, many Web browsers will display the URL to the frameset document itself. (In some browsers, this problem can extend to printing the individual frames.)

When you're Web surfing, you can usually get around this issue by right-clicking the frame in Windows, or Ctrl-clicking it in the Mac OS. You'll probably see an option such as Open Frame in New Window, which enables you to view the page, view its URL, and create a bookmark of that document.

The other issue is more basic—some people just don't like visiting sites that use frames. They'd prefer not to be forced to scroll around on different parts of their Web browser page, or be overwhelmed with different frames that act independently. Because framesets access a number of different URLs at once, they can be slower than typical Web pages. Your users with slow connections might find them annoying for that reason.

The solution, generally, is to use HTML frames only when you have a good reason, and not just because the technology is there. You can also take pains not to load another Web site's page into your frameset, which really tends to irritate people. You'll see how to avoid that in this chapter. Finally, when you do use frames, they should be as simple and cleanly designed as possible.

When Should You Use Frames?

So, you've seen the "don'ts"—what are the "dos"? While you're never *required* to use HTML frames, it's not a bad idea under a few particular circumstances:

- **Making documents available by index**—One common use for frames is to make many similar documents available using a convenient interface (as shown in Figure 12.1). Using frames in this way enables you to keep the index or table of contents readily available to the viewer, while the main frame is updated with different content.

- **Discussions or annotations**—Another reason to use frames is that it enables you to load two different pages at once on the same page. For instance, you could add annotations or explanations in one frame while the other frame holds a historical text or document that's being studied.

- **Fixed elements**—Let's say you'd like to place a banner image at the top of your Web page and have the content of the page (or the content of multiple pages) scroll beneath the banner image, instead of having the banner image move offscreen when you scroll the page. If you have two frames, one of them can hold that banner image (or anything else, such as hyperlinks or contact information) while the other frame holds a document that can scroll independently of that image. Figure 12.2 shows an example.

FIGURE 12.2

With the banner image fixed at the top of the page, it's possible to scroll another document beneath it.

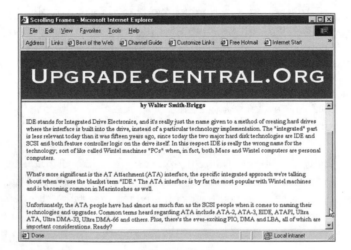

With HTML frames, you should always offer options to your visitors. In effect, you can do a few simple things that enable your visitors to "opt out" of the frames interface, if desired. You have a few different ways of doing this, which we'll explore later in this chapter.

Adding Frames to Your Site

As you've already seen, creating HTML frames means adding some elements to your repertoire, including the `<frameset>` and `<frames />` elements. Before you do that, however, you'll need to specify a new DTD and set up your Web document accordingly.

To work with framesets and be XHTML-compliant, you'll need to use the XHTML Frameset DTD, which enables you to create frames while using the transitional set of elements and attributes. The frameset DTD is added in the same way that the strict or transitional DTDs are added to your page, using a short entry at the top prior to the `<html>` open tag:

```
<!DOCTYPE html PUBLIC "-//W3C//DTD XHTML 1.0 Frameset/EN"
 "http://www.w3.org/TR/xhtml1/DTD/frameset.dtd">

<html xmlns="http://www.w3.org/1999/xhtml">
```

Creating the Frameset

Now you've defined this HTML document as a frameset document. The next step is to actually add the frameset by simply replacing the `<body>` element with the `<frameset>` element:

```
<!DOCTYPE html PUBLIC "-//W3C//DTD XHTML 1.0 Frameset/EN"
 "http://www.w3.org/TR/xhtml1/DTD/frameset.dtd">
<html xmlns="http://www.w3.org/1999/xhtml">
<head>
<title>Review.Central.Org</title>
</head>
<frameset>
</frameset>
</html>
```

The `<frameset>` element can accept two attributes: `cols` and `rows`. With an individual `<frameset>`, you can only define it as being broken into columns or rows. If you need both, you'll use multiple `<frameset>` elements, as you'll see in a moment. For now, though, notice what happens if you include a frameset definition that looks like this:

```
<frameset cols="25%, 75%">
</frameset>
```

The result is shown in Figure 12.3. (Note that if you try this example in a browser, it won't work until you've added some `<frame />` elements inside the `<frameset>` container. This is the basic structure, though.)

FIGURE 12.3

Here's an example of using a `<frameset>` element to create columns.

The `<frameset>` element will accept as many rows or columns as you want to create, and they don't need to be percentages, either. You can use specific pixels, such as `rows="10,200,30,300"`. This would create four rows. The top row will be 10 pixels high, beneath that will be a row that's 200 pixels high, and so on. Also, you can use an asterisk ("*") as a placeholder, which tells the `<frameset>` element to create a row or column that fills the rest of the space. For example, `cols="200, 400, *"` would create a third column that takes up any space that's left after the first 600 pixels. It works just as well with percentages, as in `rows="25%, 35%, *"`, with the added advantage of not forcing you to perform actual arithmetic.

`<frame>` and `<noframes>`

The `<frameset>` container doesn't do much for you on its own—you need to add additional elements before anything appears on the page. The `<frameset>` element supports two major elements: `<frame />` and `<noframes>`. The `<frame />` element is used to define frames within the document, while the `<noframes>` element is used to offer text and markup that can be seen by browsers that don't support frames. The first you might consider adding is the `<noframes>` element, such as

```
<frameset>
<noframes>
<p>This site requires HTML frames support. If your
browser doesn't support frames, you can access the
<a href="/articles/index.html">article index</a>
directly.</p>
</noframes>
</frameset>
```

Technically, the <noframes> container element could hold an entire page's worth of markup, if you thought that would be appropriate. In practice, however, you'll probably find it useful to create a special page that supports visitors who can't view frames. For instance, you could create an index that's loaded in the left column of your frameset, but that could also be used, in a browser window all by itself, as an index for accessing other pages. We'll discuss this idea more in the section "Offering Options to Users."

Meanwhile, the next step within that frameset container is to add <frame /> elements that define the rows or columns that you'd like to add to your page. For instance, if you've defined the frameset as having two columns, you'll add two <frame /> elements, one for each column's definition:

```
<frameset cols="25%, 75%">
<frame src="index.html" />
<frame src="viewer.html" />
<noframes>
<p>This site requires HTML frames support. If your
browser doesn't support frames, you can access the
<a href="/articles/index.html">article index</a>
directly.</p>
</noframes>
</frameset>
```

Generally speaking, the <frame /> element is used to define the original source HTML document that is to be displayed in that frame of the frameset via the src attribute. The src URL can be either a relative URL, as shown in the example, or an absolute URL, such as http://www.fakecorp.com/index.html.

Those source files should be full-fledged HTML or XHTML documents, complete with a DTD, <html> container, <head> and <body> containers, and so on, just like all the XHTML-compliant documents you've created thus far. For example, the page index.html might look like this:

```
<!DOCTYPE html PUBLIC "\//W3C//DTD XHTML 1.0 Strict//EN"
"DTD/xhtml1-strict.dtd">
<html xmlns="http://www.w3.org/1999/xhtml">
<head>
<title>Index Frame</title>
</head>
<body>
<h1>index.html</h1>
</body>
</html>
```

Granted, this is not a terribly useful index page, but it shows you how the frameset works, as shown in Figure 12.4.

Naming and Targeting Frames

So far this frames thing is interesting, but you might have noticed one problem—the frame definitions are static. In other words, how do you go about actively loading a new page in a particular frame? It's a two-step process. First you name the frames, and then you target those frames with your URL.

By using the name attribute, you assign the frame a name in a way that's similar to naming a section of a page for an internal link. (If you're working under the XHTML frameset DTD, you should also include the id attribute with an identical value as the name attribute for future compatibility. The name attribute was officially replaced by id, but most browsers still recognize name and will for a long time.)

Here's our example as it's progressing:

```
<frameset cols="25%, 75%">
<frame src="index.html" />
<frame src="viewer.html" name="doc_viewer" id="doc_viewer" />
<noframes>
<p>This site requires HTML frames support. If your
browser doesn't support frames, you can access the
<a href="/articles/index.html">article index</a>
directly.</p>
</noframes>
</frameset>
```

Note that I've named the second frame "doc_viewer" while leaving the first frame unnamed. In this scenario, that first frame doesn't need a name because it will always be the index page that's assigned by default. However, I'll be creating links on that index page that will target the "doc_viewer" frame.

Note

When you name frames, you're free to do just about anything except start the name with an underscore ("_"). That's because there are reserved targets that begin with underscores. (They're discussed in the "Special Targets and Removing Frames" section later in this chapter.) The most important thing is to make sure that each name is unique but efficient—don't make the name overly long.

Targeting is done with the `target` attribute to the `<a>` anchor element. On the index page (in this example), I create a hyperlink that looks something like this:

```
<a href="story1.html" target="doc_viewer">Read Story #1</a>
```

Now, when that link is clicked on the left side, the right side will display the URL referenced in the anchor. Figure 12.5 shows an example that includes a few additional targeted links. In each case, the href URL is different, but the target is always that named frame.

FIGURE 12.5

On the left side are targeted links. On the right side is the named "viewer" frame.

Tip

What should you use as the default source file for your viewer window? Figure 12.5 shows a default document that explains the interface. You might do something similar, or you can simply display the first article, image, or whatever it might be that you're using frames to display.

Note that the anchors can link to any URL that you'd like. For instance, you could create a link to a remote page:

```
<a href="http://www.w3.org/html/" target="doc_viewer">Learn more about
➥HTML</a>
```

That page will appear in the target frame. (This is what can annoy some people about frames—they allow you to place other site's documents within your frameset, and users can't always tell where a page is coming from.)

An anchor element that's in a named frame can target its own frame if desired, although it doesn't have to. If you're viewing a document in the "doc_viewer" frame, for instance, and you click an untargeted hyperlink on that document, the resulting page will load in the same frame.

Options for `<frame>`

While the `src` attribute is the only one that you really need to worry about when creating frames, you'll find that a few other optional attributes can be handy for customizing the look of your frameset. Those attributes include the following:

- `noresize="noresize"` can be used to make it impossible for your visitors to change the size of a frame by dragging its frame border.
- `frameborder` can accept either a 1 or a 0 (as in `frameborder="1"`). A 1 means that the frame has a border, while a 0 means it does not.
- `scrolling` can accept `yes`, `no`, or `auto` as values that enable you to decide whether or not a particular frame displays scroll bars. `yes` means always, `no` means never, and `auto` means scroll bars appear only when they're needed.
- `marginwidth` and `marginheight` attributes can be used to change the margins at the left and right (`marginwidth`) and top and bottom (`marginheight`) of the frame. Each accepts a value in pixels.
- `longdesc` takes an URL as its value. This enables you to include a link to an HTML document that describes the contents of the frame, which is ideal for assistive (Braille- or speech-enabled) browsers.

Once you've worked with the frames a bit, you'll start to see the value of some of these attributes for making your frameset pages look exactly as you'd like them to.

Nesting Framesets

One issue that's bound to come up is that you may want both rows and columns on your frameset document. For instance, you might want a row along the top of the document for a banner image that displays your site's name and/or logo, and then two columns below it that are used as index and viewer. You would do this by nesting the <frameset> elements.

You really want two things here. First, you want two rows—a row at the top of the page and a row at the bottom of the page. Then, in that second row, you want to split it into two columns. You can accomplish that second feat by placing a second frameset within the first frameset, like so:

```
<frameset rows="100, *">
   <frame src="banner.html" scrolling="no" noresize="noresize" />
   <frameset cols="25%, 75%">
   <frame src="index.html" noresize="noresize" />
   <frame src="viewer.html" marginwidth="5" marginheight="5"/>
   </frameset>

<noframes>
<p>This site requires HTML frames support. If your
browser doesn't support frames, you can access the
<a href="/articles/index.html">article index</a>
directly.</p>
</noframes>

</frameset>
```

In this example, the second <frameset> element is nested within the first. In fact, it replaces the second <frame /> element that would be required in that first frameset. That's because the nested <frameset> element *is* the second row of that first frameset, and it's defining that row as two columns. See Figure 12.6 for an example of how all this is coming together.

FIGURE 12.6

With nested <frameset> elements, you can define rows within columns and vice versa.

Advanced Frames

Beyond the basics of creating framesets and defining frames are some techniques that you can use to load items in different frames, or even in new windows. This section will also explore some tips and tricks for making frames a little less annoying, and for giving your visitors the option of opting out of frames. Finally, you'll take a look at the inline frame element that can be used in regular (non-frameset) HTML documents.

Special Targets and Removing Frames

I mentioned earlier that there are reserved target values that begin with an underscore. These values allow you to target particular frames or portions of the frameset without referring to them specifically by name. You can also use a special target to cause a Web document to appear in a new Web browser window, if desired. Here are those special targets:

- _self—Using this as the target value in an anchor element enables you to target the frame in which the current document appears.

- _parent—This value causes an anchor to attempt to target the frameset that's a parent of the current frame.

- _top—Using this value causes the anchor to attempt to target the current window, removing the frameset and loading the Web page referenced in href in the full browser window.

- _blank—This target is arguably the most fun; it allows you to open the referenced Web document in a new window.

These may seem a bit confusing. Consider the following listing, which shows a simplified version of the frameset we've been working with in previous examples and figures:

```
<frameset rows="100, *">
   <frame src="banner.html" />
   <frameset cols="25%, 75%">
   <frame src="index.html" />
   <frame src="viewer.html" name="doc_viewer" id="doc_viewer" />
   </frameset>
</frameset>
```

Now consider the following links, which could be a part of the index.html document that's loading in the second row, first column of that frameset. Here's what each of the various targets could do:

```
<!--Targets the third frame -->
<a href="newpage.html" target="doc_viewer">
<!-- Targets the frame where index.html was originally -->
<a href="newpage.html" target="_self">
<!-- Targets the first frameset, placing the page in the top row -->
<a href="newpage.html" target="_parent">
<!-- Targets the top of the page, removing the framesets -->
<a href="newpage.html" target="_top">
<!-- Opens newpage.html in a new browser window -->
<a href="newpage.html" target="_blank">
```

So, aside from all the cool possibilities for targeting frames, selves, and parents within a frameset document, we have two ways to remove the framesets altogether. `target="_top"` places the referenced page at the top of the current browser window, and `target="_blank"` creates a new page.

The `target` attribute and these special target values can be used with a few other elements as well. The `<base>` element discussed in Chapter 7, "Building Hypertext Links," can accept a target, as can the `<area>` element that's discussed in Chapter 11, "Advanced Web Images and Imagemaps." And you can use `target` with the `<form>` element, which is introduced in Chapter 15, "Adding HTML Forms."

Offering Options to Users

Working with what you now know about frames, you may begin to see some of the options for helping visitors to your site who don't want to use the frameset interface. If you manage things correctly, you may find that it's simple to create a site that uses both frames and non-frames interfaces.

The Index Page

In many cases, one of your frames will be used to hold a document that includes a series of hyperlinks—the remote control, if you will. That's true for document-centric frames, image-centric frames, and many others. If this is the case for your page, you may find it handy to make that page available to the user directly (see Figure 12.7).

If you have a link on that page or elsewhere in your frameset, you can allow users to load that index page in a full browser window. This gives them access to the documents or images listed on that page. It'll be a little less convenient for them (they'll have to use the Back button in their browser quite a bit), but *they're* the ones who don't like frames! Here's some sample code:

```
Click to <a href="index.html" target="_top">view this index</a> in the
➥full browser window.
```

Note

The link could also be to a different index, which might be more attractively designed or add other non-frames elements or styles. Still, you can see how easy it is to remove the frameset and load a different page in its place.

Self-Referential URLs

Another issue that tends to annoy detractors of frames are pages that are viewed in a frame without any reference to that page's URL. That makes it difficult to book-mark the page for later reference. It may also make that document difficult to print in some browsers.

The solution is simple. On all your pages that are destined for a frame, include their URLs as hyperlinks somewhere on the document. (The very bottom or top should suffice.) That way, the viewer knows the URL that references a particular page.

If you make a self-referential URL a hyperlink with a blank page as the target, you also make it easy for the user to print that page:

```
<p>Click to print or view
<a href="article2.html" target="_blank">
http://www.review.central.org/articles/article2.html</a>
in its own browser window.</p>
```

Outlinks

Finally, the last major issue with frames is "framing" someone else's content. Although you may find it handy to place a document from another Web site in a frame on your site, it can be considered rude at best (or a legal matter at worst). To avoid any potential problems, it's best to use a `target="_blank"` attribute for any link on your framed site that reaches out to another server computer. That way the page appears in a blank window, just as that other Web author intended it to look.

Note Some popular Web sites, such as About.com and Ask.com, make a habit of framing content from other sites. Both of them provide an obvious Turn Off This Top Frame or Remove Frame button, generally using a `target="_blank"` attribute. I don't know if that's enough to keep them from legal trouble or user outrage, but you can at least check out their implementations of frames if you're curious.

The `<iframe>` Element

Interestingly, this element is related to the `<frame />` element without being related to the `<frameset>` element at all. How is that? What `<iframe>` does is enable you to have an independent frame, called an *inline frame*, within a regular HTML document. The `<iframe>` container can appear inside the `<body>` element of a typical window, but it's used to display another Web page, just like a frame is within a frameset. Here's an example of how it works:

```
<iframe src="extra.html" width="300" height="300"
frameborder="1" scrolling="yes" align="right">
If you're seeing this text, then your browser
doesn't support inline frames. Click to read
<a href="extra.html">this frame's content</a>.
</iframe>
```

The `<iframe>` element supports most of the `<frame>` element's attributes, including `frameborder`, `marginwidth`, `marginheight`, and `scrolling`. It adds to those the `height` and `width` attributes that are used to set the inline frame's size in pixels. And `<iframe>` can accept an `align` attribute that can be used to make the `<iframe>` a floating element when set to `left` or `right`, just as with an `<img>` element's `align`. You'll also notice that it's a container element—the text that it contains is displayed when the browser doesn't support inline frames. Figure 12.8 shows the preceding example in a Web browser window.

The `<iframe>` element can only be used with the transitional DTD, incidentally, because it isn't supported under strict XHTML. (A similar effect can be achieved with the `<object>` element, which is supported in strict XHTML and is discussed in Chapter 13, "Adding Multimedia and Java Content.")

FIGURE 12.8

The `<iframe>` element can be used to add markup from a different Web document in a frame within your document.

Summary

In this chapter, you learned about HTML frames and how they can be used to divide a Web browser window so that multiple Web pages can be displayed on the screen at once. You also learned why some people dislike frames and that it's important to only use them when there's a strong advantage to them, and even then it's usually prudent to allow your visitors to opt out of the frames interface.

Once you've decided to work with frames, adding them is fairly easy. The `<frameset>` element is used, in place of the `<body>` element, to define the columns or rows that make up the frame-based page. You then add `<frame />` elements to define the default URL for the frame along with other attributes. One of those attributes is the `name` or `id`, which is used to identify the frame when it is to be used as a target for hyperlinks from elsewhere in the frameset.

Beyond that, you saw how to dig deeper into the `<frameset>` specification, including the nesting of framesets to create more complicated pages. You also learned how to use the special targets to launch Web pages in parent frames, without frames, and in a new browser window. Then you saw the different ways to let your visitors opt out of the frames interface. Finally, you learned about the `<iframe>` element, which can be used to create an inline frame, similar to an image, on an otherwise regular HTML document that's using the transitional DTD.

In the next chapter, you'll learn how to add multimedia content to your pages, including movies, animations, and Java applications.

ADDING MULTIMEDIA AND JAVA CONTENT

ver time, the Web has become increasingly used for communicating via video and audio, as well as formatted text and images. In this chapter, we'll take a look at popular video formats such as QuickTime and Windows Media along with portable documents, flash animations, and so on. Meanwhile, audio has moved along as well, with the advent of technologies such as the popular MP3 format, which makes CD-quality audio available over the Internet at reasonable download speeds.

We'll also take a look at Java, a popular programming language and technology that many Web browsers can implement right in the browser window, making it possible for you to interact with your users programmatically.

This chapter discusses the following:

- Understanding the different types of multimedia and why you might want to add them
- Using portable documents, Flash animations, Word documents, and other multimedia objects on your site
- Understanding Java and adding Java applets to your pages

Understanding Multimedia

What is multimedia? You've likely heard the term countless times, but it's still useful to define it. *Multimedia* generally refers to a computer-based presentation of data that makes use of more than one medium—text *and* sound, for instance, or video *and* sound. In common usage, however, *multimedia* really suggests a medium beyond basic text and images. In other words, a soundless video stream that you view via a Web browser is still a multimedia presentation, because it's something beyond the text and images that you typically see on a Web page.

Most of the multimedia items that you encounter on the Web are composed of time-based data—video, audio, or animation that you can start, stop, and play much like a video- or audiocassette. Some of those multimedia presentations will have interactive portions—buttons to click, for instance. But for the most part, the multimedia you encounter will be similar to other forms of media you find around the house—video, audio, and so on.

Consider, for example, a video using QuickTime or Windows Media formats. Such a movie file is really a series of images, shown in rapid succession, that give the appearance of motion, somewhat like the animated GIF image discussed in Chapter 11, "Advanced Web Images and Imagemaps." Computer movie technology is a little more sophisticated than that, and movie files generally also have synchronized audio tracks, but the basics are simple—images that change over time. The same is true of audio files—thousands of sound *samples* are played per second to reproduce, at various levels of quality, a recording that has been *digitized* (turned into computer data) and saved in the form of a computer file.

Three issues are important to you as a Web author:

- First, why would you want to include multimedia elements on your Web site (and if you want to do so, should you)?

- Second, you need to know the multimedia file formats you'll be working with and how likely it is that your visitors will be able to display those types of files. The type of multimedia technology you'll be using can dictate the percentage of your users who will be able to experience the multimedia.

- Third, and related to the second, is how you're going to add the multimedia element to your page. Will it be handled by the Web browser, or by a second application (called a *helper* application)? Or can the multimedia file be *embedded* in your page and played by a third-party *plug-in* to the Web browser? Let's look at these issues more closely.

Why Include Multimedia?

The first issue is whether or not you should include the multimedia content on your page at all. In general, the trade-off with multimedia is similar to the trade-off with images—you need to decide if the information conveyed is important enough to justify the amount of time your visitor will need to wait for the file to download and appear in the browser window. If there's a difference with multimedia files, it's that they can take tens or hundreds of times more storage space than a typical image file.

Video can require the largest files—even a one-minute movie trailer that takes up only a portion of your screen and plays for thirty seconds can require 10MB, 20MB or more of storage. Most Web users won't download such a movie over a modem-based connection. Audio files don't take as long to download, although a CD-quality song of three minutes can be up to 3.5MB in size. Animations destined for the Web tend to be a bit more optimal, but they can still be hundreds of kilobytes in size, often much larger than a typical Web image.

So, you have to decide if the multimedia item you'd like to add to your page communicates something vital. If so, you'll probably want to include it, and you may want to cause it to appear in your visitor's browser window by default. If the multimedia item isn't that important, you may want to give your visitor the choice of viewing it or skipping it. If it's only interesting because of the technology and not because of its content, you might decide not to include it at all.

Understanding Multimedia File Types

You've already seen some of the basic types of multimedia we're discussing in this chapter—video, audio, and animations. Some of the popular file types have also been mentioned—QuickTime and Windows Media for video (and/or audio, in some cases), WAV and MP3 for audio, and Macromedia Flash for interactive animations. Aside from these, there exist a number of other file formats that you may run across, as shown in Table 13.1. This table isn't exhaustive, but it does include the majority of the formats you'll encounter on the Web.

TABLE 13.1 Multimedia File Formats

File Format	Type of File	Extension
Sun Systems sound	Digital audio	.au
Windows sound	Digital audio	.wav
Audio Interchange	Digital audio	.aiff, .aifc
MPEG/MP3 audio	Digital audio	.mpg, .mp3
MIDI audio	Audio instructions	.mid, .midi

TABLE 13.1 (continued)

File Format	Type of File	Extension
RealMedia	Audio/video stream	`.ra, .rm, .ram`
CompuServe GIF	Graphics	`.gif`
JPEG (compressed)	Graphics	`.jpg, .jpeg`
TIFF	Graphics	`.tif, .tiff`
Windows bitmap	Graphics	`.bmp`
Macintosh picture	Graphics	`.pict`
Fractal animations	Animation	`.fli, .flc`
MPEG video	Video	`.mpg, .mpeg`
QuickTime	Video	`.mov, .qt`
Microsoft video	Video	`.avi`
Digital video (DV format)	video	`.dv`
Macromedia Shockwave Director	Multimedia presentation	`.dcr, .dir`
Macromedia Shockwave Flash	Multimedia animation	`.swf`
ASCII text	Plain text	`.txt, .text`
Postscript	Formatted text	`.ps`
Adobe Portable Document Format	Formatted text and images	`.pdf`
Microsoft Excel documents	Spreadsheet data	`.xl, .xls`
Microsoft Word documents	Formatted text	`.doc`

One thing you'll notice about the table is that it includes the filename extension that's related to the multimedia file type. That's because filename extensions are very important for the cross-platform world of the Web. While some operating systems deemphasize or hide these extensions, it's important to get to know them if you'll be adding such files to your Web site. The filename extension is the primary mechanism that most Web browsers use to determine what a multimedia file's format is and how the file is to be dealt with.

Table 13.1 also includes some file formats you might not expect, such as the Microsoft Word and Excel file formats. While they might not be multimedia formats (arguably), they are *rich media* formats that can sometimes be downloaded and viewed over the Web, particularly using viewer applications that Microsoft has written for that purpose. Also, the ubiquity of Microsoft's applications means that most visitors will have access to Word or an application that can translate a Word document. So, allowing a user to download a Word document is one option for making formatted documents available over the Internet, particularly if, for instance, you want the visitor to be able to edit and print the document.

Finally, it's worth noting that Table 13.1 doesn't show the depth of all the formats. For instance, both QuickTime and Windows Media can be *streaming* formats, like RealMedia. *Streaming* simply means the video and/or audio is played as it's received from a server computer, instead of waiting for the entire multimedia file to arrive at the user's computer before playback. Also, QuickTime and Windows Media can be used exclusively for audio, if desired, as can RealMedia formats.

So, how does a single Web browser handle all these file formats? In most cases, it doesn't, as you'll see in the next section.

Linking Versus Embedding

Most Web browsers can deal with a limited number of file types. In general, Web browsers can display HTML documents, plain text documents, and the popular image file formats. Many Web browsers also know how to access and display information from other Internet server computers, such as File Transfer Protocol (FTP) and Usenet news servers.

On top of that, some browsers can play basic sound file formats, such as the WAV audio format. But for the most part, multimedia capabilities aren't built into Web browsers. Instead, they're the responsibility of supporting applications, either in the form of *helper applications* or Web browser *plug-ins*. A *helper application* is an application that the Web browser launches automatically to deal with a particular type of multimedia. In these cases, you're said to be linking to the multimedia file—such a link is sometimes called a *hypermedia* link.

A *plug-in* actually works with the browser application to display the multimedia file within the Web browser window, making it appear to be a part of the Web page, much like an image. In those cases, the multimedia document is said to be *embedded* on the page. Plug-ins are small files of programming code that are stored in a special folder on your hard disk—usually it's a subfolder of the Web browser's folder. When you start up your Web browser, it looks in this special folder and notes which plug-ins are installed. Then, when the browser encounters the `<embed>` or `<object>` XHTML elements, it will attempt to use one of the plug-ins to display the multimedia file in the Web browser window.

Whether you choose hyperlinking or embedding depends first of all on whether or not a plug-in is available for a particular type of multimedia file. If the plug-in doesn't exist at all, it's a moot point and you'll want to link to the multimedia file. If a plug-in does exist, there are still some other issues to consider, including how pervasive the plug-in is, how likely your visitor is to have that plug-in, and how easily the plug-in can be obtained and installed if the visitor doesn't have it already.

For instance, QuickTime movies are often embedded in Web pages. Nearly all Macintosh users have some form of QuickTime system software installed, and the QuickTime plug-in is standard with most Macintosh Web browsers (see Figure 13.1). Likewise, millions of Windows users have QuickTime installed, and it's reasonably simple to install the Web plug-in component, which is updated regularly by Apple at http://www.apple.com/quicktime/.

FIGURE 13.1

Here's an example of a QuickTime movie being played within the browser window.

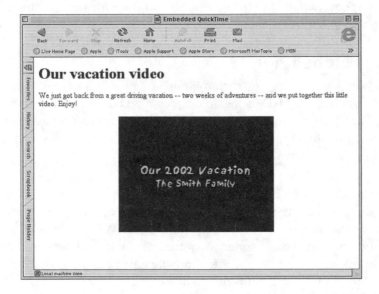

Windows Media files are also embedded in many Web pages, for the obvious reason that the majority of computer users are running Windows and can easily view a Windows Media movie or listen to Windows Media audio.

Another of the most common plug-ins is Macromedia Flash, which enables interactive animations that you'll see often on high-dollar sites designed to sell cars or introduce new movies and television shows. A high percentage of Web users have the Flash plug-in installed, so you can often embed a Flash animation in your page without much worry. Although Macromedia Director isn't as pervasive, you can also embed Director presentations in your Web pages, as well as RealMedia presentations. Both formats offer easy-to-download plug-ins for Web users who haven't already installed them.

Some other types of files and documents are more commonly linked to, however, causing a helper application to launch. For instance, PDF documents can be embedded (there's an Adobe Acrobat plug-in that's fairly common). But more often they're linked to so that the document can be more easily saved on the user's hard disk and printed, where appropriate. MP3 files can be linked to, particularly when you want the user to be able to download the file to his hard disk and use it again later. Other sound, video, and text documents are often made available via hyperlink.

Note   A PDF (portable document format) document is a type of application-independent document that includes font information and sometimes images embedded in the document itself. This makes it possible for the PDF document to look almost identical on different computers and computer platforms, even if those computers don't have the same fonts and internal graphics capabilities.

In the end, though, the decision is usually fairly simple. If you'd like your multimedia item to look like it's part of your Web page, and the element's file format is one that commonly offers a plug-in, you can consider embedding it in the page. If the multimedia item would look better or offer the user more benefits in its own window or running in its own helper application, your best plan is to create a link to it. You'll see how to do each in the following sections.

Adding Multimedia to Your Pages

In this section, let's take a general look at the two approaches to adding multimedia to your pages—the hyperlink and embedding. Then, we'll take a slightly closer look at some of the most popular technologies, including a discussion of streaming technologies.

Adding Hyperlinks

A hypermedia link really isn't much different from any other kind of link, except in one detail—instead of linking to another HTML document, you link to a multimedia file. The browser has to recognize the kind of file you've linked to and then load a helper application. The helper application takes over from the browser and displays the multimedia file.

Hypermedia links can look like any other hyperlink—they can be text, clickable graphics, or hot zones on imagemaps. All you have to do differently is enter an URL for a multimedia file in place of an URL to an HTML document. Hypermedia links are created like other links, too. Here's an example for a Windows sound file in MP3 format:

```
<a href="media/greeting.mp3">Greeting from Our Fearless Leader (1.2
➥MB)</a>
```

When your user clicks the link, the file is downloaded to the user's computer. After that, it's up to the browser and the user's available helper applications to actually play the file. If a helper application isn't available (or isn't configured), generally the user will have the option of downloading the file to disk and storing it for later viewing or listening.

Note

Two recommendations:

First, you should include the approximate size of the multimedia file in the highlighted text that describes that link. That way, a visitor can get an idea of how large the file is and how long it may take to download.

Second, it's important to have permission before you link to a multimedia file on another person's or organization's site. Multimedia files can slow down Web servers while adding greatly to the total *byte count* that's transmitted by a site. With some sites, exceeding a certain transfer limit can cost money because ISPs charge for certain thresholds. For that reason, and for legal and intellectual property reasons, you should only link to multimedia files you've stored on your own server, unless you have explicit permission.

So how does this work? Every Web browser keeps a table of hypermedia file types and the helper applications associated with each type. Whenever the browser is told to link to a file that isn't an HTML document—and it's a file that the browser doesn't otherwise know how to display—it will load a helper application to display the file.

There are a number of multimedia files that the typical browser can handle:

- Graphics such as .GIF, .JPEG, and .PNG, as discussed previously
- Sound files, especially .MIDI and .WAV for background sounds
- Plain text files with a .TXT extension

Files that don't fall into these categories generally require a helper application. Figure 13.2 shows the table that Internet Explorer for Macintosh uses to determine what helper application is invoked or what other behavior takes place when a particular file is encountered in a link. You can reach this dialog box by selecting Explorer, Preference, Helpers in Mac OS X. Nearly all other browsers have similar preference settings. In Windows, later versions of Internet Explorer use the File Types options that are built into the OS to recognize and manage helper documents.

FIGURE 13.2

Internet
Explorer's Helper
preferences
are used to
determine
how particular
multimedia file
formats are
handled.

When the user clicks a link, the file format is noted and the preference table is consulted. If that user has set a special preference for this type of file—that it should be launched in a particular helper application, or immediately downloaded to disk—generally the browser will move ahead with that instruction. If the browser encounters a file for which it has no preference setting, it will probably pop up a dialog box and ask the user what to do with the file.

Note

For the record, these preferences are often set automatically. For instance, when you install some graphics applications, they'll ask if you'd like to use it as the default application for this particular file type. In some cases, that will extend to having it set as a default helper application in your Web browser. Likewise, selecting an application the first time your visitor asks for help with a new document type may automatically set the selected application as the default for that file type.

So, with hyperlinks, you aren't even limited to particular types of files or formats. If you'd like to make a TIFF image or a Microsoft Word document or a ZIP archive available via your Web page, you can link to it. When the link is scrutinized by the user's browser, either the file will be handled automatically by the browser or the user will be asked what he or she wants to do with the file.

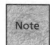

Note

Again, recall that the only way the browser knows what type of file it's dealing with is the filename extension. So, if you're making available a multimedia file of some sort, make sure it has a filename extension that's accurate for that file type.

Embedding Multimedia

The other approach to adding multimedia to your Web page is to embed it directly in the page itself. This is very similar to adding an image using the `<img />` element. In essence, embedding a multimedia file in a Web document simply defines a certain part of the Web browser window that is given over to the plug-in application, which is then responsible for displaying, playing, and otherwise controlling the multimedia element.

Note It's worth noting that, in general, embedding multimedia in a Web page can make the controls for the movie less accessible to special-needs users, particularly those that rely on keyboard controls instead of the mouse. If accessibility is a concern, you should consider always linking to multimedia files instead, because the standalone media players generally offer better accessibility. Likewise, embedded movies cause more problems with cross-browser compatibility than hyperlinks do. If you can sacrifice the coolness of embedding multimedia in the interest of better accessibility and features, consider a simple hyperlink to the media file.

How does one accomplish this embedding magic? Actually, this gets a little interesting. The problem is that the entire plug-in approach, which is very popular with Web authors, is not XHTML-compliant. Instead, it relies on a Netscape-created element that's still in fairly wide use. That element is the `<embed>` element, and using it means you need to specify a transitional DTD for your page.

In a way, `<embed>` is sort of an `<img />` element on steroids. When you add an item via the `<embed>` element, you do so by specifying the name of the item, its URL, and, if desired, its height and width. Here's an example:

```
<embed name="Movie1" src="movie1.mov" width="240" height="120"
➥    pluginspage="http://www.apple.com/quicktime/download/">
</embed>
```

Note that the element supports a name attribute (useful for accessing via JavaScript), as well as width and height attributes. In a way, it's very similar to an `<img />` element, with the exception of the required closing tag. That similarity can be a bit deceiving, however, because each individual browser plug-in can support additional non-XHTML attributes that will affect the playback of the multimedia (as discussed in the upcoming technology-specific sections).

Tip The `pluginspage` attribute is a handy one to include because it helps the user's browser locate the correct download page for a plug-in that isn't currently installed.

In the meantime, there is an XHTML-compliant element that can be used for adding some plug-in media—the `<object>` container. As you'll see later in this chapter, `<object>` is more often used for Java applets, as well as other embedding possibilities. For instance, you can embed another HTML document within the current document, producing something that's similar to an inline frame (`<iframe>` is discussed in Chapter 12, "Creating Sites with HTML Frames"). The `<object>` element can also get a bit complicated, but you'll see some examples in the following sections.

Note — Internet Explorer 5.5 and higher no longer support the `<embed>` element, instead opting to focus entirely on the `<object>` element (and, more to the point, on Microsoft's own ActiveX technology). To add embedded multimedia, you'll need to use the `<object>` element, as discussed in the next few sections.

You should consult any documentation you have for the multimedia technology you're using (QuickTime, RealMedia, and so on) to see the various ways that you can add the technology. For instance, some technologies offer both a Netscape-style plug-in and an ActiveX or Java control that makes it possible to add the multimedia item using `<embed>`, `<object>`, or both.

Embedding QuickTime

If you'd like to embed a QuickTime movie in your Web document so that it appears in the browser window, you can begin with the `<embed>` element:

```
<embed name="NewMovie" src="newmovie.mov" height="320"
➥width="240"></embed>
```

Beyond this example, however, Apple offers a slew of additional attributes that you can use to customize how the QuickTime movie and player will appear in the browser window. Some of those attributes, and their recommended values, are shown in Table 13.2.

TABLE 13.2   Commands for a QuickTime `<embed>` Element

Command	Value	What It Does
autoplay	true	Causes movie to begin automatically
controller	false	Hides movie controls
loop	true	Loops movie over and over
playeveryframe	true	Plays every frame, even if movie is too slow
volume	0 - 256	Chooses the volume level; 256 is highest
hidden	true	Movie is hidden (useful for sound-only movies)
href	URL	Allows user to click movie to move to another URL; works only if `controller=false`

These special attributes are added to the `<embed>` element only when it's being used for a QuickTime movie. Here's a simple example:

```
<embed src="movie1.mov" autoplay="true" height="320" width="240"></embed>
```

In this example, the movie would appear immediately in the Web browser window and begin playing as soon as the movie file was downloaded to the user's computer. The `<embed>` element is often used in a slightly different way with QuickTime movies, however, making the playing of the movie a two-step process. Here's the slightly more complicated example:

```
<embed src="post_movie.mov" autoplay="true"
    controller="false" href="full_movie.mov">
</embed>
```

The way this `<embed>` command is set up, the first movie loaded (`post_movie.mov`) should actually be a *poster movie*, or a movie file that only has one frame. Then, when the user clicks that poster frame, the actual movie (`full_movie.mov`) is launched, as specified in the `href` attribute. This is useful for enabling your users to verify their intent to view the movie (and therefore commit to a long download) by clicking the poster movie.

Because of the `controller="false"` attribute, the user won't be able to control the playback of the movie. Once downloaded, the QuickTime movie would begin playing all the way through without requiring any input from the user.

Tip

Aside from the attributes in Table 13.2, you can add quite a few other attributes and options to the `<embed>` element for QuickTime. See `http://www.apple.com/quicktime/authoring/embed.html` for details and instructions.

Apple notes that some browsers—notably Internet Explorer for Windows 5.5 and higher—don't support the `<embed>` element, but they do support ActiveX, a Microsoft technology for embedding programming functionality. For those browsers, you should include the `<object>` element along with the `<embed>` element, if appropriate. (Using JavaScript, discussed in Chapter 17, "Introduction to JavaScript," and Chapter 18, "JavaScript and User Input," you can determine the type of browser that you've encountered and then serve a compatible page, which might be a better solution.) Here's how Apple recommends that you add the `<object>` element:

```
<object classid="clsid:02BF25D5-8C17-4B23-BC80-D3488ABDDC6B"
    width="320"HEIGHT="240"
    codebase="http://www.apple.com/qtactivex/qtplugin.cab">
<param name="src" value="movie1.mov" />
<param name="autoplay" value="true" />
```

```
<param name="controller" VALUE="false" />
<embed src="movie1.mov" width="320" height="240"
➥    autoplay="true" controller="false"
➥    pluginspage="http://www.apple.com/quicktime/download/">
</embed>
</object>
```

This does a number of things. First, the `<object>` element will not only display the QuickTime movie in compatible browsers, but it will actually cause the ActiveX control to be downloaded to the browser automatically, if necessary. Then, with the `<embed>` element inside the `<object>` element, `<embed>` will be recognized by browsers that don't support ActiveX, while the QuickTime movie will play in those browsers that do require ActiveX.

For more on these instructions, see `http://www.apple.com/quicktime/products/tutorials/activex.html`.

Finally, it's important to note that QuickTime movies can be streaming media as well as the downloadable movie type. As mentioned earlier, *streaming* means that the movie data arrives just in time to be played back to the user. Streaming media feeds can be live events and broadcasts, or they can be regular QuickTime movies that begin playing in the Web browser more quickly than a downloaded movie.

If you're adding a streaming movie to your Web page, you'll need to make only minor tweaks to the HTML elements on your page. The real effort comes in acquiring the appropriate streaming server software, which is required to make QuickTime streaming work.

The major difference with QuickTime streaming is that you're sending a different type of URL to the end user, one that uses the realtime streaming protocol (rtsp://). You're also sending a different type of movie—if it's a downloadable movie, it needs to be saved as a Hinted QuickTime movie, which is something you can do in most QuickTime-compatible editing software. (In fact, you can do it with QuickTime Pro, which is an inexpensive upgrade to QuickTime.)

A *hinted* movie file is one that's saved in a special way so that streaming server software is more effective. The "hints" tell the server how the data should be put together for optimal playback.

So, for a downloadable movie file stored on a QuickTime Streaming Server computer, you'll first save the movie as a hinted movie, and then use the same `<embed>` and/or `<object>` elements to make it available. As you can see, there isn't much difference in the element, aside from the URL's protocol:

```
<embed src="rtsp://www.fakecorp.com/movies/hintedmovie.mov"
➥  width="240" height="180"
➥  pluginspage="http://www.apple.com/quicktime/download/">
```

Windows Media Movies

Windows Media offers embedding options in the form of both ActiveX controls and Netscape-style plug-ins, so you'll find that the basic elements for including a Windows media movie or a streaming media feed are about the same. In my experience, the Netscape-style plug-ins that Microsoft has created for Macintosh aren't all that effective. In many cases, your best plan for cross-platform support is to offer Windows Media movies and feeds as hyperlinks that appear in the Windows Media player.

But, if you'd like to embed a Windows Media feed in a browser window using the Netscape-style plug-in, you can use the familiar `<embed>` element:

```
<embed src="mymovie.avi" width="240" height="180" autoplay="-1">
</embed>
```

The `<embed>` element for Windows Media player embedding includes a number of parameters, discussed in Table 13.3.

TABLE 13.3   `<embed>` Parameters for Windows Media Movies

Parameter	Value	Meaning
showcontrols	0 or non-zero	0 means don't show controls; any other number means controls should be shown
autosize	0 or non-zero	0 means don't automatically size according to the movie's requirements
showstatusbar	0 or non-zero	0 means don't show the status bar
autostart	0 or non-zero	0 means don't automatically start the movie after download

As with other `<embed>` elements, you can use the `pluginspace` attribute to specify a location for the Windows Media plug-in, as well as `src` for the movie itself. Also, `type` is used with many `<embed>` element definitions to help specify which sort of media is to be expected, particularly since the Windows Media player can accept a number of different movie formats.

Note In programming circles, `true` and `false` are sometimes represented as *non-zero* and *zero*, where `0` means false and –1 is customarily (but not necessarily) the non-zero value meaning true.

For the ActiveX version of the Windows Media player, you can use the `<object>` element (wrapped around the `<embed>` element, if desired):

```
<object id="Player" type="application/x-oleobject"
    classid="CLSID:6BF52A52-394A-11d3-B153-00C04F79FAA6"
    standby="Loading Windows Media Player components..."
    width="320" height="240"
    codebase="http://activex.microsoft.com/activex/controls/
    mplayer/en/nsmp2inf.cab#Version=6,4,7,1112">
  <param name="autoStart" value="true">
  <param name="URL"
    value="http://www.fakecorp.com/movies/mymovie.avi">
  <embed src="mymovie.avi" width="320" height="240"
    showstatusbar="-1" showcontrols="-1" showdisplay="-1"
    pluginspage="http://www.microsoft.com/netshow/download/player.htm">
  </embed>
</object>
```

Within the `<object>` definition, you can see that the `codebase` attribute is used to automatically locate and install the ActiveX component if it isn't already available. The `<embed>` element appears within the `<object>` element—just as with QuickTime, you now have both the Netscape-compatible plug-in and ActiveX scenarios covered.

The last issue with Windows Media is the case of streaming media. Using the Windows Media Encoder (`http://www.microsoft.com/windows/windowsmedia/wm7/encoder.asp`), you can encode a movie so that it streams using a Windows Media-compatible streaming server. (If you don't have such a server available, you'll need to make your movies available as regular downloadable movies instead.) You then link to the encoded file, but with one other important step in between. You first need to create what's called a *metafile* that points to the encoded file.

Generally, you feed the `.avi` file to the Windows Media Encoder, which then transforms it into an encoded Windows Media file with the extension `.wmv`. You then save that file on the Windows Media Server computer, and you create a metafile by opening a text editor and creating a new document that includes only the components that this example does, including the special `mms://` URL protocol:

```
<ASX version = "3.0">
<Entry>
    <Ref href = "mms://www.myfakeserver.com/movie/encodedmov.wmv" />
</Entry>
</ASX>
```

Save that file with a `.wvx` filename extension, which identifies it as a streaming Windows Media video file. (If you're creating an audio-only stream, you can save the metafile with a `.wax` extension.)

With that metafile created, you can store it anywhere on your regular Web server (assuming the metafile has an absolute URL to the movie file) and then access it just as if it were an AVI file. The `href` or `src` attributes of the anchor (`<a>`) element, `<embed>` element, and `<object>` element can also be pointed at that metafile, which in turn will launch the streaming media movie you've created.

RealMedia Movies

Next up is RealMedia. As a format, RealMedia doesn't give you the option to distribute downloadable multimedia—instead, it's all about streaming audio and video. So, you'll need some tools handy for encoding QuickTime or AVI movies into RealMedia, and then you'll need a RealMedia server to use as your jumping-off point for the streamed multimedia. See `http://www.realnetworks.com/products/producer/index.html` for information on RealSystem Producer Basic (free) or RealSystem Producer Plus, which is Real's commercial encoding solution.

Note RealNetworks, Inc. appears to make its Basic versions much more difficult to find than their Pro versions. If you can't find Producer Basic at `http://www.realnetworks.com/products/producer/basic.html`, try to locate an "A-to-Z" product listing at `http://www.realnetworks.com/` and track down a free version that you can at least test before committing to the high-dollar solution.

Once the movie is encoded, you'll have a file with an `.rm` extension (in most cases), which can be stored either on a Real Media server of some kind or on a standard HTTP server. In the latter case, you simply copy the `.rm` file to your server and create a link to that file:

```
<a href="rams/realmovie.rm">Click to view the streaming file</a>
```

This approach offers limited functionality and requires a Web server that recognizes the `.rm` extension and file type, but it causes the RealMedia player to be launched for the user and the feed to be displayed.

For higher-end serving, you'll need a RealMedia server. If you've got one, you can then link or embed in a number of different ways—consult the Real Producer documentation for a good look at them. The most basic way is to use the `<embed>` element to access the `.rm` file that's stored on a Real Media server computer. Here's an example:

```
<embed src="http://realserver.fakecorp.com:8080/ramgen/realmovie.rm?embed"
    width="320" height="240" type="audio/x-pn-realaudio-plugin"
    controls="ControlPanel" console="one" autostart="true">
</embed>
```

You'll notice a few differences from other types of media, including the `?embed` portion of the URL that's required to tell the RealMedia plug-in to embed the playback instead of launching the RealPlayer helper application. The `controls` and `console` attributes are also specific to the RealPlayer plug-in, enabling you to specify the look of the controls and how they interact with any other controls you embed. This example should serve you well in most cases, however—consult the documentation for other options.

Flash Controls and Movies

Macromedia Flash multimedia presentations are still often called *movies*, but generally they're a bit different from a QuickTime or Windows Media movie. Instead of a linear stream of video and audio data, a Macromedia Flash movie is often an interactive animation. In other words, you'll find yourself pointing and clicking within the Flash movie to decide what you'd like to view next.

Creating Flash movies is the subject of plenty of books, so I won't cover that in this book. But once you have a Flash movie created, you'll likely want to embed it in your Web document, which you can do using one of the two elements we've grown familiar with: `<embed>` or `<object>`. If you're using Macromedia Flash software, you may be able to generate automatic templates that give you the required HTML code. For the record, though, here's an example of both elements, used to cover all the bases for embedding Flash:

```
<object classid="clsid:D27CDB6E-AE6D-11cf-96B8-444553540000"
➥   width="100" height="100"
codebase="http://active.macromedia.com/flash5/cabs/swflash.cab#version=5,0
➥,0,0">
➥<param name="movie" value="flashmovie.swf" />
<param name="play" value="true" />
<param name="loop" value="true" />
<param name="quality" value="high" />
   <embed src="flashmovie.swf" width="100" height="100"
➥   play="true" loop="false" quality="high"
➥   pluginspage="http://www.macromedia.com/
➥   shockwave/download/index.cgi?p1_prod_version=shockwaveflash">
   </embed>
</object>
```

If you've seen the elements used for QuickTime, you'll notice that Flash's use of these elements doesn't vary much. Flash does offer a litany of additional attributes that aren't covered here, but they're for specific preferences and controls. For details on the Flash-related attributes that work with `<embed>` and `<object>`, see `http://www.macromedia.com/support/flash/ts/documents/tag_attributes.htm`.

Flash movies can also be saved as QuickTime movies, which can retain some Flash interactivity. If you feel that you'll have better compatibility by saving a Flash movie in QuickTime format, you can consider that an option for embedding your movie.

Working with Java

If you've spent much time on the Internet, you've probably heard at least a little something about Java. In a nutshell, Java is a full-fledged computer programming language that's designed to work a lot like some other popular languages—notably a programming language called C++. Many popular Macintosh and Windows applications are written in C++.

The difference is that Java is designed to run on nearly any sort of computer that might be connected to the Internet. It's popular for programmers who want to write programs for use on the Web, because once the Java program is downloaded, it can be run by nearly anyone who visits the Web site.

Java Applets

For the most part, Java programs end up being very small when they're used on Web sites, for the same reason that Web authors try to keep everything else small—it takes time to download files from the Internet. These small programs are often called *applets* because, unlike full-sized computer applications, they generally perform a specific function. That's not to take away from Java, however, as some more complex applications are written and available in that language. Figure 13.3 shows one of the Java applications that Sun makes available for free at http://java.sun.com.

FIGURE 13.3

Java applications tend to be a little less full-featured than applications on your hard disk, but they can still be fairly sophisticated.

If you're not going to write Java applets yourself (or have someone else do it for you), you might want to check out what the Web has to offer in the way of freeware and shareware Java applets for your site. A good place to start is `http://www.yahoo.com/Computers_and_Internet/Programming_Languages/Java/Applets/` from Yahoo! or `http://java.sun.com/openstudio/` from Sun Microsystems, the developer of Java.

For the most part, Java applets are small games, Web communications enhancements, or ways to display data from internal databases on Web sites. It's also typical to see Java applets for presenting animated information screens, online classrooms, or even virtual meeting spaces. There are more sophisticated Java applications available online, including financial applications, business applications, and even productivity applications for word processing and similar tasks. While Java may never completely take over the Web, it's not a bad idea to understand how to work with and add Java applications to your site.

Add Applets Using `<object>`

As you've seen with other multimedia items, the `<object>` element is king in HTML 4.01, XHTML 1.0, and higher. While `<applet>` is an older element, it's still around for backward compatibility; it would require a transitional DTD. Instead, most modern browsers recognize `<object>` for Java applets, which is probably the best approach.

Here's a sample of the `<object>` element for Java:

```
<object codetype="application/java"
➥    classid="java:myapplet.class" standby="Applet Loading..."
➥    width=400 height=350>
</object>
```

In this example, the applet should be named `myapplet.class` and stored in the same directory as the document. You can also use a `codebase` attribute, if desired, to create a full URL to the applet, which would alter the element slightly:

```
<object codetype="application/java"
➥    codebase="http://www.fakecorp.com/applets/"
➥    classid="java:myapplet.class" standby="Applet Loading..."
➥    width=400 height=350>
</object>
```

That's all it takes. If the user's browser has Java enabled (not all of them will), the applet will be launched and displayed in the browser window, just as with other embedded content.

Summary

In this chapter, you learned what multimedia content is and how it relates to the Web page. You saw the different reasons for adding multimedia content to your pages, along with a few reasons to avoid it. From there, you learned how to include multimedia content by either linking to it or embedding it in the page. The chapter continued with a discussion of some specific multimedia formats—QuickTime, Windows Media, RealMedia, and Flash. Finally, it ended with a discussion of Java applets and how they, too, can be embedded in your Web pages.

In the next chapter, you'll learn a little about designing an entire Web site, including the creation of style sheets and site-wide styles that can be used to make the appearance of your Web site uniform.

SITE-WIDE STYLES: DESIGN, ACCESSIBILITY, AND INTERNATIONALIZATION

In this chapter, let's look a little deeper into that site-wide style sheet concept. You'll take a look at some additional style sheet properties to alter the table elements you may use when designing your pages.

This chapter shows the CSS specification and offers help on the evolving HTML and XHTML specifications with special support for browsers that respond to aural (sound) style sheet entries. If your goal is to create a complete, site-wide style sheet, you may want to include accessibility styles within that sheet for the sake of completeness.

Finally, we'll discuss some of the issues that involve internationalization and language properties on your pages.

This chapter discusses the following:

- Building and implementing a site-wide style sheet
- Working with accessibility styles to further the goals of your style sheet
- Special international considerations, including different languages and changing the direction of text

The Site-Wide Style Sheet

The idea of linking to a style sheet was touched on in Chapter 10, but not fully explored. If you're designing a large Web site, particularly if you're starting from the ground up and the appearance and professionalism of the site are important to you, I fully encourage you to begin with a site-wide style sheet. Not only will this keep the text of your pages cleaner, it will also make it possible to quickly change or update the styling of nearly every page on your site. In my own experience, I can tell you that it's a pain to update all your older pages when a site goes through a redesign. If you focus your design efforts on a site-wide style sheet, however, you'll find that making changes will be much easier in the future.

And if you already have a site you're working on, you can transform it fairly easily into a site that relies on style sheets for its design. This has the added advantage of cleaning up the actual markup of the page, particularly if that page is littered with `<font>` elements and other elements that have been used for visual design. By removing those elements, you can make your pages easier to edit, update, and interpret when you return to the page at a later date—or, when another person goes in to update or edit the page. With a site-wide style sheet in place, the markup can look simpler because styles are defined separately for the basic block and text elements.

Once you've gone through your site and determined the styles that you'd like to use, you'll create a single style sheet document. Then, that document will be linked to all of your documents, using the `<style>` element, so that each page uses the same style sheet for its visual presentation.

In this section, let's take a look at how a site-wide style sheet approach can change the look and feel of a basic Web site that we'll use as a case study.

The Basic Site

We'll begin with a look at a sample basic site before redesign. Actually, this site has already existed for quite some time. For this example, it's being redesigned and updated for a site-wide style sheet approach. Until now, it has used a hodgepodge of visual elements and attributes, which means that various pages look slightly different from one another (see Figure 14.1).

However, with a bit of a redesign and a style sheet, these pages can be made to look much the same with very little effort. What's more, the pages can also be designed so that a small change to the style sheet can make a big difference in how every page on the site looks—without even opening all those other pages. The changes are automatic because of the linked style sheet.

FIGURE 14.1

These two pages from the same Web site have subtly different styles for headlines and text.

Here's a sample portion of HTML code from one of the pages on the site:

```
<head>
<title>No Styles Example</title>
</head>

<body>
<hr width="50%">

<h2><font face="arial, helvetica">From the Editor...</font></h2>

<h4><font face="times, times new roman" size="+1">Good-bye Sick
Leave</font></h4>

<blockquote>
<p><font face="times, times new roman"><b>Hello all,</b></font></p>
<p><font face="times, times new roman">How goes it in the writing world?
Things are good on this end -- especially now that I've survived my bout
with the flu currently sweeping the nation. Ouch.</font></p>
<p><font face="times, times new roman">I'm not usually one to belly ache
to strangers about being sick, but allow me some leniency this month.
Besides, my illness offers some valuable lessons for all you would-be
free-lance writers.</font></p>

<p><a href="letter.html">Editor Letter continued...</a></p>
```

```
</blockquote>

<hr width="50%">
</body>
```

As you can see, the page's markup is pretty messy, but it looks okay in a browser window, as shown in Figure 14.2. (And, in fact, I even cheated a little and put the HTML elements in lowercase—they were uppercase on the original. That was a different era of HTML...). The first thing this page can use is some cleaning up. With a style sheet, however, we should be able to change the preceding to something much simpler. First, let's consider the style sheet.

FIGURE 14.2

Here's how this small snippet looks in a Web browser.

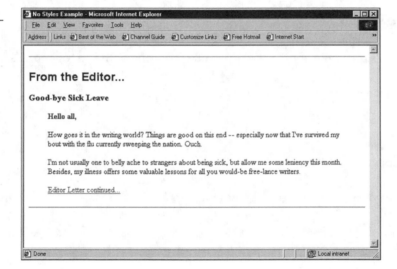

Planning the Styles

Building a site-wide style sheet will definitely take some planning, because you'll need to consider all the different elements you'll use on the page and how they should be styled. You'll also need to consider how many different styles you'll have for the same element. For instance, you might find yourself with four or five different styles that can be used with the <p> element. As you might guess, you'll probably be adding styles to your style sheet for a while as you're designing your Web site. While it's important to keep the style sheet as simple as you can, it's better to have a slightly complicated style sheet if the result is less complicated pages.

For now, let's look at that last example and see what we can come up with for style sheet entries. Here are some highlights of the process:

- If it's the "look" for the site, we can set all `<hr />` elements to 50% width with `hr {width: 50%}` instead of `<hr width="50%">`.

- Let's make all headings Arial, Helvetica, and Sans-Serif, as in `h1, h2, h3, h4, h5, h6 {font-family: Arial, Helvetica, Sans-Serif}`.

- In the original, `<h2>` was used for the first heading. This isn't recommended, but it was done so that the font was a little smaller. Instead, we can define a smaller `<h1>` if that makes sense for the whole site, as in `h1 {font-size: 18pt}`.

- The original is using `<h4>` immediately after an `<h2>`. This isn't recommended and was only done for visual reasons, because the `<h4>` is supposed to represent a subhead. Instead, we'll define a particular type of paragraph for subheads, as in `p.subhead {font-family: Times, Times New Roman, Serif; font-size: 16pt; color: blue}`.

- We'll define a special indented paragraph style so that we don't have to use the `<blockquote>` container inappropriately, as in: `p.indent {font-family: Times, Times New Roman, Serif; font-size: 12pt; margin-left: 50px; margin-right: 50px}`.

Okay, all that effort lands us a style sheet that looks something like this:

```
hr { width: 50% }
h1, h2, h3, h4, h5, h6 { font-family: Arial, Helvetica, Sans-Serif }
h1 {font-size: 24pt }
p.subhead { font-family: Times, Times New Roman, Serif;
font-size: 14pt; font-weight: bold }
p.indent { font-family: Times, Times New Roman, Serif;
font-size: 12pt; margin-left: 50px; margin-right: 50px }
```

We can even go further with this and make the style sheet a bit more efficient. Let's work from the assumption that all `<p>` containers will be Times, Times New Roman, and 12 point. We can define that, and then use the style sheet's assumption of *inheritance* so that we only need to change the properties that need changing for additional style sheet definitions.

Note

Inheritance simply means that once you've defined styles for an element, any classes subsequently defined for that element will also include the new styles. If you define paragraph text as 24 points tall and define a class of paragraph text that is red, the red text will also be 24 points tall. The only exception would be if you specifically overrode the paragraph size in the red text class definition.

Then, the style sheet would look more like this:

```
hr { width: 50% }
h1, h2, h3, h4, h5, h6 { font-family: Arial, Helvetica, Sans-Serif }
h1 {font-size: 24pt }
p { font-family: Times, Times New Roman, Serif; font-size: 12pt }
p.subhead { font-size: 14pt; font-weight: bold }
p.indent { margin-left: 50px; margin-right: 50px }
```

Notice how this makes the styles a little easier to read. The main <p> element is defined, and then the subsequent class definitions need only define the difference from the main <p> definition.

Save this style sheet as default.css, or something similar, and store it in your main Web site directory. Now the following listing should yield results that are nearly identical to Figure 14.2:

```
<head>
<title>Style Sheet Example</title>
<link rel="stylesheet" href="default.css" />
</head>

<body>
<hr>

<h1> From the Editor...</h1>

<p class="subhead">Good-bye Sick Leave</p>

<p class="indent"><b>Hello all,</p>
<p class="indent">How goes it in the writing world?
Things are good on this end -- especially now that I've
survived my bout with the flu currently sweeping the
nation. Ouch.</p>
<p class="indent">I'm not usually one to belly ache to
strangers about being sick, but allow me some leniency
this month. Besides, my illness offers some valuable
lessons for all you would-be free-lance writers.</p>

<p class="indent"><a href="letter.html">Editor Letter
continued...</a></p>

<hr>
</body>
```

How does that look? As you can see, the markup is already quite a bit cleaner, it isn't using elements that aren't recommended (such as `<h4>` and `<blockquote>` in the wrong places), and if the page is viewed by a non-graphical browser, it won't choke on all the extra visual elements. It took a little work up front, but this will make the page markup a little more readable, and the page (and the rest of the site) will be easier to revise in the future. Plus, as you can see in Figure 14.3, it's a dead-ringer for Figure 14.2.

FIGURE 14.3

Here's the style sheet version of the page in the browser window.

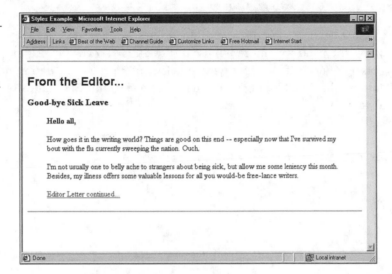

Style Sheet Power

So, you've seen some of the advantages of using style sheets. But their real strength is that you can now use this style sheet for all pages in the Web site. Once you've defined the main elements and some additional classes in the style sheet, you can generate very clean, XHTML-compliant documents that will be styled according to your defaults. Of course, you can also define more than one style sheet for your Web site and switch between them using different `<link />` elements, if desired.

And then there's my favorite advantage to style sheets—experimentation. Once you have a basic style sheet defined, you can continue to refine it as desired, experimenting to see what the overall changes would look like on your page and your site. With a few simple tweaks and additions, for instance, consider what this style sheet will do to the newly defined sample Web site:

```
a:hover { color: yellow; background-color: blue }
.indent { margin-left: 100px; margin-right: 100px;
```

```
padding-left: 10px; padding-right: 10px;
background-color: ffccff }
hr { width: 50% }
h1, h2, h3, h4, h5, h6 {font-family: Arial, Helvetica, Sans-Serif;
font-variant: small-caps}
p {font-family: Times, Times New Roman, Serif; font-size: 12pt}
p.subhead {font-family: Courier, Courier New, Monaco;

font-size: 16pt; color: blue}
```

With these changes, again saved to the same style sheet document `test.css`, I can clean up the page even more. I'll use a `<div class="indent">` (since the `indent` class has been defined without specifying an element) to cover the entire indented section of paragraphs. And I'll play with the look and feel a bit (see Figure 14.4). Here's the final version:

```
<head>
<title>Style Sheet Example</title>
<link rel="stylesheet" href="test.css" />
</head>

<body>
<hr>

<h2>From the Editor...</h2>

<div class="indent">
<p class="subhead"> Good-bye Sick Leave</p>
<p><b>Hello all,</b></p>
<p>How goes it in the writing world?
Things are good on this end -- especially now that I've
survived my bout with the flu currently sweeping the
nation. Ouch.</p>
<p>I'm not usually one to belly ache to strangers
about being sick, but allow me some leniency this month.
Besides, my illness offers some valuable lessons for
all you would-be free-lance writers.</p>
<p><a href="letter.html">Editor Letter continued...</a></p>
</div>

<hr>
</body>
```

FIGURE 14.4

Here's the page after a little experimenting.

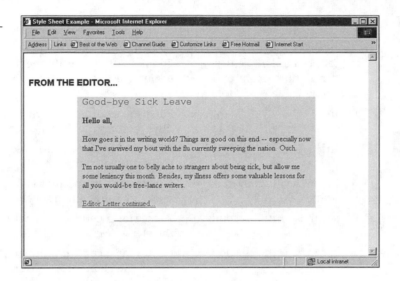

Of course, experimentation can get you in about as much trouble as it saves you. (I call this "Murphy's Law of Vertical Hold. The more you mess with something, like the knobs on a TV, the worse it looks.") But being able to change massive styling elements without digging into your page each time acts as a remote control over the design of your pages, which can be very powerful.

Accessibility Through Style Sheets

If your Web site is aimed at a sight-challenged audience, or if you'd simply like the most complete and accessible page possible, you should dig into the aural styles that the CSS2 specification makes available to you. These styles should be particularly easy to add to a site-wide style sheet that you've used to define the styling for the bulk of your elements. If you've already gone that far, adding these extras can be incredibly simple and helpful to your audience.

Note   As was mentioned in Chapter 10, CSS2 is as different from CSS1 as it is an add-on to it. Aside from aural elements, CSS2 adds styles for tables and the CSS positioning capabilities discussed in Chapter 19, "Adding Dynamic HTML."

CSS2 offers a number of styles that are specifically designed to control the output to aural browsers that speak text aloud. Table 14.1 shows many of these properties.

TABLE 14.1 CSS2 Aural Properties

Property	Values	Description
azimuth	left, center-left, center, center-right, right or an angle value (–360 to 360)	Enables you to specify the angle from which a sound seems to be coming
cue-after	url	Plays the sound file at the specified URL after reading the attached content
cue-before	url	Plays the specified sound file before reading the specified content
elevation	below, level, above, angle value (–90 to 90)	Enables you to specify the angle of a sound, above or below the listener
pause-after	seconds or milliseconds	Pauses for a certain number of seconds after the element is spoken
pause-before	seconds or milliseconds	Pauses for a certain number of seconds before the element is spoken
pause	seconds or milliseconds	Pauses before and after the element is spoken
pitch	low, medium, high, number (Hertz)	Chooses the pitch, or frequency, of the spoken text
pitch-range	0, 50 or any number	The inflection of the spoken text; 0 is monotone, 50 is normal
play-during	url	Plays a sound file while the text of the element is being read
speak	none, normal, spell-out	Sets how the element's text is spoken
speak-numeral	digits, continuous	Sets whether numbers are read as digits ("1-2-3-4") or words ("one thousand," "two hundred and thirty four")
speak-punctuation	none, code	If it's code, punctuation, then it is read aloud, as in "period" and "exclamation point"
speech-rate	slow, medium, fast, number	Sets how quickly text is read; if it's a number, the number represents words per minute
voice-family	male, female, child, Zervox, Princess	Specifies the name of the voice to be used for speech (similar to font families, the voice must be installed on the user's computer)
volume	silent, soft, medium, loud	Sets the volume of the spoken text

You use these properties within a style definition the same way you'd use any other properties. For instance:

```
h1 { volume: loud; voice-family: male; pause: 1; speak-numeral: digits }
p { volume: medium; voice-family: female; speak-punctuation: none }
```

Most of these properties should make sense. The `voice-family` property works much like the `font-family` property, specifying voices that are installed on the user's system. The generic values—`male`, `female`, and `child`—should map to certain specific voice files on the user's computer.

The `azimuth`, `elevation`, and `pitch` properties are a bit more esoteric, but essentially they're used to fine-tune the playback of the spoken text. It's possible to have headings, paragraphs, and other elements coming at different stereo "angles" from one another, making them easier to distinguish (or at least more entertaining).

Note Of course, you'd need an aural Web browser to test all these tags, and currently no mainstream browser supports them. It's still a young standard, though, so hopefully support is forthcoming. You can test your page for accessibility issues, however, using Bobby WorldWide at `http://www.cast.org/bobby/`.

International Issues

Another step you may want to take as you're developing a plan for your overall Web site is specifying languages for your pages. XHTML supports this with a special `lang` attribute, the `<q>` element, and some special instructions for table and text blocks.

`lang` and `<q>`

The `lang` attribute can work with a number of different elements to specify the language of those elements. It accepts a two-letter code to specify the language, as in

```
<p lang="es">Eso es en Espanol.</p>
```

The `lang` attribute can help the browser make decisions about how the element is rendered, including how to hyphenate words, how speech synthesizers should treat the text, and how search engines should recognize the page. By default, you specify a language as part of the XML definition of the page (as discussed in Chapter 4, "Creating Your First Page"), so generally the `lang` attribute is used to change languages mid-page.

Some of the possible language codes include ar for Arabic, de for German, es for Spanish, fr for French, he for Hebrew, hi for Hindi, it for Italian, ja for Japanese, nl for Dutch, pt for Portuguese, ru for Russian, sa for Sanskrit, ur for Urdu, and zh for Chinese.

The `lang` attribute can also be used with the `<q>` element to define quotation marks according to the attributed language. For example:

```
<p><q lang="en">I can't believe he said that,</q> Phillip said.</p>
<p><q lang="es">Si, es verdad,</q> Marcia replied.</p>
```

Table and Block Directions

Finally, it's interesting to note that you can specify the direction of text, using the `dir` attribute to most container tags. The result specifies the direction in which text flows, as in

```
<p dir="rtl">This text goes from right to left, instead of from left to
➥right.</p>
```

The `dir` attribute can be assigned to `<tr>` or `<td>` elements to change the direction of text within them. While you could change the language for any block of text, this is most useful for languages that are read from right to left, such as Hebrew.

Again, this relies on implementation of the `dir` attribute by the browser, which isn't terribly reliable even in the latest browser versions.

Summary

This chapter gave you a closer look at creating a style sheet that can be implemented site-wide, and explained the advantages of doing so. Using a site-wide style sheet gives you a consistent-looking site, while making your XHTML code cleaner and enabling you to experiment freely with the look of the page. You also saw how this approach to style sheets can be incorporated with CSS2's aural styles to make your Web pages more accessible. And, at the end of the chapter, you saw some of the elements and attributes that enable you to specify the languages used on your pages.

In the next chapter, you'll learn about the elements used to create interactive forms on your page, including entry fields, pop-up menus, and other elements you can use to enable your users to make choices and communicate with you.

PART IV

INTERACTING WITH YOUR USERS

ADDING HTML FORMS

HTML allows you to add interface elements to your pages, such as menus, radio buttons, and text areas, that make it possible for your visitors to send you information or data. The data can be as simple as an e-mail address sent to you for inclusion in your Web guest book. Or, the interaction can be as complex as enabling the user to make choices for an online computer application, such as those that locate doctors at HMO Web sites or that help you rent a car at a nationwide auto rental Web site.

In this chapter, let's take a look at how you can create HTML forms and make them look good. In Chapter 16, "CGIs and Data Gathering," you'll see how to create the back-end scripts that are used to process these forms.

This chapter discusses the following:

- The basics of HTML forms
- Adding form fields, buttons, and controls
- Using other elements to organize your forms
- Designing forms with lists, tables, and CSS

The Basics of HTML Forms

The idea behind an HTML form and its components is simple—they enable you to ask for and accept information or answers from your users with varying levels of guidance. Users can be asked to

- Type answers, either in small boxes (such as for name or address) or in full sentences (such as for comments or complaints)

- Choose answers from a list of possibilities you create, including via a menu or check box

- Choose one answer from a number of options that you specify, using the radio buttons interface that you'll commonly find in Windows and Macintosh dialog boxes

The form is created using a series of XHTML elements that define the entry boxes, checkboxes, and other controls. Each of the form elements that you create will have a name, and that name will be used to create a variable where the user's response is stored. For instance, if you assigned the name city to an entry box and the user typed Boston, then Boston will be stored as the value for the variable city.

Those variables and their associated values are then passed on to the Web server computer, which in turn passes it along to a small computer program, called a *script*. The script is designed to interpret the data, act on the data, and (in most cases) respond with XHTML markup and text that are used to create an automatic Web page in response to the data. This page might contain the results of the data-crunching, or a simple "thank you" response.

To deal with forms data, then, you need to understand a little something about creating these scripts (which are Common Gateway Interface scripts and can be written in many different programming languages). While you probably won't learn enough from this book to produce incredibly complicated scripts, we will discuss creating them in Chapter 16. You can also use HTML form elements with JavaScript in various ways, as is discussed in Chapter 17, "Introduction to JavaScript," and Chapter 18, "JavaScript and User Input."

In the meantime, Figure 15.1 shows a basic form you might decide to create for your Web site. As you can see, the HTML form can appear on a page with other markup, and textual (and other) cues can appear within the form area itself. In some ways, HTML forms are very similar to HTML tables, in that they require a chunk of the page but not the whole thing. As you'll see, you can even use tables to help lay out your form, if desired.

FIGURE 15.1

This form might
be used to
accept survey
results.

The `<form>` Element

In an HTML document, forms are created using the `<form>` element, which acts as a
container. The form container works as follows:

```
<form method="get_or_post" ACTION="URL to data destination">
...form elements and markup...
</form>
```

The most basic `<form>` element has two attributes: `method` and `action`. The `method`
attribute is used to determine how that form's data will be sent to the server. The
attribute's possible values are `post` or `get`. The `get` method causes the data from the
form to be appended to the URL for the data's destination. In most cases, it's very
limited in length, often less than 100 characters. For a single form element or two,
such as a quick search box or a single check box answer, `get` works fine. For
example:

```
<form method="get" action="/cgi-bin/search">
```

If you plan to create a long form with multiple entry boxes and menus, you'll probably opt to use the `post` method. It sends the data separately, without any practical
limit on the amount of data that can be transferred. You use a form opening tag
that looks like this:

```
<form method="post" action="/cgi-bin/survey.pl ">
```

The second attribute is `action`, which simply accepts as its value the URL for the script that will process your form's data. Most often, the script is stored in a directory called `bin/` or `cgi-bin/` located on your Web server. (Chapter 16 discusses the particulars of CGI scripts in much more detail.)

An example of the `<form>` element, then, would be the following:

```
<form method="post" action="http://www.fakecom.net/cgi-bin/survey.pl">
</form>
```

As with any HTML container element, this example of the `<form>` element has actually created a complete form (just like the `<p>` and `</p>` tags create a complete paragraph). Of course, this one doesn't do much, but it is complete. It's also worth noting that the `<form>` element can't be nested within other `<form>` elements—you need to start and end one form container before beginning another.

Other `<form>` Attributes

Aside from the two basic attributes, the `<form>` element can accept a few others. While none of these attributes are required, you may find them useful under certain circumstances. (In fact, while you're creating your first few forms, you may want to move directly to the section "Creating the Form." These attributes are a bit dense.)

The first of these is `enctype`, which accepts a MIME type entry that specifies the type of content that will be submitted. This is really only worth worrying about if you will be asking the visitor to upload a file to your server (using a special `input` element, discussed later in this chapter.) If that's the case, you should specify `enctype="multipart/form-data"`, which makes it possible to send a file (such as an image file) via an HTML form.

The `name` and `id` attributes can be used to identify the form for either scripting or for style sheets. Remember that `id` is the XHTML-compliant attribute, although `name` is sometimes still recommended for backward-compatibility. You can have both, as in `name="myform" id="myform"`.

The `<form>` element can accept a few other odd-duck attributes. The `accept` attribute can be used to specify, in a comma-separated list, the types of files that the server can handle correctly, using MIME names such as `image/jpg` and `video/quicktime`. You can view a list of MIME types at `http://www.isi.edu/in-notes/iana/assignments/media-types/media-types`. In isolated cases where you're asking the visitor to upload a file, the browser can check the `accept` attribute to make sure that the visitor is uploading a file type that's on the specified list. If the user is trying to upload a file of a type that isn't in the `accept` attribute, the browser can opt to deny the upload and display an error message.

The accept-charset attribute is similar. What it does is allow you to specify the character encodings that the server is prepared to accept when processing the form's data. For instance, if you wanted to be able to process characters that are specific to Spanish, you might need to include accept-charset="es" as part of your <form> element. Character set values can be found at http://www.iana.org/assignments/character-sets on the Web.

> By default, most Web browsers assume that the character encoding type that the page uses is the same one that any forms would accept. So if the page is set to Spanish already, the browser will most likely assume that Spanish-language characters are acceptable.

Creating the Form

Now that you've seen how to begin and end a <form> element, you're probably just about ready to start adding some substance to it. You can add all sorts of elements to your forms, including areas for entering text, menus for selections, check boxes, and radio buttons for options. You'll also need to add at least a few buttons, including the special buttons that enable your visitors to submit the form's data to your Web server computer.

Text Fields and Attributes

One of the more common uses for forms is to accept multiple lines of text from a user, perhaps for feedback, bug reports, or other uses. To do this, use the <textarea> element within your form. You can set this element to control the number of rows and columns it displays, although it will accept as many characters as the user desires to enter. It takes the following form:

```
<textarea name="name" rows="number" cols="number">
default text
</textarea>
```

The <textarea> element is a container element. What's contained between the tags is the *default text*, which is text that you can use to tell your users what you'd like them to type in. For instance:

```
<form method="post" action="/cgi-bin/form1.pl">
<textarea name="comments" rows="4" cols="40">
Enter your comments about our Web site.
Include your e-mail address if you'd like a response.
</textarea>
</form>
```

The default text appears in the text box just as typed. In Figure 15.2, notice that text inside the `<textarea>` element is formatted as if it were inside a `<pre>` container. Any returns or spaces you add to the text are displayed in the browser window.

FIGURE 15.2

The `<textarea>` element in action.

The `name` attribute is used to assign a unique identifier to the text area. When the data is passed on to the processing script, the name is used as a label for the data associated with that text area. You'll need to include instructions in the processing script itself for processing this data, but at least you'll have a name to go by.

The `rows` and `cols` attributes can accept different numbers to change the size of the `<textarea>` box, but you should make sure that the majority of browsers can see the entire box onscreen. Handheld browsers and some text-based browsers only display 40 or 60 characters in width.

Among some of the other attributes that `<textarea>` can accept is `readonly` (which should be added as `readonly="readonly"` for XHTML compliance). This attribute prevents the text area from being edited and makes it so the text between the two `<textarea>` tags is sent as the data associated with the text area.

The `<input>` Element

The `<textarea>` form element is a fairly basic data entry tool, allowing your users to type whatever text they feel is appropriate, within a certain number of characters. Often, however, you'll find it useful to limit the responses that your users can give. The `<input>` element lets you be a bit pickier about the type of input you're going to accept from the user. It enables you to create a number of different types of controls, including

- **Text boxes**—(`type="text"`) Users can type shorter entries, such as name and address information.

- **Passwords**—(type="password") In these special text boxes, what is typed by the user isn't shown onscreen.

- **Check boxes**—(type="checkbox") With these controls, you let the user select or deselect a particular item.

- **Radio buttons**—(type="radio") With these controls, the user can select one, and only one, of a series of options.

- **Hidden fields**—(type="hidden") This special type of input element is simply a field that can be sent with the form using a prespecified value.

- **Control buttons**—(type="reset" or type="submit" or type="button") Finally, the <input> element enables you to create a number of different types of buttons that are used for submitting the form, resetting the form, and other tasks you designate.

The <input> element follows this format:

```
<input type="type_of_input control" name="name" size="number"
�maxlength="number" />
```

The only required attributes are type and name. Some other types of the <input> element will also accept the attribute value, which is used to set the value or values that the individual can select. The <input> element can also accept a variety of other attributes, but they come up when you're creating different types of controls, so we'll cover them in turn.

Text Boxes

The first possible value for the type attribute is text, which creates a single-line text box of a length you choose. Notice that the length of the box and the maximum length entered by the user can be set separately. It's possible to have a box that's longer (or, more often, shorter) than the maximum number of characters you allow to be entered. Here's an example of a text box:

```
Last name: <input type="text" name="last_name" size="40" maxlength="40" />
```

When entered in a proper <form> container, this <input> element yields a box similar to the one shown in Figure 15.3. If desired, the attribute value can be used to give the text box a default value, as in the following example:

```
City: <input type="text" name="city" size="50" maxlength="50" value="New
⬍York" />
```

Password Entry Boxes

Setting `type="password"` is nearly identical to setting `type="text"`, except that using the password entry box usually causes the Web browser to respond to typed letters by displaying bullet points, asterisks, or similar characters to keep the words from being read over the user's shoulder. Here's an example:

```
Enter User Name: <input type="text" name="username" size="25"
➥maxlength="25" />
Enter Password: <input type="password" name="password1" size="10"
➥maxlength="10" />
```

When characters are typed in to this text box, they are displayed on the screen as shown in Figure 15.4.

It's important to note, however, that the only *security* that is really provided is the bullets or asterisks. The password itself is passed on by the browser in *clear text*—it is not encrypted or masked in any particular way.

For better security, you should use a secure HTTP (shttp) connection that encrypts transmissions so that they can't be intercepted. Secure servers are discussed briefly in Chapter 22, "Web Publishing Services."

Check Boxes

Setting `type="checkbox"` in the `<input>` element enables you to offer a check box "on/off" or *Boolean* control for your forms. This is best used when there are two possible values for a given choice—and no other values. You can also decide ahead of time whether or not a check box will be checked already (so that it must be unchecked by the user if desired) by using the attribute `checked="checked"`. Here's an example of adding check boxes to a form:

```
Where you heard about us:<br />
<input type="checkbox" name="web" checked="checked" />Web Search or Link
<input type="checkbox" name="advert" />Radio or TV Ad
<input type="checkbox" name="press" />Article or press mention
<br />
Check here to join our mailing list: <input type="checkbox" name="mailing"
➥/>
```

In this example, each of the values is *standalone* in the sense that more than one of these boxes can be checked at once. In the case of the first three, all three options could be selected. That may or may not be the desired result. The fourth check box is also evaluated separately from the first three, so it doesn't really matter that it appears on its own line and has a different label.

FIGURE 15.5
Each check box is evaluated separately; note the prechecked option below the other three.

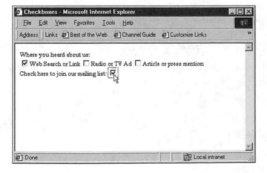

Radio Buttons

Like `checkbox`, `radio` is designed to offer your user a choice from predetermined options. The difference is that `radio` also forces the user to select only one response from among options. Whereas `checkbox` is Boolean or true/false, `radio` is multiple choice.

While `radio` is similar to `checkbox`, you'll notice one major difference—it uses the same `name` attribute value for each of the elements in the same grouping. In other words, among the multiple options from which the user will select only one value, all of them must have the same `name` value so that the browser knows that they're grouped.

The `radio` input type also requires you to use the `value` attribute, and each `value` attribute must have a unique value that can be assigned (to the variable created by `name`) if selected. For instance, look at the following example:

```
Where you heard about us:<br />
<input type="radio" name="where" value="web" checked="checked">Web Search
➥or Link
<input type="radio" name="where" value="advert">Radio or TV Ad
<input type="radio" name="where" value="press">Article or press mention
<input type="radio" name="where" value="other">Other
```

This example is shown in Figure 15.6. With `radio`, it's important to assign a default value because the user may simply skip the entry altogether. While the user can't check more than one, he or she might not check any of them. So, choose the value that you think makes sense as the default and set it as `checked="checked"`, just so the form-processing script doesn't have trouble.

FIGURE 15.6

Radio buttons limit the user to one choice among many.

Hidden Fields

This `input` type really isn't "input" at all. Rather, it's designed to allow you, the form designer, to pass along a preset value to the Web server or the script that will be processing the form. This is generally done when you're using the same script for a number of different forms or pages and you'd like the script to know which form is accessing it. The `<input type="hidden" />` element can accept the attributes `name` and `value`, as in

```
<input type="hidden" name="identify" value="form2" />
```

> *Hidden* in this context doesn't really mean *covert*, because an intrepid user could simply use the `View Source` command in most any Web browser (usually under the Edit menu) to see the value of the hidden field. It's more useful from a programmer's standpoint.

The Reset Button

Aside from entry boxes, checkboxes, and hidden fields, you can also use `<input>` to create buttons. Using the `reset` type of the `<input>` element, you can automatically add a button to your form that clears all other elements of entered data when clicked. When the user clicks this reset button, it resets all the entries and selections that the user has made to that point. For example:

```
<input type="reset" value="Reset the Form" />
```

The `value` attribute isn't required, but it's used to give the button a unique name. If you don't include it, the button will simply say Reset.

The Submit Button

The `<input>` element also has a type that creates a button to enable the user to submit the data that's been entered into the HTML form. This is how the user signals that he or she is done with data entry and ready to send it to the server. The `submit` type accepts only the attribute `value`, which can be used to rename the button. Otherwise, the only purpose of the Submit button is to send off all the other form information that's been entered by your user. See the following two examples:

```
<input type="submit" />
<input type="submit" value="Send it in!" />
```

You can use just about anything you want for the `value`, although it's best to remember that really small words such as "OK" don't look great as buttons. To make a button larger, you can create a `value` with spaces on either end, like in the following:

```
<input type="submit" value="   Submit   " />
```

The form already knows how and where to submit the data, thanks to the form's own `method` and `action` attributes. So, the Submit button itself is rather simple.

The Image Submit Button

If you'd like to use an image for your Submit button, you can use `type="image"` with the `<input>` element. The element also needs an URL to the image file and alternate text for non-graphical browsers, so it ends up looking like this:

```
<input type="image" src="images/buttons/submit.gif" alt="Submit Form" />
```

That's easy enough. But you should know that there are other ways to add custom buttons that are more highly recommended, so I'll focus on those.

Other Buttons

HTML 4.01 and higher offers another element for creating form buttons, the `<button>` element. It offers three `type` values: `reset`, `submit`, and `image`. What's different about the `<button>` element is that it's actually a container, and it enables you to use markup within the button itself. For example:

```
<button name="submit" type="submit">
<span style="font-family: Courier; font-variant: small-caps; font-size:
➥14pt">Send</span></button>


<button name="reset" type="reset">
<img src="reset.gif" alt="Reset" />
</button>
```

The `<button>` element can accept `name`, `type`, and `value` attributes, although `type` is the only one required for Reset and Submit buttons. However, for the best coding, you should at least include a `name` attribute. Figure 15.7 shows these enhanced buttons.

Tip

Transparent GIFs or PNGs make the best buttons when you're using the `<button>` element.

FIGURE 15.7

These customized buttons use the `<button>` element and include markup and style information.

Creating Menus

Another type of input control that you can offer to users revolves around the `<select>` element, which can be used to create different types of pop-up menus and scrolling menus. This is another control designed specifically for allowing users to make a choice—they can't enter their own text. The `<select>` element requires a `name` attribute and allows you to decide how many options to display at once with the `size` attribute.

Also notice that `<select>` is a container. Options (using the `<option>` element) are placed between `<select>` and `</select>`, each with a particular value. When one of those options is chosen, its value gets assigned to the name that's specified in the opening `<select>` tag.

The attribute `selected="selected"` sets the default value in a given list. An example of all this might be

```
Select how often you visit this site:
<select name="frequency">
<option selected="selected" value="first">First Time</option>
<option value="monthly">Monthly</option>
<option value="weekly">Weekly</option>
<option value="daily">Daily</option>
</select>
```

You can also use the `size` attribute to display the menu in its entirety. Simply change the first line of the example to the following:

```
<select name="frequency" size="4">
```

Both examples are shown in Figure 15.8.

FIGURE 15.8

A pop-up select menu and a scrolling list, thanks to the size attribute.

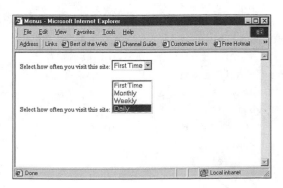

In the first example, selecting the menu item with the mouse causes the menu to pop up on the page. The user can then select from the choices. In the second example, it's necessary to click the desired item.

But what if you want to allow users to select more than one option at a time? Another attribute for the `<select>` element allows the user to select more than one option from the menu. Using the `multiple="multiple"` attribute forces the menu to be displayed as a scrolling list, regardless of the existence of a `size` attribute. (You should still use `size` to specify the number of items that appear at once in the list.) An example might be the following:

```
<p>What topics do you enjoy reading about online (pick all that
➥apply):</p>
<select name="topics" multiple="multiple">
<option value="upgrade">Upgrading computers</option>
<option value="repair">Repairing computers</option>
<option value="apps">Application How-Tos</option>
<option value="tricks">Tips and Tricks</option>
<option value="news">Industry news</option>
<option value="rumor">New Product rumors</option>
<option value="none" selected="selected">None</option>
</select>
```

In this case, the user can select multiple options, or none.

Note

Different browsers can auto-select options in different ways—some will submit `<select>` results that have no value, while others will select the first value in the menu as the default. So, it's best to create your own default using `selected="selected"`, particularly if you want to avoid inaccuracies when your scripts are processing form data.

Before we get away from `<select>` controls, there's one other element that you can toss into the mix: `<optgroup>`. This element enables you to group disparate options within the same `<select>` control. Consider this example:

```
<p>Where did you hear about us (pick all that apply):</p>
<select name="refer" multiple="multiple">
<option value="npr">Public Radio</option>
<option value="netrad">Network Radio News</option>
<option value="satrad">Satellite Radio</option>
<option value="travel">Travel TV</option>
<option value="food">The Food Channel</option>
<option value="pbs">Public Broadcasting</option>
<option value="times">The Times</option>
<option value="news">The News-Hearld</option>
<option value="none" selected="selected">None</option>
</select>
```

There's nothing particularly wrong with this list, except that we might be mixing apples and oranges a bit. As it gets longer and longer, it becomes more unwieldy. The solution is to use `<optgroup>`, which accepts a `label` attribute that can be used to label groups within the list:

```
<p>Where did you hear about us (pick all that apply):</p>
<select name="refer" size="15" multiple="multiple">
<option value="none" selected="selected">None</option>
<optgroup label="Radio">
<option value="npr">Public Radio</option>
<option value="netrad">Network Radio News</option>
<option value="satrad">Satellite Radio</option>
</optgroup>
<optgroup label="TV">
<option value="travel">Travel TV</option>
<option value="food">The Food Channel</option>
<option value="pbs">Public Broadcasting</option>
</optgroup>
<optgroup label="Newspapers">
<option value="times">The Times</option>
<option value="news">The News-Hearld</option>
</optgroup>
</select>
```

If your user's Web browser is compatible, it should display the list in a slightly different layout, which should make it easier to make selections (see Figure 15.9). Note that not every browser recognizes `<optgroup>`. When it doesn't, you're not any worse off than with a full list.

FIGURE 15.9

Here's a list organized by `<optgroup>` elements.

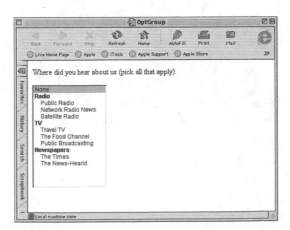

Sample Feedback Form

At this point, let's take the bulk of what's been discussed and toss it all together into a sample form. We'll be putting together a feedback survey form, using the elements that have been discussed so far:

```
<form method="post" action="mailto:surveys@fakecorp.com">
First name: <input type="text" name="first_name" size="40" maxlength="40"
➥/><br />
E-mail address: <input type="text" name="e-mail" size="40" maxlength="40"
➥/><br />
Where you heard about us:<br />
<input type="radio" name="where" value="web" checked="checked">Web Search
➥or Link</input><br />
<input type="radio" name="where" value="advert">Radio or TV Ad</input>
➥<br/>
<input type="radio" name="where" value="press">Article or press
➥mention</input><br />
<input type="radio" name="where" value="other">Other</input><br />
<p>Enter your comments about our Web site.<br />
<textarea name="comments" rows="10" cols="40">
Include comments or questions in this area.
</textarea>
</p>
Check here to join our mailing list: <input type="checkbox" name="mailing"
➥/><br />
<button name="submit" type="submit">
<span style="font-family: Courier; font-variant: small-caps; font-size:
➥14pt">Submit Survey</span>
</button>
<button name="reset" type="reset">
<span style="font-family: Courier; font-variant: small-caps; font-size:
➥14pt">Clear Page</span>
</button>
</form>
```

You can see how this looks in Figure 15.10. Overall, the form still doesn't look all that great as far as alignment and design. We'll cover those topics in the rest of this chapter.

FIGURE 15.10

Here's the sample form, functional if not pretty.

Tip

A lot of users like to move through HTML forms using the Tab key. If you'd like to specify which direction a press of the Tab key will take a person, you can add the `tabindex` attribute to any form element, using any number between 0 and 32767 as a value. (For the item that should be first, set `tabindex="1"`, for the second item, set `tabindex="2"`, and so on.) Once you've added those numbers, elements will be reached in the order specified by the `tabindex` attribute when the Tab key is pressed.

You may also have noticed that the `<form>` element itself uses an interesting `action` attribute—it includes a mailto: style URL. This makes it possible for the form's data to be mailed to a given e-mail address instead of being processed by a script. You may find this useful if you want to go through the forms by hand, or if you have an e-mail-based processing solution. (See Chapter 16 for more discussion of e-mail processing.)

Designing Forms Well

You've seen how to create forms, but we haven't covered how to make those forms attractive. It takes a little thought and quite a bit of XHTML markup to make the form elements look good, logical, and interesting to your users—interesting enough that they dive in and use the form. In this section, let's take a look at some approaches to designing useful forms.

Form Design Issues

Central to the idea of form design is making the form easy for users to understand so that they follow through and fill it out. The less incentive you give them to fill out the form, the less likely they are to try. A short, clean form is more likely to entice users than a long, confusing one.

Here are some guidelines you should consider when building your forms so that they're easier to use and more effective:

- **Use other XHTML elements to make things clear**—You can use `<br />`, `<hr />`, and paragraph tags to set apart different chunks of your form, while emphasis (`<em>`, `<strong>`) can be used to make labels and other parts of the form easier to read.

- **Keep your forms short**—This isn't always possible, but even when your forms are long, it's important to at least use `<hr />` and similar elements to break them up a bit. Splitting up forms into smaller sections makes them easier on the eye.

- **Use intuitive design**—Common sense is sometimes the key to a good form. For instance, putting the Submit button in the middle of the form will keep people from filling out the rest of it. Often it's best to use `<select>`, radio buttons, and check boxes to keep your users from guessing at the type of data you want them to enter.

- **Warn users of unsecured transactions**—You should tell your users if your Web server is secure—and how they can make sure that the connection is current. If you ask for credit card numbers or similar personal information over an unsecured connection, let them know that, too.

Finally, you can use style sheets just as effectively with forms as with other elements. In some cases, you might find them even more useful, particularly for breaking up parts of the form into chunks. And, as you'll see in this section, HTML offers some accessibility elements to help make forms easier for assistive browsers.

Line Breaks, Paragraphs, and Horizontal Lines

Unlike text-oriented XHTML, your best friend in form design is not really the paragraph element as much as it is the `<br />` element. This is because you want to directly affect the layout of the forms, instead of leaving it up to the browser. Therefore, you've got to be a little more proactive. You'll end up with a lot of line break elements before your form is through.

Consider the following example:

```
<form>
Enter your name and phone number:
First Name: <input type="text" name="first" size="30">
Last Name: <input type="text" name="last" size="40">
Phone: <input type="text" name="phone" size="12">
</form>
```

To get each of those text boxes on a separate line, and thus make them more pleasing to the eye, you need to add a few instances of <br />:

```
<form>
Enter your name and phone number:<br />
First Name: <input type="text" name="first" size="30"><br />
Last Name: <input type="text" name="last" size="40"><br />
Phone: <input type="text" name="phone" size="12"><br />
</form>
```

Adding the <br /> element forces each subsequent text box to the next line. This is a more attractive form, and the <br /> elements make it a little easier for the user to understand, as shown on the bottom half in Figure 15.11.

FIGURE 15.11

Simply adding <br /> makes the form a little easier to look at and use.

Notice the use of instructional text for these text boxes. Most of your forms will need instructions throughout, just as any paper-based form does. It's a good idea to standardize your instructions. You may also want to use bold, italic, or other emphasis to make the instructions or labels stand out from your other text.

Horizontal Lines

By placing `<hr />` elements in your form, you make it clear that new instructions are coming up, or that the form has reached the next logical chunk of entry. The `<hr />` element simply makes the form easier to look at as it guides the user through the different parts of the form. In the following, I've added `<hr />` at the logical breaks:

```
<form method="post" action="/cgi-bin/form1.pl">

First name: <input type="text" name="first_name" size="40" maxlength="40"
➥/><br />

Last name: <input type="text" name="last_name" size="40" maxlength="40"
➥/><br />

E-mail address: <input type="text" name="e-mail" size="40" maxlength="40"
➥/><br />


<hr />

Where you heard about us:<br />

<input type="radio" name="where" value="web" checked="checked">Web Search
➥or Link</input><br />

<input type="radio" name="where" value="advert">Radio or TV Ad</input>
➥<br />

<input type="radio" name="where" value="press">Article or press
➥mention</input><br />

<input type="radio" name="where" value="other">Other</input><br />

<hr />

<p>Enter your comments about our Web site.<br />

<textarea name="comments" rows="5" cols="40">

Include comments or questions in this area.

</textarea>

</p>

Check here to join our mailing list: <input type="checkbox" name="mailing"
➥/><br />

Check here if you'd like a sales call: <input type="checkbox" name="call"
➥/><br />

Check here if you'd like a print catalog: <input type="checkbox"
➥name="catalog" /><br />

<hr />

<button name="submit" type="submit">

<span style="font-family: Courier; font-variant: small-caps; font-size:
➥14pt">Submit Survey</span>

</button>

<button name="reset" type="reset">

<span style="font-family: Courier; font-variant: small-caps; font-size:
```

```
14pt">Clear Page</span>
</button>
</form>
```

The `<hr />` elements make the form a little longer, as shown in Figure 15.12. But you haven't sacrificed the approachability by adding `<hr />` elements. Increasing the white space and organization in a form is nearly as important as keeping it short enough so it isn't intimidating to users.

FIGURE 15.12
Adding a few horizontal lines makes the form a bit more logical.

Using Paragraphs

Paragraph containers are good for keeping form data together in smaller chunks. As always, a paragraph element will add space on each side of the text that it encloses. This makes it possible to create visual chunks without the full break that a `<hr />` suggests. The extra spacing also makes the page a bit less cluttered and easier to follow. Figure 15.13 shows how the following `<p>` additions change the page for the better:

```
<form method="post" action="/cgi-bin/form1.pl">
<p>
First name: <input type="text" name="first_name" size="40" maxlength="40"
➥/><br />
Last name: <input type="text" name="last_name" size="40" maxlength="40"
➥/><br />
```

```
E-mail address: <input type="text" name="e-mail" size="40" maxlength="40"
➥/><br />
</p>
<p>
Where you heard about us:<br />
<input type="radio" name="where" value="web" checked="checked">Web Search
➥or Link</input><br />
<input type="radio" name="where" value="advert">Radio or TV Ad</input>
➥<br />
<input type="radio" name="where" value="press">Article or press
➥mention</input><br />
<input type="radio" name="where" value="other">Other</input><br />
</p>
<p>
Enter your comments about our Web site.<br />
<textarea name="comments" rows="5" cols="40">
Include comments or questions in this area.
</textarea>
</p>
<p>
Check here to join our mailing list: <input type="checkbox" name="mailing"
➥/><br />
Check here if you'd like a sales call: <input type="checkbox" name="call"
➥/><br />
Check here if you'd like a print catalog: <input type="checkbox"
➥name="catalog" /><br />
</p>
<hr />
<button name="submit" type="submit">
<span style="font-family: Courier; font-variant: small-caps; font-size:
➥14pt">Submit Survey</span>
</button>
<button name="reset" type="reset">
<span style="font-family: Courier; font-variant: small-caps; font-size:
➥14pt">Clear Page</span>
</button>
</form>
```

Other Elements for Form Formatting

One of the most annoying parts of setting up a form so far has been the inability to line up text box fields as they go down the page. For instance, whenever the Name: and Address: fields have been used in examples, they've always looked a little ragged.

One solution is the `<pre>` element. Because anything between the two `<pre>` tags uses the same spacing and returns, this element does two things. First, it allows you to line up your text boxes. Second, it eliminates the need for `<br />` elements at the end of `<input>` elements, because the browser will recognize your returns. The following is a ragged-looking example:

```
<p>
First name: <input type="text" name="first_name" size="40" maxlength="40"
➥/><br />
Last name: <input type="text" name="last_name" size="40" maxlength="40"
➥/><br />
E-mail address: <input type="text" name="e-mail" size="40" maxlength="40"
➥/><br />
</p>
```

To improve this situation, you can put form elements inside a `<pre>` container and format them yourself:

```
<pre>
```

```
First name:       <input type="text" name="first_name" size="40"
➥maxlength="40" /><br />
Last name:        <input type="text" name="last_name" size="40"
➥maxlength="40" /><br />
E-mail address:   <input type="text" name="e-mail" size="40" maxlength="40"
➥/><br />


</pre>
```

Remember that you need to use the spacebar, not the Tab key, to create the space between the name of the box and the text box itself. As before, you may need to play with the formatting a little to get things lined up like they are on the bottom of Figure 15.14.

FIGURE 15.14

Use the <pre> container to align elements of your form, as shown in the bottom three rows.

If you can, set your text editor to a monospaced font (like Courier) for editing text inside your <pre> container. This will allow you to see exactly how <pre> text will be displayed when viewed in a browser, because <pre> forces your browser to use a monospaced font.

Using Lists for Forms

Another form design trick involves using the list tags to create organization for your forms. Nearly any form element can be part of a list, and there are often good reasons to use them. Consider the following example:

```
Where you heard about us:<br />
<dl>
<dd><input type="radio" name="where" value="web" checked="checked">Web
➥Search or Link</input></dd>
<dd><input type="radio" name="where" value="advert">Radio or TV
➥Ad</input></dd>
```

```
<dd><input type="radio" name="where" value="press">Article or press
➥mention</input></dd>
<dd><input type="radio" name="where" value="other">Other</input></dd>
</dl>
```

You've used lists in this way before, to create indented lists or outline formats that help you communicate a little better. In this case, it also makes the form look better.

Using Tables for Forms

You may also find it useful to align and manage your form elements with table cells. They can give you some fine control over the placement of text and form controls. For example:

```
<form>
<table>
<tr>
<td>First Name</td> <td><input type="text" name="first_name"></td>
</tr>
<tr>
<td>E-mail Address</td> <td><input type="text" name="e_mail"></td>
</tr>
</table>
</form>
```

This basic approach can be improved upon in any way you see fit, including removing borders (so that the organization appears to be created without table cells), cell padding, row or column spanning, and so on.

Form Structure

Later iterations of the HTML standard have added two elements, `<fieldset>` and `<legend>`, that can be used for creating structure within a longer form. As it turns out, they're also handy for assistive browsers and can be used with style sheet properties.

The `<fieldset>` element is used simply to create groupings of form elements and markup. In many browsers, you'll see border lines drawn around the defined fieldsets. In our example form, one `<fieldset>` might be the personal information at the top, while another might be the questions section. The `<fieldset>` element, because it's similar to a `<div>` element, is also very useful for style sheet properties.

The `<legend>` element is used to label a particular fieldset or otherwise add a textual label to the underlying structure of the form. `<legend>` will not only appear in a browser window, but can be read aloud or otherwise rendered by assistive browsers as well. Listing 15.1 shows an example that includes these elements, along with many of the others discussed in this section. Note that this example is the XHTML used to generate the survey page shown in Figure 15.1.

Listing 15.1 A Full Survey Page

```
<!DOCTYPE html PUBLIC "-//W3C//DTD XHTML 1.0 Strict//EN"
"http://www.w3.org/TR/xhtml1/DTD/strict.dtd">
<html xmlns="http://www.w3.org/1999/xhtml">
<head>
<title>Site Survey</title>
</head>

<body>
<form method="post" action="/cgi-bin/form1.pl">

<h1>Web Site Survey</h1>

<fieldset style="background-color: #CCCCCC">
<legend><b>Contact Information</b></legend>

<table cellpadding="5">
<tr>
<td>First name:</td> <td><input type="text" name="first_name"
➥size="40" maxlength="40" /></td>
</tr>
<tr>
<td>Last name:</td> <td><input type="text" name="last_name"
➥size="40" maxlength="40" /></td>
</tr>
<tr>
<td>E-mail address:</td> <td><input type="text" name="e-mail"
➥size="40" maxlength="40" /></td>
</tr>
</table>
</fieldset>

<fieldset style="background-color: #FFFFFF">
<legend><b>Questions and Comment</b></legend>

<p>
<b>Where you heard about us:</b></p>
<input type="radio" name="where" value="web" checked="checked">Web Search
➥or Link</input><br />
```

Listing 15.1 (continued)

```
<input type="radio" name="where" value="advert">Radio or TV Ad</input>
<br />
<input type="radio" name="where" value="press">Article or press mention</input><br />
<input type="radio" name="where" value="other">Other</input><br />
</p>

<p><b>Enter your comments about our Web site:</b></p>
<p>
<textarea name="comments" rows="5" cols="40">
Include comments or questions in this area.
</textarea>
</p>
</fieldset>

<fieldset style="background-color: #CCCCCC">

<button name="submit" type="submit">
<span style="font-family: Arial, Helvetica; font-variant:
➥small-caps; font-size: 12pt">Submit Survey</span>
</button>
<button name="reset" type="reset">
<span style="font-family: Arial, Helvetica; font-variant:
➥small-caps; font-size: 12pt">Clear Page</span>
</button>
</fieldset>
</form>
</body>
</html>
```

Accessibility: Labels and Access Keys

Recent iterations of HTML and XHTML have added an element and an attribute to help with accessibility issues. The `<label>` element is used to create a relationship between a `form` element and the text that precedes it. It also requires the use of an `id` attribute to the form element itself. The `<label>` container surrounds the text that labels the form element. It has a `for` attribute, which references the `id` of that form element. For example:

```
<label for="first">First Name:</label><input type="text" name="first_name"
➥id="first">
```

This element specifically indicates the text that is a label for a particular form element. This is considered assistive because it can tell speech synthesizers how to render the labels in a particular way. It's also useful because it specifies which text is a label for which form element, even when lists or tables are being used to format the form.

You can also label a form element *implicitly* by surrounding it with the `<label>` element, as in

```
<label>
First name:
<input type="text" name="first_name">
</label>
```

This makes it possible to specify the label text without using the `for` and `id` attributes.

Along with `<label>`, the entire repertoire of form elements can be used along with the `accesskey` attribute to enable form elements to be selected with a single keypress. For instance:

```
First name: <input type="text" name="first_name" accesskey="f">
```

This example will enable some browsers to move the user directly to the First Name entry box when the F key is pressed on the keyboard, usually in combination with another key. (On Microsoft Windows computers, generally it's the Ctrl key; on Macs, it's often the command key.)

Summary

In this chapter, you learned how to add HTML forms and form elements to your pages. The chapter began with an overview of how forms work and which items need to be present in the `<form>` element itself. You learned how to add text areas, text entry boxes, radio buttons, check boxes, password fields, hidden fields, and menus to your HTML form. From there, the discussion turned to creating attractive, easy-to-understand forms through certain layout and labeling techniques. This included some methods that can be used to better organize your form and make it more accessible to assistive browsers.

In the next chapter, you'll see how Common Gateway Interface scripts work, and how to use scripts to work with HTML form data.

CGIS AND DATA GATHERING

*I*n Chapter 15, "Adding HTML Forms," you got an in-depth look at creating and formatting HTML forms. In this chapter, you'll see the other side of HTML forms—gathering the data and reporting back to the user. This is accomplished using *scripts*, small programs that are stored on the Web server computer. Form data is sent to these scripts, as specified in the action attribute to the <form> element. Once the script receives the form data from the Web server, it should look through that data, compute what it needs to compute, and reply to the user. In this chapter, we look at the components that make up this back-end system, and you'll get a taste of the scripting that's required to make this all work.

This chapter discusses the following:

- The fundamentals of the Common Gateway Interface, including the languages you can use and why you'd use them
- How scripts work, how data is passed to a script, and how the script replies to the user's browser
- Finding and using scripts on the Web, or writing your own

What Is CGI?

Fill-in forms for your Web pages don't do anything by themselves. Your readers can fill them in, but when they click the Submit button, the data won't go anywhere unless you've written a special script to process the data. (As you'll see in Chapter 17, "Introduction to JavaScript," and Chapter 18, "JavaScript and User Input," you can also use JavaScript and client-side scripting to process some types of data.)

So how do you get data from the HTML form to the script? That's where the Common Gateway Interface (CGI) comes in. By developing CGI scripts, you can make your forms interactive.

CGI scripts bring your static Web pages to life—returning requested data, responding to user input, and making a record of how many people access your site. In this way, the script interacts with your user, responding to what they enter in forms instead of simply displaying static Web pages.

In practice, a link to a CGI script works the same way a link to an HTML page works. But under the hood, a CGI script is much more than a normal Web page. When a typical Web page's URL is requested via hyperlink, a file is read, interpreted, and displayed by the browser. When an URL to a CGI program is requested, it causes a program to be executed on the server, and that program can do just about anything you want it to: scan databases, sort names, or send e-mail. CGI scripts allow for complex back-end processing. In the case of an HTML form, generally the CGI will receive the values in that form, process them, and then reply to the user.

CGI changes the definition of what a Web page is. While normal pages are static and unchanging, CGI programs enable a page to react to the user's input, making them dynamic.

CGI Languages

You do not write CGI scripts in HTML, CSS, or even JavaScript, which are all languages that can be used in Web documents. CGI scripts are written in other computer languages, such as Unix shell scripting, Perl, C, AppleScript, and Visual Basic, so you need knowledge of at least one of these languages. You then store the script separately, in its own file, on your Web server computer. Here's a look at some of the languages you can use for CGI scripting:

- Unix shell scripts (or the similar Windows batch files) are a good choice for small or temporary CGI programs. They are easy to write and you can see results immediately, but they aren't designed for high-volume use by multiple users, as might occur with a shopping-cart application on a busy commercial Web site. A shell script often has a filename with a .sh suffix.

■ Perl is a good choice for medium-complexity programs, and most platforms support it. It's fast, easy to program, and *interpreted*, meaning that it doesn't need to be *compiled* into a fixed, formal application as with the C programming language. Also, Perl libraries exist that automatically translate any data sent to your CGI program into a usable form. Information on Perl itself is available all over the Web, including at `http://dir.yahoo.com/Computers_and_Internet/Programming_and_Development/Languages/Perl/` and `http://www.yahoo.com/Computers_and_Internet/Internet/World_Wide_Web/Programming/Perl_Scripts`.

Note

Interpreted languages are those that don't require that a script or program be translated into *machine code* before it's executed. The script stays exactly as written until it's executed. Only when the script is put into action does the interpreter quickly change its typed commands into machine language that the server computer can recognize. This extra step makes interpreted scripts a little slower, but they're also easier to edit and tweak when necessary.

■ For very complex data manipulation, it's best to use a full-fledged compiled language, such as C. It will give you the fastest response and let you work with your information in the most flexible way. C libraries also exist for using Web data. Other C variants, such as Objective C and C++, are popular on some platforms.

■ Macintosh Web servers are popular alternatives to Windows and Unix/Linux, and easy-to-create hooks exist between the Web server applications and Mac scripting languages such as AppleScript. You might start with the AppleScript-focused `http://www.scriptweb.com/`.

A Simple CGI Script

Although CGI programs can become extremely complex, they can also be quite simple. One of the simplest is the Unix shell script shown here:

```
#!/bin/sh
echo "Content-type: text/html"
echo ""
echo "<html><head><title>CGI Generated Page</title></head>"
echo "<body>This page was generated by a <em>simple</em> CGI
script.</body></html>"
```

Even if you aren't familiar with Unix, you may be able to see what this simple script is doing. The first line of this script (`#!/bin/sh`) tells Unix which shell this program is written for. If the program were a Windows NT batch file, the line could be excluded. (For our purposes, you can ignore that first line if you aren't familiar with shell scripting at all, and move on to the next line.)

The second line (`echo "Content-type: text/html"`) uses the `echo` command to tell the Web server what type of information is to follow in *MIME (Multipurpose Internet Mail Extension)* format. (The `echo` command is a common way for batch and shell scripts to "type" text as if a person were at the keyboard.) MIME is a method of delivering complex binary data using only ASCII text characters. There are hundreds of standard MIME formats now registered, but the two most common for CGI applications are text/html (for HTML/XHTML output) and text/plain (for plain ASCII output).

The third line (`echo ""`) is simply an empty space to tell the server that what follows is the data described by the "Content-type."

Finally, the fourth and fifth lines are the actual HTML data. These are sent through the server to the browser and interpreted just the same as instructions would be if they'd been read from an HTML file.

In other words, this simple script begins by telling the Web server to expect some HTML, and then it sends the server a few lines worth of text and HTML markup. Whenever this script is executed, these lines are sent to the remote browser, where they'll be interpreted and displayed just like any other Web document.

Referencing CGIs

Although conventions differ between servers, most require CGI programs to be installed in a special CGI directory. This is a subdirectory of the main directory on the Web server's hard drive, and it's usually called cgi-bin. If you aren't allowed to install your program in that directory (or if you're not sure), talk to your system administrator or your ISP.

You may also need to ask your administrator or ISP how to install the script itself, which is usually a matter of copying it from your own computer to the appropriate directory of the main Web server. The cgi-bin directory may not be called exactly that, and it may be located in an odd place on your Web server. (For instance, on many Mac OS X servers, which are Unix-like at their core, CGI scripts are stored in the /Library/WebServer/CGI-Executables/ folder even though they're referenced using a standard call to the cgi-bin directory in an URL.)

After your CGI script is in place, you can reference it from a browser like any other URL. For example, if you installed a program called script.sh in the cgi-bin directory, its URL would be as follows:

```
http://www.fakecorp.com/cgi-bin/myscript
```

These URLs can be used like any others, including as href URLs in anchor elements or as src URLs for images.

Note | Not all ISPs require that you have a special CGI-BIN directory; one of the servers I use on a regular basis allows CGI scripts to be launched from anywhere within my assigned directory space. When that's the case, however, you'll often find that you need the script to have an accurate filename extension, such as .pl for Perl scripts, .sh for shell scripts, and .exe for executable programs (such as compiled C language programs). Often a script stored in the CGI-BIN directory doesn't require a filename extension.

How Scripts Work

Although creating detailed CGI scripts can get complicated, the basic theory behind what's going on isn't that tough to understand. Scripts are designed to accept data and/or generate HTML documents in response. It all begins when the script is called, via an URL, often as the action of a <form> element. When the server notes this call, it locates the script in the cgi-bin directory and tells that script to execute. The script then checks the method used to send the data (if any) and then retrieves that data. The script begins to cull through that data looking for important information. When it finds what it's looking for, it computes, stores, or does whatever else it needs to with that data. Then, in most cases, it returns an HTML document to the user's browser, with the results of the computation, a thank-you page, or something similar.

Scripts can also be called directly, without a <form> acting as the intermediary. Instead, the script might be part of a hyperlink, or it might even be the URL in an <img> element. When that happens, it's often designed to either launch a very simple script or a complex one. A fairly simple script might be one that returns a "quote of the day," a random number, or a page counter. A very complex script might be responsible for an entire Web application, such as those used to take online merchandise orders or manage travel reservations.

In either case, eventually the script will need to check for data from the user and evaluate that data using some set methods. Let's take a look at how that works from the point of view of the script, as well as what the script will see when data is submitted to it.

Receiving Form Data

You may recall from Chapter 15 that there are two different methods to pass data to your CGI script. These two methods, get and post, cause data to be sent in different ways.

The method used to send the data is stored in an *environment variable* called REQUEST_METHOD on the Web server. (Environment variables are those that the Web server stores so that their values can be accessed by scripts.) The get method simply appends your form data to the URL and sends it to the server. Most servers will then store these appended data elements in another environment variable called QUERY_STRING. This *string* is generally limited to less than one kilobyte of data (approximately 1,000 characters), which explains why the get method is less popular.

The term *string* is used in programming to suggest a single series of characters, generally accessible using a *variable name*. In this case, it's the environment variable QUERY_STRING. So, a script can be written to check the QUERY_STRING variable for relevant data and then act on that data.

Using the post method causes the length of the data string to be stored in a variable called CONTENT_LENGTH, while the data itself is redirected to stdin ("standard in"). In effect, the data is made to appear to your script or program as if it was typed in to the server using a keyboard. Your script must then be designed to *parse* that input.

In English, *parsing* means to explain the grammatical form or function of a word. In computerese, *parsing* means something more like breaking up unreadable computer data into something that people (or at least programs written by people) can work with.

There are actually two steps to receiving the input: decoding and parsing. Data sent from your Web browser is encoded to avoid data loss—essentially, by turning spaces into plus signs (+) and non-text characters (such as an exclamation point) into a percent sign (%) and a hexadecimal code. For instance, ! is turned into %21.

There are programs designed specifically for decoding Web data. cgi-bin.pl is the Perl library for this on Windows and Linux servers. Mac Web servers might use Parse CGI for AppleScript CGI scripts.

Once you've worked through the decoding process, you're left with a text input that follows this format (where the ampersand simply separates each pairing of name and value):

```
NAME1=VALUE1&NAME2=VALUE2&...
```

An example of this might be

```
address=1234 Elm Ave&city=Atlanta&state=GA
```

And so on. You might notice that these entries actually pair up nicely with the names you specified in your HTML form for each of the elements used to receive input. For instance, let's say you have the following form snippet:

```
<p>
Last name: <input type="text" name="last_name" size="40" maxlength="40" />
<br />
City: <input type="text" name="city" size="50" maxlength="50" value="New
York" />
</p>
<p>
Where you heard about us:<br />
<input type="radio" name="where" value="web" checked="checked">Web Search
or Link
<input type="radio" name="where" value="advert">Radio or TV Ad
<input type="radio" name="where" value="press">Article or press mention
<input type="radio" name="where" value="other">Other
</p>
```

The values parsed from the data stream might be something like this:

```
last_name=Smith&city=Denver&where=advert
```

Or something similar, according to the choice made by your user. Those are really the basics of how to use form data in scripts.

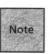

Note

If you're not using a parsing program or library (which, ideally, would allow you to easily reassign the values in this file to variables in your script), your script will need to accept this data stream, strip the ampersands, and reassign the values to appropriate variables. That's a tougher requirement, and it's beyond the scope of this text. You might consider Que's *Special Edition Using XHTML*, ISBN: 0-7897-2431-6, *Special Edition Using XML*, ISBN: 0-7897-1996-7, and *Special Edition Using Java 2, Enterprise Edition*, ISBN: 0-7897-2503-7 if you'd like to learn more about writing CGI scripts that parse input.

The mailto: Option

This section may seem like something of an aside, but it makes sense in this context. Chapter 15 mentioned the possibility of using a mailto: URL in your `action` attribute instead of referencing a CGI script directly. What happens then is simple—the unparsed, undecoded form data is sent directly to the specified e-mail address (assuming the user's Web browser is equipped to send mailto: messages). Here's an example of a mailto: URL in a `<form>` element:

```
<form action="mailto:surveys@fakecorp.com" method="post">
```

When your user clicks the Submit button, the results of the form are now forwarded to the specified e-mail address instead of being sent to a CGI script. And that's great if you don't have access to your Web server's CGI directory. The only downside is figuring out what exactly you should do with the e-mail message once you receive it. Most likely, it isn't yet ready for easy reading.

The first problem is that the e-mail message is still encoded in the post format that forms use to send messages to scripts. Figure 6.1 shows an example of a typical received message—it's not a very pretty sight.

FIGURE 16.1

Here's what an e-mail message looks like when it's sent from an HTML form.

Note   Interestingly, some versions of Internet Explorer will send form data in a decoded format when IE recognizes a mailto: URL. Unfortunately, you can't count on all your users to have IE when they're accessing your form, so you'll still likely have to deal with this encoded data sometimes.

The second problem is an extension of the first: You're either going to have to process all these e-mails by hand or write a program that interacts with your e-mail program to handle these messages. Either approach is probably fine for the small-business or home Web designer; at least you get the form data from users without requiring you to implement a CGI script. In some cases, there may be an easy solution—many modern e-mail programs can interact with scripting languages such as Visual Basic Scripting or AppleScript. Those scripts then parse the output and do something automatically (such as make a computation based on the data and respond to the user via e-mail).

You might also notice one last problem—once the user clicks Submit and data is sent by e-mail, the page just sits there because there isn't a CGI script that can respond to the form page with an acknowledgment page. Instead, you'll need to include a Back button or hyperlink on the page to let users move back to a previous page. Add a clickable image, for instance, that says something like "Click after submitting," and then hyperlink that button to another page.

Another solution is a little more automatic: You can use JavaScript to respond to the user's click, launching a new page at the same time. See Chapter 18 for details.

| Note | If you have access to the cgi-bin directory but you aren't much of a programmer, you can install a generic forms-to-e-mail gateway, like the one available at `http://www.worldwidemart.com/scripts/formmail.shtml`. This solution is a bit more elegant because it will redirect the user to a new page after the form has been submitted. Plus, you'll receive the form data fully parsed and ready to read. |

Your Script's Output

Creating output with a script is probably the easiest part. Because `stdout` ("standard out") is redirected to the HTML browser, you simply need to use `print` (Perl and other languages), `echo` (Unix shell and Windows batch scripts) `lprint` (C language), or similar commands that print directly to the screen, terminal, or console. You use the print command to output HTML codes, just as if you were using your text editor.

Here's a short snippet of a Perl script to do just that:

```
print "Content-type: text\html\n\n";
print "<html>\n<head><title>Submission - Thank You!</title></head>\n";
print "<body>\n<h1>Success</h1>\n<p>Thank you for your submission<\p>\n"
print "<p>Click to go back to the <a href="index.html">main page</a>.
➥<\p> \n</body></html>"
```

Remember that all this "standard in" and "standard out" stuff is so your script seems as if it's typing something into the server computer. In this case, when sending to standard out, it's as if an HTML document is being typed and sent to the Web browser, which will then interpret the text and markup as it would any HTML document.

In a number of programming languages, `\n` is the *newline* character, which simply feeds a return to standard out, as if you had pressed the Return or Enter key while typing. Otherwise, this should look rather familiar; it's basic HTML.

Whatever the programming language's "print" command is, as long as it's designed to print to `stdout`, you should be able to create automatic Web pages in this way. In fact, you can use the same approach, along with variables you define and use within your script, to print out pages that include information about the user's computer, information from the form that was submitted, or information that has been calculated in response to items that were submitted on the form. For instance, Figure 16.2 is the output generated from a call to a sample CGI script called `printenv` that's included with many different operating systems. It's used to print the environment variables that a given Web server makes available to you for scripting purposes.

FIGURE 16.2

The output of the printenv script shows you how variables can be used in output, as well as how many variables there are for your scripts to use.

Finding and Using Scripts

While a tutorial on any particular scripting language is outside the scope of this book, we can take a quick look at some other resources you might want to consider when it comes to CGIs. In fact, if you're lucky at all, you may come across scripts that don't require much or any programming. If they're reasonably well documented, you can sometimes even edit publicly available scripts a bit to get them to work with your site.

In this section, you'll see some of the Web sites you can visit to learn more about scripting and to get scripts you can use on your own server. You'll also see a few sample scripts and resources that will give you a sense of how all this scripting stuff works and, frankly, if it's the sort of thing you're interested in pursuing for your site. In some cases, you may find it easier to just download and use prebuilt CGI scripts with your site. You may also want to explore JavaScript or similar options that will be discussed in Chapter 17.

Working with Other's Scripts

As with any programming endeavor, there are people who love to create scripts and people who, well, could do without it. Regardless of the category you fall into, you may find it helpful to visit some sites on the Web that focus on CGI scripting, including those that make sample scripts available for download. In some cases, scripts are available for free and can be freely altered, so that you can turn a given script into something you find more useful. In other cases, you may come across commercial solutions that enable you to purchase and use a script on your site or server.

One great place to start is the CGI Resource Index at `http://cgi.resourceindex.com`. This site includes links to thousands of different CGI scripts—both freebies and commercial scripts—that you can use to alter your site. They run the gamut from Web counter scripts to full-fledged site management applications. For instance, you can use a downloadable script for processing an HTML form. Some scripts will work with a backend database, for instance, while others can be used simply to parse the form data and send it to you in e-mail. One such script is Form Processor from FreeScripts.com (`http://www.freescripts.com/scripts/`).

Installing the Script

Once you've downloaded a script you'd like to use, such as Form Processor, it needs to be installed in your cgi-bin directory. (Most scripts available on the Web work on Unix-based servers, but you'll find scripts designed for Windows- or Mac-based servers as well.)

When installing the script in your cgi-bin directory, you may need to set permissions so that the script can be properly accessed and executed by the Web server. For Unix-based servers, this is generally done using the `chmod 755 scriptname.pl` command at a command-line prompt or in a terminal window. (If that last sentence doesn't make much sense to you, consult your system administrator or ISP.) You may also find that your FTP application will allow you to change permissions for scripts.

Note

Not all Web servers require you to place CGI scripts in a cgi-bin directory. Some will execute the CGI script wherever you store it on the Web server. You may still need to set permissions for the script, however. For Unix-based servers, you'll probably set the permissions to *read*, *write*, and *execute* for the owner, and *read* and *execute* for others (group and world). (This means, in the interest of security, you're giving yourself permission to alter the script, but nobody else can.) Again, consult your administrator or ISP for specific instructions regarding your particular Web server, as permissions are sometimes set differently on different servers.

Once installed, the script will likely require some special configuration. In many cases, you'll edit a text-based configuration file that's stored somewhere on your server computer. This file will be used to set options, choose default directories, and determine other behaviors. In the case of Form Processor, the script mentioned earlier, a few simple configuration options are built into the script, including options that determine whether an e-mail with the form data is sent or whether a text file is saved. Other options enable you to append data to a contact file or to send a confirmation e-mail to users when they submit the form.

Along with this configuration, Form Processor also uses a series of hidden fields to choose preferences such as to whom the processed form data should be e-mailed:

```
<input type="hidden" name="admin" value="admin@fakecorp.com">
<input type="hidden" name="subject" value="Web Order">
<input type="hidden" name="redirect"
value="http://www.fakecorp.com/orders/confirm.html">
```

Along with these hidden fields, the script uses a system of codes for the `name` attributes within the forms. Those codes make it possible to set the order of the fields that are reported to the user. And, using particular name entries (such as user_email) enables the script to recognize the e-mail address for use with the auto-generated reply.

If there's one issue you'll occasionally encounter when using other's scripts, it's some level of incompatibility. If you're installing Perl scripts, you may need to know the version of Perl (such as Perl 5) that's installed on your server computer, and occasionally you may need to ask your administrator or ISP to turn on a particular preference or enable some secondary level of support, such as a particular library or directory path. For the most part, though, you'll find that installing somebody else's scripts is fairly painless, and you'll soon get used to the configuration files and preferences, particularly if you read any included documentation carefully.

Using a Hosted Script

Another approach to using outside scripts is something called a *hosted script*, which simply means the script remains on the host's server computer. Because a form `method` statement or the `src` attribute for any sort of link can point to a remote URL, you can actually have your forms processed (or other CGI scripts invoked) on another server. This is particularly useful if you don't have access to the cgi-bin directory on your server and/or you are limited in the number or types of CGI scripts that you can run from your server. (Such limits aren't completely uncommon, particularly on free or inexpensive servers.) In that case, the best solution might be a hosted script of some sort.

The CGI Resource site includes a page that links to various hosted options at `http://cgi.resourceindex.com/Remotely_Hosted/`. Again, the types of CGIs vary greatly, from counters to bulletin boards to online chats. As you might expect, a number of them exist for processing forms. For basic form processing, a service such as Form Buddy at `http://www.formbuddy.com/` might do the trick. You create a form and use Form Buddy's CGI script URL as the method of your form. Then, when the user submits the form, the data can be e-mailed to you, or it can be stored on the server and you can access it later. Also, the CGI can send an acknowledgment e-mail message to the user who submits the form (assuming that user also submits a valid e-mail address). Of course, the site is ad-supported, but that may be a small price to pay if you can't otherwise install CGI scripts on your server.

Hosted CGIs can get more complex, too. For instance, Formsite.com can be used to create a variety of different forms using templates as a guide. Depending on the level of service (in some cases, you'll have to pay), you can either create a form and link to Formsite.com for the CGI processing, or host the entire form (or forms) on its site. Formsite.com's templates range from guest books and password protection to order-taking e-commerce pages.

You'll find other third-party scripts discussed elsewhere in the book, particularly Chapter 21, "Forums, Chats, and Other Add-Ons," which covers a number of different community-building scripts and applications for creating bulletin boards, chat rooms, and so on.

Creating Your Own Scripts

If you plan to create your own scripts, you'll need to start by learning a compatible language (if you don't already know one). Far and away the most popular language is Perl, although many Mac users opt for AppleScript, and simple CGIs are often written as Unix shell scripts. For a high-end overview on many Web authoring and programming topics, see Que's *Special Edition Using XHTML*, *Special Edition Using XML*, and *Special Edition Using Java 2, Enterprise Edition*. To learn more about Perl, check out *Perl 5 by Example*, ISBN: 0-7897-0866-3, also published by Que.

When you're creating Perl scripts, you'll often do so in standard text editors, such as Emacs or Pico. If you aren't developing in Unix, programming text editors for Windows or Macintosh will work just as well. Perl is an *interpreted* language. This means that scripts don't need to be compiled ahead of time, so you won't need development environments or compilers such as those required for C or similar programming. You will need to test your scripts, however. The easiest way to do that is probably to run a local, Perl-capable Web server on your computer (or over your local network). Enable CGIs on that Web server, install them in the appropriate directories, and begin your testing.

If you're testing your scripts on your home or office computer instead of on a remote server, you should consider shutting down your Internet connection while your Web server software is active. Even if you're only playing around with a Web server and scripts, others could access that server over the Internet and gain access to your personal data. It's not a huge risk, but to be safe, a computer that's used for testing Web servers and scripts should be isolated from the Internet to avoid remote tampering.

Although Perl is designed for a command-line Unix environment (which is broad enough to include any Linux-variant FreeBSD versions and their progeny, such as Mac OS X), it's available for other platforms as well. The Classic Mac OS (Mac OS 9.x and earlier) has MacPerl (`http://www.macperl.com/`), which can be used for slightly modified Perl scripting and Mac-based CGIs. For Windows, Indigo Perl (`http://www.indigostar.com/indigoperl.htm`) is a freeware solution that includes a built-in Apache server that enables you to test your Perl scripts. Another popular option for Windows is ActivePerl (`http://www.ActiveState.com/Products/ActivePerl/`).

For more on Perl programming, you may want to visit Perl.com. There you'll find articles, discussions, How-To's, and tools. Other resources include the Perl Mongers (`http://www.perl.org/`) and the Perl Monks (`http://www.perlmonks.org/`), two different groups of Perl programmers and aficionados banding together to share information, code snippets, and other resources. For even more, check out Yahoo!'s Perl pages at `http://dir.yahoo.com/Computers_and_Internet/Programming_and_Development/Languages/Perl/`.

For other CGI programming, generally you need to choose a language that your Web servers (both your testing server and your target, final Web server) are comfortable dealing with. If that's Unix, you can use many of the aforementioned languages—Perl, C, or shell scripts. For Windows, you might opt for Visual Basic or a language supported by the particular server application—that may also be Perl or C. For Macintosh, use AppleScript, MacPerl, or a similar scripting environment, such as Frontier technologies (`http://www.userland.com/`), which is also available for Windows.

Summary

This chapter continued the discussion from Chapter 15, focusing on the Common Gateway Interface scripts and programs that are required to process HTML form data. You learned what CGI scripts are and how they work. You learned how form data is submitted to the script, parsed into useful data, and stored in variables. You also saw how such form data can be sent, if desired, via e-mail.

The second part of the chapter focused on getting and installing CGI scripts, including a discussion of some online resources and some representative scripts for form processing. There was also a brief discussion of what's in store for you if you opt to learn a scripting language and attempt to write your own scripts.

In the next chapter, you'll be introduced to JavaScript, a language that enables you to embed scripting commands directly within your HTML documents, making them dynamic and more responsive to users.

INTRODUCTION TO JAVASCRIPT

*T*he last few chapters showed you how to use HTML forms and CGI scripts to interact with the user. CGI requires access to the server computer (at least the cgi-bin folder). JavaScript, on the other hand, works within the browser (assuming the browser is compatible with it). That means you can use it for small scripting tasks or for very complex tasks that don't involve the server at all.

It's also a pretty involved topic. See Chapter 18, "JavaScript and User Input," to take a closer look at some of the tasks you can perform with JavaScript that have to do specifically with user interaction. Then, in Chapter 19, "Adding Dynamic HTML," the use of JavaScript is shown with dynamic HTML.

This chapter discusses the following:

- The basics of JavaScript—what it is, why you might want to learn it, and what your options are
- Creating your first JavaScript: embedding and linking
- Creating and using JavaScript functions
- Inside the lingo: variables, comparisons, conditionals, and loops
- How objects and methods work, and a few objects you can use in your scripts

What Is JavaScript?

JavaScript is a scripting language that's similar to AppleScript, Visual Basic Scripting (VBScript), and languages such as Unix's shell scripting languages. Although JavaScript is similar in on the surface in some ways to full-fledged programming languages, such as C, C++, and Java, it doesn't require you to worry as much about the program's underlying structure. It's a bit limited in that way, but still very useful.

JavaScript was specifically designed by Netscape to work together with HTML (and XHTML) to create more dynamic Web pages. Netscape and Internet Explorer browsers tend to support JavaScript from the 3.0 level on up, while other browsers have spotty support for JavaScript—some are better than others. In most cases, you can't rely on your user to have JavaScript capabilities, so it's important to design your pages to support all possible users. We'll discuss that throughout this section.

Note

Microsoft's implementation of JavaScript is called JScript, and its basic operation is about the same as JavaScript. It offers some different commands, but there's a strong overlapping pool of commands and logic. Both, in turn, are relatives of ECMAScript (`http://www.ecma.ch/ecma1/STAND/ECMA-262.HTM`). It's the "official" standard set by the European Computer Manufacturers' Association, to which JavaScript and JScript conform.

JavaScript is designed to work with the different elements on your page, reacting to user input, feeding form values to equations and formulas, and otherwise making it possible to turn a Web document from a static page into something that more closely resembles a computer program's interface. If you get hooked on JavaScript, you'll find it handy in many different situations, including such things as automated HTML frame interfaces and form data checking (see Figure 17.1).

FIGURE 17.1

JavaScript can be used to check an HTML form before it's ever submitted to a CGI script, making sure it has all the requisite data filled in and accounted for.

JavaScript isn't part of the HTML or XHTML standards, although it's used almost exclusively within HTML documents, and both standards have a special `<script>` element that's used in tandem with JavaScript. Plus, JavaScript (or a similar scripting language) is at the heart of what's called *Dynamic HTML*, which uses JavaScript, style sheets, and other technology to create interesting and interactive pages.

The JavaScript/Java Relationship

Java and JavaScript are not the same and aren't really even related in any significant way, despite their names. Java is a full-fledged programming language, invented by Sun Microsystems, in the spirit of C++. Designed for the more advanced programmer, Java has a number of strengths:

- It's a very modern programming language that's still familiar to the legions of C and C++ programmers who are interested in using a newer language.

- It has been designed to be more than a computer language. It's also a *virtual machine* technology, which means that Java applications can run on a variety of computer platforms.

- Web browsers often support Java much as they do multimedia plug-ins. A Java application can take over part of the Web browser window and interact with the user almost as if the user had launched the Java application from his or her hard disk.

The virtual machine concept is the reason that at one time, many thought that the computing world would eventually be overtaken by Java. The idea behind the virtual machine is that every computer in the world can pretend to be a less sophisticated "Java-standard" computer.

Usually a computer is defined by the sort of hardware it's composed of and the operating system it uses. For instance, you can't run Macintosh applications on a typical Microsoft Windows-based computer. Part of that is because Macintosh applications are designed for a different operating system, the Mac OS, which in turn is designed for different processors and hardware from Microsoft Windows.

But Java creates a standard computer—a virtual machine—completely in the software. Instead of programming specifically for Windows or the Mac OS, programmers simply write the program for the virtual machine, which is nearly the same on all computer platforms. Because Web browsers can create this machine, it's possible to run Java programs (which are called Java *applets* in this context) from within the Web browser, making sites more interactive and entertaining.

The truth is that, so far, Java's virtual machine hasn't really taken over desktop computers, and Windows, Macintosh, Unix, Linux, and other operating systems still require applications written (or at least *compiled*) directly for them. That said, there are some Java applications available for use on the desktop, and Java is popular in Web browsers. Beyond that, Java is also popular simply as a computer language, and many applications—both on the desktop and for the Web—are now written in Java.

So, why do Java and JavaScript have similar names? Aside from confusing novice computer users, there is a reason for the similar names—JavaScript was designed to use a fairly Java-like syntax. That's it. Even though JavaScript isn't nearly as powerful or complex, and it's only designed to work within Web browsers, it uses some commands and syntax that are similar to Java. Of course, that's not really saying much, because Java is similar to C++, and C++ is based on C. In essence, JavaScript is easy to learn for anyone who's ever programmed in one of these modern object-oriented programming languages.

JavaScript Versus VBScript

JavaScript is certainly the most popular scripting language for Web documents, but it isn't the only one. VBScript runs a distant, but occasionally significant, second place in the Web scripting world, despite the fact that it's a Microsoft-only technology that's only supported in Internet Explorer for Windows.

VBScript has two things going for it: It's the scripting language recommended for ActiveX controls (which are sort of Microsoft's proprietary version of Java applets), and it's very much like Visual Basic, the popular Windows programming language. Whereas both Java and JavaScript are platform-neutral, VBScript and ActiveX have made a very Windows-centric play for control of the Internet.

This chapter and the next two focus on JavaScript because it's the more widely accepted of the two, it's already cross-platform, and it uses a slightly more approachable syntax. Still, if you plan to implement Web sites that are Microsoft-only (such as intranets), if you're working with ActiveX controls, and/or if you're already a proficient Visual Basic programmer, you may want to look further into VBScript for scripting within your Web documents.

How Web Scripts Work

With the preliminaries out of the way, now we can move on to two basic concepts in Web scripting with JavaScript: *functions* and *event handling*.

In most of the scripts you create using JavaScript, you'll have two distinct sections—code within the `<head>` of your document, and code within the `<body>` of your document. The stuff in the `<head>` will usually be functions, while the code in the `<body>` will often comprise *function calls*.

Function calls don't do a lot of actual processing. Instead, they're in the `<body>` of the document to either respond to user input or follow a set path of statements. The function calls usually take a particular value and send it up to the functions that are stored in the `<head>` of the document. Those functions then process the data, do some math (or some other sort of computation), and then return the value to the function call in the body of the script.

Of course, this whole process would be silly if the function calls simply happened in order—at that point, you might as well put the whole script in one part of the document. But the value of functions is that they can be reused at different points in a script, in different orders. That's where *event handling* comes into play. In essence, the script is able to wait for certain events to happen—such as the user clicking a particular link or button, or entering data in an HTML form. When that happens, the script can respond to the event, send data to a function, and get a returned value.

Instead of a procedural program that guides the user from step A to step B to step C, the function/event approach means that the script waits for the user to do something, and then reacts to it. When a particular piece of information needs to be retrieved from the user, or if a certain calculation needs to be performed, a function is called to solve that problem. But functions are only invoked when the user does something that the script needs to react to. That's why it's called *handling* events.

Note

Note that *events* aren't always something the user does—a script can be programmed to react to other events, such as a certain time or date, a page being loaded, or in response to one of the server's variables changing. These events are things that the script can react to as well, by automatically generating XHTML markup, changing the content of a frame, or any number of other reactions.

Entering Scripts in Your Web Documents

JavaScript is simply more plain-text markup that you're adding to your Web pages, so you don't need any new applications or tools. That said, a text-based editor that includes a JavaScript reference is always helpful, and you may want to have the JavaScript guide from Netscape open in a Web browser window as you work (it's at `http://developer.netscape.com/docs/manuals/js/client/jsguide/index.htm`). It's also important to test your scripts carefully in as many Web browsers as you can—including Internet Explorer, Netscape, and others—in different version numbers, and for different computing platforms. If you're using JavaScript for business or organizational use, testing is very important.

JavaScript authoring involves a new element, the `<script>` element. Although the element is your typical XHTML container element, what isn't typical is that you'll need to hide the `<script>` element within your page.

The `<script>` Element and Script Hiding

The `<script>` element is used to add JavaScript commands to your HTML pages. This is done so that JavaScript-compatible browsers can determine which text is actually scripting commands and which text should be displayed in the browser window. `<script>` is a container that can accept the attribute `type`, which enables you to specify the scripting language used. (Generally, JavaScript is the default.)

Note | For backward compatibility, particularly for browsers that predate the 3.0 level of IE and Netscape, you may want to include the `language="JavaScript"` attribute as well. It isn't necessary for later browsers, but using both `type` and `language` is the most complete approach.

Here's how it works:

```
<script type="text/javascript">
Script function definitions
</script>
```

Although some old browsers that don't recognize JavaScript may just skip over the `<script>` element and its contents, it's also possible that an old browser will attempt to interpret your script commands or other text as HTML markup. So, you've got to be careful about how you hide the script stuff.

For non-JavaScript browsers, you do that hiding with the scripts commands within the opening and closing brackets of the HTML comment element:

```
<script type="text/javascript">
<!--
script commands
// -->
</script>
```

To keep scripts from causing trouble in older browsers, we've got to add all these special commands. You might have even noticed that you have to put two slashes (`//`) in front of the closing XHTML comment tag. This is because JavaScript will generate errors when it sees `-->`; it will try to interpret that as scripting code. (To JavaScript, that looks like two minus signs and a greater than sign.) So, you need to comment the comment, using JavaScript's comment command, which happens to be those two slashes.

Of course, the primary purpose of JavaScript comments is to include information about the script itself. Using JavaScript's two comment types, you can add information about how the script works and why it does what it does:

```
<script type="text/javascript">
<!--
script command     // A comment about this command
...script commands...
/* If you have longer comments, you can place then
between these two comment elements */
// this JavaScript comment precedes the HTML comment closing tag -->
</script>
```

The two types of comments are the *single-line* JavaScript comment and the *multi-line* comment. Single-line comments start with two forward slashes and must completely fit on a single line with a return at the end. Multi-line comments can be enclosed in an opening comment element (/*) and a closing comment element (*/), with as much space and comments inside as desired.

With all these comments and hiding, it's not a bad idea to create a template for starting out with your script-based pages. You can use that template to begin pages from scratch, or you can cut and paste all the default scripting comments and elements to get a head start.

Strict Versus Transitional

If you're hiding scripts within your Web document, you'll need to use the XHTML Transitional DTD. If you want to use the strict DTD with scripts, you can, but only if you link to your script's function definitions instead of embedding them in the page (more on that in a moment), or if you take an additional hiding step within the page.

The reason for this type of hiding is that certain common characters used in JavaScript are interpreted differently in XML. (And XHTML is HTML cast in XML, remember?) As a result, the characters < and & can be mistaken for XML items instead of the scripting elements they're intended to be. The solution is to include another layer of hiding to prevent an XML interpreter from interpreting the scripting as XML commands. Here's how:

```
<!DOCTYPE html PUBLIC "-//W3C//DTD XHTML 1.0 Strict//EN"
    "http://www.w3.org/TR/xhtml1/DTD/xhtml1-strict.dtd">

<html xmlns="http://www.w3.org/1999/xhtml">
<head>
<title>Strict Scripting</title>

<script type="text/javascript">
<![CDATA[
 ...script commands...
]]>
</script>

</head>
```

In this case, the `<![CDATA[` and `]]>` tags are used to tell the XML parser to ignore what comes between them. At least, that's the official recommendation. The problem is that this method of hiding is still somewhat theoretical. It may be the desired approach for future Web browsers, but right now it simply doesn't work. So, using the strict DTD with the `<script>` element in your pages is tough.

If you really want to use the strict DTD, there is another solution. You can place the script function declarations (the script portions that appear in the `<head>` of your document) in a separate document and link to it. That would look something like

```
<head>
<title>Linking to JavaScript</title>
<script type="text/javascript" src="script_functions.js">
</script>
</head>
```

The document `script_functions.jp` would be a simple text file that starts with the first JavaScript command, just as if it were enclosed in the `<script>` container. This is by far the best way to get around all the scripting hiding issues.

Note

To avoid all this, you might want to simply use the transitional DTD on your JavaScript pages. (That's how I'll do it in examples throughout this chapter and the next two.) Also, be aware that at some point in the future, aspects of scripting on the page—particularly the event handling bits—may have to change before the Web can go fully XHTML Strict.

Script Meta Type and `<noscript>`

Technically, each instance of the `<script>` element should include a `type` attribute (although not all Web browsers require this to the letter). You can get around that, however, by declaring a default using the `<meta>` element in the `<head>` of your document:

```
<head>
<title>JavaScript By Default Page</title>
<meta http-equiv="Content-Script-Type" content="text/javascript">
</head>
```

Doing this will be particularly important as you get deeper into scripting. JavaScript's event handlers (where a script function is called from within the Web page itself) don't allow you to specify script `type`, so they rely on the `<meta>` definition (or force the browser to guess).

Finally, XHTML also offers the option of a `<noscript>` container that can be used within a `<script>` element to offer alternative text and markup for browsers that don't support scripting. That looks something like

```
<body>
<script type="text/javascript">
<!--
//<![CDATA[
 ...functions...
// ]]>
// -->
</script>

<noscript>
<p>It appears your browser doesn't support JavaScript. Please visit
<a href="noscript.html">the no-script page</a> to see a non-JavaScript
version of this page.</p>
</noscript>
</body>
```

Let's put it all together in a template and a quick example.

The "Hello World" Example

Whenever you learn a new programming language, traditionally the first example you encounter is a "Hello World" script or program. This Hello World example will show you the basics of the hiding and scripting commands and how the `<script>` elements work.

For the purpose of this example, you need to know one command you haven't been introduced to yet. It's `document.writeln()`, and it's called a method in JavaScript. A *method* is a function that's built into a particular object, enabling it to do something automatically. In this case, it can automatically "write" to the object "document." In other words, the method `document.writeln()` writes text to your Web page.

Listing 17.1 is a complete HTML document that includes some basic JavaScript.

LISTING 17.1 Hello World Example

```
<!DOCTYPE html PUBLIC "-//W3C//DTD XHTML 1.0 Transitional//EN"
    "http://www.w3.org/TR/xhtml1/DTD/xhtml1-transitional.dtd">

<html xmlns="http://www.w3.org/1999/xhtml">
<head>
<title>Hello World</title>
<meta http-equiv="Content-Script-Type" content="text/javascript">
</head>
<BODY>
<script language="JavaScript">
<!-- hide script
document.writeln("<h1>Hello World!<\/h1>")
// end hiding -->
</script>
<noscript>
<p>Your browser doesn't appear to support JavaScript.</p>
</noscript>
</body>
</html>
```

This example offers a few things worth discussing:

- The `<script>` container has been added in the `<body>` of the document. That's typical when you're using the script to create something within the document's body, instead of defining functions, which happens in the `<head>`. In more complicated scripts, you'll likely have `<script>` containers in both sections.

- Within the `document.writeln()` command, the closing `</h1>` tag actually looks like `<\/h1>`. That's because the closing `/` would otherwise be misinterpreted by the `document.writeln()` method as the beginning of a special character, such as the newline (`/n`) character. So, you need to *escape* the forward slash using the backslash.

■ Because you're using the `<meta>` element to specify the scripting content, you don't need a `type` attribute for `<script>`. However, the `language` attribute is still there for backward compatibility.

Save this document as something like helloworld.html and then open it using a Web browser. If your browser is capable of dealing with JavaScript, your output should look something like Figure 17.2. If it's not, you'll just see the `<noframes>` text.

FIGURE 17.2

Here's the result of the Hello World script in all its glory.

Creating Functions in JavaScript

A *function* can be thought of as a mini-program within your script. Generally, a function is designed to accomplish one particular task and then return a value to the main body of the script. Functions start by being *passed* a particular value. That value is then used in calculations or as part of a procedure. Then, in most cases, the function will return a new value to the body of the script, where something else may or may not happen.

Although it's perfectly possible to have an entire script in the body of your document (and you will, occasionally), you'll find that this sort of *procedural* programming is both wasteful and limited. By breaking your scripts into functions and function calls, you gain two advantages.

First, the functions don't have to be used in any particular order, just like you don't have to click the icons in Microsoft Windows or Macintosh applications in any particular order. So, a script can be changed around or used with event handlers to call the functions in any order.

Second, functions can be reused. You can use different data with the same function to get different results. If the function is flexible enough, it will save you quite a bit of programming to simply call the function whenever its particular capabilities are required.

However, functions do need to be declared, or defined, usually in the <head> of your Web document. Then, the functions have to be called, or launched, usually from within the Web page itself.

Declaring Functions

Declaring a function is when you tell the browser, "I'm going to have this function, and this is what it's going to do." When the browser loads a page, it will make note of the different functions that you've declared so that it knows to return to them when they're called.

Most script authors will declare their JavaScript functions in the <head> of their Web documents, although that isn't strictly required. They can be declared anywhere within the document. The function declaration needs to appear inside a <script> container, and you're free to place more than one <script> container in a document. In fact, JavaScript is a little weird because all the <script> elements, taken together, comprise the script. (In most programming, your script isn't broken up with HTML and XHTML markup in-between the functions and function calls.)

Here's the basic format for a function call:

```
<script type="text/javascript">
<!-- hide script
  function function_name(incoming_value) {
  ...function code...
  return (new_value)
}
// end hiding -->
</script>
```

Remember that when a script calls a function, it often sends along a value. In your function definition, you'll need to assign a name to that passed value, which is represented by *incoming_value*. If the function is designed to perform simple math, for instance, you might call the incoming value *first_num* or something similar. You can then use that name in formulas, such as new_num = first_num * 3.

When you give the incoming value a name, you're creating a *variable*. Then the computer reserves some memory for that variable and gives it a name. You can then assign a certain value to that name and use that name in your script. For instance:

1. In the body of your script, you send the value 5 to a function.

2. The function receives that value and creates a variable called my_number to which that value is assigned.

3. Then you tell the script to "add 10 to my_number" using a formula such as
new_number = my_number + 10

4. If you did it right, the script returns the answer using the variable new_number
to the body of the script.

5. The body of the script accepts that new value, and the answer is 15.

Along with that variable, note the keywords function and return. The function keyword is always the beginning of a function declaration, followed by the name of the function and, in parentheses, the variable name to be assigned to the incoming value. The return keyword is used to end the function declaration—it's telling the function to return the parenthetical value to the portion of the body of the script that called this function in the first place.

Also, notice that the entire calculating part of the function is between curly brackets, between the two keywords. An example of a function declaration might be

```
<script type="text/javascript">
<!--
function getSquare (num)
{
    squareNum = num * num;
    return (squareNum);
}
// end hiding -->
</script>
```

In this example, you've created a function called getSquare, which accepts a value, names it num, and then multiplies that value by itself and assigns the resulting value to a variable named squareNum. Finally, it returns that value to the body of the script.

At least, that's what the function has been declared to do. It won't actually do it yet because it doesn't know which actual values to work with until you call the function from within the body of the script.

Function Calls and Value Return

Generally, the body of your script will be just a series of function calls. There isn't a whole lot of calculating done in the guts of your script. You send a value out to a function to be computed and then receive the results back in the body. A function call either appears inside a <script> container, in an event-handler attribute (see Chapter 18), or in an URL. A typical function call looks like this:

function_name(value);

You can put a variable name, an actual number, or a string of text in the parentheses, as long as the function is designed to accept such a value. (Function calls in the body of your document need to be surrounded by `<script>` tags, just like the function definitions in the head of the document.)

Note Your function calls must always pass a value type that the function expects. If you pass a string of text to a function designed to perform math functions, you won't get anything useful in return.

As an example, consider the following script that might appear in the body of a document. This script will call the `getSquare` function created in the previous section:

```
<script type="text/javascript">
<!--
myNum = 10;
mySqr = getSquare (myNum);
document.writeln ("The square of " + myNum + " is " + mySqr + ".");
//-->
</script>
```

Here's what is happening in this function call:

1. You've assigned the value `10` to the variable `myNum`.
2. Then that variable (and hence the value `10`) is passed to the function `getSquare`. (This example assumes we're using the same function created in the previous section, "Declaring Functions.")
3. When that number gets up there to the function, it's assigned to the variable `num` and then the computation occurs.
4. After the computation, the new value is passed back to the function call in the body of the script.
5. Here's the interesting part. The entire function call is replaced with the value that is passed back from the function declaration. In this example, the entire call `getSquare (myNum)` is replaced with the value of `25`.
6. As a result, the variable `mySqr` is assigned the value of `25`, thanks to that equals sign in the script line.

In JavaScript (and in most computer programming), a variable followed by an equal sign is an assignment. In this case, there are actually two. First, you assign `myNum = 10`, and then you assign `mySqr = getSquare (myNum)`. What you're telling the script is, "Set the variable `mySqr` equal to the value of the function `getSquare` when we send it the value `myNum`."

In JavaScript, the equal sign is used to assign values to variables. So when you type countNum = 12, it isn't a question. You've told the browser that the number 12 is now the value of the variable countNum. This is in contrast to a comparison, which is represented by two equal signs (==). You use the comparison when you want the script to decide whether or not two values are equal. You'll see more on variables and comparisons later in the section "Controlling Your JavaScript."

Function Call Example

Building on the function call and return process that we've discussed so far, let's take a look at a sample document that incorporates the entire script that's been used as an example in this section. Listing 17.2 shows the whole thing coming together.

LISTING 17.2 Function Call and Return

```
<!DOCTYPE html PUBLIC "-//W3C//DTD XHTML 1.0 Transitional//EN"
    "http://www.w3.org/TR/xhtml1/DTD/xhtml1-transitional.dtd">

<html xmlns="http://www.w3.org/1999/xhtml">
<head>
<title>Get Squared</title>
<meta http-equiv="Content-Script-Type" content="text/javascript">

<script type="text/javascript">
<!--hide scripting
function getSquare (num)
{
    squareNum = num * num;
    return (squareNum);
}
//end hiding -->
</script>
</head>

<body>
<h1>Here's the answer:</h1>
<script type="text/javascript">
<!--hide scripting
myNum = 10;
mySqr = getSquare (myNum);
document.writeln ("The square of " + myNum + " is " + mySqr + ".");
// end hiding -->
```

LISTING 17.2   (continued)

```
</script>

<noscript>
<p>Your browser doesn't appear to support JavaScript.</p>
</noscript>

</body>
</html>
```

As you can see, you can incorporate regular markup with the script's function call. After the processing, the variables all have values and the document.writeln() method is able to put the answer onscreen in the browser window, as shown in Figure 17.3.

FIGURE 17.3

This Web page's second line is the result of a function call and returned value.

Working with Variables

In your scripts, you'll work with two basic types of data: *literals* and *variables*. Literals are simply values that don't change, such as 5 or "Love hurts" or 6.02. These represent different types of values that you can use directly in the assignments and computations (both of which, together, are called *expressions* in programming) that make up your script.

You've already had a brief introduction to variables in JavaScript, but they're worth looking at a bit more closely. Variables in JavaScript are probably easier to work with than those in many other programming and scripting languages, because you don't need to be explicit about declaring the variables and setting them with a certain *type*. You'll find that there are four types of values that you can work with in JavaScript: integers, floating-point numbers, text strings, and Boolean values.

Integers are plain, non-decimal values such as 4, 17, and 2546. They can be positive or negative, such as -57. Floating-point numbers are those that include a decimal point, such as 3.2, 2456.24, and 1.45674e10 (which would be 14,567,400,000 using exponent notation). Boolean values simply mean true or false; you can use these values in certain comparisons within your script.

Strings are a special type of value that represents a series of characters that appear between quotation marks. These values can be words, sentences, data series, and even numbers. The difference between a string and an integer or floating-point is that strings can't be used in arithmetic. (They can be converted to numbers when necessary, however.) For instance, City = "Miami" and Zip = "33140" are both string assignments, because they are strings of characters in quotation marks.

Variable Names

There are rules and conventions for naming variables that you should consider following when you're creating your JavaScript code.

Variable names must start with either a letter or the underscore character. Otherwise, they can be composed of upper- and lowercase letters and the digits 0–9. Variable names are case-sensitive, so myVar and Myvar are two different variables.

So, how do you pick the names? Different script writers will take different approaches, but I recommend making your names as meaningful as possible. You can often do that by compressing words together to make variable names such as NewNum or TotalSales. You can also use an underscore to create variables like oct_sales or fish_count. Either is acceptable, although I'd recommend keeping your variable names reasonably short, because you're going to have to type them repeatedly.

It's also fairly common to use short, one-letter variables in certain situations, usually when you want a "toss-away" variable that's used for counting something. Throughout the examples in this section, you'll see cases where a simple variable letter is used. As long as it's a letter, and not a number or punctuation of some kind, it's legal.

Variables, Math, and Assignments

As you might guess, particularly if you have an experience with algebra, these variables are used in a lot of math. You can add (+), subtract (-), divide (/) or multiply (*) variables and literals, such as

```
myNum * 5
x + 1
12%5
```

In that third example, you get the remainder—2—after division between the two values takes place. In fact, you'll see this sort of math going on a lot in scripts and programming. However, you may have noticed something about those examples—they're pretty much useless. Again, as with algebra, math in scripting is really only handy when you assign the *result* to some variable:

```
newNum = myNum * 5;
x = x + 1;
```

These are assignments, and they're used to further the cause of the script. (They're also valid JavaScript expressions, which is why each one has a semicolon at the end.) Now that the new value is assigned to a variable, it can be used later in the script.

Variable assignments can be simpler, if desired:

```
myName = "Mike";
x = 4;
carColor = "light blue";
```

JavaScript also enables you to *declare* a variable without immediately assigning a value to it. This can be handy when you need to create a variable, but you don't want it to have a particular value yet:

```
var x;
var myVariable;
```

By the way, you're free to declare new variables as part of an assignment, too, as long as the variable hasn't already been created. So, the following is valid:

```
var mileageCount = 10000;
```

Incrementing and Decrementing Variables

As you've seen, math is pretty easy to accomplish in JavaScript. One of the most typical operations is to increment a particular variable, sometimes to count how many times something happens within a script. One way that's done has been shown already:

```
x = x + 1;
```

The plus sign in this equation is called a *binary* operator because it requires two items that can be added together. In this particular instance, the old value of x is added to 1, and the result becomes the new value of x. For instance:

```
var y = 5;
y = y + 1;
```

After the first line, the value of y is 5; after the second line, the value of y is now 6.

JavaScript allows you to do this particular operation in another way, using *unary* operators. A unary operator requires only one operand, as in the unary increment operator:

```
x++;
```

In fact, you can increment with either x++ or ++x. The difference is in when the increment occurs. For instance, if x equals 2:

```
y = x++;
```

y will be assigned the value 2, and then x will be incremented to 3. Consider the following example, though:

```
y = ++x;
```

x is incremented first, to 3, and then that value is assigned to y, so that they both now equal 3.

Decrementing (subtracting from) variables works the same way, with both x-- and --x as possibilities. Both work similarly to x = x - 1, except that --x will decrease before being assigned.

It is also possible to assign the value to variables at the same time you increment or decrement. Generally, you would do this with an expression like the following:

```
x = x + 3;
```

However, this is also possible with the unary operators += and -=. For instance, the preceding could be written as

```
x += 3;
```

If x was originally 5, it would now equal 8. Similarly, these two expressions yield the same result:

```
y = y - 2;
y -= 2;
```

Understanding Arrays

Before we leave this discussion of variables, there's another type of variable we should discuss. It's called the *array*, and it's actually a technique by which you can store more than one value within the same variable name. In other words, you can create a list of values within one variable. Here's an example:

```
var player = new Array ("Bob", "Steve", "Marcia", "Dinah");
```

Now, the player variable is actually an array, meaning it's storing those four values at once. So, how do you access one of those variables? Using an index number, as in

```
document.writeln ("The winner is " + player[2] + "!")
```

Arrays are indexed from 0, so in this example, player[2] would equal "Marcia" and that name would be used in the println method. You can use a special property, called length, to determine the number of items that are stored in an array:

numPlayers = player.length;

Note that, because the array index starts at zero, you can't simply use the number stored in the length property as the index. For instance, if there are 5 items in the list (and thus the length value is 5), the last item is index [4], because the first one has index [0]. So, you need to compensate for that in the script.

Once the array is created, you can use the index to add players, or you can use the index to change the value of a player using a standard assignment. This script sample shows a number of these array issues at once:

```
<script type="text/javascript">
<!--hide scripting
var player = new Array ("Bob", "Steve", "Marcia", "Dinah");
document.writeln ("<p>Player #3 is: " + player[2] +"<\/p>");
player[2] = "Roger";
player[4] = "Susan";
document.writeln ("<p>Player #3 is now: " + player[2] +"<\/p>");
var newIdx = (player.length - 1)
document.writeln ("<p>Our newest player is: " + player[newIdx] +"<\/p>");
// end script hiding -->
</script>
```

Figure 17.4 shows the results in a browser.

FIGURE 17.4

Here's a script that accesses different values stored in an array.

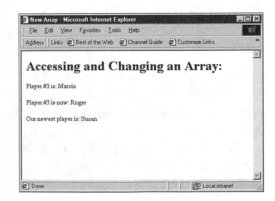

Controlling Your JavaScript

So far you've seen quite a few of the basic JavaScript programmer's tools, including variables, functions, assignments, and math. The next step is using those items together with some of JavaScript's built-in *statements* to create meaningful expressions that help you get things done in your scripts. This section discusses some of the statements you use to control the script.

If you have any experience with programming languages, JavaScript's statements should be familiar: the `if...else` construct and the loop statements `for`, `while`, `break`, and `continue`.

The key to many of these statements is called the *condition*, which is simply a bit of JavaScript code that needs to be evaluated before your script decides what to do next. You can think of a condition's logic as, "If something is true, then something else will happen." A similar condition might be, "Until something is true, continue trying to make it true." And so on.

Often, these conditions require a *comparison* of some kind—is one value equal to another, or is a value greater than another? That works together with the conditional to create a statement along the lines of, "If x is greater than y, then return the value of x."

So, before you look at JavaScript conditional statements, take a look at the comparison operators that JavaScript recognizes.

Comparison Operators

Comparisons are generally enclosed in parentheses, and they are always small snippets of code designed to evaluate as `true` or `false`. For instance, the following is a conditional statement:

```
(x == 1)
```

This may look like an assignment, but note carefully that there are two equal signs. That means this is a comparison to see if the two values really are equal to one another. If x does equal 1, this condition is `true`.

Now, believe it or not, an assignment can also have a value—it's always `true`. The following condition will always evaluate to `true`, because it's an assignment:

```
(errorLevel = 1)
```

Although it may seem to make sense to use an equal sign to create the "does x equal 1" comparison, if you don't use the proper operator, you'll accidentally change it to "set x equal to 1." That isn't what you want. In this instance, you actually need to use the comparison operator `==` for this condition.

Table 17.1 shows a listing of the comparison operators.

TABLE 17.1   Comparison Operators in JavaScript

Operator	Meaning	Example	Is True When
==	Equal to	x == y	x equals y
!=	Not equal to	x != y	x is not equal to y
>	Greater than	x > y	x is greater than y
<	Less than	x < y	x is less than y
>=	Greater than or equal to	x >= y	x is greater than or equals y
<=	Less than or equal to	x <= y	x is less than or equals y

All these operators can be used to create expressions that can be evaluated as either true or false. Some examples are

```
(countVar == 5)
(testAver > 85)
(itemType != "shirt")
```

As the examples show, comparisons can test strings as well as numerical values. When a comparison is evaluated, the actual comparison itself—the parentheses and all—is set to either true or false. It's given a value that could be assigned to a variable if necessary. Just remember to picture those parentheses as replaced by "true" or "false" when you're scripting and you'll have a good sense of how the comparisons are actually working.

The `if…else` Condition

So how do you put these comparisons and operators to use? JavaScript offers the if…else conditional statement as a way to create either/or situations in your script. Here's how it works:

```
if (condition) {
  script statements }
else {
  other statements }
```

The condition can be any comparison that evaluates to either true or false. The statements can be any valid JavaScript statements. For example:

```
if (x == 5) {
  document.writeln("The variable X equals 5.");
  return;
  }
  else {
  document.writeln("The variable X does not equal 5.")
  }
```

The else statement and related statements are not required if you simply want the if statements to be skipped and the rest of the function executed. An example might be

```
if (totalValue == 0) {
   return (0)
   }
```

In this case, if the condition is false (totalValue does not equal 0), the if statement is skipped completely and anything that comes after it is executed. If the condition is true, the return (0); command is executed and this particular function has ended abruptly.

Looping Conditionals

The next two conditional types are used to create loops—script constructs that repeat until a condition is met. These loop statements are for and while.

A for loop looks like this:

```
for (counter variable; condition; increment_counter variable) {
    JavaScript statements
    }
```

This is how it works:

1. You'll generally start a for loop by initializing your *counter* variable.
2. Then, you'll evaluate the counter within a condition to see if it's reached a certain level.
3. If it hasn't, the loop will perform the enclosed statements.
4. Once the statements have been performed, the counter variable is incremented.
5. If the counter has reached your predetermined value, the for loop ends. If not, the loop continues with step 2.

For example:

```
for (x=0; x<10; x=x+1) {
   totalNum = 2 * x;
   document.writeln ("Two times " + x + " equals " + totalNum + "<br
➥\ />");
   }
```

You start by initializing a counter variable (x=0) and then evaluating the counter in a conditional statement (x<10). If the condition is true, the loop will perform the enclosed scripting. Then it will increment the counter—in this case, add 1 to it. The loop begins again and the new value of x is compared to 10; when the counter reaches 10, the loop ends.

The while loop is similar to the for loop, except that it offers a little more freedom. It's used for a great variety of conditions. The basic while loop looks like

```
while (condition) {
  JavaScript statements
  }
```

As long as the condition evaluates to true, the loop will continue. An example would be the following:

```
x = 0;
while (x <= 5) {
   x = x + 1;
   document.write (X now equals " + x + "<br \/>")
   }
```

As long as the condition remains true, the while statement will continue to loop. In fact, the risk with while statements is that they can become *infinite loops* if the expression never evaluates to false. Here's a common mistake:

```
while (x = 5) {
  x = x + 1;
  document.write (X now equals " + x + "<br \/>")
  }
```

The condition is actually an assignment, not a comparison, so it will always evaluate to true. In this example, the loop would continue indefinitely, and the output would always be X now equals 6.

Break and Continue Your Loops

Two other keywords, break and continue, can be used in for and while loops to change the way a loop operates when certain conditions occur.

break is ideally used when you're not sure which values are coming—for instance, when the values are being input by a user, via XHTML form elements. Consider a bit of script like this:

```
for (x=0; x < 10; x=x+1) {
    z = getInput ();
    if (z == x)
       break;
    }
```

In this case, a function called `getInput()` is being called. Assuming that function asks the user for a number and that number is assigned to `z`, the break occurs if the values of `z` and `x` happen to be the same. Otherwise, the `for` loop continues until `x` reaches `10`.

The `continue` statement is used within a loop to skip a particular increment. For instance:

```
<script>
var x = 0
while (x < 10) {
    x = x + 1;
    if (x == 5) continue;
    document.writeln (x + " does not equal 5. <br \/>");
    }
</script>
```

In this case, when the condition `(x == 5)` evaluates to true, the `continue` statement will cause the loop to move directly back to the `while` statement, thus skipping over the last line that writes out the statement. When the condition is `false`, as it will be most of the time, the last line will execute, resulting in another line of XHTML text and markup.

Loops and Arrays

Although there are plenty of reasons to use loops in your scripting, one reason that may not have jumped out at you yet is working with arrays. It turns out that loops and arrays are natural helpmates. Loops are great at counting from one number to the next, and arrays store multiple values using a numerical index.

Let's consider the example of a `while` loop designed to extract values from an array:

```
<script type="text/javascript">
<!-- Hide scripting
student = new Array("Bill", "Wendy", "Susan", "Barry", "Olga", "Narice");
numStudents = (student.length);
document.writeln ("There are " + numStudents + " students in the class <br
➥\/>");
var x = 0;
while (x < numStudents) {
    document.writeln ("Student #" + (x+1) + ": " + student[x] + "<br \/>");
    x++;
}
// end hiding -->
</script>
```

Because of the funny way arrays work, we need to do a little math with the x variable. It's used to count through the `while` loop, as well as to fill in with the student number and as the index for the array. Because `student #1` equals `index [0]`, we need to change the student number to `(x+1)`. Otherwise, everything else hums along swimmingly, as you can see in Figure 17.5.

FIGURE 17.5

Loops make a lot of sense when you need to work with arrays.

Understanding JavaScript Objects

So far in this chapter, you've been introduced quickly to creating scripts that perform logical computing tasks using JavaScript. In this last section, we'll be focusing on JavaScript's use of *objects* or collections of properties.

JavaScript, as with many other modern-day computer languages, is *object-oriented*. This means you can create these special named collections of properties that include variables and special built-in functions, called *methods*. You'll find that these objects can make working with chunks of data quite a bit easier.

In more practical terms, an object is a named container of sorts. In most cases, you create an object with a special function, in a way that's similar to creating an array. You can then refer to the object using special notation that enables you to dig into the object and access certain variables or methods. You've already seen a few instances of this, such as

```
document.writeln()
```

This command is actually a call to the `writeln()` method that is part of the `document` object. As you'll see in Chapter 19, an HTML document is actually one large object with many different variables that you can access and change. Changing aspects of the document is one of the really cool things that JavaScript enables you to do.

You can also create your own objects and use them to store values. As an example, consider an object called home01. This particular object is designed to store information about a real estate listing, so it might have the following variables as part of it:

```
home01.price = 125000
home01.sqfoot = 2300
home01.beds = 3
home01.baths = 2
home01.base = true
home01.descrip = "Great location, good schools."
```

What's happened here is simple—values have been assigned to variables that all happen to be associated with one another, because they're all properties of the home01 object. Because they're all part of a single object, you can use the object for such things as function calls:

```
<script>
showListing (home01);
</script>
```

And then you can use the pointer to that object to access each of the individual variables:

```
<script>
function showListing (home) {
    document.writeln ("Home Price = " + home.price + "<br \/>">);
    document.writeln ("Square Footage = " + home.sqfoot + "<br \/>");
    document.writeln ("Beds/Baths = " + home.beds + "/" + home.baths + "<br
➥\/>");
    document.writeln ("Description = " + home.descrip + "<br \/>");
    return;
    }
</script>
```

Of course, for this example to work correctly, you'd need to actually create the object home01, which I haven't gotten around to telling you how to do yet. Let's look at how that's done before moving on.

Creating New Objects

Creating objects is done in two steps. First, you need to create a template for the object, which is done using a function declaration. Then, you need to create an instance of a particular object so that you can begin to work with it.

For instance, to create the template for your `home` object, you need to create a function:

```
function home(price, sqfoot, beds, baths, base, descrip) {
   this.price = price;
   this.sqfoot = sqfoot;
   this.beds = beds;
   this.baths = baths;
   this.base = base;
   this.descrip = descrip;
   }
```

Notice the use of the word `this`. In JavaScript, `this` is a special keyword that's used to refer to the current object. It's used throughout object manipulation, particularly with forms, as you'll see in Chapter 18.

Meanwhile, note also that the object will be created, based on the function template, using the `new` keyword. Using `new` is the second step in creating your new object. The following is an example:

```
home01 = new home(125000, 2300, 3, 2, true, "Great location, good
➥schools.");
```

The `new` keyword creates a new object. It also tells the object-creating `home` function that the price of this new object will be 125000, and so on. When the `home` function is called, `home01` will replace `this` and the assignment will work like this:

```
home01.price = 125000
home01.sqfoot = 2300
home01.beds = 3
home01.baths = 2
home01.base = true
home01.descrip = "Great location, good schools."
```

Of course, you won't see any of this happen. But, it's now possible for you to access this data just like a regular object:

```
document.writeln ("This house is priced at: $" + home01.price);
```

What if you only want to create one object? If that's the case, you don't need a template. Instead, you can simply use an assignment to create the object:

```
myhouse = {price:125000, sqfoot:2300, beds:3, baths:2,

base:true, descrip:"Great location, good schools."}
```

And while you're working with individual objects, you're free to add properties to an object at any time. For instance:

```
home01.location = "midtown"
```

This is perfectly okay. It won't affect any other objects that have been created, even if those objects used the same function template that this one did.

More on Methods

Just as an object's properties are simply variables that are associated with that object, methods are basically functions associated with objects. For instance, one of the methods you've used quite a bit is document.writeln(), which is really just a function provided by JavaScript that allows you to write XHTML marked-up text to the current document object.

Notice that writeln() is the function, and document is the associated object. JavaScript-compatible browsers define certain basic objects, like document, so it's easier to access them and change their properties.

You can even create your own methods by simply assigning a function name to an object variable:

```
object.methodname = function_name
```

Or, in an object definition function, you can create a method like this:

```
function showListing () {
    document.writeln ("Home Price = " + this.price + "<br \/>">);
    document.writeln ("Square Footage = " + this.sqfoot + "<br \/>");
    document.writeln ("Beds/Baths = " + this.beds + "/" + this.baths + "<br
➡\/>");
    document.writeln ("Description = " + this.descrip + "<br \/>");
    return;
    }


function home(price, sqfoot, beds, baths, base, descrip) {
    this.price = price;
    this.sqfoot = sqfoot;
    this.beds = beds;
    this.baths = baths;
    this.base = base;
    this.descrip = descrip;
    this.showListing = showListing;
    }
```

Then, for instance, if you've defined an object named `home01`, calling the method `home01.showListing()` would cause the `showListing` function to execute, using `home01` in the place of the `this` keyword in the function.

> Note that you need to include the parentheses when you're calling methods, even if you don't have data to pass to that method. If that's the case, just opened and closed parentheses "()" are appropriate.

Built-In Objects

When you're authoring scripts, there are a number of things you're likely to do over and over again. JavaScript includes some of these often-used calls in the language itself, instead of forcing you to write your own functions and create your own objects. The built-in objects tend to store useful values or offer convenient methods. The functions usually perform some fairly intensive calculating that you'll often need to use.

You'll learn about three major built-in objects available for you in JavaScript:

- The first is the String object, which helps you manipulate your strings.

- The Math object holds certain constant values for you to use in your script and methods, making it a little easier to perform some mathematical functions.

- The Date object can be used to get the current date or to create a date object for any date or time in the past or future.

> These are only a few of the built-in objects, shown here because they're often used and they're representative of the other objects. For more on built-in objects, see the Objects chapter of the JavaScript reference at `http://developer.netscape.com/docs/manuals/js/client/jsguide/obj.htm`.

The String Object

The String object is interesting if only because you don't actually have to use the notation `string.property` to use it. In fact, any string you create is a String object. You can create a string as simple as this:

```
mystring = "Here's a string"
```

The string variable `mystring` can now be treated as a String object. For instance, to get a value for the length of a String object, you can use the following assignment:

```
stringlen = mystring.length
```

When you create a string, and JavaScript makes it a String object, the value of its length is stored in the property length. (Note also that, because length is a property and not a method, you don't need the parentheses.) It also associates certain methods with the object, like toUpperCase(). You could change a string to all uppercase letters with the following line:

mystring = mystring.toUpperCase()

If the string had the value "Here is a string", this assignment would change it to "HERE IS A STRING". Table 17.2 shows some of the other methods available with string objects.

TABLE 17.2 Methods for Strings in JavaScript

Method	What It Does	Example
anchor	Creates a target anchor	mystring.anchor(*section_name*)
big	Displays string as big text	mystring.big()
blink	Displays string as blinking text	mystring.blink()
bold	Displays string as bold text	mystring.bold()
charAt	Selects an individual character	mystring.charAt(2)
fixed	Displays string in teletype font	mystring.fixed()
fontcolor	Displays string in color	mystring.fontcolor("red")
fontsize	Displays string in new font size	mystring.fontsize(2)
indexOf	Finds index # of a letter	mystring.indexOf("w")
italics	Displays string as italic	mystring.italics()
lastIndexOf	Finds last occurrence of letter	mystring.lastIndexOf("w")
link	Creates a link from the string	mystring.link()
small	Displays string as small text	mystring.small()
strike	Displays string as strikethrough text	mystring.strike()
sub	Displays string as a subscript	mystring.sub()
substring	Selects part of the string	mystring.substring(0,7)
sup	Displays string as a superscript	mystring.sup()
toLowerCase	Displays string as lowercase	mystring.toLowerCase()
toUpperCase	Displays string as uppercase	mystring.toUpperCase()

You'll notice that the table often says that the string is displayed as *something*, because the methods don't actually change the original value of the string. Instead, they return a value that's appropriate to their functions. That is, the small() method returns the string as small text, while the `toUpperCase()` method returns the string as uppercase text. So, the following example doesn't really accomplish anything because the `small()` method doesn't change the original string:

```
<script type="text/javascript">
<!-- hide scripting
var testString = "Testing 1, 2, 3";
document.writeln (testString + "<br\/>");
testString.small()
document.writeln (testString + "<br\/>");
// end hiding -->
</script>
```

A better way to do this would be as follows:

```
<script type="text/javascript">
<!-- hide scripting
var testString = "Testing 1, 2, 3";
document.writeln (testString + "<br\/>");
var smallString = testString.small()
document.writeln (smallString + "<br\/>");
// end hiding -->
</script>
```

Now, with the returned value assigned to a new variable, you'll find yourself with something a bit more useful.

So what are these methods doing? For instance, the following two script lines would have the same results:

```
document.write("<big>" + mystring + "</big>");
document.write(mystring.big());
```

Some of the other tags need explaining—especially those that deal with indexes. Every string is *indexed* from left to right, starting with the value 0. So, in the following string (which has been assigned to the variable `howdystring`), the characters are indexed according to the numbers that appear under them:

```
Howdy, you
0123456789
```

In this case, using the method `howdystring.charAt(4)` would return the value y. You could also use the method `howdystring.indexOf("y")`, which would return the value 4. Notice that there are two instances of y, however. Using `howdystring.lastIndexOf("y")`, you could find out that the index of that second y (as it's also the last one in the string) is 7.

The `Math` Object

The `Math` object just holds some useful constants and methods for use in mathematical calculations. Its properties are mathematical constants like *e*, *Pi*, and *log10e* (logarithm, base 10, of *e*). You can use these by simply adding the name as the `Math` property, as in the following example:

```
var pi_value = Math.PI;
area = Math.PI*(r*r);
```

Table 17.3 shows you the various properties for the `Math` object.

TABLE 17.3   Properties for the `Math` Object

Property	Value
PI	Pi (approximately 3.1416)
E	e, Euler's constant (approximately 2.718)
LN2	Natural log of 2 (approximately 0.693)
LN10	Natural log of 10 (approximately 2.302)
LOG10E	Base 10 log of e (approximately 0.434)
SQRT1_2	Square root of 1/2 (approximately 0.707)
SQRT2	Square root of 2 (approximately 1.414)

Of course, the properties are simply values that are conveniently stored within the `Math` object. Along with those properties, the `Math` object offers methods that you can use for a variety of mathematical hoop-jumping. The `Math` object's methods are called like any other methods. For instance, the *arc sine* of a variable can be found by using the following:

```
Math.asin(your_num);
```

Table 17.4 shows the methods for the `Math` object.

TABLE 17.4   Methods for the Math Object

Method	Result	Format
abs	Absolute value	Math.abs(*number*)
acos	Arc cosine (in radians)	Math.acos(*number*)
asin	Arc sine (in radians)	Math.asin(*number*)
atan	Arc tangent (in rads)	Math.atan(*number*)
cos	Cosine	Math.cos(*num_radians*)
sin	Sine	Math.sin(*num_radians*)

TABLE 17.4 (continued)

Method	Result	Format
tan	Tangent	Math.tan(*num_radians*)
ceil	Least integer >= num	Math.ceil(*number*)
floor	Greatest int <= number	Math.floor(*number*)
exp	e to power of number	Math.exp(*number*)
log	Natural log of number	Math.log(*number*)
pow	Base to exponent power	Math.pow(*base, exponent*)
max	Greater of two numbers	Math.max(*num, num*)
min	Lesser of two numbers	Math.min(*num, num*)
round	Round to nearest integer	Math.round(*number*)
sqrt	Square root of number	Math.sqrt(*number*)

These methods should come in pretty handy in creating the functions for your scripts, especially if you'd like to do some serious scientific or mathematic calculations on your Web pages. That is to say, if you know more about math than I do.

The Date Object

Finally, let's quickly look at another object you may have reason to use in your JavaScript—the Date object. You can use the Date object to set the current date, perform math between different dates, and so on.

To use the Date object, you'll need to create a particular instance of that object:

```
todayDate = new Date();
```

If you create a Date object that doesn't include anything in the parentheses, it uses the current date and time, in this format:

Day Mon Date HH:MM:SS ZNE Year

Here's an example:

```
Thu Nov 29 13:57:46 CST 2001
```

You can use methods for the Date object to extract different portions of the date, such as todayDate.getDay(), or todayDay.getDate() and todayDate.getHours(). If you'd like to place the current date and time in your page, for instance, the following would do that:

```
<script type="text/javascript">
<!-- begin hiding
var todayDate = new Date();
```

```
document.writeln ("Today is: " + " " + todayDate.getMonth() +
"/" + todayDate.getDate() + "/" + todayDate.getYear() + "<br>");
document.writeln ("The time is: " + todayDate.getHours() + ":" +
todayDate.getMinutes() + "<br>");
// end hiding -->
</script>
```

The results would look something like this:

```
Today is: 10/5/2002
The time is: 14:31
```

Summary

In this chapter, you learned quite a bit about the basics of JavaScript, beginning with how to add scripting elements to your pages, how to hide them from incompatible browsers, and how to create comments within the script. You then saw a brief "Hello World" example, which showed you a working JavaScript.

From there, you were introduced to functions, how they're declared, and how they're called from the body of the script. Then you learned about variables, how they're created, how values are assigned to them, and some special ways in which they can be incremented and decremented. In that same section, you were introduced to arrays.

After variables came comparisons, including a look at many of the comparison operators and how they differ from mathematical operators. In that section, you also learned about the comparisons that can be done and how they're used together with the conditionals and loops to control the flow of a JavaScript.

Finally, you learned about objects within JavaScript, including how to define objects and how to create and use methods. The chapter ended with an overview of three important built-in objects: the String object, the Math object, and the Date object. You can use all this knowledge in Chapters 18 and 19 as you create more advanced scripts and solutions with JavaScript.

JAVASCRIPT AND USER INPUT

*I*n this chapter, we'll focus on some tasks you can accomplish with JavaScript. You'll see the different ways that you can handle events that occur when people use your HTML documents and how you can react to those events with scripted responses.

After that, you'll see how to react to data that's been entered into HTML forms, calculate values based on that data, and return values to the user. You'll also see how to use JavaScript with full-fledged HTML forms to check for errors or trouble with input before those forms are submitted to CGI processing scripts.

Finally, we'll look at some other JavaScript automation possibilities, including automatic page redirection, launching new pages with JavaScript, and working with an HTML frames interface using a JavaScript control.

This chapter discusses the following:

- What events are and how they are handled
- Using object pointers and accessing objects
- Using JavaScript and HTML forms for interaction with the user
- Using JavaScript to check HTML form data for errors
- Automating the browser to redirect pages, create special links, and manage HTML frames

Understanding JavaScript Events

In Chapter 17, you saw numerous references to event handling. One of JavaScript's main functions is to react to what the user does on the page, whether that's selecting buttons, clicking hyperlinks, or even hovering over items with the mouse. Anything that the user does is considered an event, as is anything that happens automatically or that occurs within the browser. For instance, when a page loads, that's an event. When the page is unloaded so that another page can appear, that's an event, too.

To deal with these events, you'll need to add *event handlers* to certain XHTML elements. You'll follow this general format:

```
<element event_handler="JavaScript code or function call"> </element>
```

Most `<form>` elements, hyperlinks, and some other elements can accept the various event handler attributes. For instance, a few of the event handlers are designed specifically to work with the `<body>` element, so that things can happen automatically when the page is first loaded into a browser window.

The `<form>` elements are where you'll see a lot of event handlers, however. Take the following example, which enables you to use a form button not to submit the form to a CGI script, but rather to submit the entry to a JavaScript function:

```
<h1>Computing the Entry:</h1>
<form>
Enter a number: <input type="text" name="userEntry" size="5" /> <br />
Here's the result: <input type="text" name="result" size="5" /> <br />
<input type="button" value="Calc" onclick="result.value =
➥compute(userEntry)">
</form>
```

In this snippet of code, the user is asked to enter a number in the top form element (a text entry box) and then click the Calc button. When that button is clicked, an event handler, called `onClick`, is invoked. That event handler calls a function, called `compute`, and sends a pointer to the `<input>` object named `userEntry` so the function can find that data and use it for the calculation. Then, when the function returns a value, it's assigned to the variable `result`, and that result appears in the second entry box, which happens to be named `result`. You can see how all this looks in Figure 18.1. (Note that the function isn't shown in the preceding sample, but it simply adds 100 to the number.)

FIGURE 18.1

Using event handlers and form elements, JavaScript can return values without worrying about CGI scripts.

Types of Event Handlers

Sometimes called *intrinsic events* to suggest that they're scripting attributes without the formal requirement of the `<script>` element, these event handlers are focused on form elements. However, they can be used for a number of other elements on the page that a user might interact with. Some events are used exclusively with certain elements, while others can be used with a wide range of elements. You'll see both types in Table 18.1.

TABLE 18.1 Event Handlers and Their Purposes

Event Handler	The Event Is Triggered When...
onfocus	The user enters a form element (`<input>`, `<select>`, `<textarea>`, and `<button>`) or other input element (`<a>`, `<label>`) using the mouse or keyboard.
onblur	The user leaves a form element, hyperlink, or other input element (same elements as for onfocus), either by using the mouse or pressing a key.
onclick	The user clicks an element.
ondblclick	The user double-clicks an element.
onchange	The user changes a value and leaves a form element (used with `<input>`, `<select>`, and `<textarea>` only).
onkeypress	The user presses a key while an element has the focus.
onkeydown	The user holds a key down while an element has the focus.
onkeyup	The user releases a key while an element has the focus.
onload	The page loads (used with `<body>` or `<frameset>`).
onunload	The page is exited (`<body` or `<frameset>`).
onmouseover	The user points the mouse at an element.

TABLE 18.1 (continued)

Event Handler	The Event Is Triggered When...
onmousedown	The user holds the mouse button down while pointing at an element.
onmouseup	The user releases the mouse button while pointing at an element.
onmousemove	The user moves the mouse while it's over an element.
onmouseout	The user moves the mouse pointer away from an element that it had been pointing to.
onselect	The user selects either an `<input>` or `<textarea>` form input field.
onreset	The user resets a form (works only with the `<form>` element).
onsubmit	The user submits a form (works only with the `<form>` element).

Creating an event handler is simply a question of adding one of these handlers as an attribute to the element that will be the focus. Then, inside the handler's quotation marks, you either include scripting code or a function call. Here's an example that calls a built-in function:

```
<body onunload="alert('Thanks for visiting!')">
```

Incidentally, this example is the major reason that JavaScript will allow you to use either single or double quotes in your scripting, as long as you're consistent. If you used double quotes in this `alert` function (the function is being passed a string value), the `onunload` handler's quotes will be closed early, thus creating an invalid handler.

As noted, one way to respond to a user's input is through an alert box, which is similar to a dialog box except that it has only one button for a response. An alert box communicates directly with the user, often blocking the main document window until it's dismissed.

Tip

The newline character, \n, allows you to add a hard return in the middle of a text string used to create an alert box.

Aside from using built-in functions, such as `alert()`, you could call your own function from within the handler:

```
<input type="text" name="phoneNumber" onchange="checkPhone (this.value)"
 />
```

In this example, the `checkPhone()` function is called and passed the value of the `<input>` text entry box named `phoneNumber`. It does this by sending a *pointer* to that value, using the `this` keyword, which is discussed in the next section.

The `this` Keyword

The `this` keyword is probably one of the odder ducks you'll encounter while trying to learn JavaScript. What it does, in essence, is stand in for the current object that has focus relative to the handler. Here's an example like the one discussed in the previous section:

```
<form name="myForm">
<input type="text" name="phoneNumber" onchange="checkPhone (this.value)"
➥/>
</form>
```

`this` is used to suggest "this input element," and `value` is a property that stores the value associated with this form element. You could also access that same value as the following in order to pass along the value:

```
<form name="myForm">
<input type="text" name="phoneNumber"
onchange="checkPhone (document.myForm.phoneNumber.value)" />
</form>
```

Note that the name of the form and the name of the `<input>` element are both vital in getting at the correct value. That's one reason for the `this` keyword; another is simple convenience.

Introducing the Document Object Model

The `this` keyword is also an insidious harbinger of a concept that you must grasp before you get too deep into forms—the Document Object Model (DOM). The DOM extends the concept of objects—which you learned about in Chapter 17—until it covers the documents that you're creating in XHTML and working with in JavaScript. In other words, it makes the document itself into objects, which you can then use for JavaScript.

You've just seen an example of the DOM in action. In the most recent example, you saw the following as the event handler for an `<input>` element:

```
onchange="checkPhone (document.myForm.phoneNumber.value)"
```

That series of references inside the function call—`document.myForm.phoneNumber.value`—is a reference to the DOM. Beginning with the first object name, `document`, you then work through a number of objects that have been created in the course of the XHTML authoring for this page. First is the `myForm` object, which holds all the different elements' named objects; then the `phoneNumber` object, which stores a number of properties for that particular `<input>` element; and finally the `value` property of `phoneNumber`, where the number entered by the user is stored.

It turns out that the DOM also enables you to work with a set of properties between a function call and a function without actually passing any values between the two. Listing 18.1 is an example of this—notice that neither the function nor the function call requires any parameters. That's because the form data is stored in the DOM, which can be accessed using the correct object syntax.

LISTING 18.1   Working Directly with Your Document's Object Properties

```
<!DOCTYPE html PUBLIC "-//W3C//DTD XHTML 1.0 Transitional//EN"
    "http://www.w3.org/TR/xhtml1/DTD/xhtml1-transitional.dtd">

<html xmlns="http://www.w3.org/1999/xhtml">
<head>
<title>Passing the Pointer</title>
<meta http-equiv="Content-Script-Type" content="text/javascript">
<script>
<!-- Begin hiding
function compute()
{
    var myNum = document.myForm.userEntry.value;
    myNum = eval(myNum)
    var myResult = myNum + 100;
    document.myForm.result.value = myResult;
    return;
}
// End hiding -->
</script>
</head>

<body>
<h1>Computing Form Data:</h1>

<form name="myForm">
Enter a number: <input type="text" name="userEntry" size="5" /> <br />
Here's the result: <input type="text" name="result" size="5" /> <br />
<input type="button" name="Calc" value="Calc" onclick="compute()" />
</form>

</body>
</html>
```

Here's how this works:

1. The user enters a number in the userEntry text box.

2. Then, when the user clicks the Calc button, the `compute()` function is invoked.

3. The function looks up the value of that user entry and assigns it to `myNum`. Next, it accesses a built-in function, `eval()`, which evaluates that entry into a number. (Otherwise, it would think the value is text, even though we asked for a number.)

4. Some arithmetic happens and the answer is assigned to `myResult`.

5. `myResult` is assigned to the `value` property for the `result` entry box that's down in the form. The answer automatically appears in the `result` entry box, and hence is made visible to the user. (This is the same example you saw back in Figure 18.1.)

One thing to watch out for when you're working on this sort of script is when to use the `value` property and when to ignore it. In most cases, if you're trying to assign something to a particular element with a form, you'll need to use the value property. That's because the named element—say, `userInput`—has more than just a value associated with it. It also has a `type` property, for instance, which was set in the original `<input>` element. So, you can't just use `document.form.userInput = x;` because `userInput` is an object, not a property.

Note

The DOM has only recently been standardized by the W3C, and Internet Explorer, Netscape, and other browsers have varying implementations of it. Throughout this chapter and the next, I'll try to touch on only cross-platform DOM issues (those that work in both browsers). Chapter 19, "Adding Dynamic HTML," will offer some platform-specific discussion of other DHTML issues, though.

Understanding Scope and Pointers

One of the issues that can be something of a pain with the DOM is constantly referring to items by their full DOM paths. In general, you need to start at the highest object and move through them, with a period between each one, to get down to a particular property or method. In fact, we've already been using a shortcut. The highest-level object is actually `window`, so most of our references in the previous section could have looked like this (or something similar):

```
window.document.form.userInput.value
```

As it turns out, though, these paths have something called a *scope*, which means you can use a shorthand within certain boundaries. Because our scripts aren't affecting any other windows at this stage, we can start with the document object because the current window is assumed.

Along with scope comes another interesting concept, called the *pointer*. In essence, a pointer is a variable that holds the location of an object. This allows us to cut down the amount of typing we do by assigning a variable to a particular object's path:

```
function compute()
{
    var theForm = document.myForm;
    var Num = theForm.userEntry.value;
    Num = eval(Num)
    var Result = Num + 100;
    theForm.result.value = Result;
    return;
}
```

With this simple change to Listing 18.1, we're able to substitute theForm for document.myForm in each of the object references, which makes life just a little bit easier.

These assignments don't have to happen up top, either. Instead, you could create the pointer in the transaction between the function call and the function. First, consider the function call:

```
<form name="myForm">
...other elements...
<input type="button" name="Calc" value="Calc" onclick="compute(myForm)" />
</form>
```

Notice that this is a little different from Listing 18.1, because now you're going to pass the name of the current form to the function. Because of scoping, you don't have to use the entire DOM path to myForm—because you're in myForm, you can go ahead and simply use myForm in the function call. Now you have to rewrite the function to accept the value and create a pointer:

```
function compute(theForm)
{
    var Num = theForm.userEntry.value;
    Num = eval(Num)
    var Result = Num + 100;
    theForm.result.value = Result;
    return;
}
```

Creating the pointer isn't tough at all. All you have to do is give the pointer a name in the parentheses following the function name and you're set. When the function is called, the pointer is created and it's assigned the location of the form. Now, when you access objects and values using that pointer, you can work with them just as if you were using the entire DOM path.

Working with High-Level Objects

So far what we've dealt with are form objects, and we'll get back to those later in this chapter. In the meantime, however, you may be interested to see some of the other DOM objects that you can use in your scripting. In particular, let's take a look at the `window` object, the `location` object, and the `document` object.

The `window` Object

The `window` object is something you're already familiar with, even if you don't know it. One familiar method of the window object is the `alert()` method, which you've seen in sample scripts up until now. The full reference to that method is `window.alert()`, but unless you're trying to open an alert for another window, scoping allows you to drop the full reference. What `alert()` does is pop up a dialog box that must be dismissed—by clicking the OK button—before anything else can happen in that window. A string in the parentheses determines what text will appear in the alert dialog box.

As with any other object, the `window` object has both properties and methods. For the most part, the properties can only be read—you can't change many of them, because the window already exists. Those properties include `name` (in the title bar), `length` (number of frames in the window), `self` (which points to the current window), and `status`. This last one can actually be used to change the Web browser's status line, which is the little description line at the bottom of the window. Here's an example:

```
<a href="products.html" onmouseover="status='See our full line of
products'" onmouseout="status=''">Products</a>
```

The `window` object offers a number of methods that you can use to change things about the window. These include both `alert()` and the `eval()` methods, which you've been introduced to. The `eval()` method, which we used to turn a string into a number, can actually be used to turn any string into JavaScript code, not just into a number.

Other methods that you can use with the window include `confirm()`, which, like `alert()`, pops up a dialog box with the enclosed string as its message. Instead of just an OK button, however, the user can also choose a Cancel button. If Cancel is clicked, a value of `false` is returned; if OK is clicked, `true` is returned. For example:

```
var keepGoing = confirm("Do you want to continue?");
```

The `prompt()` method is also similar to `alert()` and `confirm()`, but it's used to receive a value from the user. You can include both a string for the dialog box text and an optional sample value:

```
var numberGuess = prompt("Enter a number", 5);
var emailAddress = prompt("Enter your e-mail address",
➥"myadd@fakecorp.com");
```

The `open()` method can be used to open a new window, and you can include parameters to govern how that window is opened and what URL it displays. To open a window and display a particular URL, simply use `window.open("URL")`.

The `resizeTo()` method is a fun one—you can automatically resize a browser window to a particular width and height in pixels. For instance, if your site is best viewed in 800×600, you might opt for a line such as this:

```
<body onload="window.resizeTo(800,600)">
```

Along with those properties and methods, the window object has a number of sub-objects, such as `location`, `document`, and `history`. The first two have their own sections coming up, but `history` is worth looking at here. You can use the `history` object to access different URLs stored in the browser's history (the pages that have been visited recently). Properties for history include `current`, `previous`, and `next`, which can be used to get the URLs of recently visited pages. The `length` property can be used to determine the number of URLs that are stored in the history, and then the `history.go(x)` method can be used to go to a particular entry, where `x` is the number of entries to go backward in the history. (To go forward, make `x` a negative number.) Other methods include `back()` and `forward()`, as in the following:

```
<a href="" onclick="history.back()">Go back</a>
```

The `location` Object

As mentioned, the `location` object is actually part of the `window` object, so it's technically referenced using `window.location`. In practice, scoping generally enables you to leave off the `window` and just use `location`, as in `location.href`.

You can access a number of different properties of the `location` object, all of which are designed to help you learn different portions of the URL of the current page. For instance, `location.href` is used to display the entire URL of the current page:

```
document.write("The current URL is: " + location.href);
```

The rest of location's properties hold portions of the page's URL that can be accessed separately. They include the following:

href	Holds the full URL
protocol	Stores the protocol, as in http:
hostname	Stores the name of the computer that is hosting the current document, as in www.fakecorp.com
port	Stores the port number, if relevant
pathname	Stores the path statement, including the directories, the subdirectories, and the name of the current document

You can use this information for something as simple as a command to place the current URL on every page, perhaps near the top or the bottom of the page. For instance:

```
document.writeln("This page's URL is: " + location.href);
```

You can also cause a new page to load in the browser window with a command such as this:

```
location.href = "http://www.fakecorp.com/newpage.html";
```

The document Object

The document object is another child of the window object, but it's a child that's all grown up. This one is really the main object you'll be dealing with when it comes to JavaScript, and particularly HTML forms. That's not to say other objects aren't accessible, but the document object is where all the other objects and elements on your page are stored. So it's through the document object that you'll access and alter those elements.

The document object's properties include

domain	Stores the domain at which this document is located (as in www.fakecorp.com)
URL	Stores the URL to the current document
referrer	Can be used to determine the URL of the page from which this page was linked (the page that *referred* the user to this page)
lastModified	Stores the date when the document was last changed
title	Stores the title of the document (as defined between the <title> tags)

`anchors`	This is an array, which stores each of the anchors in the document that has a name associated with it
`images`	Another array that stores all the images on the page
`forms`	Yet another array, designed to make different forms on the page accessible

Most of these are fairly self-explanatory. The last few arrays can be accessed using the same approach to arrays that was discussed in Chapter 17. For instance, to find out the URL to the first image on the page, you could use this:

```
alert(document.images[0].src);
```

You could also set that image to a new URL, which would actually substitute the image on the page. This is something we'll look into more in Chapter 19, as it's considered a "dynamic HTML" trick:

```
document.images[0].src = "images/new.gif"
```

The `document` object includes a few methods with which you are already familiar, such as `document.writeln()`, which is used to write a line of text and markup to the page. Similarly, `document.write()` can also be used for this purpose—the only difference is that `writeln()` includes a hard return at the end of each line. (Generally that isn't important in XHTML markup, unless the return occurs inside a `<pre>` element or inside some other element definitions.)

Another method enables you to clear out the current markup first, and then write to the page. It's the `document.open()` method, which clears the page. Follow it with `document.write()` or `document.writeln()` methods and the `document.close()` method, and you've got a new page, as shown in Listing 18.2.

LISTING 18.2   Using a Form Value for Personalization

```
<!DOCTYPE html PUBLIC "-//W3C//DTD XHTML 1.0 Transitional//EN"
    "http://www.w3.org/TR/xhtml1/DTD/xhtml1-transitional.dtd">

<html xmlns="http://www.w3.org/1999/xhtml">

<head>
<title>Personalization Page</title>
<script type="text/javascript">
<!-- Begin hiding
function personalizePage ()
{
var userName = personalForm.myName.value;
```

LISTING 18.2   (continued)

```
document.open()
document.write("<html><head><title>New Document</title></head>")
document.write("<body><h1>Welcome, " + userName + "</h1>")
document.write("<p>This page has been customized for your personal enjoyment.</p>")
document.write("</body></html>")
document.close()
}
// End hiding -->
</script>
</head>

<body>
<h1>Personalize the Page</h1>
<p>Enter your name, then click the Personalize button. The content of the
page will change.<br /> Note that the URL will not change, only this page's
content.</p>

<form name="personalForm">
Enter your name: <input type="text" name="myName"> <input type="button"
name="personalButton" value="Personalize " onclick="personalizePage()">
</form>
</body>
</html>
```

Note that this example not only demonstrates the `document.open()` method, but it also demonstrates that you're not actually changing documents. The statement `var userName = personalForm.myName.value;` shows that the document is still the ultimate scope—it's able to access the `personalForm` object without a more strict object reference. If this were a new page (changed using `location.href`, for instance), you'd have a tougher time accessing that form value. Figure 18.2 shows Listing 18.2 in action.

FIGURE 18.2

On the left is the original page; on the right is the page after the `document.open()` method has been invoked.

JavaScript and HTML Forms

In the previous section, you saw a number of the DOM objects you can access and alter using JavaScript. In this section, we're going to focus on one subset of the `document` object, the `form` object, and the various ways it can be manipulated.

The `form` Object

First, we should get the issue of multiple forms out of the way. In most cases, your forms will have names, thanks to the `name` attribute you use in the `<form>` element. If you give your form a name, as in `name="myForm"`, you can easily access the elements of that form:

```
var name = document.myForm.custName.value
```

Likewise, you've seen the steps you need to take to either pass a value to a function, pass a pointer to a function, or pass nothing to a function and let the function directly access the form via the `document` object. Easy enough.

But, as was mentioned, the `document` object has a property called `forms` that's actually an array of the forms stored in that document. Assuming `myForm` in the preceding example is the first form in the document, it could also be accessed in this way:

```
var name = document.forms[0].custName.value
```

That's perfectly valid. And at times, you may find it useful to access forms using the array, particularly if you need to access them automatically:

```
for (x=0; x<3; x=x+1) {
 var formName[x] = document.forms[x].name
}
```

With that sort of `for` loop, you could set each form's name to an array, making them individually accessible using the `formName` array.

Each form object (whether it's accessed as an array or by name) has a number of properties, just like the document and window objects do. The `form` object's properties include the following:

`action`	The action URL, as set in the `<form action=" ">` attribute
`method`	The `method` attribute's value (`get` or `post`)
`name`	The name of the form, as set in the `<form name=" ">` attribute
`length`	The number of elements (`input`, `textarea`, and `select` elements) in the form
`target`	The window or frame that is targeted by the form
`elements`	An array that holds all the elements (`input`, `textarea`, and `select` elements) in that form

The form object also includes some methods, including reset() and submit(), which can be used as if the Reset or Submit buttons were clicked by the user.

Form Error Checking with JavaScript

JavaScript and event handling are ideal for checking your user's form entries. As users type, JavaScript can be working in the background to make sure that the users' entries are correctly coded, have the right number of characters, and so on. You'll find that you can check pretty much any form element, although you'll most likely want to focus on entry boxes and textarea elements.

Let's start with an example script. Listing 18.3 shows you an entire page that has been designed to enable form entry, while checking the user's input in the ZIP Code entry box to make sure the ZIP Code is a valid number.

LISTING 18.3   Verifying Form Data with JavaScript

```
<!DOCTYPE html PUBLIC "-//W3C//DTD XHTML 1.0 Transitional//EN"
    "http://www.w3.org/TR/xhtml1/DTD/xhtml1-transitional.dtd">

<html xmlns="http://www.w3.org/1999/xhtml">
<head>
<title>Checking the Zip</title>
<meta http-equiv="Content-Script-Type" content="text/javascript">

<script>
<!--

function zipCheck()
{
  var zipStr = custForm.zipCode.value;

  if (zipStr == "") {
    alert("Please enter a five digit number for your Zip code");
    return(-1);
    }
  if (zipStr.length != 5) {
    alert ("Your Zip code entry should be 5 digits");
    return(-1);
    }
  return(0);
}

function checkSend()
```

LISTING 18.3 (continued)

```
    {
    var passCheck = zipCheck();
    if (passCheck == -1) {
        return;
    }
    else {
        custForm.submit();
    }
}

// end hiding -->
</script>

</head>

<body>

<h1>Please fill out the following form:</h1>

<form action="cgi-bin/address.pl" method="post" name="custForm">

<pre>

Name:    <input type="text" size="20" name="name">
Address: <input type="text" size="50" name="address">
City:    <input type="text" size="30" name="city">
State:   <input type="text" size="2" name="state">
Zip:     <input type="text" size="5" NAME="zipCode"
            onBlur = "zipCheck()">
Email:   <input type="text" size="40" Name="email">

<input type="button" value="Send It" onClick = "checkSend()">
</form>
</body>
</html>
```

This form works by using the onblur event handler to notice when the user moves away from the ZIP entry box—either by clicking in another box or by pressing the Tab key. The event handler then invokes the zipCheck function, which makes sure that the ZIP Code has been entered correctly. First, if nothing has been entered, an alert pops up, letting the user know that the ZIP Code is required. This is done by checking if the zipStr variable is empty:

```
if (zipStr == "") {
```

Next, the function checks that the ZIP Code entered is five characters long—not longer or shorter. It does so with this `if` statement:

```
if (zipStr.length != 5) {
```

If the ZIP Code is the correct length, nothing happens and the user can continue entering items on the form. If the ZIP Code isn't the correct length, an alert pops up.

Of course, the user could either ignore the alert or change the ZIP Code but still get it wrong. In that case, the `zipCheck` function gets called a second time, from within the `checkSend` function:

```
var passCheck = zipCheck();
```

If the ZIP Code is still incorrect, the `zipCheck` function will return the value -1, which the `checkSend` function is on the lookout for:

```
    if (passCheck == -1) {
        return;
    }
```

So, if the ZIP Code is still not correctly entered, the `checkSend` function will return to the form so the user can try again.

If the user did enter a correctly sized ZIP Code this time, the form is submitted:

```
    else {
        custForm.submit();
    }
```

See Figure 18.3 for an example of what happens when the user enters a ZIP Code incorrectly.

FIGURE 18.3
If the ZIP Code isn't entered correctly, an alert box appears.

Actually, we haven't completely checked for a valid ZIP Code. Indeed, this could get as complicated as you want it to be. For instance, you could add code that makes sure the ZIP Code is made up of numbers, thus disallowing characters. One way to do that is using the charAt() method of the String object, which can check each character to make sure it falls within the correct range of 0 through 9. Here's the expanded zipCheck function:

```
function zipCheck()
{
  var zipStr = custForm.zipCode.value;

  if (zipStr == "")
    {
    alert("Please enter a five digit number for your Zip code");
    return(-1);
    }
  if (zipStr.length != 5)
    {
    alert ("Your Zip code entry should be 5 digits");
    return(-1);
    }

  for (x=0; x < 5; x++)
  {
    if ((zipStr.charAt(x) < "0") || (zipStr.charAt(x) > "9"))
    {
      alert("All characters in the Zip code should be numbers.");
      return(-1);
    }
  }
  return(0);

}
```

Now, with this one, we've added another check, just in case the user squirms by the first two. This third check begins with a for loop, so that the script can move through the length of the ZIP Code and check each character:

```
for (x=0; x < 5; x++)
  {
```

Using the `for` loop, we can move through each index value (from 0 to 4) of the `zipStr` array. Then, using a clever little `if` statement, the function checks each character to see if it's a number (that is, it makes sure the character isn't below 0 or above 9):

```
if ((zipStr.charAt(x) < "0") || (zipStr.charAt(x) > "9"))
    {
```

The `||` means "or," by the way. This expression evaluates as "if the character is less than zero *or* if the character is more than 9." If one of those is true, the alert is triggered:

```
alert("All characters in the Zip code should be numbers.");
        return(-1);
```

If the alert isn't triggered, the `if` statement is over and the user is none the wiser for having been checked.

Client-Side JavaScript

Another advantage of JavaScript is that it gives you an option for dealing with forms without ever worrying about a CGI script. In some cases, you'll find that you don't have access to the CGI directory on your server. In other cases, you simply don't want to go to the hassle of creating a CGI script. Listing 18.4 shows an example of such a script.

LISTING 18.4   The Completely Client-Side Form

```
<!DOCTYPE html PUBLIC "-//W3C//DTD XHTML 1.0 Transitional//EN"
    "http://www.w3.org/TR/xhtml1/DTD/xhtml1-transitional.dtd">

<html xmlns="http://www.w3.org/1999/xhtml">
<head>
<title>Customer Survey Form</title>
<script>
<!--
function processform () {
    var newline = "\n";

    var result_str = "";
    var Form1 = document.form1;
    result_str += Form1.first_name.value + " " + Form1.last_name.value + newline;
    result_str += Form1.email.value + newline;
```

LISTING 18.4   (continued)

```
        for (x = 0; x < Form1.where.length; x++) {
            if (Form1.where[x].checked) {
            result_str += Form1.where[x].value + newline;
            break;
            }
        }

        if (Form1.desktop.checked) result_str += "desktop computers" + newline;
        if (Form1.notebook.checked) result_str += "notebook computers" + newline;
        if (Form1.peripherals.checked) result_str += "peripherals" + newline;
        if (Form1.software.checked) result_str += "software" + newline;

        document.form2.results.value = result_str;

        return;
        }

// -->
</script>
</head>

<body>

<h1>Web Site Survey</h1>

<form name="form1" id="form1">

<table cellpadding="5">
<tr>
<td>First name:</td> <td><input type="text" name="first_name" size="40" maxlength="40"
➥/></td>
</tr>
<tr>
<td>Last name:</td> <td><input type="text" name="last_name" size="40" maxlength="40"
➥/></td>
</tr>
<tr>
<td>E-mail address:</td> <td><input type="text" name="email" size="40" maxlength="40"
➥/></td>
</tr>
```

LISTING 18.4   (continued)

```
</table>

<p>
<b>Where you heard about us:</b></p>
<input type="radio" name="where" value="Web" checked="checked">Web Search or
➥Link</input><br />
<input type="radio" name="where" value="Advertisement">Radio or TV Ad</input><br />
<input type="radio" name="where" value="Press Mention">Article or press
➥mention</input><br />
<input type="radio" name="where" value="Other">Other</input><br />
</p>

<p>
<b>What products would you like more information about? (check all that apply)</b><br />
<input type="checkbox" name="desktop"> desktop computers
<input type="checkbox" name="notebook"> notebook computers
<input type="checkbox" name="peripherals"> peripherals
<input type="checkbox" name="software"> software
</p>

<button name="submit" type="button" onclick="processform ()">
<span style="font-family: Arial, Helvetica; font-variant: small-caps; font-size: 12pt">
Submit Survey</span>
</button>
<button name="reset" type="reset">
<span style="font-family: Arial, Helvetica; font-variant: small-caps; font-size: 12pt">
Clear Page</span>
</button>


</form>

<hr />

<form name="form2" id="form2" action="mailto:survey@fakecorp.net">

<p>Check the entries below for accuracy. If they're accurate, then enter a comment on
the last line (if desired) and click Send It to send the form via e-mail.</p>
<textarea name="results" cols="40" rows="10">
</textarea>
<button name="submit" type="submit">
```

LISTING 18.4 (continued)

```
<span style="font-family: Arial, Helvetica; font-variant: small-caps; font-size: 12pt">
Send It!</span>
</button>

</form>

</body>
</html>
```

This script isn't too terribly complicated, but it's worth examining. First, the script accepts values from the user via the survey form. Then, it translates those values, via the script up top, into text values, which are fed into the second form's text area. Then, the user is able to edit the data (add a comment, for instance, as shown in Figure 18.4) and click the Send It! button to send the form as an e-mail message.

FIGURE 18.4

Here the user can edit the data before sending it.

Note   The data will still arrive in the post format (see Chapter 15, "Adding HTML Forms"), but there's only one field to worry about working with once the text has been parsed.

This example shows that it's important to get the correct values from checkboxes and radio buttons. Listing 18.4 shows two different ways to do that. To begin, let's look at radio buttons. You need to determine which of the radio buttons has been checked, and then you can work with that value. With radio buttons, the values are stored in a special array, so we use a loop to access them:

```
for (x = 0; x < Form1.where.length; x++) {
        if (Form1.where[x].checked) {
        result_str += Form1.where[x].value + newline;
        break;
        }
    }
```

All the radio buttons are stored in an array of objects that are named for the `name` attribute used to create the radio buttons—in this case, that's `where`. Within each `where` object, the property `checked` can be used to determine if that value has been selected. When you find the checked `where` object, the associated `value` property is what you're interested in. So, the preceding loop looks at each `checked` property. When it finds one that's true, that value is used (in this case, it's added to `result_str`) and the `for` loop stops, thanks to the `break` command.

The second example shows how to deal with a series of checkboxes. Again, you test the `checked` property. Because each checkbox has its own `name` attribute, however, you don't need an array or a loop. Each checkbox is evaluated individually to see if it's checked. If it is, its value is used:

```
    if (Form1.desktop.checked) result_str += "desktop computers" +
➥newline;
    if (Form1.notebook.checked) result_str += "notebook computers" +
➥newline;
    if (Form1.peripherals.checked) result_str += "peripherals" + newline;
    if (Form1.software.checked) result_str += "software" + newline;
```

If the box is checked, a string is added to the `result_str`; if it isn't checked, the script moves to the next `if` statement.

JavaScript for Redirection and Frames

You've seen how to access and alter some of the main objects of the DOM, and you've seen how to verify form data and use JavaScript to alter form data and for client-side processing. In this section, let's take a quick look at some other little JavaScript tricks, including redirecting a browser, building links in JavaScript, and using JavaScript with frames.

Browser Redirection

It can be useful to figure out which browser your user is using and redirect that user to a particular page. Not only is it sometimes important to know if the browser is Internet Explorer, Netscape, or another brand, but you can also use browser redirection to determine whether or not a browser supports JavaScript and make sure your user automatically visits the appropriate page.

For browser redirection, you'll use another object we haven't touched on much, the navigator object. Using this object and its properties, you can get a sense of which browser version you're dealing with. The `navigator.appName` property stores a string that tells you the full name of the application, the `navigator.userAgent` object tells you the general level that the browser is compatible with (as in `Mozilla/4.0`, which could be any Netscape-compatible 4.0-level browser), and the `navigator.appVersion` property reports the version number.

So, the first thing you can do with this knowledge is create a document that will show you all the properties of the browser that access that document:

```
<script type="text/javascript">
document.writeln ("navigator.appName: " + navigator.appName + "<br \/>");
document.writeln ("navigator.userAgent: " + navigator.userAgent + "<br
➥\/>");
document.writeln ("navigator.appVersion: " + navigator.appVersion + "<br
➥\/>");
</script>
```

Although this information is useful, it can be a bit more difficult to turn it into a perfectly useful browser redirection script—one that notes the version and loads a particular URL in response. That's because you need to actually have the script parse those names and figure them out so you know which browser is which. This can be done with a series of `if` statements, as shown in Listing 18.5.

LISTING 18.5   Browser Redirection

```
<!DOCTYPE html PUBLIC "-//W3C//DTD XHTML 1.0 Transitional//EN"
    "http://www.w3.org/TR/xhtml1/DTD/xhtml1-transitional.dtd">

<html xmlns="http://www.w3.org/1999/xhtml">
<head>
<title>Browser Detector</title>
<script type="text/javascript">
<!--
var browserAppName = navigator.appName;
if (browserAppName == "Netscape") {
    window.location = "net_index.html";
    }
else {
  if (browserAppName == "Microsoft Internet Explorer"){
    window.location = "ie_index.html";
    }
```

LISTING 18.5 (continued)

```
else {
   window.location = "index.html";
   }
}
//-->
</script>
</head>

<body>
<h1>Browser Detector</h1>
<p>If this page doesn't refresh, then you may have a browser that isn't JavaScript
compatible, or you may have JavaScript turned off. Please click to visit our
<a href="index.html">non-JavaScript index</a> page.</p>
</body>
</html>
```

Of course, you already may have figured out that if your goal is simply to detect JavaScript versus non-JavaScript, the best way is to include a JavaScript redirect command—just a simple `window.location = "newpage.html"` command will suffice. If that page doesn't redirect, you can assume the user doesn't have a JavaScript-capable browser, so you can offer him a link to the non-scripted part of your site.

Note

Sometimes you'll need to know more than simply the brand of browser. In that case, you may also want to test the `.appVersion` property to see what version of the application you've encountered. Also, Chapter 19 has a more sophisticated look at browser detection (often called browser *sniffing*) in the section "Cross-Browser DHTML Example."

The JavaScript Link Menu

One of the form elements we haven't yet discussed is the `<select>` element, partly because it's the odd duck of form elements and JavaScript. In this example, though, we'll create a navigation menu that you can use on your pages to allow your users to quickly move to a different page. And we'll use a `<select>` menu to create that navigation menu. Listing 18.6 shows this in action.

LISTING 18.6   The `<select>` Menu and JavaScript

```
<!DOCTYPE html PUBLIC "-//W3C//DTD XHTML 1.0 Transitional//EN"
    "http://www.w3.org/TR/xhtml1/DTD/xhtml1-transitional.dtd">

<html xmlns="http://www.w3.org/1999/xhtml">
<head>
<title>Change Page</title>
<script type="text/javaScript">
<!--
 function changePage(theSelect) {
     var x = theSelect.selectedIndex;
     window.location.href = theSelect.options[x].text;
     }
// -->
</script>

</head>
<body>
<div align="center">

<form name="changeForm">

<p>
<select name="changeSelect" onchange="changePage(this)">
<option selected="select">Choose a Page</option>
<option>index.html</option>
<option>products.html</option>
<option>service.html</option>
<option>about.html</option>
<option>help.html</option>
</select>
</p>

</form>
</div>

<hr />

<h1>Welcome to the Site!</h1>

<p>Markup...</p>

</body>
</html>
```

With a `<select>` menu, there are no assigned values, as with most other form elements. Instead, the text of the menu itself is what is stored, in a `text` property of the select menu's object. Also, the selected value is stored in a `selectedIndex` property. So, using the following function, the script simply consults the `selectedIndex` property, and then uses that index to access the text of the selected option (which is stored in the `options` array):

```
function changePage(theSelect) {
     var x = theSelect.selectedIndex;
     window.location.href = theSelect.options[x].text;
     }
```

Programmatically, that's how you get items out of a `<select>` element. Figure 18.5 shows this page in action.

FIGURE 18.5

Changing pages with a `<select>` menu and JavaScript.

Of course, the way this script and menu are set up, you'll need to copy them to each of the pages involved if you want the menu as a fixture on your Web site. There is another option—you could use frames, as discussed next.

JavaScript and HTML Frames

So, assuming you are working with a browser that's capable of JavaScript, wouldn't it be interesting to use it for the entire interface? One way to do that is to use HTML frames to create the interface, while offering your users a pull-down menu for navigation. In this section we'll create such a site, which will be designed as an archive of Web articles, easily accessed via a menu.

As with any frames interface, you're going to need a number of different documents to make this interface work. First, a `<frameset>` document will be used to bring the whole thing together. Second, you'll need a navigation page that includes a `<select>` menu, as discussed in the previous section. With just a few tweaks, that menu can be used for this frames-based approach as well.

In addition to those two elements, you'll need a document that loads when the frameset appears. In this case, it will be the default page that explains the interface. And of course, you'll need all the content pages that are to appear in the frames interface.

To begin, Listing 18.7 shows the frameset document.

LISTING 18.7   The Frameset Document

```
<!DOCTYPE html PUBLIC "-//W3C//DTD XHTML 1.0 Frameset//EN"
    "http://www.w3.org/TR/xhtml1/DTD/xhtml1-frameset.dtd">

<html xmlns="http://www.w3.org/1999/xhtml">
<head>
<title>The Article Viewer</title>
</head>

<frameset rows="150, *">
    <frame src="navigate.html" />
    <frame src="default.html" name="main_viewer" />
</frameset>
```

Next up, we need `navigate.html`, which will be the top frame of the frameset and is based on the `<select>` menu example used in the previous section. Listing 18.8 shows that example, now tweaked to target the `main_viewer` frame of the frameset, using the object reference `top.main_viewer.location.href`. As you may remember from Chapter 12, "Creating Sites with HTML Frames," `top` is a special target that means, ultimately, the browser window. It's also an object in the DOM, which includes all the frames of the frameset, so that those frames can be assigned URLs programmatically.

Note, also, that this version of the navigate page has been altered so that the user, instead of seeing URLs, sees a description, which is translated into the appropriate URL. That's done simply by creating an array of URLs, which are referenced using the index number of the selection in the menu. You'll need to carefully construct this array (to make sure that the `<option>` entries in the `<select>` element correspond to this list of URLs in the array), but it's a tricky way to make the menu a little more readable.

LISTING 18.8 The navigate.html Page

```
<!DOCTYPE html PUBLIC "-//W3C//DTD XHTML 1.0 Transitional//EN"
    "http://www.w3.org/TR/xhtml1/DTD/xhtml1-transitional.dtd">

<html xmlns="http://www.w3.org/1999/xhtml">
<head>
<title>Navigate Page</title>
<script type="text/javaScript">
<!--
 function changePage(theSelect) {
     pageArray = new Array("default.html", "article1.html", "article2.html",
"article3.html", "article4.html", "article5.html");
     var x = theSelect.selectedIndex;
     top.main_viewer.location.href = pageArray[x];
     }
// -->
</script>

</head>
<body style="background-color: yellow">
<div align="center">

<h1>FakeCorp Article Archive</h1>

<form name="changeForm">

<p>What article would you like to read?</p>

<p>
<select name="changeSelect" onchange="changePage(this)">
<option selected="select">Default Page</option>
<option>The Skinny on RAM</option>
<option>Hard Drive Technologies</option>
<option>Choosing a Monitor</option>
<option>Upgrading and Swapping Processors</option>
<option>Troubleshooting the OS</option>
</select>
</p>

</form>
</div>

</body>
</html>
```

Now, we need a `default.html` page that can appear when the frameset is first loaded. This page is a simple XHTML document that tells the user a little about the interface, offers any news or updates, and enables incompatible browsers to avoid the frames interface. Listing 18.9 shows the page.

LISTING 18.9   The `default.html` Page

```
<!DOCTYPE html PUBLIC "-//W3C//DTD XHTML 1.0 Transitional//EN"
    "http://www.w3.org/TR/xhtml1/DTD/xhtml1-transitional.dtd">

<html xmlns="http://www.w3.org/1999/xhtml">
<head>
<title>Default Page</title>
</head>

<body style="margin: 24pt">
<h1>Welcome to the Article Viewer!</h1>

<p>Using the menu above, select the article that you'd like to view.
It should load automatically in this window. If you'd like to return
to this page, choose Default Page from the menu. </p>

<p>If you'd prefer to view this site without a frames interface, or if
your browser doesn't support JavaScript, please visit or
<a href="noframes.html">no-frames interface</a> to read these articles.</p>

<h2>Latest Additions</h2>

<p><strong>10/13 --</strong> We've just posted an article that looks
into the various RAM technologies to help you decide which is right
for your model of computer. Check it out for in-depth coverage of the
numbers and statistics you need to know to buy reliable RAM.</p>

<p><strong>10/5 --</strong> Check out Upgrading and Swapping Processors
for step-by-step discussion on deciding whether it's time to upgrade your
PC's processor and, if so, how you should go about it.</p>

</body>
</html>
```

Now, assuming the other articles are in place (those referenced in the array that was created for the `navigate.html` page), we're ready to put this frameset to use. Figure 18.6 shows the final frameset in action.

FIGURE 18.6

Using a frameset and a special `<select>` menu navigation page, you can create a JavaScript-based interface.

Summary

In this chapter, you saw some advanced JavaScript issues focusing on how to react to user input. The chapter began with a discussion of event handlers and how they're used in conjunction with JavaScript function definitions to create scripts that respond to the user. The chapter then took a fairly in-depth look at some of the main objects of the Document Object Model, all of which can be useful for altering document, window, and page properties using a script.

After that, the chapter turned to using the DOM, event handlers, and JavaScript to respond to user's input in HTML forms. You saw how to check the data that is input into form elements, as well as how to create a form that is completely processed in JavaScript and then sent via e-mail, bypassing the CGI script approach that was discussed in Chapter 16, "CGIs and Data Gathering."

Finally, the last section of the chapter focused on using JavaScript to change the page automatically. You saw how to redirect pages based on the Web browser brand, how to create a menu of URLs for page switching, and how to build a fairly sophisticated menu-based interface using JavaScript and HTML frames.

In the next chapter, you'll learn more about JavaScript and how it can work together with the CSS technology to become something that's often called Dynamic HTML.

ADDING DYNAMIC HTML

hen JavaScript, the Document Object Model, and Cascading Style Sheets are brought together on a single page, the result is often called *Dynamic HTML*. Ideally, using Dynamic HTML helps you create a page that responds to user input with special effects that can make your information engaging and entertaining, as well as informative.

Dynamic HTML varies somewhat from Web browser to Web browser, with Netscape and Microsoft in particular offering slightly different features. In this chapter we'll spend most of our time looking at the Dynamic HTML elements that the two browsers have in common, focusing on using JavaScript and style sheets together to create pages that can change automatically.

This chapter discusses the following:

- What Dynamic HTML is, and what the implications are of using it on your page
- The "greatest hits" of Dynamic HTML—using mouseovers to change images and positioning
- Exploring, understanding, and scripting layers
- Working with style sheets—scripting styles and classes

What Is Dynamic HTML?

Let's begin the definition of Dynamic HTML by discussing what it *isn't*—it isn't an official standard. HTML has become XHTML, and CSS is a standard, as is the Document Object Model. But Dynamic HTML is really something more of a marketing term, or an unofficial name, meant to suggest using scripting and the DOM together to do things on the page—usually visual tricks. *Dynamic HTML* sometimes means that you're using scripts to alter your style sheet properties. It can also sometimes mean you're incorporating technology called *layers*, which enable different parts of a document to overlap and even hide one another.

In fact, you have already seen some minor examples of Dynamic HTML in Chapter 18, "JavaScript and User Input," when you saw the images array being accessed and the document object being opened and rewritten. We'll take those examples further in this chapter, and we'll cover some new technologies. First, let's complete the definition of Dynamic HTML by taking another look at the DOM, as well as some other important technologies.

Note

In the past, *Dynamic HTML* has been used to mean some other things as well. Netscape used the term to cover downloadable font technology, which both Microsoft and Netscape offer in incompatible ways. DHTML has also been used to refer to some special filter effects that Microsoft had offered in its browser. In this chapter, I'll stick to the CSS and CSSP (CSS Positioning) aspects of DHTML. For more on all other aspects, see *Sams Teach Yourself DHTML in 24 Hours* or a comprehensive text such as Que's *Platinum Edition Using XHTML, XML, and Java 2*.

The Document Object Model Revisited

Perhaps the most important thing to recognize about the DOM is that it's only recently become a standard. The W3C has standardized the DOM, with the latest version being a working draft of DOM level 3. The latest Web browsers (Internet Explorer 6.x and Netscape 6.x) incorporate aspects of DOM level 2, which is a great start. It means that those browsers are much more compatible with one another than IE and Netscape have been in the past.

At about the 4.0 level of both browsers, the DOM was introduced for public consumption. It varied quite a bit between the two browsers, because there were no guiding standards and each company wanted to make a variety of object properties and methods available to the user. The result was a bit chaotic, as it was difficult to really decide whose DOM implementation to use.

Although the basic document objects discussed in Chapter 18 are safe, the 4.0 level of Internet Explorer and Netscape offered many other objects that could be altered. IE made nearly every element on the page an object, and hence scriptable. IE has also had support for reformatting pages without reloading them, so that you could change an element's content (even a paragraph or a bullet point) using a script, and the page would reconstitute itself on the fly. Netscape 4.x doesn't support that, although Netscape 6 does, and arguably offers a more complete implementation of the W3C's DOM.

Browser Compatibility

These different approaches have also slowed the adoption of some of the DHTML techniques, as has the unbalanced adoption of CSS and JavaScript implementations by Netscape's and Microsoft's browsers. For the sake of practicality, that means you probably should only use DHTML when you also offer the same information in other formats. Otherwise, your users may not see everything you're trying to communicate. You should also encourage your users to download and install the latest versions of their Web browsers. IE 5.5 and 6 and Netscape 6 are much more standards-based, and cross-platform DHTML tricks are easier when you can assume that your users are surfing with one of those two browsers (or a third-party browser that's compatible).

In this chapter, we won't cover too much of the Netscape 4- or IE-specific technology—we'll stick closer to the W3C standards. But, if you do opt to use browser-specific approaches, you'll want to either automatically redirect incompatible browsers (as discussed in Chapter 18 or later in the section "Cross-Browser DHTML Example") or provide links to non-DHTML pages that users can choose. In the past, many pages were developed with small badges or lines of text saying "Best Viewed in Netscape" or "Best Viewed in Internet Explorer." You can take that route too, although in today's Web development world, cross-browser compatibility is encouraged.

For more on the two main browser's DHTML capabilities, I recommend you visit their respective developer Web sites. Netscape offers DOM- and DHTML-related discussions for Netscape 6 at `http://developer.netscape.com/tech/dom/` and coverage of DHTML issues in Netscape 4.x at `http://developer.netscape.com/tech/dynhtml/index.html`. Microsoft's site for HTML and DHTML is `http://msdn.microsoft.com/library/default.asp?url=/workshop/author/dhtml/dhtml_node_entry.asp`.

Note | I'm editorializing here, but Microsoft's approach to URLs on its Web site (like the one above) is a wonderful example of how *not* to arrange your pages if you want them to be convenient for your users. Whenever possible, you should try to have direct paths to documents that can be jotted down, or some other way to make the reference easy, such as simple article numbers.

CSS and CSS Positioning

Both Netscape and Microsoft have supported a great deal of the CSS standard since their 4.0 browsers, and both support a lot of scripting of those elements. You'll find that CSS is the overlapping Dynamic HTML principle we can focus on.

Beyond the type of style sheet information discussed in Chapter 10, "Get Splashy: Style Sheets, Fonts, and Special Characters," there's another level of CSS, called CSS Positioning or CSSP. CSSP takes the style sheet approach and enables you to choose the exact position of elements on the page, including ways that enable them to overlap or hide one another. In addition, both browsers (particularly IE 6 and Netscape 6) offer support for scripting those positioned elements, even to the point that you can move them around in the browser window. We'll discuss some of that in this chapter, as well.

Mouseovers: Changing Things Without Clicks

One of the more popular uses of DHTML is to create mouseover scripts that enable you to change either an image or a text property when you place the mouse pointer over it. These scripts are actually fairly easy to create, with the JavaScript and CSS knowledge you already have.

Although CSS-based mouseovers (using the pseudo-classes such as a.hover) work in Netscape 4, these DOM-based mouseovers work only in Internet Explorer 4 and above, and in Netscape 6 and above. If you use the mouseovers to communicate important information, you may need to offer another page for users of earlier browsers.

Basic Image Mouseover

To begin, let's look at a very basic mouseover, which simply causes an image to change when you place the mouse over it. This might not sound like much, but it can actually be quite handy. Not only is it a visual cue to show users that the mouse is hovering over the image, but it can also be used to display two images in the space of one image—for real estate or classified ad pages, for instance.

Listing 19.1 shows the code for the image mouseover.

LISTING 19.1   A Basic Image Mouseover

```
<!DOCTYPE html PUBLIC "-//W3C//DTD XHTML 1.0 Transitional//EN"
    "http://www.w3.org/TR/xhtml1/DTD/xhtml1-transitional.dtd">

<html xmlns="http://www.w3.org/1999/xhtml">
```

LISTING 19.1   (continued)

```
<head>
<title>Mouseover Image Demo</title>
</head>

<script type="text/javascript">
<!--

function changeImage () {
    document.images.myImage.src="second.jpg";
    }

function changeBack () {
    document.images.myImage.src="first.jpg";
    }

// -->
</script>

<body>
<p>Mouse over the image to change it:</p>
<img src="first.jpg" id="myImage" onmouseover="changeImage()" onmouseout="changeBack()"
➡/>

</body>
</html>
```

When the user places the mouse pointer over the image, it changes from the first.jpg image to the second.jpg image. When the user removes the mouse pointer from the image, the first.jpg image returns. This is shown in Figure 19.1.

FIGURE 19.1

On the left, the image before mousing over; on the right, the image is being pointed to with the mouse pointer, so it changes.

For this to work, particularly for cross-browser compatibility, your images need to be the exact same size, down to the pixel. If they're even a little off, you'll get odd results. IE may reformat the page, which looks bad, while earlier Netscape versions may have trouble rendering the images at all.

As you can see, this is a fairly simple script that relies on something you've already seen, the `images` object that's part of the `document` object:

```
function changeImage () {
    document.images.image01.src="second.jpg";
}
```

In this case, the image was given an object name via the `id="image01"` attribute that was added to the `<img>` element, which makes it possible to refer to the image by name in this object reference. This is convenient, but not entirely necessary. The `images` object is an array, which can be accessed using an index. So, for instance, you could have used

```
function changeImage () {
    document.images[0].src="second.jpg";
}
```

This gives you the same result, because `image01` and `images[0]` refer to the same image—in this case, it's the first and only image on the page.

Remote Image Mouseover

Another step up in the "Wow" department is the remote image mouseover. This simply means that you can encourage your users to mouse over an element—a hyperlink, for example—and that changes an image on another part of the page.

For this example, a table will be used for layout. On the left side of the table are links that can receive the mouseovers; on the right side is the image. If the user decides to click a link, the full page for that link will load.

The way this example is done, it will still work well in earlier versions of Netscape and Internet Explorer (at least, those that support tables). While the image won't swap in some versions, the user is still free to click the hypertext link to see more about each item (in this case, a house). Presumably, they'd be able to see more traditional images on those pages.

Listing 19.2 shows the code for this page.

LISTING 19.2   Remote Mouseover for Images Swapping

```
<!DOCTYPE html PUBLIC "-//W3C//DTD XHTML 1.0 Transitional//EN"
    "http://www.w3.org/TR/xhtml1/DTD/xhtml1-transitional.dtd">

<html xmlns="http://www.w3.org/1999/xhtml">

<head>
<title>Dynamic Image Demo</title>
</head>

<style>
a, h1 {font-family: Arial, Helvetica}
</style>


<script type="text/javascript">
<!--

function changeImage (indexNum) {
    if (indexNum == 1) document.images.image01.src="1980main.jpg";
    if (indexNum == 2) document.images.image01.src="1730maple.jpg";
    }

function changeBack () {
    document.images.image01.src="logo.jpg";
    }

// -->
</script>

<body>

<h1>Featured Listings</h1>

<table border="0" width="600" cellpadding="10">

<tr>
<td width="380">
<p><a href="1980main.html" onmouseover="changeImage(1)" onmouseout="changeBack()">1980
➥Main Street</a></p>

<p>This beautiful 3/2 farmhouse is right in the heart of Old Towne, taking you out of
```

LISTING 19.2   (continued)

the suburbs and back to within walking distance of not only the drug store, but the drug store's soda fountain! Put life back the way it's supposed to be, at $125,000.</p>

```
<p>
<a href="1730maple.html" onmouseover="changeImage(2)" onmouseout="changeBack()">1730
➥Maple Avenue</a></p>
```

```
<p>
Not only does this neighborhood have good schools and good shade trees, it's got great
sidewalks. Get out and meet your new neighbors, or strap on that helmet and get back on
that bicycle you haven't ridden in years. The bike path in front of this property takes
you right along Creekside Drive and into the county park! This 2/2 cottage has two
porches and a two-car garage with studio apartment. Only $135,000.
</p>
```

```
</td>
```

```
<td width="200">
```

```
<div align="center">
```

```
<img src="logo.jpg" id="image01">
```

```
</td>
</tr>
</table>
```

```
</body>
</html>
```

You'll notice that this script is actually pretty similar to Listing 19.1—particularly the script functions, which perform the same basic image assignment using an object reference. The only difference up top is the series of if statements, which are used to determine what image should be loaded depending on the hyperlink that receives the mouseover event. Each individual hyperlink is designed to send its own index, so you know which image to load. Figure 19.2 shows this script in action.

FIGURE 19.2

On the left, the page before a mouseover event; on the right, the pointer is over a hypertext link and the image has changed.

Preloading Images

Before we move on to some other DHTML topics, we should cover the notion of *preloading* images. When you preload an image for mouseover use, that image is stored in the browser's cache. That means the browser won't have to retrieve the image when the mouseover occurs, which can result in delays that confuse the user. To get around that, you need to tweak the approach a little bit, as shown in Listing 19.3.

LISTING 19.3 Preloading Images for a Mouseover

```
<!DOCTYPE html PUBLIC "-//W3C//DTD XHTML 1.0 Transitional//EN"
    "http://www.w3.org/TR/xhtml1/DTD/xhtml1-transitional.dtd">

<html xmlns="http://www.w3.org/1999/xhtml">
<head>
<title>Preload Image Mouseover Demo</title>
</head>

<script type="text/javascript">
<!--

function loadImages () {
    image01 = new Image();
    image01.src = "first.jpg";
    image02 = new Image();
    image02.src = "second.jpg";
    }

function changeImage () {
    document.images.myImage.src=image02.src;
    }

function changeBack () {
```

LISTING 19.3 (continued)

```
        document.images.myImage.src=image01.src;
        }

// -->
</script>

<body>

<script type="text/javascript">
<!--
loadImages();
// -->
</script>

<p>Mouse over the image to change it:</p>
<img src="first.jpg" id="myImage" onmouseover="changeImage()"
onmouseout="changeBack()" />

</body>
</html>
```

The major difference in this script is the new `loadImages()` function, which is called from the main body of the script so that the images load into the browser's cache. That's done by creating a new `Image` object (using the `new Image()` command) and assigning it a particular image file as a source. (The `Image` object is a preset object that's built into JavaScript implementations.) Now, these image objects can be used in the `changeImage()` and `changeBack()` functions, with the added advantage that the images are already loaded when called—the user won't have to wait to see the images change.

CSS Positioning and Layers

The most cross-compatible DHTML technology is *CSS Positioning*, which is an extension of the CSS style script standard that enables you to be very specific about the position of elements on your page. As long as everything is stable, your pages will look very similar in IE, Netscape 4, and Netscape 6.

When you decide to move an element or change its position, however, you find yourself in a different situation. Each browser has a slightly different DOM implementation, meaning you need to access the CSSP elements slightly differently.

Adding more confusion is Netscape 4, where it's easier to dynamically alter items on the page if they're formatted using two elements that Netscape created, the `<layer>` and `<ilayer>` elements. These elements enable you to place content on top of other content, set the visibility of the layers, and hide and show content dynamically.

Unfortunately, the `<layer>` elements also aren't standard—the W3C never incorporated them, and Netscape has moved away from them. We'll look at them briefly in this section, but I recommend you stick to CSSP for your positioning. As you'll see at the end of this section, you can create a page based on CSSP that works in all three browser versions.

Basic CSS Positioning

Ultimately, the point of CSS Positioning is that the content and appearance of a Web page should be separated and separable. With regular CSS style sheets, you've seen how that's true—the style sheets make the page look good, but without them, a browser could still access the information on that page.

CSSP takes that same theory a little bit further. Although CSSP enables you to precisely position elements on the page—even more precisely than with table elements—it does so without interfering with the regular markup. You can create pages that look completely different in CSS-compatible browsers, and yet those same pages could be viewed in a non-graphical or incompatible browser.

CSSP really isn't all that odd if you've gotten used to regular CSS properties—it's just more of the same. In most cases, you'll create a new class to specify a particular position for an element. Then you can either add the `class` attribute to a particular element or use the `<span>` or `<div>` elements to assign that position class to a number of elements. First, though, you need to know the CSS properties that are useful for positioning. They're shown in Table 19.1.

TABLE 19.1 CSS Positioning Properties

Property	Possible Values	Example
position	absolute, relative, static	position:absolute
left	number and units	left:100px
top	number and units	top:50px
width	number and units	width:250px
height	number+units	height:5in
clip	rect (top, right, bottom, left)	rect (100px,50px,50px,100px)

These properties enable you to work with an individual element, division, or span as a single box. You can define that box at a particular size and have it begin at a particular spot on the page, either relative to where it would have appeared on the page without the styling (the relative position), or relative to the top-left corner of the page itself (the absolute position).

Note If you use the position: static property, the item acts as if it were a regular XHTML element without any particular CSSP markup.

If any of these properties is a bit odd, it's the clip property, which is used to make only portions of a particular division visible. It works a little like cropping an image in an image-editing application, by hiding any part of the element that's not enclosed in the rectangle that's created by the property. An example might be

```
.story_text {
    position: absolute;
    left: 25px;
    top: 80px;
    width: 210px;
    clip: rect(10px, 200px, 500px, 10px);
}
```

Tip When you type in and test Listing 19.4, try substituting the preceding class definition to see how clipping can change things. The result is shown in Figure 19.3.

FIGURE 19.3

The clipped story looks almost as if it were cropped in a photo application.

To see some of these items in action, let's begin with a simple example that uses positioning to place a headline and a story on the page in a newsletter style. Listing 19.4 shows this page.

LISTING 19.4   Positioning a Headline and News Story via CSSP

```
<!DOCTYPE html PUBLIC "-//W3C//DTD XHTML 1.0 Transitional//EN"
    "http://www.w3.org/TR/xhtml1/DTD/xhtml1-transitional.dtd">

<html xmlns="http://www.w3.org/1999/xhtml">
<head>
<title>CSSP Basic Example</title>
</head>

<style type="text/css">

.headline1 {
   position: absolute;
   left: 25px;
   top: 20px;
   width: 200px;
   height: 50px;
   }

.story_text {
   position: absolute;
   left: 25px;
   top: 80px;
   width: 210px;
   }


</style>

<body>

<h1 class="headline1">Man Bites Cat</h1>

<div class="story_text">
<p><strong>Orwitz, Nevada</strong> -- In a bizarre story that has local officials
scratching their heads, an Orwitz man has been questioned in an alleged biting attack
on a feline. Rich Cutter, 42, a noted local physician, apparently scrambled up a tree
in his backyard in pursuit of the cat, which lives with a neighbor. It was in that tree
that the alleged biting incident took place.</p>
```

LISTING **19.4**   (continued)

```
<p>The cat is known to prowl Cutter's neighborhood, often singing, say some residents
of the calm suburban division, into the early morning hours.</p>

<p>"It's a sweet cat," said Muffy Einstein, a local school teacher. "It's just crazy
what that man did."</p>

<p>Others, like former professional athlete Hugh Ballhandler, call the cat's
vocalizations "screeching" and "loud meowing."</p>

<p>"That cat got what it deserved," said Ballhandler. "No jury in their right mind
would convict. That noise had to stop!"</p>

<p>The cat was available for comment, but seemed too agitated to make much sense.</p>
</div>

</body>
</html>
```

As you can see from Figure 19.4, the CSSP properties give you some interesting control over the page. The measurements used in Listing 19.4 use pixels, which is probably the most convenient way to parcel up the browser window and figure out how to position things. Note also that the appearance of the fonts in the browser could affect the ultimate layout, too. You might want to couple the CSSP properties with the standard CSS properties to keep things as uniform as possible.

FIGURE 19.4

Here's a nice CSSP layout thanks to Listing 19.4.

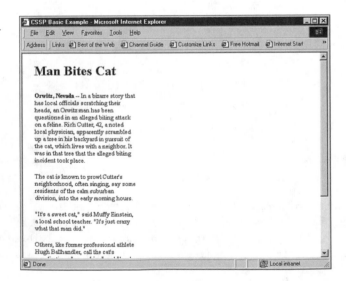

Overlapping Elements and `z-index`

CSSP gives you the tools to lay out boxes and elements on your page with exacting specifications. That includes overlapping those elements, if desired. In fact, something as simple as changing Listing 19.4 so that the `story_text` class begins a bit higher causes the two elements to overlap:

```
.story_text {
   position: absolute;
   left: 25px;
   top: 25px;
   width: 210px;
   }
```

Figure 19.5 shows what that overlap looks like.

FIGURE 19.5

Using CSSP to cause items to overlap on the page.

That might not seem terribly useful. However—aside from visual collage—there are a few instances where overlapping elements could be useful. For instance, you might want to place text on top of an image, which could be done with CSSP. Listing 19.5 is an example.

LISTING 19.5   Overlapping Items Using CSSP

```
<!DOCTYPE html PUBLIC "-//W3C//DTD XHTML 1.0 Transitional//EN"
    "http://www.w3.org/TR/xhtml1/DTD/xhtml1-transitional.dtd">

<html xmlns="http://www.w3.org/1999/xhtml">
```

LISTING 19.5   (continued)

```
<head>
<title>Overlap Text and Images</title>
</head>

<style type="text/css">

.image {
   position: absolute;
   left: 25px;
   top: 20px;
   width: 300px;
   height: 225px;
   z-index: 0;
   }

.cutline {
   position: absolute;
   left: 125px;
   top: 200px;
   width: 210px;
   z-index: 1;
   font-face: courier;
   font-weight: bold;
   color: white;
   }

</style>

<body>

<img src="house.jpg" class="image" />

<p class="cutline">12:04 P.M: Grandma's House</p>

</body>
</html>
```

In this example, the text is positioned over the image, making it appear as if it is part of the image (or at least that you did this on purpose). Figure 19.6 shows this example.

FIGURE 19.6

The text has
been placed on
top of the
image.

Want to specify which element appears on top of which other elements? By default,
later elements are piled on top of earlier elements, so text that appears in the Web
document after an image will appear on top of that image. By using another CSSP
property, z-index, you can change that order by giving each element or class a number. The higher the number, the closer to the top of the pile that element will be.
(Note that z-index is recognized in Netscape 6 and IE, but not in Netscape 4, which
uses the <layer> element for this sort of thing.)

With some minor adjustments to the style definition for the previous example, you
can change the z-index order so that the image appears on top of the text. (You'll
also change the size and color of the text so that you can see it back there.)

```
<style type="text/css">

.image {
  position: absolute;
  left: 25px;
  top: 20px;
  width: 300px;
  height: 225px;
  z-index: 1;
  }

.cutline {
  position: absolute;
  left: 200px;
  top: 100px;
  width: 400px;
```

```
        z-index: 0;
        font-face: courier;
        font-size: 36pt;
        color: blue;
        }
</style>
```

Figure 19.7 shows what this looks like in a browser.

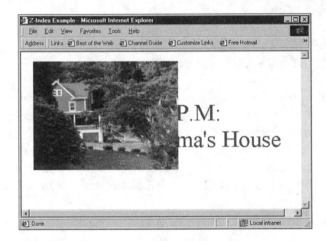

Nesting Positioned Elements

So far we've dealt strictly with elements and boxes that are completely discrete—one ends before the next begins. But what happens if you nest a positioned element within another one? If you use absolute positioning (position: absolute, as in the last few listings), all elements are positioned relative to their *parent* elements. In all the examples thus far, the parent has been the <body> element.

If you nest one element within another, however, the nested element becomes a child of the element within which it is nested. That means suddenly the child's coordinate system is based upon the parent element's, so the top and left properties, in particular, will be relative to the parent.

Let's see what happens with the basic positioning example you saw in Listing 19.4 if you change it around and make one of the elements the child of another. That's shown in Listing 19.6. (For the sake of space, I've cut the text of the example article, which was shown in Listing 19.4.)

LISTING 19.6 Nesting CSSP Elements

```html
<!DOCTYPE html PUBLIC "-//W3C//DTD XHTML 1.0 Transitional//EN"
    "http://www.w3.org/TR/xhtml1/DTD/xhtml1-transitional.dtd">

<html xmlns="http://www.w3.org/1999/xhtml">
<head>
<title>Nesting Example</title>
</head>

<style type="text/css">

.headline1 {
   position: absolute;
   left: 25px;
   top: 20px;
   width: 200px;
   height: 50px;
   }

.story_text {
   position: absolute;
   left: 25px;
   top: 80px;
   width: 210px;
   }

</style>

<body>

<div class="headline1">
<h1>Man Bites Cat</h1>

<div class="story_text">
<p>Body of article.</p>
</div>
</div>

</body>
</html>
```

The classes have been assigned to two different `<div>` containers, with the first one containing the second one. The result is a slightly different layout, as shown in Figure 19.8.

FIGURE 19.8

Because the second `<div>` is nested in the first, the coordinate system for the second `<div>` has moved down and to the right.

Relative Positioning

So far we've worked with absolute positing, but sometimes relative positioning (with `position: relative`) can be a useful property to set as well. Generally, you do that when you want a particular box to flow with the rest of the document for some reason, but you'd like to specify some of the box's position parameters, such as the width or the `z-index`.

For instance, building on Listing 19.6, you could change the second style class definition to

```
.story_text {
    position: relative;
    top: 5px;
    }
```

Because it's a child of the first `<div>` element (remember, that's what was introduced in Listing 19.6), the story text is still bound to the coordinates specified by `<div class="headline1">`. So, its definition can be much simpler—all it needs to do is position itself 5 pixels below where it normally would be (below a `<h1>` element) to make it look good in the layout.

Note

It can take a while to get used to the differences between absolute and relative positioning. I recommend that you play with them in these examples, changing values and so on to see what the result is. Also, in my experience, relative positioning can vary a bit from browser to browser, even among the 6.0-level browsers.

Dynamic Positioning and Layers

Up until now, we've discussed using CSSP to create divisions of elements that can overlap one another. You saw how you can use the z-index to change the relative position of each layered element, and how individual elements or boxes can be placed at absolute and relative points in the browser window. In this section, we'll look at how to use this knowledge to work with DHTML *layers*.

First, it's worth noting that layers are more of a concept than a particular set of parameters that you need to learn. In the previous section, you saw layers of elements that could be absolutely positioned. In CSSP, that's really the extent of what a layer is. The term is commonly used, however, when you're specifically using the <div> element to create each layer, and more to the point, when you use scripting to make the positioning of those layers dynamic in some way.

There is a special case where the term *layer* takes on more significance—when you're dealing with Netscape 4.x, which includes support for a <layer> element. (Netscape 6 also supports it for backward compatibility, but it's not recommended.) Because the <layer> element is obsolete, I'll only touch on it briefly. But you should know it exists, particularly in case you come across some preexisting code for managing layers.

CSSP Layers

When you're creating CSSP-based layers, the only real difference from what you've seen so far in this chapter is a matter of convention rather than a matter of rule. When you're creating a layer, you'll generally use the ID selector (#) in your <style> definitions, instead of a class definition, because each layer you create needs a unique ID. That's accomplished using a combination of the # symbol and, again by convention, the <div id="layer_name"> element.

Listing 19.7 is an example of two layers defined using the ID selector and the <div> element.

LISTING 19.7   Creating CSSP Layers

```
<html xmlns="http://www.w3.org/1999/xhtml">
<head>
<title>CSSP Layers</title>

<style type="text/css">
#mydiv1 {
position:absolute;
```

LISTING 19.7   (continued)

```
top:50px;
left:50px;
height:300px;
width:500px;
}

#mydiv2 {
position:absolute;
top:350px;
left:50px;
height:300px;
width:500px;
}
</style>
</head>

<body>

<!--Begin first layer -->
<div id="mydiv1">

<img src="1980main.jpg" />

<p>This beautiful 3/2 farmhouse is right in the heart of Old Towne, taking you out of
the suburbs and back to within walking distance of not only the drug store, but the
drug store's soda fountain! Put life back the way it's supposed to be, at $125,000.</p>


</div>
<!--End first layer -->

<!--Begin second layer -->
<div id="mydiv2">

<img src="1730maple.jpg" />

<p>
Not only does this neighborhood have good schools and good shade trees, it's got great
sidewalks. Get out and meet your new neighbors, or strap on that helmet and get back on
that bicycle you haven't ridden in years. The bike path in front of this property takes
you right along Creekside Drive and into the county park! This 2/2 cottage has two
porches and a two-car garage with studio apartment. Only $135,000.
```

LISTING 19.7 (continued)

```
</p>

</div>
<!--End second layer -->

</body>
</html>
```

The result is two nice, well-defined <div> elements that can be used to alter the positioning, or even visibility, of the enclosed elements, as you'll see in the next two sections. As a quick example, though, all you would have to do is swap the names of the ID selectors in the style definition:

```
<style type="text/css">
#mydiv2 {
position:absolute;
top:50px;
left:50px;
height:300px;
width:500px;
}

#mydiv1 {
position:absolute;
top:350px;
left:50px;
height:300px;
width:500px;
}
</style>
```

If you did that and tested the result in a browser, you'd see that the two layers had switched places, with the second <div> container on top and the first <div> container below it.

Dynamic Positioning

Now that you've seen how to position elements on the page, the next step is to introduce some JavaScript to your pages, thus making them truly dynamic. (Otherwise, it isn't really *Dynamic* HTML, is it?) As a simple demonstration, you can take a single object, set its positioning, and use a simple JavaScript to change that position dynamically, thus animating the object in the browser window.

Let's try it. Listing 19.8 shows the script in action. (Note that, as written, this script will only work in Internet Explorer versions 4 and 5.)

LISTING 19.8 Moving an Item on the Page

```
<!DOCTYPE html PUBLIC "-//W3C//DTD XHTML 1.0 Transitional//EN"
    "http://www.w3.org/TR/xhtml1/DTD/xhtml1-transitional.dtd">

<html xmlns="http://www.w3.org/1999/xhtml">

<head>
<title>Dynamic Animation</title>
<style>
#headblock {
position: absolute;
left: 25px;
top: 100px;
width: 200px;
}
</style>
</head>

<script type="text/javascript">
<!--

function moveHeading(x, y) {
   x = x + "px";
   y = y + "px";
   headblock.style.left = x;
   headblock.style.top = y;
}

// -->
</script>

<body>

<form>
<pre>
Enter x coordinate: <input type="text" id="xcoord" />
Enter y coordinate: <input type="text" id="ycoord" />
<input type="button" value="Click to Submit" onclick="moveHeading(xcoord.value,
➥ycoord.value)">
```

LISTING 19.8   (continued)

```
</pre>
</form>

<div id="headblock">
<h1>Man Bites Cat</h1>
<p><strong>Orwitz, Nevada</strong> -- In a bizarre story that has local officials
scratching their heads, an Orwitz man has been questioned in an alleged biting attack
on a feline. Rich Cutter, 42, a noted local physician, apparently scrambled up a tree
in his backyard in pursuit of the cat, which lives with a neighbor. It was in that tree
that the alleged biting incident took place.</p>
</div>


</body>
</html>
```

When you enter values and click the Click to Submit button, the function assigns those values to the appropriate style values. Note that the left and top properties require values that specify the units (in this case, px for pixels), so they need to be added to the value before it's assigned to the properties. Figure 19.9 shows this.

FIGURE 19.9

Enter figures and click the Click to Submit button, and the layer is moved to a new location on the page.

So why doesn't this work in Netscape? Basically, because Netscape references individual objects from the DOM a bit differently from IE. To work in Netscape version 6.0 (as well as IE 5.5 and higher), you would need to change the function slightly:

```
function moveHeading(x, y) {
    headblock = document.getElementById("headblock");
    x = x + "px";
    y = y + "px";
    headblock.style.left = x;
    headblock.style.top = y;
}
```

Netscape 6 uses the W3C's DOM approach to storing elements in the document object. This is different from Microsoft's 4-level approach, which is to place each named element in the document object automatically. A hybrid approach would require that you first detect which browser your user has, and then assign the substitute object variable (headblock=) for Netscape. We'll discuss how to do that a little later in this chapter in the section "Cross-Browser DHTML Example."

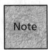

Note Just because Netscape 6's approach is different from the IE4-compatible approach doesn't mean Netscape 6 is wrong—it's actually closer to the W3C's standard for the DOM. In fact, Internet Explorer 5.5 supports the getElementById() method as well. But if you want to be compatible with IE4 and up, you need to use the older IE method.

CSSP Visibility

There's one other new property that CSSP brings to the style sheet: visibility. The options are visible, hidden, and the default, auto. By adding the property to your script class definition, you can determine whether or not any elements that have that class will appear in the browser window:

```
#mydiv1 {
position:absolute;
top:50px;
left:50px;
height:300px;
width:500px;
visibility: hidden;
}
```

By adding this to the sample script shown in Listing 19.7, you end up with a page that looks like Figure 19.10. Suddenly, the story text is gone. (Actually, only the first paragraph is gone, which is the only one that I've given this particular class for the example.)

FIGURE 19.10

With the first
`<div>` set to
`hidden`, there's a
gap on the
page.

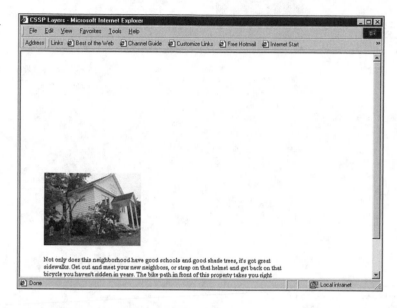

Hiding the text and elements you've sweated over in your XHTML authoring probably doesn't seem all that appealing. But the `visibility` property gets more interesting
when you mix in some JavaScript.

Using the two together, you could set up a page somewhat akin to the image-swapping
page back in Listing 19.2, except that you're able to swap an entire layer of content
instead of an image. You do this by defining a division of content, giving it an ID,
and then assigning a `visibility` property to that division. In Listing 19.9, you'll also
find that the blocks have been positioned absolutely, and positioned so that they
exactly overlap one another.

Note

Again, as written, this example only works in Internet Explorer 4.0 up to version 5.5
because of the way it references the object model.

LISTING 19.9   Using Visibility to Swap Content

```
<!DOCTYPE html PUBLIC "-//W3C//DTD XHTML 1.0 Transitional//EN"
    "http://www.w3.org/TR/xhtml1/DTD/xhtml1-transitional.dtd">

<html xmlns="http://www.w3.org/1999/xhtml">
<head>
<title>Changing Visibility</title>

<style type="text/css">
```

LISTING 19.9 (continued)

```
#mydiv1 {
position:absolute;
top:50px;
left:50px;
height:400px;
width:500px;
visibility:visible;
}

#mydiv2 {
position:absolute;
top:50px;
left:50px;
height:400px;
width:500px;
visibility:hidden;
}
</style>

<script>
<!--
function changeVis () {
   if (mydiv1.style.visibility != "hidden") {
       mydiv1.style.visibility = "hidden";
       mydiv2.style.visibility = "visible";
       }
   else {
       mydiv1.style.visibility = "visible";
       mydiv2.style.visibility = "hidden";
       }
}
// -->
</script>
</head>

<body>

<form>
<input type="button" value="Click me" onclick="changeVis()">
</form>
```

LISTING 19.9 (continued)

```
<!--Begin first layer -->
<div id="mydiv1">

<img src="1980main.jpg" />

<p>This beautiful 3/2 farmhouse is right in the heart of Old Towne, taking you out
of the suburbs and back to within walking distance of not only the drug store, but
the drug store's soda fountain! Put life back the way it's supposed to be, at
➥$125,000.</p>


</div>
<!--End first layer -->

<!--Begin second layer -->
<div id="mydiv2">

<img src="1730maple.jpg" />

<p>
Not only does this neighborhood have good schools and good shade trees, it's got
great sidewalks. Get out and meet your new neighbors, or strap on that helmet and
get back on that bicycle you haven't ridden in years. The bike path in front of this
property takes you right along Creekside Drive and into the county park! This 2/2
cottage has two porches and a two-car garage with studio apartment. Only $135,000.
</p>

</div>
<!--End second layer -->

</body>
</html>
```

The page creates the two `<div>` elements and renders the content for both, hiding the
second `<div>` because of its `visibility` property. When the button is clicked, the `script`
function is invoked. It checks the first `<div>` element to see if it's currently visible. If it
is, that `<div>` is hidden and the second `<div>` is made visible. If the first `<div>` is
already hidden, the opposite takes place. The result is that every time the button is
clicked, the images and text swap places, as shown in Figure 19.11.

FIGURE 19.11

On the left, the
page before
clicking the but-
ton; on the
right, the page
after clicking
reveals the sec-
ond `<div>` ele-
ment's contents.

Again, this doesn't work in Netscape because of the DOM differences between the
two. To make it work in Netscape version 6.0 and IE 5.5 or higher, you would need
to change the function slightly:

```
function changeVis () {
    mydiv1 = document.getElementById("mydiv1").style;
    mydiv2 = document.getElementById("mydiv2").style;
    if (mydiv1.visibility != "hidden") {
        mydiv1.visibility = "hidden";
        mydiv2.visibility = "visible";
        }
    else {
        mydiv1.visibility = "visible";
        mydiv2.visibility = "hidden";
        }
```

Note

As mentioned, there's more on these issues in the "Cross-Browser DHTML Example"
section later in this chapter.

Netscape Layers

In Netscape 4.x browsers, a different approach to layers was taken with the `<layer>`
element. That element never was terribly popular, and more to the point, it wasn't
accepted as a standard HTML or XHTML element. In version 6 of its browsers,
Netscape has moved to CSSP standards for positioning, although the `<layer>` element
is still around for backward compatibility.

There are a few key differences between the `<layer>` element and its CSSP counter-
parts:

■ It doesn't require a style definition before it's used. Although it does have an
ID, it's assigned differently from in CSSP.

■ It works like other page elements, meaning it has typical attributes such as
id, top, and left. These attributes accept an equal sign and a value in quotes,
not colons and semicolons like style markup.

■ It has a src attribute that can load an HTML document into the layer, as well
as pagex and pagey attributes that don't have equivalents in CSSP.

Once you've seen the CSSP positioning approach at work, the <layer> approach
doesn't seem terribly foreign. Listing 19.10 is an example.

LISTING 19.10   Using Netscape Layers for Positioning

```
<html xmlns="http://www.w3.org/1999/xhtml">
<head>
<title>Netscape Layers</title>
</head>

<body>

<layer id="mydiv1" top="50" left="50">

<img src="1980main.jpg" />

<p>This beautiful 3/2 farmhouse is right in the heart of Old Towne, taking you out of
the suburbs and back to within walking distance of not only the drug store, but the drug
store's soda fountain! Put life back the way it's supposed to be, at $125,000.</p>

</layer>

<layer id="mydiv2" top="500" left="50">

<img src="1730maple.jpg" />

<p>
Not only does this neighborhood have good schools and good shade trees, it's got great
sidewalks. Get out and meet your new neighbors, or strap on that helmet and get back on
that bicycle you haven't ridden in years. The bike path in front of this property takes
you right along Creekside Drive and into the county park! This 2/2 cottage has two
porches and a two-car garage with studio apartment. Only $135,000.
</p>

</layer>

</body>
</html>
```

Like <div>, the <layer> container surrounds all the text and markup that will be on that layer. Unlike <div>, the style changes are added as attributes to the <layer> element instead of via a style sheet definition. The positioning is absolute in nature—the specified coordinates are relative to the browser window.

You've seen some of the attributes that <layer> can accept, but let's take a closer look at them and some others not yet mentioned. You'll notice that most of them mirror the CSSP property names:

id	This attribute gives the layer a unique identifier.
left and top	These attributes determine how far from the left and top of the layer's parent element the layer will appear. With the <layer> element, all positioning is similar to absolute positioning in CSSP. Units are assumed to be pixels, so no px is needed.
pagex and pagey	These attributes can be used to arrange the layer based on the page's dimensions, even if another parent element is present. (That is, even if the <layer> element is nested in another element.)
src	With the <layer> element, you can use the src attribute to specify an outside file for the layer.
width and height	Set the dimensions of the layer's box. These attributes assume the dimensions are in pixels, but they can also be a percentage of the page, as in height="50%".
clip	With this attribute, you can decide that only a portion of the layer will be visible, using four values that represent the left, top, right, and bottom points of the clipping region. An example would be clip="5,5,100,100".
z-index	As with the similar CSSP property, z-index is used to determine where a layer fits above or below other layers. The higher the number, the closer the layer is to the top.
visibility	Again similar to the CSSP property, the visibility attribute can accept three values: show, hidden, and inherit. The inherit value is used to set the current layer to the same visibility as its parent.
bgcolor and background	The <layer> element can accept a background color setting (using color names or color hexadecimal values). The background attribute accepts the URL to an image to be placed in the background of the layer.

In addition to all these attributes, there is also the `<nolayer>` container, which displays its contents in browsers that don't recognize the `<layer>` element. For example:

```
<nolayer>
This page is only viewable in Netscape 4.0-level browsers or higher.
</nolayer>
```

Netscape's Inline Layer

Netscape's answer to the relatively positioned CSSP element is the `<ilayer>` element, which can be used to specify an *inline* layer. Just as with a relative-positioned CSSP layer, an `<ilayer>` begins at the place it generally would as the next logical element, but then the top and left attributes can be used to move it from that position.

This code snippet is an example:

```
<body>
<p>This is a regular XHTML paragraph.</p>
<ilayer id="para2" left="10">
<p>This paragraph began at its natural origin, then moved ten pixels to
➥the right.</p>
</ilayer>
<p>This paragraph is another regular paragraph, back at the "natural"
➥origin.</p>
</body>
```

Scripting Netscape's Layers

As with CSSP layers, you can use JavaScript or a similar language to manipulate Netscape's layers. The layer object model is slightly different from the CSSP object model (which is also different between browser versions), so it's a little tricky to learn. Fortunately, on its own, accessing Netscape layer properties is pretty easy. They follow this basic structure:

layerName.propertyName

Netscape includes a number of methods for the `<layer>` element, which are accessed using this familiar structure:

layerName.methodName()

Unlike many objects and elements rendered in Netscape 4, layers can be changed dynamically. You can use them in Netscape 6 as well, although the CSSP properties also allow for dynamic changes and are closer to cross-platform.

The `layer` object's properties mirror the attributes almost exactly, such as `layer1.top`, `layer1.visibility`, and so on. The one major difference is the `clip` attribute, whose properties are accessed individually at `layer1.clipleft`, `layer1.clipright`, `layer1.cliptop`, and `layer1.clipbottom`.

The layers themselves are actually held in an array of layers that are part of the `document` object. To access a particular layer, you can use the name of the layer as the index for the array:

```
document.layers["layer1"]
```

In many cases, you'll want to set the layer in question to a new variable that can be accessed as a standalone object:

```
myLayer = document.layers["layer1"];
```

The properties and methods of that particular layer can then be accessed using the new layer variable:

```
myLayer.top = 5;
```

The `layer` object also includes a number of methods that don't have corollaries in the CSSP world. These methods are used to directly manipulate layers, making it a little easier to animate them and make them visible or hidden. Table 19.2 shows many of the methods available for use with layers.

TABLE 19.2   Layer Object Methods

Method	Description
`moveBy(x,y)`	Moves the layer by the number of pixels
`moveTo(x,y)`	Moves the layer to particular pixel coordinates, relative to the layer's parent
`moveToAbsolute(x,y)`	Moves the layer to the specified coordinates on the page
`resizeBy(width, height)`	Grows or shrinks the layer by the number of pixels specified
`resizeTo(width, height)`	Changes layer size to the exact specified pixel values
`moveAbove(layerName)`	Places this layer above the specified layer
`moveBelow(layerName)`	Stacks this layer below the specified layer
`load(src, width)`	Changes the source of a layer to the contents of a file

In Netscape 4, note that resizing layers doesn't reposition the text and markup like you might think it would. Instead, it acts more like the `clip` attribute, in that it simply makes more or less of the layer visible. Methods are used in the same way that they are in any JavaScript code:

```
layer1.resizeTo(250, 500);
```

Now you're ready to toss in some JavaScript. In this example, the approach is similar to the layer movement shown in Listing 19.9, where two layers are specified and clicking a button changes their visibility. Listing 19.11 shows the scripting of <layer> elements.

LISTING 19.11 Changing a Layer's Visibility

```
<html xmlns="http://www.w3.org/1999/xhtml">
<head>
<title>Netscape Layers</title>
<script>
<!--

function changeLayer () {
    window.alert(document.mydiv1.visibility);
    if (document.mydiv1.visibility != "hide") {
        document.mydiv1.visibility = "hide";
        document.mydiv2.visibility = "show";
        }
    else {
        document.mydiv1.visibility = "show";
        document.mydiv2.visibility = "hide";
        }
}
// -->
</script>

</head>

<body>

<form>
<input type="button" value="Click me" OnClick="changeLayer()">
</form>

<layer id="mydiv1" top="50" left="50">

<img src="1980main.jpg" />

<p>This beautiful 3/2 farmhouse is right in the heart of Old Towne, taking you out of
the suburbs and back to within walking distance of not only the drug store, but the drug
store's soda fountain! Put life back the way it's supposed to be, at $125,000.</p>
```

LISTING 19.11   (continued)

```
</layer>

<layer id="mydiv2" top="50" left="50" visibility="hide">

<img src="1730maple.jpg" />

<p>
Not only does this neighborhood have good schools and good shade trees, it's got great
sidewalks. Get out and meet your new neighbors, or strap on that helmet and get back on
that bicycle you haven't ridden in years. The bike path in front of this property takes
you right along Creekside Drive and into the county park! This 2/2 cottage has two
porches and a two-car garage with studio apartment. Only $135,000.
</p>

</layer>

</body>
</html>
```

You can see that this script is very similar to the script used for CSSP, with the exception of the `<layer>` elements and the object model used to access those items. In fact, you can pare that down even more, as you'll see in the next section.

Cross-Browser DHTML Example

Okay, the $64,000 question is, "Can I possibly create one page that will work in three different browsers—IE, Netscape 4, and Netscape 6?" The answer is "Yes," because they all have some things in common that may be a little surprising. In this section, we'll look at the layer-swapping example that was used in Listings 9.9 and 9.11 to see how we can bring them all together in one page.

First, let's start with Netscape 4. The surprising bit is that you don't even have to use the `<layer>` element if you don't want to! Instead, Netscape 4 will accept the `<div>` elements and allow you to create the layers using the ID identifiers in a `<style>` section. That means the cross-browser DHTML example can include the following for all three browsers:

```
<style type="text/css">
#mydiv1 {
position:absolute;
top:50px;
left:50px;
height:400px;
width:500px;
visibility:visible;
}

#mydiv2 {
position:absolute;
top:50px;
left:50px;
height:400px;
width:500px;
visibility:hidden;
}
</style>
```

Likewise, all three browsers support the same basic `<body>` container shown back in Listing 19.9. They all support the `<div>` element and the `onClick` event handler.

What needs to be different for each browser is the function that changes the layers. They need to be different for two reasons:

■ Each browser accesses the `document` object a bit differently. IE 4 and higher uses `document.all.`*`layername`*, Netscape 6 uses `document.getElementById("`*`layername`*`")`, and Netscape 4 uses `document.`*`layername`*.

■ Netscape 4 can assign the strings `visibility` and `hidden` to the `visibility` property, but it must test for the values `show` and `hide`. That's weird, but we can work around it.

Note   Technically, IE 5.5 and higher can use the Netscape 6 approach, but that would require detecting four different browser types instead of three. So, because IE 5.5 is also backward compatible with the IE 4 approach, we can use it for all IE versions.

The only way to use different functions for the different browsers is to detect the type of browser that the user has, and then work a little object magic. Here's what the testing part of the function will look like:

```
function changeLayer () {

    var isNet4;
    var isNet6;
    var isIE;
    if (navigator.appName == "Netscape") {
        if (navigator.appVersion.charAt(0) == "4") isNet4 = true;
        if (navigator.appVersion.charAt(0) == "5") isNet6 = true;
    }
    if (navigator.appName.indexOf("Microsoft") != -1) isIE = true;
```

This does a series of simple tests to determine which browsers we're working with. Here's how it works:

1. The function begins by defining three variables.

2. Then it tests to see what the name of the browser application is.

3. If "Netscape" is the application's name, we'll test for the application number. Depending on the number, either the variable isNet4 or the variable isNet6 will be assigned the value true.

4. If "Microsoft" is the application's name, the variable isIE is assigned true. (Technically, the comparison is using the indexOf method to find out if the string "Microsoft" is part of the application's name. If the indexOf value does not equal –1, that means the word "Microsoft" is in the name. It's a little convoluted, but it works.)

5. Now, we can set up the function so that it creates variables that will fit into the final formula, depending on the browser we're using. In this section of the function, we'll set the variable visTest to hold the string that corresponds to the visibility property value we're going to test against. (When you test visibility in Netscape 4, it responds with the values hide and show instead of hidden and visible. So, you have to test especially for those values. Oddly, though, it can accept the latter two values as assignments, so we don't have to do anything different for Netscape 4 in the section that actually swaps the layers.)

6. Then, two object variables (div1object and div2object) are created to circumvent the different ways that each browser accesses the visibility property of these layers:

    ```
    var VisTest;
    var div1Object;
    ```

```
        var div2Object;

        if (isNet4) {
           visTest = "hide";
           div1Object = document.mydiv1;
           div2Object = document.mydiv2;
           }

        if (isNet6) {
           visTest = "hidden";
           div1Object = document.getElementById("mydiv1").style;
           div2Object = document.getElementById("mydiv2").style;
           }

        if (isIE) {
           visTest = "hidden";
           div1Object = document.all.mydiv1.style;
           div2Object = document.all.mydiv2.style;
           }
```

Finally, the function ends with the same pattern you saw earlier in Listings 9.9 and 9.11. The `visibility` property is tested to see if the first layer is hidden. If it isn't, the first layer is hidden and the second layer is shown. If the first layer is hidden, the opposite happens:

```
    if (div1Object.visibility != visTest) {
        div1Object.visibility = "hidden";
        div2Object.visibility = "visible";
        }
    else {
        div1Object.visibility = "visible";
        div2Object.visibility = "hidden";
        }

}
```

As you can see, the `visTest` and two object variables are cleverly plugged in there to make up for the differences in the browser's approaches to the DOM. Listing 19.12 shows the whole page.

LISTING 19.12   Cross-Browser Compatible Layer Switching

```
<!DOCTYPE html PUBLIC "-//W3C//DTD XHTML 1.0 Transitional//EN"
    "http://www.w3.org/TR/xhtml1/DTD/xhtml1-transitional.dtd">

<html xmlns="http://www.w3.org/1999/xhtml">
<head>
<title>Netscape Layers</title>

<style type="text/css">
#mydiv1 {
position:absolute;
top:50px;
left:50px;
height:400px;
width:500px;
visibility:visible;
}

#mydiv2 {
position:absolute;
top:50px;
left:50px;
height:400px;
width:500px;
visibility:hidden;
}
</style>

<script>
<!--

function changeLayer () {

    var isNet4;
    var isNet6;
    var isIE;
    if (navigator.appName == "Netscape") {
        if (navigator.appVersion.charAt(0) == "4") isNet4 = true;
        if (navigator.appVersion.charAt(0) == "5") isNet6 = true;
    }
    if (navigator.appName.indexOf("Microsoft") != -1) isIE = true;
```

LISTING 19.12   (continued)

```
    var VisTest;
    var div1Object;
    var div2Object;

    if (isNet4) {
       visTest = "hide";
       div1Object = document.mydiv1;
       div2Object = document.mydiv2;
       }

    if (isNet6) {
       visTest = "hidden";
       div1Object = document.getElementById("mydiv1").style;
       div2Object = document.getElementById("mydiv2").style;
       }

    if (isIE) {
       visTest = "hidden";
       div1Object = document.all.mydiv1.style;
       div2Object = document.all.mydiv2.style;
       }


    if (div1Object.visibility != visTest) {
        div1Object.visibility = "hidden";
        div2Object.visibility = "visible";
        }
    else {
        div1Object.visibility = "visible";
        div2Object.visibility = "hidden";
        }

}

// -->
</script>

</head>

<body>

<form>
```

LISTING 19.12 (continued)

```
<input type="button" value="Click me" OnClick="changeLayer()">
</form>

<div id="mydiv1">

<img src="1980main.jpg" />

<p>This beautiful 3/2 farmhouse is right in the heart of Old Towne, taking you out of
the suburbs and back to within walking distance of not only the drug store, but the drug
store's soda fountain! Put life back the way it's supposed to be, at $125,000.</p>


</div>

<div id="mydiv2">

<img src="1730maple.jpg" />

<p>
Not only does this neighborhood have good schools and good shade trees, it's got great
sidewalks. Get out and meet your new neighbors, or strap on that helmet and get back on
that bicycle you haven't ridden in years. The bike path in front of this property takes
you right along Creekside Drive and into the county park! This 2/2 cottage has two
porches and a two-car garage with studio apartment. Only $135,000.
</p>

</div>

</body>
</html>
```

Cross-Browser APIs

In the previous section, you saw a long script that produced a reasonably simple result. You can imagine what happens when you try to create pages to do much more complicated things that work in many different browsers. Although it's perfectly common and acceptable to do all this prep work (detecting browsers and substituting pointer variables for certain DOM objects), a more sophisticated approach is to use a special *application programming interface*, or *API*.

Although APIs are usually the domain of more sophisticated programming languages, a number of cross-browser APIs for JavaScript have been developed. They give you predetermined function calls that you can use with your scripts to make things like browser detection much easier. Instead of writing the function yourself, you simply learn the API and then plug that function into your script. You'll load the API as an external script file, making its functions available to you within your own script.

If that sounds interesting, visit one of the following Web sites to learn more:

- `http://www.mozilla.org/docs/web-developer/csspapi/csspapi.html`—The Mozilla organization—the open source arm that developed the underlying Netscape browser engine—offers a freely downloadable cross-browser JavaScript API.

- `http://dynapi.sourceforge.net/dynapi/`—The DynAPI is a similar effort that offers an API for cross-browser use, as well as a few extras within the API to make certain Dynamic HTML tricks easier to accomplish.

Dynamic Styles and Classes

If you've worked through the previous sections of this chapter, these last few pages should be a cakewalk. Now that you've seen how to change the CSS Positioning elements, changing regular CSS elements using a script should be simple.

And it is, unless you want to do it in Netscape 4. That can't really be done, because Netscape 4 doesn't support dynamic rerendering of elements on pages like Internet Explorer 4 and higher does. It so happens that Netscape 6 has been updated with this capability, however, so you'll find that the ability to change styles using scripts is supported in both those later browsers.

By the way, we're discussing the scripting of CSS1—CSSP capabilities are considered part of the CSS2 standard. CSS1 is the CSS standard that includes the style sheet properties discussed in Chapter 10—font, text, border, and similar properties. In this section we'll look at scripting basic CSS1 properties in IE 5.5 and higher, Netscape 6, and other compatible browsers.

Scripting Styles and Properties

With what you already know about scripting style properties, scripting CSS1 properties is straightforward. Take this example:

```
<html xmlns="http://www.w3.org/1999/xhtml">
<head>
```

```
<title>Dynamic Image Demo</title>
</head>

<script type="text/javascript">
<!--

function changeText (p) {
        p.style.color="red";
        }

// -->
</script>

<body>

<p onmouseover="changeText(this)">Test 1</p>
<p onmouseover="changeText(this)">Test 2</p>

</body>
</html>
```

When you place the mouse pointer over either of these paragraphs, the text turns red. Using the simple `p.style.color="red";` assignment, the style of the received element pointer is changed.

You can experiment with nearly any style in CSS1 and change properties in this way. Because most property values are strings, you'll find that you can even accept entries from the user for the property values and then assign them, as in Listing 19.13.

LISTING 19.13 Changing the Color of Text

```
<!DOCTYPE html PUBLIC "-//W3C//DTD XHTML 1.0 Transitional//EN"
    "http://www.w3.org/TR/xhtml1/DTD/xhtml1-transitional.dtd">

<html xmlns="http://www.w3.org/1999/xhtml">
<head>
<title>Dynamic Text Color</title>
</head>

<script type="text/javascript">
```

LISTING 19.13 (continued)

```
<!--

function changeBack () {
    var theColor = document.forms[0].myColor.value;
    alert (theColor);
    document.getElementById("myPara").style.color = theColor;
    if (theColor == "white") document.body.style.backgroundColor = "black";
    }

// -->
</script>

<body style="background-color: gray">

<form name="form1">
<p id="myPara">What color would you like the text?</p>
<input type="text" name="myColor" /> <br />
<input type="button" value="Change It" onClick="changeBack()">
</form>


</body>
</html>
```

In this example, the user can enter a color in the myColor input box and then click the Change It button. When the button is clicked, the changeBack() function is called. In the function, the color name entered by the user is assigned to a variable (theColor), and then the style of the paragraph of text is assigned to the value of the variable. The function will also check if the new foreground color is white; if it is, it changes the background color to black so that the text can still be read.

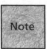

Note

This script should work, but it's a bit oversimplified because it doesn't account for a user who enters an invalid color name. If you were really going to implement this script, you might use a <select> element to limit the color choices to valid color names, or you might create another function that tests the user's entry against valid color names.

Dynamic Classes and IDs

In the previous section, you saw that you can change the individual properties of elements, regardless of whether or not they've been predefined with other style properties or even been assigned classes. But what if you want to change an element's class ID itself, so that the element changes a number of different properties dynamically? This is easily done, in both Internet Explorer and Netscape, using a script such as the one shown in Listing 19.14.

LISTING 19.14 Changing CSS Classes Programmatically

```
<!DOCTYPE html PUBLIC "-//W3C//DTD XHTML 1.0 Transitional//EN"
    "http://www.w3.org/TR/xhtml1/DTD/xhtml1-transitional.dtd">

<html xmlns="http://www.w3.org/1999/xhtml">
<head>
<title>Dynamic Classes</title>

<style>
.big {font-size: 36; color: red}
.small {font-size: 12; color: black}
</style>

<script type="text/javascript">
<!--
function changeClass () {
    theClass = document.getElementById("myPara").className;
    alert (theClass);
    if (theClass != "big") {
    document.getElementById("myPara").className = "big";
    }
    else document.getElementById("myPara").className = "small";
}
// -->
</script>
</head>

<body>
<form name="form1">
<p id="myPara" class="small">What class would you like assigned to this text?</p>
<input type="button" value="Change It" onClick="changeClass()" />
</form>
</body>
</html>
```

In this case, when the user clicks the `Change It` button, the function is invoked. It then determines the current class name that's being used with the paragraph and assigns it to `theClass`. Next, it checks if `theClass` *does not equal* big. If it doesn't, it is assigned the class big; if it does, it is assigned the class small. In this way, the script is able to compensate for either choice and switch between them repeatedly as the user clicks the button.

Figure 19.12 shows this script in action.

FIGURE 19.12

On the left, the page before clicking the button; on the right, the page after clicking has changed the class of the targeted paragraph.

Summary

In this chapter, you learned how JavaScript and CSS can come together into something that some people call Dynamic HTML. When Netscape and Internet Explorer released their 4.0-level browsers, Dynamic HTML was a buzzword on every Web developer's lips. It turned out that a great number of both browsers' implementations were incompatible with one another, making aspects of DHTML difficult to adopt.

With both browser companies now offering 5.x- and 6.x-level browser versions, that landscape has changed somewhat. Both browsers support a common overlap of CSS, both for appearance styles and for positioning elements on the page. Using those styles, it's possible to do a great deal of Dynamic HTML—programming style sheets—that will work cross-browser.

This chapter started by introducing the CSSP properties and techniques, and then showed you how to script CSSP in each of the major browsers. Also shown was how scripts can be written that take into account all CSS-compatible versions of the major browsers, including the problematic Netscape 4.x browsers.

The chapter ended with a look at scripting CSS1-level properties, including changing individual properties and changing the CSS class with which a particular property is associated.

In the next chapter, you'll see some of the popular graphical editors for HTML and XHTML. You'll learn some of the differences between them and the advantages to using a graphical editor, particularly once you've come to understand XHTML and other Web technologies.

PART V

WEB PUBLISHING TOOLS

GRAPHICAL
EDITORS

y recommended path for a Web author is to learn XHTML first. You want to know what your graphical editor is doing and how to augment its capabilities or fix any problems that crop up by digging into the code. If you've been reading the chapters of this book in order, you should have no problem managing a graphical editor.

The advantages of a graphical editor are obvious—you don't have to type all those crazy codes! Nearly all graphical editors let you lay out your page with tables, create framesets, or even add some JavaScript. At the high end, a graphical editor can enable you to work with complex style sheet configurations and CSS positioning or other DHTML procedures. Best of all, you generally do less editing of elements and tags by hand.

In this chapter, you'll take a look at some popular graphical editors; the differences and advantages of them for Web authoring.

This chapter discusses the following:

- Netscape Composer
- Adobe GoLive
- Macromedia Dreamweaver
- Microsoft FrontPage 2002

Netscape Composer

While Netscape Composer doesn't exactly belong in the same class as the other graphical editors discussed in this chapter, it's worth covering for one primary reason—it's free. It's also gotten a bad rap from some Web authors, perhaps because earlier versions were partial to Netscape-only elements and the code tended to be a bit messy. The fact that Netscape Communicator (the main version of Netscape's software in the late 1990s) went quite a while without significant updates also hurt Composer, because it was stuck at a particular support level of HTML for quite a while.

Composer has been updated for Netscape 6.x, however, and it turns in a decent performance. It's part of the standard Netscape distribution, which now incorporates all the modules (Web browsing, e-mail, newsgroups, and Composer) that used to comprise Netscape Communicator. In Netscape 6.x, all you need to do is choose File, New, Blank Page to Edit to begin working with Composer.

Where to Get It

You can get Composer simply by downloading Netscape from `http://home.netscape.com/computing/download/index.html`. Once that's downloaded and installed, Composer is available immediately.

Composer's Strengths

Composer is an HTML 4.01 transitional DTD-compliant Web browser. It doesn't follow all the rules of an XHTML document—for instance, empty elements don't include a trailing slash. However, it does follow many of the rules, including closing most container elements, avoiding most deprecated elements, and using the appropriate elements for much of the markup. Likewise, the raw markup is reasonably clean and easy to read, which was a problem with earlier versions of Composer (as with many early graphical editors).

Composer features a number of different modes that are great for the Web developer who is learning HTML code. The Show All Tags mode (see Figure 20.1) can be used to quickly see which elements are being used on a particular page. This mode enables you not only to see potential mistakes (such as the two `<div>` elements that appear in Figure 20.1), but also to double-click an element and change its attributes or add inline style or JavaScript event handlers.

FIGURE 20.1

In Show All Tags mode, Composer gives you a special view that displays the elements being used. You can also change them and add inline styles.

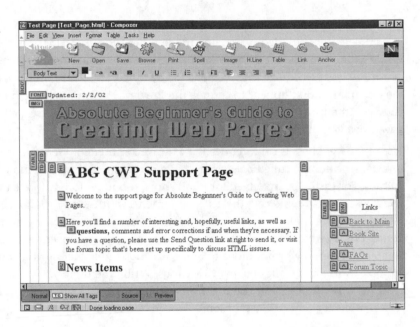

Composer offers two other modes: HTML Source and Preview. The HTML Source mode is useful for seeing the source that Composer is developing, as well as for making alterations yourself when necessary. And the Preview mode is useful because it can show you exactly how the page will look—at least in Netscape 6.x. You can also edit in Preview mode, if desired, without the guides that are shown in the Normal mode.

Composer's Weaknesses

Composer isn't really an XHTML tool, although generally Composer will create pages that validate to the HTML 4.01 transitional DTD. (And in fact, a validation tool is built into Composer.) Composer tends to use `<font>` elements for changing the size and typeface of fonts, although you can opt to add inline styles to elements one by one.

Composer is designed primarily to edit individual pages. As you'll see with the other tools discussed in this chapter, pro-level editors tend to help you manage an entire site, including uploading and downloading the site or otherwise working with the server. Composer is really a page editor, leaving most of the site management up to you.

Probably its biggest weakness is that it has very little support for adding `<style>` and `<script>` elements to the page in any mode other than the HTML Source mode. While Composer doesn't seem to damage the `<style>` and `<script>` elements, it doesn't always recognize them, either. For instance, style definitions in the `<head>` of the document don't appear to change the Preview mode presentation of the page. If you click the Browse button to see the page in a full-fledged Netscape browser window, however, the style sheet definitions are put into place.

The other weakness is an interface issue. Most commercial Web authoring packages use small windows, called *palettes*, to make common settings available as you're editing. For instance, a Web editor might have a palette for settings so that when you click inside a table cell, the cell's alignment, width, background color, and other settings are available immediately. In Composer, these settings are handled using dialog boxes, which simply adds a step to the process. You need to double-click an element, either in Normal mode or Show All Tags mode, before you can see the dialog box that governs that element's settings. While the dialog boxes tend to be powerful (as I mentioned, you can add inline style and JavaScript event handlers), all that double-clicking can get tiresome.

Composer's Highlights

If you're interested in trying out Composer, simply launch Netscape 6.x and choose File, New, Blank Page to Edit, or choose Tasks, Composer to launch Composer directly. (Netscape 6 also has a small menu bar, usually in the bottom-left corner, that has a Composer launch button.) Once it's launched, you can begin typing directly in the window. Composer considers the entire window to be within the bounds of the `<body>` of your document, unless you're editing in Source mode.

As you type, note that the menu in the top-left corner can be used to change the current paragraph on the page to a particular block style, either a paragraph style or a heading, as shown in Figure 20.2. You needn't highlight block elements to change them—simply place the insertion point in a paragraph and choose from the menu.

You can change font typefaces, sizes, and text styles by highlighting words and choosing styles from the toolbar, or by opening the Format menu and choosing from the Font, Size, and Text Style submenus.

Also on the Format menu are controls for editing table properties, as well as the Format, Page Title, and Properties menu items, where you can enter the title and some `<head>`-level elements.

FIGURE 20.2

Changing block
level styles with
the menu bar
menu.

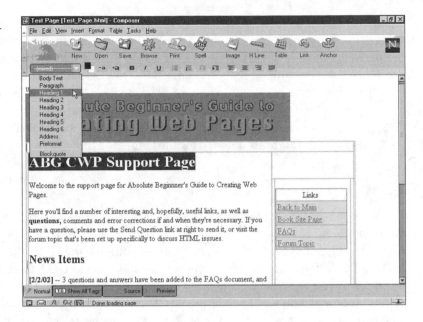

Adding other elements is accomplished via the Insert menu, where you can add images, hyperlinks, tables, and other HTML markup. For instance, choose Insert, Image and the resulting dialog box enables you to locate the image on your hard disk. (Remember, it should be in the same relative location that it will be once it's uploaded to your Web server.) The Image Properties dialog box allows you to add alternative text, specify the width and height of the image, or create an imagemap. Once you've made your settings and click OK, the image is added where the insertion point is on your page. You can then drag the image around to change its location.

Adding a table is a similar prospect. Choose Insert, Table and a dialog box appears. In that dialog box, choose the number of rows and columns for the table, the width, and the border thickness. For more advanced options, including cellpadding and cellspacing, click the Advanced Edit button. Otherwise, click the OK button to add the blank table to your page. You'll see the cells, ready for you to begin typing (or pasting) content.

As a knowledgeable Web author, you'll likely find yourself spending at least some time in the HTML Source mode. There you can edit the elements directly, and you can add <head>-level elements, scripting, or style code. Netscape Composer is fairly good at staying out of your way after you've edited the source code. (In fact, in the Preferences dialog box, you can tell Composer to maintain the original formatting of the HTML that you type in manually.)

Finally, you have a few different choices when you're ready to preview the page. Click the Preview mode tab for an editable preview of your page. Click the Browser button in the toolbar to see the page in an actual Netscape browser window, where you'll likely see even truer representations. (Plus, JavaScript and CSS will work in those browser windows.) Finally, choose Edit, Validate HTML to automatically connect to the W3C's validator page and test your document to make sure it's valid HTML. (Again, it's compared against the HTML 4.01 transitional DTD, which is similar to the XHTML 1.0 transitional DTD but slightly less strict.)

Adobe GoLive

GoLive began as its own very successful development company, creating what was at first a Macintosh-only Web editor called GoLive CyberStudio, which surpassed everything else of its time in terms of graphical editing. One of the first editors to make Web authoring more object-oriented and less code-focused, GoLive still works by enabling you to "drag in" any number of different objects and work with them without too much low-end knowledge of HTML coding. Since its early beginnings, it has gone cross-platform and hit the big time. It's now owned by graphics powerhouse Adobe, which has given it a makeover to resemble Adobe's line of graphics applications, while retaining its powerful approach.

For knowledgeable Web authors, GoLive offers a way to quickly prototype pages and then dig into the code to make them perfect. GoLive also supports tons of advanced features, including a JavaScript editor, drag-and-drop support for multimedia controls, and the ability to work easily with technologies such as CSS Positioning. It's definitely a pro-level tool, which extends to the price—currently, it's $299 for most users. Still, if you're planning to do professional work with GoLive, it's probably money worth spending.

 As with many software applications, GoLive is available in a much cheaper academic version for teachers and students (and occasionally parents). Check with your school or university to see if you qualify for educational pricing.

Where to Get It

You can get Adobe GoLive in most computer stores and superstores, or you can order it online via any number of vendors. If you're not yet sure that GoLive is right for you, Adobe offers a 30-day demo that you can download at `http://www.adobe.com/products/golive/main.html`. Be warned that the demo's archive is over 35MB for the Windows version and nearly 50MB for the Mac version, so downloading it is only recommended if you have a broadband connection.

GoLive's Strengths

If you fire up GoLive and you have existing Web sites, you might come across the first advantage immediately—GoLive can import an existing Web site quickly and easily. All you have to do is tell it where the index page is, and it can figure out the rest. Once you've imported your site, GoLive allows you to manage that site visually (see Figure 20.3).

FIGURE 20.3

Adobe GoLive enables you to manage your Web site visually.

Probably the most obvious reason to choose GoLive is its integration with other Adobe tools. GoLive can work directly with PhotoShop image files, rollover animations created with Adobe ImageReady, and files created in Adobe Illustrator or Adobe LiveMotion. This integration, as well as a shared approach to the user interface, makes Adobe GoLive a good choice for Web authors who have bought other Adobe products, or Adobe users looking for a pro-level Web development tool. In fact, you can purchase GoLive in various bundles with these other Adobe tools (one of them called Adobe Web Studio), which is much cheaper than buying each application individually.

GoLive offers many additional rich features, including strong support for programming back-end databases, the ability to create pages that work with Microsoft's ASP servers, and automatic conversion of HTML documents to XHTML. It offers particularly strong tools for editing the source code, including the ability to view elements in different ways, such as a hierarchical tree that can show you when elements are missing from the logic of your page. And GoLive includes a special feature to ensure that code you import or type directly will remain off-limits to the program so that it doesn't change items you've hand-coded.

In fact, if you happen to have GoLive or the GoLive demo available as you work through this book or explore XHTML coding further, you'll find the Source mode is a great way to work in XHTML. (You access Source mode by clicking the Source tab at the top of the editing window.) Small buttons in the button bar enable you to highlight different portions of the code—you can highlight only links, for instance, or only server-side code. You can also display line numbers. This can be handy for troubleshooting JavaScript (JScript) code in Internet Explorer, which reports errors on numbered lines. GoLive even displays a small error count at the top of the editing window, and it can alert you to errors and warn about problematic code.

Although GoLive is a strong Windows tool, its Mac roots still show through a bit. It supports AppleScript, it can work extensively with QuickTime movies, and it directly supports WebObjects technology, which is Apple's high-end Web application environment (for building high-capacity Web stores, for instance).

GoLive's Weaknesses

Reviewers and users often directly compare Adobe GoLive to Macromedia Dreamweaver (covered later in this chapter), which tends to be the category leader. Whereas GoLive relies on its Adobe family integration for some of its strengths, some feel that it continues to lag behind Dreamweaver's ease of use. GoLive requires a slightly steeper learning curve than some other editors, although it does go deeper with database-driven sites than much of the competition does.

GoLive 5 can have trouble with standards, thanks to some slightly proprietary approaches to creating pages. It doesn't always create pages that pass muster with the validators, it doesn't generate strict XHTML 1.0, and often it throws in some messy proprietary codes (such as special attributes for tables), particularly when you're working with tables and grid-based layouts.

If you plan to use GoLive, you should have a large computer display and it should run at high resolution. GoLive uses palettes for a number of solutions and tools, making it easy to fill up the screen on smaller displays. Editing Web pages at 800×600 is frustrating at best (see Figure 20.4). A better workspace for GoLive includes a large display and a good mouse—you'll be doing a lot of pointing and clicking, and contextual menus abound.

GoLive's Highlights

If you've already put together a Web site of any sort, you should allow GoLive to import that site so you can see the site-management tools. Once you grow familiar with GoLive, you'll appreciate being able to not only edit pages within it, but to manage your overall site, including the FTP process to your server. In fact, if your server supports the WebDAV protocol, you can actually edit your pages directly on the server using GoLive, which supports WebDAV.

FIGURE 20.4

These are GoLive's default palette positions—nearly impossible to work with at 800×600.

If the site is stored on your local hard disk, import it by choosing File, New Site, Import from Folder. If not, choose File, New Site, Import to import from an FTP Server. In the second case, your entire site will be downloaded via FTP, which can take a while.

Once the site is imported, you'll see the Site window. There you can inspect all the pages on the site, along with other attributes of the site's markup. For instance, you can check the Colors tab to see the different colors being used in your site. GoLive even allows you to assign your own names to particular color values, which can be handy if you have a group of designers and you want to create a custom palette of approved colors. Clicking the Font Sets tab shows you the different font families being used—again, this is helpful if you have a team of designers for your site. The Errors tab shows any URLs or other referenced files that don't exist or links that don't work.

Double-click a page in the Site window (or create a new one using the File, New command), and you're introduced to the main editing interface. Along the top of the editing window are a number of tabs that you use to change modes—Layout, Source, Preview, and others for viewing frames and viewing an element hierarchy.

Once you're working on a page in Layout mode, you'll find that most of the images, form elements, and pretty much anything else you don't type in are added by dragging an icon to your page. The Objects palette holds different icons that you can drag directly to your window. Anything from a comment, a line break, or a horizontal line, all the way up to a QuickTime or RealMedia plug-in object, can be dragged directly into the editing window. Once an element is in the window, selecting it causes its properties to be displayed in the Inspector, which you can then use to tweak the attribute settings for that element.

Perhaps the least familiar element to a seasoned XHTML author is the layout grid that GoLive can use for HTML layout (see Figure 20.5). Essentially, it enables you to lay out your page as precisely as you'd like without worrying about any particular CSS, table, or other element or property. Then, when you're done, HTML tables are created to place the elements on the page as exactly as is possible with the HTML specification.

FIGURE 20.5

You can use a layout grid to position elements without worrying about the underlying table code.

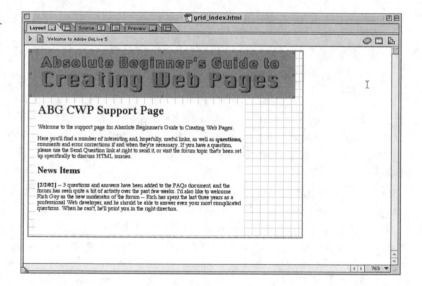

Macromedia Dreamweaver

By most accounts, Dreamweaver is the leader in professional Web authoring tools. While both GoLive and Microsoft FrontPage (discussed next in this chapter) have their strengths, those strengths tend to focus on integration—GoLive integrates well with other Adobe products, whereas FrontPage integrates well with Microsoft products. Dreamweaver, in many cases, is favored simply for its interface and its approach to Web page creation. Personally, I've come across a number of Web neophytes who have found that Dreamweaver helps them make sense of basic Web editing and updating—even the actual process of sending files to the server via FTP is made a little more bearable by Dreamweaver.

In fact, Dreamweaver's emphasis on interface design means you can work with fewer palette windows on the screen, if desired. You can actually drag tabs from one palette to another, creating a personalized interface that enables you to work with fewer windows that still have your favorite tools. This is a great way to get quick access to the tools you use regularly, particularly once you've worked with Dreamweaver a bit and gotten a sense of its capabilities.

At the same time, Dreamweaver is owned by Macromedia, a powerhouse multimedia applications company. This means it integrates well with Macromedia's tools, which include some very popular Web development tools such as Macromedia Flash. In fact, Macromedia sells Dreamweaver in different bundles that include Flash, Fireworks (for animated and optimized images), and other Macromedia applications. These bundles (Macromedia calls them Studios) can be much cheaper than buying all the included applications individually.

Where to Get It

Macromedia offers a free 30-day demo of Dreamweaver that you can download from `http://www.macromedia.com/software/dreamweaver/`. The suggested price for Dreamweaver is $299, although upgrade and "cross-grade" prices are also available.

Dreamweaver's Strengths

Dreamweaver features a good mix of visual editing and textual editing, which works well for both the novice Web author and one who has XHTML experience. The blank page offers the user a word processor-like interface, with a small taskbar that holds commonly used elements that can be dragged into the window and defined. Using that tool palette, you can add anything from a horizontal line to a plug-in object.

The word processor theme is carried through to the Properties window, which shows up at the bottom of the page by default. As you move to different elements on your page, the Properties window changes to reflect the sort of element you're working with. You can then make immediate changes that are reflected in the code that Dreamweaver generates, such as changes to the fonts, sizes, or styles of text, or to the dimensions or alternate text of images. You create hyperlinks using the Properties window by highlighting text or an image and entering an URL in the Link entry box (see Figure 20.6).

FIGURE 20.6

As you create
your page, use
the Properties
area to quickly
change values
and styles.

One favorite element of Dreamweaver's interface is a split-window option for code-level editing of the page. You can view pages in full graphical mode, source code-only mode, or a split window with source code on the top and a graphical representation on the bottom. This is great for knowledgeable Web authors. You can immediately see the changes made in one environment and tweak them in the other. If you add an element in the graphical pane, for instance, and you don't like one of the attribute settings that Dreamweaver uses, you can click in the source pane and edit it. The changes are shown immediately in the graphical representation (see Figure 20.7). Note that both sides are active at once—highlighting text in the preview pane also highlights it in the source pane. You can jump back and forth, editing freely on either side.

Dreamweaver features a Reference panel that includes content from books that offer quick reference for both HTML and CSS. Likewise, a palette is available that makes it easy to add CSS styles to your page, whether you're creating a site-wide style sheet, a redefinition of an existing element, or a class for use with various elements. Unfortunately, the Dreamweaver engine isn't fully capable of displaying those CSS styles, but you can use a button in the main window to preview your work in Internet Explorer, Netscape, or another external browser.

Aside from the windowpane approach to source code, Dreamweaver's most unique offering is the Asset panel, which is particularly useful for larger sites. The Asset panel collects the images, colors, URLs, and multimedia elements that you've already used in your site. Using the Asset panel, you can quickly drag and drop these recurring elements into your pages, making it easier to generate pages that use the standard navigational aids and other styles that you've developed for your site.

FIGURE 20.7

The split-pane approach is great for authors who know their way around HTML.

Dreamweaver's Layout mode is similar to GoLive's, but it offers some interesting visual feedback. Select the Layout icon in the View portion of the Object panel, and the Layout tools come alive. You can draw a table on the page and begin adding content, or you can draw individual cells on the page, which Dreamweaver automatically turns into cells of a whole-page table. As you draw these floating cells, you can see the rest of the table taking shape in the background. In this way, you can create very complex tables (see Figure 20.8) that can be used to create very interesting designs.

Layout tools

FIGURE 20.8

In Layout mode, you're free to draw cells all over the page, perhaps leading up to a very interesting page design.

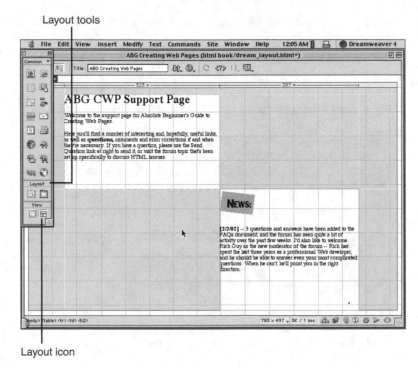

Layout icon

Other features include a JavaScript debugger for creating and editing scripts. The debugger can find specific problems with your JavaScript code and help point you in the right direction.

Finally, are you interested in adding some Macromedia Flash rollover images? Thanks to Dreamweaver's shared parentage with Flash, it can create some basic Flash text and animated buttons without requiring an outside application.

Dreamweaver's Weaknesses

Compared to the other high-end Web editors discussed in this chapter, Dreamweaver is probably the weakest when it comes to working with server-side elements. While GoLive includes a number of built-in database-access capabilities, and FrontPage supports Microsoft's servers very well, Macromedia requires you to upgrade to Dreamweaver UltraDev if you want support for anything beyond basic server-side includes. The UltraDev package is powerful, with support for ASP, JSP, and Cold Fusion—names that should mean something to Web application developers. The UltraDev pacakge is more expensive than the others. If you're looking for a graphical editor that also works with various server front-ends, shop carefully.

Dreamweaver may be a bit frustrating if you're shooting for 100% strict XHTML 1.0 code because it tends to use a transitional DTD approach. However, Dreamweaver's plug-in architecture makes it possible for third-party software to fill that gap. You'll find such tools for XHTML compliance at `http://www.macromedia.com/exchange/dreamweaver/`, where Macromedia highlights the plug-ins.

Otherwise, Dreamweaver has few weaknesses, if you like the interface. FrontPage offers a more comfortable interface for users who are accustomed to Microsoft Office products, and GoLive is sometimes more comfortable for Mac users, Photoshop users, and those who are familiar with Adobe's products. But Dreamweaver tends to appeal to all sorts of customer profiles. It's simply a very impressive tool.

Dreamweaver's Highlights

Dreamweaver's Site window is a great place to start if you've already begun work on a Web site. Choose Site, Define Sites from the menu to begin converting an existing site to a Dreamweaver site. In the Site Definition window, you can name the site, choose its local root folder, and specify the URL that the site will use when it's available online. When defining the site, notice that you can do much more—under Remote Info, you can enter information about your FTP server or any other mechanism for updating the site that you choose. When the Design Notes feature is enabled, it lets you share notes with others who are working on the site.

Click OK in the Site Definition window to create your site. Now you can use the Site, Open Site command to open this Web site whenever necessary. If you've set up FTP access, you can even use the Site window (see Figure 20.9) to quickly log in and transfer files to and from the server.

FIGURE 20.9

The Site window is great for quickly managing your Web site.

To edit an individual page, double-click in the Local Folder pane of the Site window. (Or, for individual pages, use the File, New or File, Open command.) Now, if you're like me, you'll immediately switch to the split-window view. (It's the center of three buttons in the button bar at the top-left of the editing window. Or you can choose View, Code and Design.) If the page is something you've worked on previously, you can scroll the source code view to see if any of it is highlighted. If so, that suggests the code is incorrect in some way. Make the corrections, click the Refresh button in the toolbar (or choose View, Refresh Design View), and you can see if you've fixed the error.

Adding elements to your pages is a simple drag-and-drop from the Objects bar, if that's how you want to do things. You can also use the Insert menu to add many types of objects, such as images (Insert, Image), tables (Insert, Table), or form elements (Insert, Form and Insert, Form Elements). You can even create layers (CSS- or Netscape-compatible) and add server-side includes.

As you're working, you can use the Properties window (it's at the bottom of the screen by default) to alter just about any of the markup you're working with in your document. If you highlight text, the Properties window changes to show text options. (Watch out—some of them may be using transitional elements such as the `<font>` element.) If you highlight a table cell, you'll see table-related choices.

Also, while you're working, it's handy to have the CSS Styles window open so you can edit and update CSS styles, many of which will be updated immediately in the Dreamweaver editing window. And with the Assets window open, you can easily drag and drop images, colors, and other elements that you've already used elsewhere in the site. This makes it convenient to keep your site looking uniform.

When you're done editing a site, choose Site, Check Links Sitewide for a quick report on any broken links that your site may have. You can then use that report to dig back into the site and fix the problems.

Microsoft FrontPage 2002

FrontPage 2002 is a popular Web-editing application, particularly among users who are partial to Microsoft Office-like applications and those who are creating Web pages specifically for Microsoft's Internet servers. FrontPage 2002 is designed specifically to work well with Microsoft Word, Excel, and the rest of the Office package, while at the same time integrating Web-application creation with Microsoft's languages, proprietary scripting, and interface hooks.

Where to Get It

FrontPage isn't available as a downloadable demo, presumably because it's too big for the download. It's available in a trial version, but only via CD-ROM. Check your local computer store to see if they have the demo in stock. If not, you can order it directly from Microsoft at `http://www.microsoft.com/frontpage/evaluation/trial.htm`. Unlike all the other tools discussed in this chapter, FrontPage 2002 is only available for Windows—there is no Mac version (or Unix or Linux versions, which Netscape Composer does offer). FrontPage 2002 is packaged in a number of Microsoft Office bundles, or it can be purchased separately at a retail price of $169.

FrontPage's Strengths

The obvious strength of FrontPage 2002 is its integration with Microsoft Office. It looks very much like a Microsoft application, with a toolbar very similar to Word's, the ability to directly import Word documents, and even that ubiquitous little paper-clip for getting help. It includes wizards to help you create and manage pages, as well as wizards to help you create a particular type of page or site.

FrontPage 2002 has been reworked to place many more tools on the main interface, including tools that enable you to look at your Web site in different ways. For instance, the Hyperlinks tool can show you the different ways that each page is linked to the main page, while the Navigation view can be used to quickly see the navigational structure of your site.

FrontPage focuses its ease-of-use on the beginning user by making it easy to pull off some complex tasks. For instance, adding a DHTML mouseover event is something you can accomplish simply by displaying the DHTML formatting toolbar (Format, Dynamic HTML Effects) and then highlighting an item for which you'd like to create the effect.

FrontPage integrates well with Microsoft's servers, allowing you to manage your Web site closely. You can check statistics such as page hits, the operating systems being used, and the referring URLs, essentially enabling you to monitor Web log stats from within the FrontPage interface. FrontPage also allows you to integrate content and technology from Microsoft Web sites, such as bCentral.com (for Web site revenue and traffic), Expedia (for online travel links), and even MSNBC (for placing news headlines on your page).

One of FrontPage's real strengths is making tedious things simple to do. For instance, one special Web component (Insert, Web Component) is a photo gallery (also via Insert, Picture, New Photo Gallery), which is really a wizard to help you create a thumbnail gallery of images that can be clicked and enlarged for viewing. Using templates provided by FrontPage, you can create a montage, a slide show, or a page of images and descriptive text (see Figure 20.10).

FIGURE 20.10

The Photo Gallery Properties window helps you put together a quick page of thumbnails.

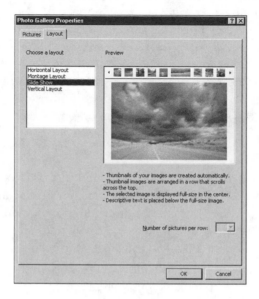

Likewise, FrontPage includes a number of templates, both for Web pages and for entire Web sites, that can make setting up a basic Web presence fairly simple and quick. In fact, you can even use FrontPage to create more complicated sites—such as a guest book, discussion forums, feedback pages, or HTML forms—as long your Web server is running FrontPage Extensions.

Note FrontPage Extensions is a set of applications that run server-side on capable servers. (That's mostly Microsoft servers, although they can be added to Unix-based servers as well.) FrontPage can then use those server extensions to add interesting interactive items to pages, such as hit counters, bulletin boards, and form submissions. Those same pages won't work on a server that doesn't support FrontPage Extensions, however.

FrontPage's Weaknesses

FrontPage's interface is something you'll either love or hate. If you're not a fan of other Microsoft Office components, you may find that FrontPage suffers from similar "featuritis"—it's filled with commands and features, which you might feel get in the way of actually editing pages. It offers a lot of templates and wizards and helpers that can sometimes seem to keep you separated from your XHTML code instead of intimately familiar with it.

It can also rely a bit heavily on proprietary features, such as FrontPage Extensions or Internet Explorer-specific codes and elements. It often makes these items available to you without making it terribly clear that they *are* proprietary. If you develop a page in FrontPage and you don't have a FrontPage Extensions-enabled Web server, you may find that the particularly cool add-ons don't work correctly or at all.

Finally, this Windows- and Office-centric approach means FrontPage is great for Windows users who are used to Office, but less interesting for Macintosh users, Unix users, and those wild-hair creative types who want to use different graphics and animation tools. Although FrontPage has its collaborative features, it's probably best characterized as a "pro-sumer" tool—one that can make personal and small business Web sites look great.

FrontPage's Highlights

The highlights begin at the beginning, particularly if you're creating a new Web site that will be hosted on a server that supports FrontPage Extensions. If that's the case, you can launch FrontPage and immediately dig into some of the templates it offers. Whenever you select File, New, Page or File, New, Web, you'll see a column on the far-right side of the FrontPage interface. There you can choose to create a blank page or an empty Web site, or you can work from templates. To explore the template options, choose Page Templates or Web Site Templates from the column.

In the Templates window, you can select one of the templates for a small preview (when applicable). If it looks like the type of page you want to work with, you can click the OK button. In some cases, a wizard will launch. In other cases, you'll be presented immediately with the page template, which you can begin to fill out.

With the page up in the FrontPage interface (whether or not you're working with a template), the next step is to begin editing. If you're familiar with Microsoft Word at all, you'll notice that some of the formatting options in FrontPage are made to look like those in Word. You can select the Bold, Italic, and Underline buttons in the toolbar as you type and edit, for instance, or you can select Format, Font to see more extensive options for changing font appearances.

Want to *really* change the look of the page? Go for a theme. Choose Format, Theme and a dialog box appears, enabling you to choose from some predesigned themes that Microsoft has thrown in with FrontPage. The themes can look professional, artistic, or just wacky. Select one, and then make a few other choices below the list of themes. The options include Apply Using CSS, which will create the theme using a style sheet instead of using `<font>` elements and other attributes. Click OK and the new theme is applied to your page—instant design!

Note Note also that the Themes dialog box gives you the choice of applying a theme to the selected page or to all pages. Choose the latter only if your pages are simple in design. Generally, complex table-based layouts get messed up by the Themes option, and it can be tough to restore your site after applying a theme.

Another fun way to create your site is to use the Web components. Choose Insert, Web Component and the Insert Web Component Wizard appears. Then you can select from among many different types of components, such as dynamic effects, tables of contents, a hit counter, and so on. You can also add components that access content from Microsoft's other Web sites and services.

Although many of these elements require FrontPage Extensions, you'll find that some of them simply make it easier to create navigation aids for your pages, such as Back and Forward links on the pages or hyperlinks to all the pages that comprise your Web site. Once you've made a selection, walk through the remaining steps of the wizard and your Web component will be added to the page.

When you're done adding themes and components to your pages (along with some good old-fashioned text and photos), you're ready to publish your Web site by selecting File, Publish Web. The Publish Destination dialog box appears—enter the URL for your server. (Use http:// if the server supports FrontPage Extensions, and ftp:// if it doesn't.) Once the server is contacted, verified, and you're logged in, the publishing process should go smoothly. Your site will be uploaded, and then you'll be ready to view it on the Web.

Summary

Quite a few Web authoring applications are available for you to try out. Although a well-trained Web author will know XHTML and related technologies at the code level, a graphical editor can be an immense help in quickly prototyping sites, as well as managing large projects and collaborating with others.

Each Web authoring package has its strengths, its weaknesses, and its affiliations. Adobe's GoLive works well with other Adobe products, Macromedia's Dreamweaver integrates with other Macromedia products, and Microsoft's FrontPage looks and acts very much like other Microsoft Office applications. Netscape's Composer may be the odd one out. But then again, it's free, and it's designed primarily for editing individual pages.

Most high-end Web authoring tools have demo versions, so you should download them and test them to see which one works best for you. After all, these tools can get a little expensive at the pro level, and having the wrong one won't help much.

In the next chapter, you'll learn to use add-on technologies to make your Web site more dynamic and interactive. You'll also learn a little more about CGI scripts and other server-side scripting options.

FORUMS, CHATS, AND OTHER ADD-ONS

*M*any different options enable you to add interactive elements to your Web site without requiring much programming knowledge. You can download and install software on your Web server that's been written by someone else or you might link to a *hosted* service, where the application resides on someone else's Web server.

You'll find Web solutions, including *forums* and *chat* applications for real-time discussions. You'll also see solutions for counting your page visitors, tracking Web statistics, and much more.

This chapter discusses the following:

- ■ Creating and hosting forums on your site, including download-able and hosted forums
- ■ Adding a live-chat capability to your Web site using third-party solutions
- ■ Adding counters and other third-party statistics tools to your site
- ■ Checking out your site's statistics and making sense of the results

Creating and Hosting Forums

Before the Internet became popular, many of the people who wanted to meet in "cyberspace" did so via online services such as America Online or dial-up bulletin board systems (BBS), most of which were locally run using a computer, a modem, and a phone line or two. The bulletin board software would answer the phone, log in the user, show some news about the BBS, and allow the user to post messages in various forum areas to participate in ongoing discussions.

While the phone-based BBS isn't quite the cutting-edge tool that it once was, much of its functionality has been moved to the Internet in the form of Web-based forums and bulletin board applications. Forums exist on all sorts of topics—computer support, politics, music, and so on.

If you want to interact with your visitors, answer questions, or try to strike up lively discussions—in other words, build up a community of repeat visitors—you'll probably want to consider a bulletin board system of some sort. Corporate or organizational sites can benefit from forums as well, if only because users will often answer each other's questions (or can find the previous answers you've supplied).

Forum Types and Technologies

As with many Web applications, there are two major types of forums—server-based and hosted. A *server-based* forum application will need to be installed on your Web server, generally as a series of CGI scripts, and will need to be maintained on that server. That may include backups, database maintenance, and occasionally reinstallation.

Server-based forums come in a vast range of technologies and capabilities, ranging from ASP (Active Server Pages) applications to CGI scripts written in Perl and C. Some will require your Web server to offer certain database capabilities, such as an ODBC (Open DataBase Connectivity) database. Others may require PHP (a server-side scripting language) or any variety of other scripting solutions that are available for different Web-hosting server platforms.

Hosted solutions are actually stored on someone else's server—usually a company devoted to that purpose. You sign up for a forum that you'd like to host, in some cases paying for the privilege. You're then given a username, password, and URL. You access the forum, set up the topics, and publicize it. You'll likely link to it from your own site, and you may be able to make it look somewhat as if it's actually part of your site. But the URL is different (because it's not on your server), and you may not have access to the actual files in which messages are stored.

Hosted forums are easy to use, but the downside is a certain lack of control. Your forums will likely have to comply with the host's terms of service, and may be subject to editing or censorship. Also, you may not be able to back up and/or transfer the messages easily if you change your mind and opt for a different solution. While many people are turning to a variety of hosted applications on the Web these days, generally the convenience comes at the expense of turning over a little power to the hosting company.

Choosing a Server-Side Forum

There's a great deal of forum software for the various Web server platforms you'll encounter on the Internet, so the first consideration in forum shopping is what sort of server you're using for your Web site. You'll need to ask the system administrator or your Web-hosting company these questions:

- Is the server based on Unix, Windows, or Macintosh?
- What access do I have to the server—can I install in the `cgi-bin` directory, or should I install somewhere else?
- What scripting technologies, CGI languages, and/or database technologies are available?
- What are the version numbers of the particular languages or scripting environments that are available?

You'll find that most ISPs (if that's who you're dealing with) are familiar with these questions and can tell you their do's and don'ts regarding Web applications. Likewise, if you're planning to implement server-side applications for your company Web site, your IT department or system administrator should be able to answer these questions.

Once you're familiar with the options and limitations of your Web server, you can start researching compatible forum software. A great place to start is the Conferencing on the Web guide (`http://thinkofit.com/webconf/`), where you'll find links to most of the Web forum packages available.

The main decision you'll likely need to make is whether or not you want to pay for the forum software. There's a fair amount of freeware available for your forums, but few of those options give you the flexibility and professional look-and-feel of the more expensive commercial software. Commercial software can vary in price, from tens to hundreds of dollars, but in many cases the price can be worth it.

Aside from the look of the software, the differences tend to be in the following areas:

- **Customization features**—Can you make the forums look like they're a part of your Web site? Can you change colors, fonts, and so on?

- **Management features**—How do you manage users and messages? Does the software offer sophisticated support for registered and non-registered users, or is everyone lumped into a single category? Can you send e-mail messages to all of your registered users? Can you block certain users or add users as moderators or forum managers?

- **User interface features**—Can visitors use HTML markup, images, emoticons, and other widgets to make their discussions a little more personal and fun?

Here are a few of the more famous and notable server-side Web forum software packages:

- **WWWBoard** (`http://worldwidemart.com/scripts/wwwboard.shtml`)—This one isn't the prettiest bulletin board system available, and it can get unwieldy if it sees a lot of action. But it's freeware and it's been around a long time, so it's popular. It's written in Perl, requiring Perl 4 or higher, and has ports to Windows and Macintosh.

- **WebBBS** (`http://www.extropia.com/applications/web_bbs.html`)—This is another popular, simple discussion system, similar to WWWBoard, with very little in the way of user interface options and user-management features. It requires Perl 5.

- **IkonBoard** (`http://www.ikonboard.com`)—Another freeware solution, this one is popular because it looks a bit like Ultimate BB (discussed below), which defines the look-and-feel standard for bulletin boards. Surprisingly, it's free, but you may need to do some tweaking and regular maintenance to get it running and stay on top of the updates. The software requires Perl 5.004.

- **YABB** (`http://yabb.xnull.com/`)—The name stands for Yet Another Bulletin Board, but this one is a great option considering it's freeware (probably thanks to the fact that it's an open source project). With the look-and-feel of a good Ultimate BB clone, YABB also offers a lot of the customization and management features of higher-end software. This requires Perl 5 and works with Unix and Windows NT.

- **Discus** (`http://www.discusware.com/`)—Discusware offers two versions of its software, a freeware offering and a commercial one. Both are good competitors in their respective markets—the freeware version is very popular, and the commercial version is reasonably inexpensive ($149). In fact, many users like the no-nonsense tree-based interface, which isn't as graphical as Ultimate and its clones but is still very well thought-out. It requires Perl 5.005 running on a Windows or Unix server.

- **Ultimate Bulletin Board** (http://www.infopop.com/)—This one has been the standard-bearer for a long time, particularly when it used to have a freeware version. Now you can download a trial version that has a limited number of uses, and the license for the full version is $199. Ultimate BB looks great, and it offers customization, e-mail options, HTML, searching, personal profiles, and much more. It uses Perl; a PHP version called UBBThreads is also available.

- **vBulletin** (http://www.vbulletin.com/)—Another Ultimate BB clone, vBulletin gets higher marks from some users than the original. It's a little less expensive ($85 a year or $160 to own it) and uses PHP and MySQL for a faster interface than most Perl solutions. PHP 3.0.9 and MySQL 3.22 are the minimum requirements. The company offers vBulletin Lite, which can be used for testing or for smaller sites (it's feature-limited, but it works). Figure 21.1 shows vBulletin's support forum, which itself uses the vBulletin software.

FIGURE 21.1

The vBulletin software offers a reasonably inexpensive commercial solution that's graphically appealing.

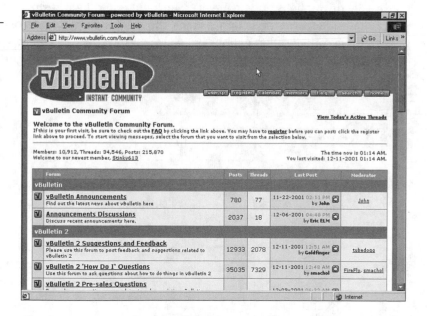

Installing a Server-Side Forum

So what does it take to install a server-side forum? Each one is a little different, and some of them can require some tedious configuration—particularly the free ones. Generally, the process goes something like this:

1. Download the software package and decompress its archive to reveal all the files.

2. Copy (or upload) files to various directories on your Web server, mostly the cgi-bin directory. You may also need to copy or upload images and other ancillary files, such as help files, to other directories on your server, according to the software's instructions.

3. Set permissions for the forum scripts, so that the scripts can be executed by the Web server software when requested by a browser. (Generally this will be done either using your FTP software or at the Unix command line, if your Web server supports a command-line login.)

Changing Web server permissions settings can be a bit unsettling because making a mistake can sometimes create a security hole. You should read the instructions for the forum software carefully, and consult with your ISP or system administrator if you're not familiar with setting file and folder permissions.

4. Set any options and preferences, including an administrative account, the original forum topics or questions, the look-and-feel, and so on. Sometimes these configuration options are done via an HTML document, and sometimes they're done by hand-editing a configuration text file (see Figure 21.2).

FIGURE 21.2

Here's a sample configuration file for YABB.

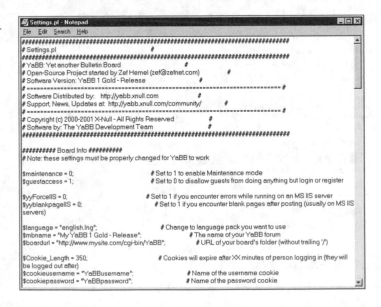

Once the system is set up, generally you access it using a straightforward CGI URL, such as `http://www.fakecorp.com/cgi-bin/forum.pl`. Then the forum application takes over and the users can begin reading and posting. The application will also likely have administrative features, which you should be able to access using the administrative account you've created.

> Remember that using a CGI application, particularly a sophisticated one that involves this much user interaction, could pose a security risk to your server. You should read the documentation for your Web forum software closely for security issues, including creating a unique administrator account and password. Likewise, because you're managing the software yourself, make sure you keep up with the updates and new versions, particularly if they fix security issues.

Hosted Forum Solutions

If you're not keen on digging into configuration files, uploading files to your server, or changing permissions and doing other admin-level things, a hosted solution might be better for you. With a hosted bulletin board, you create an account, log in, and create the bulletin board. Then, your users will be able to access the bulletin board via a special URL that points to the host's server. The software doesn't run from your server, so you have a little less control over it. A good hosted bulletin board will be run by professionals who know what they're doing, though, so hopefully it will be fairly bulletproof and convenient.

Ultimately, the decision may come down to how much control you want over the forum software. If your pursuit is commercial, backups are critical, and you can't stand the idea of another company controlling some of your content, you should probably skip a hosted solution. If you still don't want the hassle of running a board but you want more guarantees, you can go with a higher-end commercial hosting company, which may be willing to write a specific contract giving you as much control as you want.

If you're an individual, hobbyist, or non-profit, you may find that a hosting solution is the best way to quickly get your discussion groups up and running. For informal discussions, Q&As, and other less-than-critical solutions, a hosted forum might be the way to go. Figure 21.3 shows one of my hosted forums in action.

> Read any user agreements and privacy agreements carefully when you're creating or using a hosted message board. They're ripe for e-mail address gathering, generally for the purposes of *spam* or unsolicited advertising.

FIGURE 21.3

Here's my forum on Mac upgrades hosted by EZBoard. Although it's not on my server, it still matches the design of my Web site.

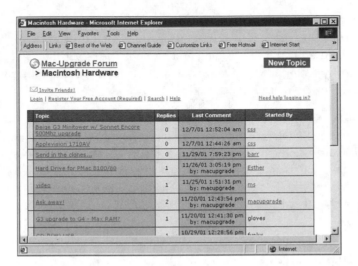

Hosted solutions range from ad-supported freebies to expensive commercial applications. Here's a look at some of the available hosted discussion group applications:

- **EZBoard** (http://www.ezboard.com/)—Discussion boards can be created for free, if you don't mind banner and pop-up ads. For a minimal fee, a discussion community can remove the ads. EZBoard even includes a donation mechanism you can use to get the money from your users. The look-and-feel is similar to Ultimate BB, and the customization options are pretty good, including backups for paid boards.

- **BoardHost** (http://www.boardhost.com/)—The bulletin board software is very basic, but some folks like it this way—threaded discussions without all the subject and topic pages. Setting up a basic board is free, with premium service options that get rid of the ads.

- **TimTyler Solutions** (http://www.timtyler.com/siteForums/)—This is a basic forum application that's a bit pricey compared to some other services. With a sign-up fee and monthly fee, the major advantage appears to be personal customer service.

- **MSN Communities** (http://communities.msn.com/)—Would Microsoft allow itself to be left out? Here you can create an ad-driven community for free. It includes more than bulletin boards, offering support for users to post photos, calendars, and chat. It's full-featured, but you can't make the forums look like an extension of your own Web site.

- **World Crossings** (http://worldcrossing.com/)—This is the hosted version of Web Crossings software, from the same company. The forums aren't graphical UBB clones, but they're functional, with "conversation" and "threaded" options for different types of boards. It's free because it's banner-ad supported, but it's a great choice if you'd like the simple, less-busy approach to useful forums.

- **InfoPop** (http://www.infopop.com/)—The company that makes UltimateBB will host UBB-based forums for you, for a price. Intended for corporate clients (it would appear), the cheapest price for this service is $299 a month.

Add Live Chat to Your Site

For years, one of the strengths of the big-name online services such as America Online was their ability to host live chats—text-based discussion groups where all participants are active at the same time. You type a comment, others respond, and so on.

For the most part, this sort of interaction is beyond the capabilities of an HTTP server or even many CGI applications, because Web technologies rely on the static approach—click a link, load a page—that HTTP offers. While that works for forums and bulletin boards, live chat requires a different technology. In the case of Web-based chat, this is usually a Java applet, although other options also abound.

You'll find that most consumer-oriented chat options are hosted by their respective companies and tend to be ad-driven. If you're looking for institutional or corporate use, some full-featured alternatives are available for a price.

Remember, too, that chatting doesn't even have to be all that specific to your Web site. Several of the Internet chat options that are popular for one-to-one communication also enable you to create your own chat groups and link to them from your Web documents:

- MSN Messenger—http://messenger.msn.com/
- Yahoo! Messenger—http://messenger.yahoo.com/
- AOL Instant Messenger—http://www.aim.com/

You have two ways to add a Java-based chat room to your Web site. The first way is to simply create a hyperlink to a hosted chat room that's configured and served on another server. The other way is to download chat server software and run it from your Web server. Unless you have physical access to your Web server, a hosted chat room is probably your best option. Even access to the CGI directory may not help you with something as sophisticated as a Java chat server.

If you want to place a Java server on your site, however, you do have a few options:

- **DigiChat** (http://www.digichat.com/)—With this server installed on your Web server computer, you can offer Java-based chat rooms to any compatible client. Features include moderated chats, content filtering, and a high level of customization. Licenses for the server start at $595 and go up depending on the number of users. You can also have the chats hosted for $25 per month and up.

- **ChatBlazer** (http://www.chatblazer.com/)—Prices start at $395 for the Gold server and go up for the Enterprise edition, which is priced depending on the number of Web sites it supports and can go as high as $9,995. Works on any server that supports Java, and supports embedding on your Web pages for a more integrated design.

- **iChat** (http://www.ichat.com/)—Focusing on the corporate customer, iChat offers service licenses starting at $495. The software includes "auditorium" modes for a moderated chat that many people can listen to, but only the people "onstage" and selected others can participate in.

- **VolanoChat** (http://www.volano.com/)—Another pricey option starting at $495, VolanoChat offers you many of the same features that the others do—moderated chats, banner ads, membership, and chat room transcripts. The company offers a free, fully operational demo limited to five users.

Beyond the big guys, you'll find a number of services that enable you to create your own hosted chat rooms for free, or nearly free. These chat services give you less control over the configuration and user management, and many are ad-based or are basic offerings that attempt to entice you into subscribing to a pay service. But they might work well for a small or growing site. Here are a few examples:

- **ChatPod** (http://www.chatpod.com/)—This ad-based service offers free Java chat rooms that you can link to from your site. ChatPod is a service of the same company that makes DigiChat software, so you can upgrade to one of their hosted solutions if desired.

- **Multicity** (http://www.multicity.com/)—Offers tiered pricing for chat rooms—a basic room supporting 25 people is free, the 50-user level is $30 a month, and a 100-people room with other pro-level features is $50 a month. It offers both Java and HTML clients so that non-Java browsers can still participate. Multicity also offers message boards, instant messaging, Web polls, and even hosted auction sites.

- **Talkcity** (http://www.talkcity.com/)—This very popular destination offers free chat rooms that you can create and use on the service, or ownership of a chat room for $3 a month. The service requires users to sign in and offers safer (content-regulated) chatting options. They'll also list your premium site to millions of users or make it completely private.

- **GroupBoard** (http://www.groupboard.com/)—Not only can you chat on this site, but you can use a whiteboard to draw pictures for the entire group to see. That might be useful for meetings or teaching, but mainly it's just fun.

- **Bravenet** (http://www.bravenet.com/)—Offers basic, hosted, ad-driven Java chat rooms, along with many other such services for improving Web sites.

Many Java-based chats offer more of the same, except for the look-and-feel. To explore other chats and pick one that agrees with you, try the Freeware Java Chat page at http://freewarejava.com/applets/chat.shtml.

Counters and Web Statistics

Most Web authors like to know how well their sites are doing—how many people visit, which pages they look at, and what about the site seems to be succeeding. That's the whole point of Web statistics, which is what we'll talk about in this section.

Most Web server applications keep fairly detailed statistics about the activities on the site, including which pages have been visited, how often, by which IP addresses, and sometimes which page the user came from most recently (the "referrer" page). If you're interested in those things, you'll need to dig into your Web server's statistics log files.

Not all Web authors have access to these log files. If you don't, or if you simply want a more visual approach to page tracking, you can add a *counter* to your pages. Most counters act a little like a car's odometer, counting up one tick every time that particular page is visited. Some are more sophisticated, only counting unique visitors, giving you more detailed statistics, and so on.

Accessing Your Web Statistics

If you run your own Web server, you probably have some idea where your Web statistics are stored—most likely you have a log file that's auto-generated by the Web server software and stored somewhere on the server computer. (Unix-compatible computers generally place a log file in the /var/log/httpd/ directory, for instance.) If you have an ISP-based Web site, the ISP probably still makes a log file available to you somewhere in your Web space, with which you can download and work.

This log file is filled with an entry for every access request, whether it's for a Web page, an image, or some other resource on your Web site. Generally speaking, just looking at such a log page will tell you next to nothing about your Web site. Instead, you'll need a program of some kind that can take that log file (or, more appropriately, a copy of that log file), analyze it, and report its findings to you.

Perhaps the most popular application for doing that is Analog (`http://www.statslab.cam.ac.uk/~sret1/analog/`), which is available for nearly any computer operating system. It's not much of an application in its own right—that is, you don't do much clicking or choosing while it's running. Instead, you launch the application and point it to the log file. (Often this simply means having the log file in the same directory as the application.) It analyzes the log and generates an HTML document that gives you an idea of how well your Web site is performing (see Figure 21.4).

FIGURE 21.4

Analog's output is a fairly uniform HTML document that shows you what's going on with your site.

Tip

Some ISPs offer automatic analog output posted somewhere in your own Web space. Others offer proprietary Web-based interfaces for checking statistics.

Analog (and other analysis programs) will tell you the total requests and the total *page views*. For most applications, the number of page views that your site receives is the most interesting because requests can include images, multimedia, and other items that don't really account for additional visitors. You'll also find that Analog offers interesting averages, such as the average number of page views per day, and other tidbits, such as which days of the week seem to have the most traffic.

Adding a Web Counter

Even if you do have access to your Web statistics, many Web authors like to post Web counters to provide a quick indication of how many people have loaded a particular page. While a counter will only give you the basics about how many people visit your site, it can be handy and entertaining.

The easiest way to add a counter is as a *server-side include (SSI)*, which is discussed later in this chapter. But if your Web server or ISP doesn't support SSI, or if you'd like more flexibility for your counter—such as graphics—you might opt for either a CGI-based counter or a Java-based counter.

A CGI counter is best if you don't want to rely on the Web browser, as you do with a Java counter. Instead, a CGI counter relies on your own server, so you know the count is always working. CGI counters can be very basic, offering only text-based results, or they can be fairly ornate, with numbers, banner advertisements, and all sorts of add-ons.

If you have access to your cgi-bin folder, you can install a CGI-based counter yourself, or your ISP may offer such a counter. CGI counters can be found online at a number of places, including Matt's Script Archive (`http://www.worldwidemart.com/scripts/`), CGIAdmin.com (`http://www.cgiadmin.com/freescripts/`), FreeCode (`http://www.freecode.com/index/`), CGIExtremes (`http://www.cgiextremes.com/`), and anywhere else fine CGIs are downloadable.

If you don't want to install a CGI, a fair number of Web counters are external, hosted services—and a number of them are free. Here's a look at a few different options:

- **Digits.com** (`http://www.digits.com/`)—This popular graphical counter is free as long as you include the Digits.com graphic and a link to the site.

- **Web-Stat** (`http://www.web-stat.com/`)—More than a counter, Web-Stat can do quite a bit of the traffic analysis that can be done with Analog and similar applications, although it doesn't require access to the log file. Instead, you place code on your page and the Web-Stat server tracks users. Web-Stat costs $5 a month.

- **CyberCount** (`http://www.cybercount.com/`)—Similar to Web-Stat, CyberCount offers a graphical counter and Web statistics tracking. It's free if you also run their banner ad on your pages, or $5 a month ad-free.

- **FastCounter** (`http://www.bcentral.com/products/fc/default.asp`)—Another popular option from Microsoft's bCentral, it's free to registered bCentral members. (bCentral is a "small business solutions" site that focuses on generating Web traffic for its members via Web rings, search engine submission, and similar options.)

These counters are simple to add—you'll be given a selection of HTML code to paste into your Web document. When you put the Web document on your server and access it via a Web browser, the counter is activated, the remote server is queried, and the statistics are tracked.

Server-Side Includes

Server-side includes, or SSIs, were among the earliest add-ons to Web servers. SSIs are used to include certain text files or server variables in your Web documents. For instance, if you store a text document (even a snippet of XHTML code) that includes the header you use for multiple pages on your Web site, you can use an SSI command to include that code on the relevant pages. Then, the server pieces the document together and sends it to the requesting browser as if it were all one file stored on the server.

Along with text files, SSIs can be used to include certain environment variables. SSIs depend entirely on your Web server software—there's no official standard, and SSIs can be implemented in any way that the server desires. Generally, these commands are fairly simple, but they can be effective. For instance, SSIs can be used to include the current date, the current URL, information about the user's browser, and other environment variables. In addition, many servers implement Web counters using SSI, and you can often execute a small CGI script and put the results on your page.

You'll find that SSI support isn't offered by every ISP, and they may be turned off by your system administrator for security or server-load reasons. If you do have access to SSIs, you'll likely need to discuss their implementation with your system administrator. The exact commands and syntax at your disposal may vary depending upon the actual Web server software in use.

As a general template, you'll need to take a few steps to use SSIs on your site:

1. Confirm with your ISP or system administrator that your Web server is capable of using SSIs and that they're turned on.

2. Save your pages with a `.shtml` or `.shtm` filename extension. That's how the server knows to expect SSIs on the page.

3. Add the SSI commands to your page. Generally, they're added using the HTML comment tag with the SSI command inside the brackets:

   ```
   <!-- #include file="banner.txt" -->
   ```

Aside from the `#include` command, SSI implementations usually have an `#echo` command, which causes the Web server to add something to your page:

```
<!-- #echo var="DATE_LOCAL" -->
```

Using that command, you could add the current date to your page. Remember that SSIs work by replacing the text within your Web document *before* it's sent to the Web browser. So, you can even place the commands inside XHTML containers, if desired:

```
<p>Document was last modified: <b><!-- #echo var="LAST_MODIFIED" -->
➥</b></p>
```

When this page reaches the Web browser, it will no longer have the `<!-- -->` command in it because the entire bracket is replaced with the value of the `echo` command. That's how SSIs work. Once the server has parsed the page, the comment brackets are completely replaced with the SSI's value. Even if the user used the `View Source` command in a Web browser, the SSI command wouldn't appear there.

The environment variables were discussed in Chapter 16, "CGIs and Data Gathering." You should be able to access those same variables from your SSI commands.

Here's how a counter, banner, or rotating "Saying of the Day" often works—using the `exec` command. This actually launches a script, with the result of that script being included at the place where the script call is on the page. So, if you have a script that calls a counter, and the script `counter.pl` is in the same directory as the page you're authoring, you could include its results like this:

```
<p>This page has had <!-- #exec cmd="./counter.pl" --> visitors since
➥March 1.</p>
```

You may have seen a line similar to this on many Web pages. What the SSI is doing is executing the script, plugging the result into the page, and thus replacing the SSI command with a number.

As with any CGI script, this script would need to be executable. On Unix and Windows servers, you'd need to set the appropriate permissions, or the script would need to be an executable application. This can be a security risk, so check with your ISP or administrator before changing permissions.

One thing that's interesting about the `exec` command is that it tends to only work for scripts that are in the same directory as the Web page you're authoring. And, for security reasons, many Web servers won't allow you to place executable scripts in a regular HTML directory. Instead, you'd need to access the `cgi-bin` directory. You can do that using the `virtual` command instead:

```
<!-- #include virtual="/cgi-bin/counter.cgi" -->
```

The `virtual` command actually works by building its relative URL based on the "virtual server" that it's dealing with—that is, the local domain name and server address. In this example, the virtual command will go to the root of the Web server's drive, locate the `cgi-bin` directory, and execute the script from there.

Tip

If your Web site uses Apache server software, visit `http://httpd.apache.org/docs/howto/ssi.html` for more on its implementation. You'll notice that you can get even more advanced with SSI, including creating variables and performing some conditional expressions!

Summary

In this chapter you saw some of the add-on products, both freeware and commercial, that you can use to make your Web site more community-focused, more automated, or just a bit more fun. For instance, adding discussion groups is a great way to foster community and participation among your users, which generally means a more active Web site. Likewise, chats are a good way to get together in real-time with your visitors and share information or simply have a good time.

This chapter also discussed the fine art of counting pages, including special counter programs you can add to your site, as well as programs you can download and use on your own computer to analyze your site's log files.

Along with CGI and Java-based solutions, this chapter discussed hosted solutions for chat, messages, and counters that are run from the hosting company's server instead of your own. The advantages are that you don't have to set up the programs and configure them to keep them running, while the disadvantage is a certain lack of control. Still, hosting is one way to add high-end applications to your site without too much trouble.

Finally, the chapter ended with a quick look at SSI technology, which lets you include files, CGI results, and other scripted solutions on your page, thanks to server-side processing.

In the next chapter, you'll learn about some of the different approaches you can take to choosing a Web server, including solutions for selling things online.

WEB PUBLISHING
SERVICES

hether you're just starting out with a new Web site or building a number of sites, eventually you'll probably want to shop around for a Web publishing service. (If you're like me, you'll probably move your favorite sites around a little bit, too.) All sorts of Web publishing services are available to you, the differences pretty much hinging on price and service. This chapter will take a look at some of the basic issues you should consider when shopping for Web services. It will also look at some specific offerings and see how they compare.

This chapter discusses the following:

- Questions you should ask and features to look for in a Web service
- Using free services—do you get what you pay for?
- How to add e-commerce solutions so that you can sell products (and maybe even make money)

Finding the Right Web Host

You might be asking, "Why is this chapter at the back of the book instead of the front?" My answer is simple: Before you can choose your Web server, you need to know a little about what you want to accomplish with your Web site. To do that, you need to know Web publishing, as this book has taught you. So, this chapter comes last.

There are so many ISPs and Internet Presence Providers that choosing one can prove incredibly difficult. In certain cases, you may use a pricier service because you know the people who manage the ISP or you've had a personal recommendation. In other cases, the cheapest (or almost cheapest) service may suffice, just to put up a quick site. You may even find use for one of the free Web hosting services, some of which offer clever templates and solutions to interesting problems.

Note An Internet Presence Provider (IPP) is a company that provides Web server space and services without offering dial-up, DSL, or other connections to the Internet that most ISPs offer.

So, to find the right Web service, you'll need to know a little something about your Web goals. You'll need to decide what's important to you, what you can skip, and what you're willing to pay for.

Let's consider the items that are likely to be important to you when you're selecting your Web service provider. They range from basic to somewhat involved, so it's probably a good idea to have a pencil and pad handy to jot down your answers.

Before we get to the list, the first question to ask yourself is, "Am I willing to spend money?" If you're not willing to spend money, you can immediately eliminate a great number of the IPPs out there that charge for their services. Instead, you're looking at two basic options—either using the ISP-provided server space that you may already have, or signing up for free server space, which is usually ad-driven. (The server company places an ad on your site.) See the section "Using Free Servers" for more details on a few of the most popular no-charge options.

The rest of the questions in this section assume that you are willing to spend a little for services.

Does the Web server platform matter to me? If it's important to you that your pages be hosted on Unix, Linux, Windows NT, or a Mac OS version, you should make that a primary consideration when you're shopping. In day-to-day terms, the Web server platform generally is irrelevant, except that sometimes it can dictate the filename extension (.html or .htm) that you use for your files. Still, some Web authors care, particularly if an ISP offers access to that OS via remote login tools, or if you want to use particular scripting and database languages.

Are CGI scripts important, and does the language matter? If you want to create scripts (as discussed in Chapter 16, "CGIs and Data Gathering,") or add CGI-based forums, chat, and other goodies (as discussed in Chapter 21, "Forums, Chats, and Other Add-Ons"), the CGI language support will matter to you. Some ISPs offer Perl and C for CGI scripting, and others offer PHP, AppleScript, Visual Basic, and so on. If you're looking for a specialty language, that may narrow your options.

Are SSIs or FrontPage Extensions turned on, and what specific commands can I use? If you want to use Service Side Includes or Microsoft FrontPage extensions on your pages, you'll need to know what's available from your ISP, or if they're offered at all.

Do I need a database solution? Many Linux- and Unix-based servers run versions of SQL or mySQL that you can use for a back-end database, often coupling it with CGI scripts for page retrieval, forums, banner ad management, and so on. Other specialty servers will offer FileMaker Pro, Microsoft Access, or other types of database backends. Even if you're simply downloading applications or scripts that you want to use with your site, check those scripts' requirements to see if you need your ISP to provide a particular database solution.

Do I need secure server capabilities? Using SSL (Secure Socket Layers) technology, you can encrypt the communication between your user's browser and the Web server. However, the Web server has to support this feature, and the IPP has to make it available to you.

Do I need e-commerce tools? If you have access to a CGI directory and the right back-end databases and/or languages, you can probably implement your own e-commerce solution to accept Web-based orders and credit card purchases. But if e-commerce is one of your goals, it can be easier to choose an ISP that already has support for e-commerce applications. Preferably, it should give you a demo of its capabilities and how they would be tailored to your Web site.

Aside from these slightly more advanced issues, you'll also need to consider the issues discussed in Chapter 3, "What You Need to Get Started," concerning storage space, throughput limits, and other basic IPP questions. And, to top it all off, you may be interested in other services the IPP can provide for particular accounts, such as e-mail accounts, e-mail forwarding, domain name registration, and so forth.

An IPP doesn't have to be in your immediate geographical area, but I can tell you from personal experience that an IPP or ISP with good customer service—people eventually answer the phone when you call, for instance—can be worth a few extra dollars. An unbiased recommendation from a current customer or a magazine article can also be worthwhile, if only to keep you away from a potentially deadbeat IPP.

There are so many Web hosts out there that Yahoo! has an entire topic devoted to the Web hosting *directory* sites. Check out `http://dir.yahoo.com/` `Business_and_Economy/Business_to_Business/` `Communications_and_Networking/Internet_and_World_Wide_Web/` `Network_Service_Providers/Hosting/Web_Site_Hosting/Directories/`.

Using Free Servers

So you're taking the cheap route? If you don't mind limited support for CGI scripts, you don't want your own domain name (or you want to add it cheaply), and you're not against a little advertising, a free server is a perfectly reasonable choice. In fact, some of them offer some interesting advantages. Often, you can add a feature or two for a few bucks—such as a personalized domain name or e-commerce tools. This may be worth it, especially as your site grows.

America Online Hometown

If you have an AOL account, you automatically have access to AOL's Hometown service (`http://hometown.aol.com/`), which enables you to post up to 12MB of HTML, photos, and other documents. The Hometown service is available to non-AOL members as well, but you're limited to using their online tools, 1-2-3 Publish or Easy Designer, if you want to place the pages online. AOL members can use a special FTP area on the service, or they can use an external FTP application while connected to AOL to upload standard HTML documents and images.

If you use Hometown, you'll have a small banner at the top of your page that includes the Hometown logo, some buttons to encourage users to join Hometown themselves, and generally a small banner advertisement. Aside from templates and the easy-to-use publishing tools, AOL features a few small scripts for users to add to their pages for a guestbook or to receive HTML data in e-mail. There is no access to other CGIs, however, and no option to pay for the privilege of a page without ads or a unique domain name.

Yahoo! GeoCities

GeoCities (http://geocities.yahoo.com/) has been popular for years as a free option for Web publishing—since well before it came under the Yahoo! banner. Today, GeoCities still provides free, ad-supported pages, with the option of paying a premium for additional features, including domain name support.

With the basic GeoCities account, you get 15MB of storage space and access to GeoCities' Web building tools. Your domain will be http://geocities.yahoo.com/ username/ and you'll have FTP access to the site, meaning you can bypass the easy-to-use tools and upload your own Web documents, images, and so forth.

The main advantage to GeoCities appears to be that you can add certain Yahoo!-powered content to your site: news, stock quotes, a Yahoo! search box, and so on. You can also select a category for your Web site, which enables Yahoo! to serve more targeted advertising. Ideally, that's an advantage for you and your user, as well as an obvious advantage for Yahoo!.

Along with the Yahoo! add-ons, you can add a guest book and a counter, and you can send HTML forms data via e-mail. Yahoo! also offers clip art, images, and games (such as video poker) you can add to your site. And the interface includes an advanced look at your site's statistics.

If you move up to premium services, you can get your own domain name, matching e-mail addresses, and even the ability to create subdomains, such as fred.fakecorp.com. Premium services aren't terribly pricey (currently starting at $9 per month) and offer the same access to the Yahoo! add-ons and so forth, without the ads.

Lycos Tripod

Tripod is another free service, but this one focuses a bit more on business pages—particularly those that participate in advertising share programs, such as affiliate programs and Web rings. Join up and you get 50MB of space, although your pages will include banner ads served by Lycos. Interestingly, the ads are customizable—you can use "ad skins" to make the advertising area at the top of the page look a little more interesting, and you can choose between banner ads and pop-up ads.

Tripod enables you to focus on scripting a bit more than other free services, with a few prebuilt CGI and JavaScript scripts that you can access. In addition, the service offers a script editor, which you can use to write JavaScript or Perl scripts and add them to your pages (see Figure 22.1).

FIGURE 22.1

Tripod includes
a script editor
that you can use
to create
JavaScript or
Perl scripts.

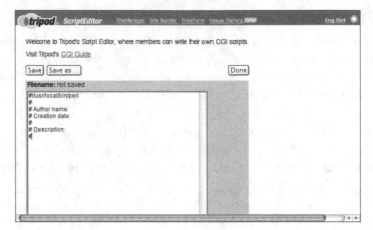

You can have a domain name forwarded to the site for free, as long as you pay $20
to register it yourself using Lycos' domain name registration partner. In fact, part-
nerships seem to abound on Tripod. You'll find links to many other Lycos services,
such as Webmonkey for Web publishing tutorials, the Online Business Center for
e-commerce advice, and Commission Central for developing relationships with affiliates and other advertisers.

Lycos offers a Tripod Plus service, which enables you to serve pages without ads. You
can also pay to upgrade the amount of storage space for your documents and the
amount of bandwidth your site can serve. At the time of this writing, prices start at
$4.95 a month.

Apple's iTools

As part of a value-added service for Macintosh users, Apple offers iTools, a suite of
Internet-based applications. It includes a Mac.com e-mail, an online storage area
called iDisk, some Internet-based greeting cards called iCards, and HomePage,
Apple's tools for Web publishing.

Note | As of this writing, Apple requires that you access your HomePage tool from a Mac-
based browser. Logging in from a Windows version of Internet Explorer won't work.

An iTools account offers 20MB of total storage to be shared between the iDisk and
the HomePage tool, and you can distribute that storage in any way you please.
Apple doesn't advertise on its pages, but it does offer you prebuilt templates and wizards for putting together your Web pages in a way that tends to have a certain
Apple-ified look to it. Not that that's bad; it's just true.

FIGURE 22.2

Apple's HomePage tool can be used to create pages based on professionally designed templates.

HomePage offers some interesting templates, including special pages that can turn a directory of images into a thumbnail gallery, a tool that posts QuickTime movies online for easy viewing, and a template that enables you to share files with other users over the Web.

What's more, Apple doesn't seem too uptight about bandwidth usage. So if you're a shareware author who wants to make your software available to the world, you might consider placing it on your Mac.com pages.

HomePages are found at `http://homepage.mac.com/username/`, and Apple doesn't let you have your own domain name. You can pay to upgrade your account, but that just gives you more storage space for the iDisk and HomePage tools.

E-Commerce Solutions

What if you want to sell something on your Web site? Again, tons of ISPs and IPPs are ready to offer you the basics of an e-commerce site, including SSL security, back-end databases, credit-card accounts, and even prebuilt "shopping cart" applications to display your products and help your customers choose them and track them. If you find a reputable local or regional IPP that's willing to help you with your online store, use it if the deal seems right. In this section, I'll be focusing on a few lower-cost national solutions that might also be interesting.

Yahoo! Store

Yahoo! offers a service called Yahoo! Store (`http://store.yahoo.com/`), which promises a turnkey online store solution. The service walks you though the process of adding products, using templates, and even getting a merchant account for accepting credit cards. The cost is currently about $50 per month, plus some other fees, such as per-product listing costs. And in certain cases, Yahoo! gets a percentage of your sales when the customers are referred from other Yahoo! pages.

While the price structure may sound a little daunting, Yahoo! Store is fairly cheap for an e-commerce solution. Plus, you can apply for a listing in the Yahoo! Shopping channel, which could be a boon to your sales. Yahoo! Stores can be "built with a single click," according the Yahoo!, so it's worth consideration if you're looking to jump into an online store immediately.

Catalog.com

Catalog.com is another intriguing low-cost service for quickly putting together an e-commerce site. As part of its basic plan (currently $25), you get a fairly solid Windows-based hosting package. It includes access to CGI scripts and the ability to run your own scripts, Microsoft Access support, VBScript and FrontPage support, ODBC-compliant database support, and even some multimedia features such as RealAudio serving. (There's also a Unix-based package for the same price that substitutes mySQL, PHP, and Python instead of the Microsoft-specific features.)

The kicker, though, is the ability to list up to 50 products in an online catalog, accept credit card payments, and so on. You can pay more to list additional items, currently $10 per 1,000 items.

Your best bet is to sign on to the site and try out the demo store to see if it works for you. This will require a bit more customization and HTML know-how than a solution like Yahoo! Stores. Then again, thanks to this book, you have that HTML know-how already!

Oracle Small Business

Oracle Small Business (`http://www.oraclesmallbusiness.com/`) began life as NetLedger.com, an online application for managing small business accounting. Since then, it's grown into a tool for managing a small business that's completely online—or a traditional business with an online store—thanks to its module-based approach.

This approach is a little different, but it could be very interesting if you already own a small business. Oracle Small Business begins by replacing your current software-based accounting system (such as QuickBooks or Peachtree Accounting) with its online application. The advantage is that you don't need special server computers. The disadvantage is that you lose some control over your data. The online application is used for accounting, payroll, inventory management, and so on.

The really interesting part is how well the online store can integrate with the accounting software. Oracle Small Business claims that its Web store can be created "in a snap"—that's partly true because it can be populated automatically using your inventory records, and sales made on the Web site can be entered into your accounting system automatically. In fact, clients can access your online accounting system to check out their invoices and pay them online. For a basic Web store of up to 100 items, plus all the accounting, customer relationship, payroll, and inventory features, the service currently starts at $99 a month.

This solution is too complex to describe in a few paragraphs, but it's worth looking into if you're running a small business, you already have accounting issues or payroll headaches, and you think you're interested in a Web-based store.

Miva Merchant Servers

Although there are many, many different e-commerce server engines out there, Miva Merchant (http://www.miva.com/) stands out because it's popular with ISPs and IPPs that offer e-commerce as a value-added solution. Also, Miva is touted as an easy add-on for regular Web authors. In fact, one approach to using Miva is the Miva Now service, which offers what's essentially a hosted e-commerce store that you can set up and test for 30 days. You're then transferred to a Miva partner IPP if you opt to keep the store. Miva-enabled accounts begin around $30 per month.

Miva Merchant can be purchased for $595, but you'll likely use Miva through your IPP for a monthly fee. (ISPs and IPPs can run Miva Empressa, a platform for multiple Miva-enabled shopping sites.) You manage your store from your Web browser, making it fairly easy to administer. You can check statistics, track your inventory, and so on.

The Miva Merchant system also makes it easy to create an *affiliate program*, which is a popular way to drive business to your e-commerce site. Under an affiliate program, other Web authors (your affiliates) place advertisements for your store on their Web sites. When a user clicks an ad, the Web author gets credit, ranging from a small amount of money per click (usually a few cents) to a percentage of the sale. In a sense, it turns other Web authors into commissioned salespeople for the store.

Perhaps the most interesting component of the Miva line of servers is their support for Miva Script. It's a proprietary Web-scripting language that enables you to add HTML-like elements for interactive forms allowing feedback, user registration, and e-commerce shopping. Using Miva Script, you can either do the scripting yourself (which you'll want to do on some level) or add third-party scripts, including some fairly sophisticated offerings that enable you to manage an entire Web site, much as you would using Perl or PHP. For more on Miva Script, see `http://www.ideablue.com/index.mv?Menu=MivaScript` or `http://www.miva.com`.

Summary

This chapter expanded on the basic ISP or IPP discussion that was begun in Chapter 3 by looking at how to choose a Web-hosting solution. Before shopping for a Web-hosting service, you should ask yourself about the complexity of scripting, databases, and add-ons you want for your site. Once you've made those decisions, you can make a more informed choice.

In particular, this chapter covered some solutions for Web hosting, from the free services offered by AOL, Yahoo!, and Lycos to some e-commerce solutions. Although many, many Web-hosting companies compete for your attention (and many more than are mentioned in this chapter deserve a look), this chapter looked at a few fairly unique e-commerce solutions that all promise to be easy to set up and administer.

Now you know how to find a host for all of the Web pages, forms, frames, JavaScripts, multimedia, and other exciting Web technologies that you've developed throughout this book. You're done!

Appendix A offers a quick reference for common XHTML elements and their attributes, as well as a reference for CSS style sheet elements and options. Good luck with your Web sites!

PART VI

APPENDIX

XHTML AND CSS COMMAND REFERENCE

This appendix is a quick reference to the bulk of the XHTML elements and attributes introduced in this book. Likewise, this appendix offers a quick reference to the CSS properties discussed in the text.

Document Elements

The elements in this section are those required for well-formed Web documents, as well as the options and attributes that go along with them.

DTD Declarations

DTD declarations begin every well-formed Web document, telling the parser what type of document to expect.

The XHTML Strict DTD Declaration is used if you intend to be strict in your use of XHTML 1.0 compliant elements and in using well-formed coding rules:

```
<!DOCTYPE html PUBLIC "\//W3C//DTD XHTML 1.0 Strict//EN"
"DTD/xhtml1-strict.dtd">
```

The XHTML Transitional DTD Declaration can be used if your page includes elements that aren't supported in the XHTML 1.0 specification, but are supported in early HTML standards:

```
<!DOCTYPE html PUBLIC "\//W3C//DTD XHTML 1.0 Transitional//EN"
"DTD/xhtml1-transitional.dtd">
```

The XHTML Frameset DTD Declaration is used for creating frameset documents:

```
<!DOCTYPE html PUBLIC "\//W3C//DTD XHTML 1.0 Frameset//EN"
"DTD/xhtml1-frameset.dtd">
```

The `<html>` Element

The `<html>` element is the first-level container for a Web document—all other elements will be placed inside the `<html>` element. This element can accept a `lang` attribute and an `xmlns` attribute, which is used to specify the XML namespace (in this case, XHTML).

Example:

```
<html xmlns="http://www.w3.org/1999/xhtml" lang="en">
```

The `<head>` Elements

The `<head>` elements include `<head>` itself, along with a number of others that are enclosed within the `<head>` of the document, including the `<title>`, `<meta>`, and `<base>` elements.

The `<head>` element is a container that wraps around these other elements (only `<title>` is required), as well as `<script>` containers, if they're used in the `<head>` of the document. The `<head>` element can also accept a `lang` attribute.

Example:

```
<head>
...head-level markup
</head>
```

The `<title>` Element

The `<title>` element is used to determine the text that will appear in the Web browser's title bar when the page is displayed. The title may also be used for the bookmarks or favorites feature employed by the Web browser, and in other situations where a name should be associated with a particular Web document. The `<title>` element can accept a `lang` attribute. It must appear inside the `<head>` container.

Example:

```
<head>
<title>Title Example</title>
</head>
```

The `<meta>` Element

This optional element is used to pass along additional information about the document, called *metadata*. This metadata can be used by the browser or other applications (such as a Web search engine's *robot* or *spider* application) to learn more about the document. The `<meta>` element accepts a `contents` attribute and either a `name` or `http-equiv` attribute, but never both. This element is used for a variety of purposes, particularly when pages are generated by graphical Web editors.

Examples:

```
<meta name="keywords" content="PC, hardware, repair, laptop, newsfeed">
<meta http-equiv="refresh" content="30";
url="http://www.fakenews.com/newpage.html" />
```

The `<base />` Element

This optional element is used to specify a base-level URL for relative URLs used elsewhere on the page. For instance, if the base URL is `http://www.fakecorp.com/products/`, relative URLs such as `href="product1.html"` will be accessed as `http://www.fakecorp.com/products/product1.html` regardless of the actual stored location of the current document. The `<base>` element accepts the `href` and/or `target` attribute. The `target` attribute is useful for specifying a default frame when using framesets.

Examples:

```
<base href="http://www.fakecorp.com/people/bob/" />
<base target="main_viewer" />
```

The `<body>` Element

The `<body>` element is used to contain all the non-`<head>` elements on the page. Specifically, this element contains all the text and markup that will appear in the Web browser window. It can accept a `lang` attribute. A typical `<body>` container simply wraps around all other content on the page.

Example:

```
<body>
<h1>Hello World</h1>
...Additional content...
</body>
```

The Comment Element

Comments can appear anywhere in your document, including the head or body. The comment element is used to hide and embed comments in your page that don't appear in the browser window.

Example:

```
<!-- This is a one line comment. -->

<!-- Comments can also stretch
over multiple lines -->
```

Styles and Scripting

Although style sheets and scripting may seem like advanced topics, they happen to appear in the `<head>` of the document in some cases, and they both add attributes that apply to nearly all XHTML elements.

The `<script>` Element

The `<script>` element is used to contain scripting language that the Web browser is not supposed to attempt to parse as XHTML. Instead, the Web browser should note the scripting commands and turn them over to a script interpreter, which is often built into the browser. The `<script>` element can accept the `type` attribute, although the `language` attribute is also sometimes used (in transitional DTDs) for backward compatibility.

Example:
```
<script type="text/javascript">
...JavaScript commands...
</script>
```

Typically, the `<script>` container will be hidden using the XHTML comment element to make sure that incompatible browsers don't attempt to render the script commands. This is called *script hiding*.

Example:
```
<script type="text/javascript">
<!--
script commands
// -->
</script>
```

The `<noscript>` Element

In documents that use `<script>` elements within the `<body>`, you can include the `<noscript>` element to enclose text and markup that should appear if the user's browser doesn't support scripting or that particular scripting language.

Example:
```
<noscript>
This page requires JavaScript. Please visit
<a href="index2.html">our text-based index</a> instead.
</noscript>
```

The `<style>` Element

The `<style>` element is a container used in the `<head>` of the document to store style and class definitions. This element accepts a `type` attribute.

Example:
```
<style type="text/css">
...CSS definitions...
</style>
```

Style, Script, and Universal Attributes

Because the scripting and style sheets can affect nearly every element that appears inside the `<body>` container on your page, a few special attributes exist to support those technologies. These attributes are useful for classifying and identifying markup elements so that they can be used with scripts or styles. In addition, a few other universal attributes can be added to nearly any element.

Note	In general, the `<head>` elements (`<head>`, `<meta>`, and so on) and the `<script>` and `<style>` elements themselves do not accept these attributes.

class

The `class` attribute is used to assign a particular style class to a markup element. Classes are defined between the `<style>` tags and can then be assigned to other elements. (The `<div>` element is a general-use block-level element that you can use to apply styles or alignment to a number of elements at once. It's discussed in the section "Formatting Blocks.")

Examples:

```
<p class="intro">paragraph text</p>
```

```
<div class="centerbold">
... text and markup...
</div>
```

id

The `id` attribute is used to assign a unique identifier to a particular element, often so that element can be referenced in a script.

Example:

```
<p id="para1">paragraph text</p>
```

style

The `style` attribute is used to assign a particular style to the element without first defining the style or class.

Example:

```
<p style="font-family: Arial">paragraph text</p>
```

dir

The `dir` attribute is used to select the direction that the text will render in compatible browsers. It works only with container elements, and not with `<frame>` or `<frameset>` elements. Possible values are `ltr` (left to right) and `rtl` (right to left).

Example:

```
<p dir="rtl">paragraph text</p>
```

lang

The `lang` attribute is used to specify the language of the enclosed text, which may help the browser render that text. The attribute accepts a two-letter language code.

Example:

```
<p lang="fr">paragraph text in French</p>
```

General Markup

The elements in this section fall into two basic categories—elements used to mark up text and those used to create blocks of text.

Formatting Blocks

The block elements are used to create blocks or chunks of text that make up paragraphs, line returns, quoted passages, headings, and other divisions on the page.

Among these elements are a series of containers that are all variations on the paragraph element, `<p>`. The `<p>` element is used to contain text and markup that make up paragraphs on the page. Each paragraph has white space before and after it.

Example:

```
<p>This is a paragraph of text.</p>
```

Other elements with similar results are shown here:

`<pre>`	The `<pre>` element is used to enclose text and markup that should be rendered with spaces and linefeeds (returns) intact.
`<blockquote>`	This element renders the enclosed paragraph as a quotation, often by indenting both margins of the paragraph.
`<address>`	This container is often used at the beginning or end of the page to give information about the page's author. Many Web browsers render this text in italics.
`<div>`	The `<div>` container is often used with style sheet markup to assign a particular style or class to the enclosed markup. The `<div>` element can also be used with an `align` attribute to align the enclosed markup to

center, left, right, or justify. (Note that align is not strict XHTML.) The <div> element, like a <p> element, creates whitespace around itself, but it can enclose more than one block-level element.

<h1>...<h6>   The heading elements are used to contain different levels of document headings, from the largest (<h1>) to the smallest (<h6>). They should be used in order, without skipping levels. Like paragraphs, white space appears above and below a heading.

In addition, a few other elements can be used to break up the appearance of a page. These elements are all *empty* elements, meaning they require only one tag and don't contain any text or markup:

    This is the break element, which creates a line return whenever it is inserted in a block-level container.

<hr />   The horizontal rule element creates a horizontal line on the page.

One final block-level element is the <span> container, which is generally used to apply a style to the enclosed text and markup. Note that <span> differs from <div> primarily in that it doesn't force white space around itself, so that the following use would not break up the paragraph:

```
<p>This text: <span class="bold">is boldface</span> and this text
➥isn't.</p>
```

Formatting Text

The text-level formatting elements are generally used to change the appearance of certain words within your text so that they stand out. These elements can be either *physical* or *logical*. The physical elements demand a particular appearance (as in **bold** or *italic*), while logical elements will allow the browser to use a different appearance if it must.

Physical Styles

The physical text style elements are

<b>   Boldface

<i>   Italic

<tt>   Mono-spaced typewriter font

<u>   Underlined

`<big>`	Make text bigger
`<small>`	Make text small
`<sub>`	Subscript
`<sup>`	Superscript

Example:

```
<p>This text is <i>italic</i>, this text is <b>bold</b>,
this text is <tt>typewriter</tt> and this text is <u>underlined.</u></p>
```

Logical Styles

The logical styles will often render as bold (`<strong>`) or italic (`<em>`), but they aren't required to. Non-graphical browsers can elect to emphasize the words in a different way.

The logical text style elements are

`<em>`	Emphasized
`<strong>`	Strongly emphasized
`<cite>`	A citation or reference to an outside source
`<code>`	Computer programming code
`<dfn>`	The primary or defining instance of the term
`<samp>`	Sample output, often rendered in a way similar to code
`<kbd>`	Representing text that should be entered at a keyboard
`<var>`	A variable or value
`<q>`	Quoted text
`<abbr>`	An abbreviation
`<acronym>`	An acronym

One element in particular, `<q>`, offers a good use of a logical style. In most browsers, the `<q>` container will appear with quotation marks around the contained text. If you include a `lang` attribute representing a language that offers alternative quotation marks (or if the page itself is already rendering in a different language), the browser may render those marks correctly, thanks to the use of the `<q>` element.

`<ins>` and `<del>`

Two other logical styles, `<ins>` and `<del>`, can be used to surround text that should be inserted or deleted. These elements are often used on collaborative documents. They can accept the attributes `datetime`, `cite`, or `title`. The `datetime` attribute is used to show the date and time of the insertion or deletion. The `cite` attribute is used to reference an URL that includes an explanation of the insertion or deletion. The `title` attribute can be used to explain it right within the tag.

Example:

```
<p>It's important for the <ins datetime="2001-12-05T09:00:00-05:00"
title="Changed after the board's vote on this matter">Board of
Directors</ins>
<del>Office of the President</del> to have an opportunity to make its case
to the shareholders.</p>
```

Creating Lists

Lists are block-level elements that contain a series of list items, each of which is individually contained in a `<li>` element. To change the style of list, you simply change the list element that's used to enclose the list items.

An ordered list, using `<ol>`, places a number in front of each list item.

Example:

```
<ol>
<li>First item</li>
<li>Second item</li>
<li>Third item</li>
</ol>
```

An unordered list, using `<ul>`, places a bullet character in front of each list item.

If you use a transitional DTD, you can use `start`, `value`, and `type` in ordered lists and just `type` in unordered lists. (These attributes have been dropped in strict XHTML 1.0.) In ordered lists, you can change the type of numbering used for each item:

`<ol type="A">`	Uppercase letters
`<ol type="a">`	Lowercase letters
`<ol type="I">`	Uppercase Roman numerals
`<ol type="i">`	Lowercase Roman numerals
`<ol type="1">`	Numbers

In unordered lists, you can change the appearance of the bullet character:

`<ul type="disc">`	Solid circle
`<ul type="square">`	Solid square
`<ul type="circle">`	Open circle

In addition, the start attribute can be used to change the starting value for an ordered list.

Example:

```
<ol start="10">
```

You can also use the value attribute to change the value of an individual list item, or to change the counting within the list itself.

Example:

```
<ol>
<li>Item #1</li>
<li>Item #2</li>
<li value="1">Item #1</li>
<li>Item #2</li>
</ol>
```

A third type of list, the definition list using <dl>, can have two different list items: a definition term, <dt>, and a definition, <dd>. You don't have to use both, but the list type is most useful when you do. A definition list does not place numbers or bullets in front of items.

Example:

```
<dl>
<dt>Term 1</dt>
<dd>Definition of term 1</dd>
<dt>Term 2</dt>
<dd>Definition of term 2</dd>
</dl>
```

Images, Hyperlinks, Java, and Plug-Ins

The elements and attributes in this section are used to add images or other multimedia to your page. Also discussed are the various elements and attributes used to create and govern hyperlinks on your pages.

Adding Images

The <img /> element is used to add images to your page by specifying either a relative or absolute URL to a compatible image file that's stored in GIF, JPEG, or (for many browsers) PNG format. The src attribute for <img> is required.

Example:

```
<img src="image1.gif" />
```

The `<img />` element offers a number of attributes, including `alt`, which accepts a string value that is displayed when the image can't be. The `longdesc` attribute is used to accept the URL to a longer text-based description of an image. This is useful for assistive browsers, particularly when an image (such as a chart or graph) requires explanation.

Example:

```
<img src="chart1.jpg" alt="chart of first quarter sales"
➥longdesc="/img_desc/chart1.html" />
```

The `<img />` element can accept the `align` attribute, which can be used to align inline images to the top, middle, or bottom of the surrounding line of text. The `align` attribute can also accept `left` or `right` as values, which cause the image to *float* so that text wraps around the image.

The `<img />` element can accept the attributes `height` and `width`, which are used to specify the dimensions of the image in pixels. This is generally done to help the target browser download the image and page more quickly, although it can also be used to scale the size of the image.

Example:

```
<img src="chart1.jpg" alt="chart #1" align="left" height="330" width="200"
➥ />
```

Adding Hyperlinks

The `<a>` anchor element is used to create a hyperlink by associating an URL with the text and markup that it contains. Creating a hyperlink `<a>` container requires the `href` attribute, which accepts a relative or absolute URL. The markup contained between anchor tags can be text, XHTML elements, images, or almost any combination of those things, as long as `<a>` elements are not nested inside one another.

Examples:

```
<a href="http://www.w3.org">Visit the W3C</a>
```

```
<a href="products/product1.html"><img src="product1.jpg" alt="product #1"
➥/></a>
```

The anchor element can also be used with the `name` attribute to create a named section within a document. That section can then be referred to using the # sign as part of the URL.

Note The name attribute isn't strict XHTML, so it's best to use a transitional DTD and then use name and id in the same <a> element for backward compatibility.

By creating a named section like this:

```
<a name="answer1" id="answer1"><h2>A: Why the sky is blue</h2></a>
```

you can use the # sign to link to that named section:

```
<a href="#answer1">Q: Why is the sky blue?</a>
```

Named anchors can also be accessed from another document using a full URL:

```
<a href="http://www.fakecorp.com/questions.html#answer1">Q: Why is the sky blue?</a>
```

Note that hyperlinks can include almost any sort of valid URL, including those that use mailto:, ftp://, and other protocols. Linking to a document that the browser doesn't understand will either cause a *helper application* to launch or prompt the user to download that document to the user's computer.

The <a> element can accept another attribute, the target attribute, which is used to tell the browser which frame of a frameset document the anchor's URL should appear in. It can also be used with special targets that can determine where the new document is loaded:

_blank	Loads the URL in a new window
_top	Loads the URL in the same browser window at the top of the page, without regard to frames (if there are any)
_parent	Loads the URL in the frame that is the immediate parent of the current frame
_self	Loads the document in the same frame in which the anchor appears

Example:

```
<a href="product1.html" target="_blank">Click to see the product
in its own browser window.</a>
```

Imagemaps

You can combine images and hyperlinks into something called the *imagemap*. This enables you to use a number of different hyperlinks and associate them with an image, so that clicking different parts of the image loads different URLs.

This is done with the usemap attribute to the <img /> element. The usemap attribute accepts a named link reference, which is used to refer the browser to the portion of the document where the imagemap is defined.

Example:

```
<img src="banner.gif" usemap="#banner_map" alt="navigation banner"
border="0" />
```

> **Note**
>
> Note the `border` attribute, which can be used with images when they're used as hyper-links or in imagemaps to avoid placing a blue (or other color) border around the image in graphical browsers.

The `usemap` attribute tells the browser to look for a map definition. That definition is created using the `<map>` element, which contains individual `<area />` elements that define each *hotzone* that you're creating on the map. The `<map>` element uses the `name` attribute to give the map definition a name.

Inside the `<map>` element, an `<area />` element is used to create each hotzone's shape, using the `shape` attribute. The `<area>` element also includes the `coords` attribute to define the shape and the `href` attribute for the linked document's URL. Three different shapes are supported:

- `rect`—The rectangle requires four coordinates: a set that defines each of the left, top, right, and bottom coordinates.
- `circle`—A circular hot zone requires three different coordinates: center-x, center-y, and a radius.
- `polygon`—The third shape, a polygon, enables you to specify a shape with any number of sides. Each vertex requires a pair of points (x,y) as its definition.

Example:

```
<map name="banner_map">
<area shape="rect" coords="0, 0, 100, 100" href="index.html" alt="Index"
➥/>
<area shape="rect" coords="100,0,200,100" href="products.html"
➥alt="Products" />
<area shape="rect" coords="200, 0, 300, 100" href="about.html" alt="About
➥Us" />
</map>
```

If you plan to use a server-side imagemap, you can use the `ismap="ismap"` attribute to the `<img />` element. Then, wrap the `<img />` in an anchor that points to the map file on the server.

Example:

```
<a href="/maps/topbanner.map">
<img src="topbanner.gif" ismap="ismap" alt="Banner image" />
</a>
```

Multimedia Content

The typical way to link to multimedia documents is to use the `<a>` element. In certain cases, however, multimedia elements can be *embedded* in the document window. This means they're made to appear much as if they were images added using the `<img />` element.

One way to do this is to use the `<embed>` element, which is not strict XHTML, so it requires a transitional DTD be in effect. The `<embed>` element is used to load a *plug-in* that provides extra functionality to Netscape-compatible browsers. The `<embed>` element can have quite a few different attributes, depending on the media that's being embedded. Some of the more common attributes are `src`, `width`, `height`, `pluginspage`, and sometimes `autoplay`. You'll need to check the documentation of the particular plug-in (and Chapter 13, "Adding Multimedia and Java Content") to see the specific attributes.

Example:

```
<embed name="Movie1" src="movie1.mov" width="240" height="120"
pluginspage="http://www.apple.com/quicktime/download/">
</embed>
```

Java Applets

Java applets are small Java-language programs designed to be executed within a portion of the Web browser window. The Java applet actually uses the Web browser as a *virtual machine*, thus enabling it to run.

Java applets are best added using the XHTML-compliant `<object>` element, although the older Netscape-specific `<applet>` element is still popular. The `<object>` element should include a `classid` attribute, which points to the Java applet's file. It can include a `codebase` attribute as well, if you need a full URL to the Java applet.

Example:

```
<object codetype="application/java"
codebase="http://www.fakecorp.com/applets/" classid="java:myapplet.class"
standby="Applet Loading..." width=400 height=350>
</object>
```

Creating Tables

The table elements enable you to place content in rows and columns on the page. These elements can be used to display sections of tabular information on the page or to lay out the entire page in rows and columns, as discussed in Chapter 8, "Basics Tables," and Chapter 9, "Advanced Table Elements and Table Design."

Tables are created using the `<table>` element, which can accept a number of attributes:

width	Sets the relative width (percentage) of your table as part of the browser window or an absolute width, usually in pixels
border	Defines the width, in pixels, of the border surrounding the table
cellspacing	The amount of space, in pixels, between individual cells
cellpadding	The amount of space, in pixels, used to *pad* data elements from the walls of the cell
rules	Determines where lines are drawn between cells (none, groups, rows, cols, or all)
frames	Determines where lines are around the table (above, below, hsides, lhs, rhs, vsides, box, or border)

Tables can also accept an `align` attribute, but it isn't strict XHTML. The `align` attribute accepts `right` or `left` to cause the table to float on the page (text wraps around it).

Example:

```
<table border="1" cellpadding="5" cellspacing="5" width="50%">
</table>
```

The `<table>` element can accept another attribute, called `summary`, which is useful for non-graphical and assistive Web browsers.

Example:

```
<table summary="This table shows that sales in the Western region were 500
in spring and 600 in summer; sales in the Northern region were 300 in
spring and 400 in summer and sales in the Southern region were 200 in
spring and 650 in summer.">
```

Inside the `<table>` container, you can add the `<caption>` element, which is used to contain the text and markup for the table's caption.

Example:

```
<table>
<caption><b>Sales (in thousands) for Spring and Summer
➥Quarters</b></caption>
</table>
```

Inside the `<table>` definition, you use the `<tr>` container to create rows, the `<th>` container to create heading cells, and the `<td>` container to create data cells.

Example:

```
<table>
<caption><b>Sales (in thousands) for Spring and Summer
➥Quarters</b></caption>
<tr><th>Quarter</th><th>West</th><th>North</th><th>South</th></tr>
<tr><th>Spring</th><td>500</td><td>300</td><td>200</td></tr>
<tr><th>Summer</th><td>600</td><td>400</td><td>650</td></tr>
</table>
```

Both table rows and cells can accept the attributes `valign` and `align`. The `valign` attribute is used to vertically align the data with the cell, with values of `top`, `middle`, and `bottom`. The `align` attribute aligns elements horizontally with the `left`, `center`, and `right` values. If you use the values with the `<tr>` element, then using different values with the `<th>` or `<td>` element will override the settings for the `<tr>` element.

Example:

```
<table border="1">
<tr valign="top">
<td><img src="image1.gif"</td>
<td valign="bottom"><img src="image2.gif"></td>
<td><img src="image3.gif"></td>
</tr>
</table>
```

Table data and heading cells can accept the `rowspan` or `colspan` attributes to cause that cell to take up more than one row or cell when necessary.

Example:

```
<table>
<tr><th>Student</th><th colspan="2">Test Scores</th></tr>
<tr><td>Mike</td><td>100</td><td>90</td></tr>
<tr><td>Sarah</td><td>85</td><td>100</td></tr>
<tr><td>Susan</td><td colspan="2">95</td></tr>
</table>
```

Note

Rows and individual cells can use the `bgcolor` attribute to accept a color name or color hexadecimal value (such as #FFFFFF for white), but only under a transitional DTD because this attribute has been dropped in strict XHTML.

In addition to these elements, tables can include a few others: `<thead>`, `<tbody>`, and `<tfoot>`. These elements are particularly useful when used with a Web browser that recognizes them and is able to scroll the body (`<tbody>`) of the table independently of the header (`<thead>`) and footer (`<tfoot>`). The XHTML specification recommends that `<tfoot>` come immediately after the `<thead>` element, so that browsers can render them correctly. (Note that doing so will occasionally cause the footer's contents to appear out of order with the rest of the table in earlier browsers.)

Example:

```
<table>
<thead>
    rows of data in the header
</thead>
<tfoot>
    rows of data in the footer
</tfoot>
<tbody>
    rows of data in the body
</tbody>
</table>
```

Creating Framesets

Using the `<frameset>` and `<frame>` elements, you can create a browser window that has different HTML documents loaded into different portions of the interface. You can then use the `target` attribute to load new URLs into the various frames.

To begin a frameset document, you need to use the frameset DTD at the top of the page, followed by the `<frameset>` element, which acts much like the `<body>` element in non-frameset documents. The `<frameset>` element can accept two attributes: `rows` and `cols`. With each `<frameset>` element, you define either rows or columns; if you need one within the other, you'll use multiple framesets. The `rows` and `cols` attributes can accept pixels, percentages, or the * sign, which means "the rest of the window."

Example:

```
<!DOCTYPE html PUBLIC "-//W3C//DTD XHTML 1.0 Frameset/EN"
"http://www.w3.org/TR/xhtml1/DTD/frameset.dtd">
<html xmlns="http://www.w3.org/1999/xhtml">
<head>
<title>Frameset</title>
</head>
```

```
<frameset cols="150, *">
</frameset>
</html>
```

Within each frameset, you'll use the `<frame>` element and the `<noframe>` element. You should have as many `<frame>` elements as you've defined columns or rows in the `<frameset>` element (unless you're nesting framesets, as is discussed in a moment). You should have one `<noframes>` element per page, used for browsers that don't recognize frameset markup.

The `<frame>` element accepts a `src` attribute that specifies the URL for the default page for this frame. Optionally, the `<frame>` element can accept an `id` attribute, which is used to give the frame a target name.

 Note While the `id` attribute is appropriate for XHTML compliance, you should also include the `name` attribute for backward compatibility with earlier browsers.

The `<noframes>` element contains text and markup that you want to display in browsers that don't support frameset markup.

Example:
```
<frameset cols="150, *">
<frame src="index.html" />
<frame src="viewer.html" name="main_viewer" id="main_viewer" />
<noframes>
<p>If your browser doesn't support frames, you can access the
<a href="/articles/index.html">article index</a> directly.</p>

</noframes>
</frameset>
```

The `<frames>` element can accept a number of optional attributes:

`noresize="noresize"`	Size of frame cannot be changed by users
`frameborder`	Accepts either a 1 or a 0 (as in `frameborder="1"`); a 1 means that the frame has a border, while a 0 means it does not
`scrolling`	Can accept `yes`, `no`, or `auto` as values that enable you to decide whether or not a particular display has scroll bars
`marginwidth`	Changes the left and right margins of the frame, in pixels
`marginheight`	Changes the top and bottom margins of the frame, in pixels

longdesc Used to include a link to an HTML document (via URL) that describes the contents of the frame; this is ideal for assistive browsers

You may also want to nest `<frameset>` definitions, particularly if you need to have two rows appear within a column, or something along those lines. You do that by replacing one of the `<frame>` elements with a second `<frameset>` element.

Example:

```
<frameset rows="150, *">
   <frame src="topbanner.html" />
   <frameset cols="25%, 75%">
      <frame src="leftcol.html" name="left_col" id="left_col" />
      <frame src="default.html" name="viewer" id="viewer" />
   </frameset>
</frameset>
```

As mentioned earlier in this appendix, frames are used in conjunction with the `target` attribute for the `<a>` element (and other elements that accept URLs) to cause a page to load in a particular named frame. For instance, in the preceding example, a link in the `leftcol.html` document might look like

```
<a href="newpage.html" target="viewer">Click to see the new page</a>
```

This would cause the document `newpage.html` to appear in the frame labeled `viewer`.

Creating Forms

Using the XHTML forms elements, you can create pages that interact with your user, responding to typed information, menu choices, checkbox choices, and button clicks. This data can then be sent to a server-side script for processing, sent via e-mail, or processed "client-side" using JavaScript or a similar scripting language.

The `<form>` Element

The main element of the forms specification is the `<form>` container, which accepts the attributes `method` and `action`. The `method` attribute accepts either `get` or `post` as its value. The `get` method causes the data from the form to be appended to the URL for the data's destination. The `post` method sends the data separately, without any practical limit on the amount of data that can be transferred.

The second attribute is `action`, which simply accepts the URL for the script that will process the data from your form. Most often the script is stored in a directory called `bin` or `cgi-bin`, located on your Web server.

Example:

```
<form method="post" action="http://www.fakecom.net/cgi-bin/survey.pl">
</form>
```

Aside from the two basic attributes, the `<form>` element can accept a few others:

enctype	Accepts a MIME type entry that specifies the type of content that will be submitted
name and id	Used to identify the form for either scripting or style sheets (id is XHTML-compliant; name is recommended for backward compatibility)
accept	Used to specify, in a comma-separated list, the types of files that the server can handle correctly, using MIME names
accept-charset	Used to specify the character encodings that the server is prepared to accept when processing the form's data

`<textarea>`

The `<textarea>` element enables you to accept multiple lines of text from a user. This element is a container that wraps around the default text you'd like to have in the area. It accepts the `rows` and `cols` attributes to specify the size of the text area, as well as the `name` attribute, which is used to give it a unique identifier for scripting.

Example:

```
<textarea name="comments" rows="4" cols="40">
Enter your comments about our Web site.
Include your e-mail address if you'd like a response.
</textarea>
```

The `<textarea>` element can accept the `readonly` attribute, making the area so that it can't be edited.

The `<input />` Element

The `<input />` element accepts a `type` attribute that is used to determine the type of input control that will be created. Possible values for the `type` attribute include the following:

text	Creates a short text entry box for typed input
password	Like text, but letters are shown as asterisks when typed

checkbox	Creates a checkbox interface that can be clicked on or off
radio	Creates a radio button interface, where only one of many options can be selected
hidden	Creates a hidden field whose value can't be altered by the user
reset	Creates a reset button to clear the form of its current input
submit	Creates a Submit button for sending the form to the URL specified in the action attribute of the `<form>` element

The `<input />` element also accepts the name attribute, which is used to give it a unique identifier, and the value attribute, which is used to set a default value (used for the text on Submit and Reset buttons) for the input element.

Tip

For text and password types, the `<input />` element can also accept the size attribute (for the size of the box) and the maxlength attribute (for the maximum number of typed characters).

Example:

```
<form method="post" action="cgi-bin/form.pl">
<pre>
Name: <input type="text" name="name" length="40" />
Check the prizes you'd like:
<input type="checkbox" name="car" />New car
<input type="checkbox" name="cash" />Cash
<input type="checkbox" name="land" />Real Estate
Do you want us to contact you about subscriptions:
<input type="radio" name="subs" value="yes" checked="checked" />Yes
<input type="radio" name="subs" value="no" />No
<hr>
<input type="submit" value="Submit Form" />
<input type="reset" value="Reset Form" />
</pre>
</form>
```

Notice that checkbox elements all have different name attribute values, while radio buttons that are grouped have the same name attribute. Also note the checked attribute, which can be used on either radio button or checkbox elements to determine that they're selected by default.

The `<select>` Element

The `<select>` element is used to create pop-up and scrolling menus. It requires a `name` attribute and allows you to decide how many options to display at once with the `size` attribute. The `<select>` element is a container. Each `<option>` element, representing a menu option, is placed between `<select>` and `</select>`, and each `<option>` element can have an initial value. When one of those options is chosen, it gets assigned to the name that's specified in the opening `<select>` tag. The attribute `selected="selected"` sets the default value in a given list.

Example:

```
Choose your hobby:
<select name="hobby">
<option selected="selected">Golf</option>
<option>Jogging</option>
<option>Web Publishing</option>
<option>Cooking</option>
</select>
```

You can also use the `size` attribute of `<select>` to display the menu as a scrolling menu instead of as a pop-up menu. Another attribute of the `<select>` element, `multiple="multiple"`, allows the user to select more than one option from the menu.

Finally, you can create groupings of options within a `<select>` element using the `<optgroup>` element. The `<optgroup>` element accepts a `label` attribute that can be used to label groups within a `<select>` control. The `<optgroup>` elements are used by some browsers to arrange a `<select>` control.

Example:

```
<p>Choose your hobby :</p>
<select name="hobby" size="15" multiple="multiple">
<option value="none" selected="selected">None</option>
<optgroup label="Indoor">
<option>Cooking</option>
<option>Computing</option>
<option>Arts&Crafts</option>
</optgroup>
<optgroup label="Outdoor">
<option>Travel</option>
<option>Hiking</option>
<option>Biking</option>
</optgroup>
```

```
<optgroup label="Sports">
<option>Golf</option>
<option>Basketball</option>
<option>Swimming</option>
</optgroup>
</select>
```

CSS

In this section, I've reproduced some of the tables in Chapter 10, "Get Splashy: Style Sheets, Fonts, and Special Characters," and Chapter 14, "Site-Wide Styles: Design, Accessibility, and Internationalization," that discuss CSS styles. Text style properties are shown in Table A.1.

TABLE A.1 CSS Text-Style Properties

Property	Value	Example(s)
word-spacing	Number and units	1pt, 4em, 1in
letter-spacing	Number and units	3pt, 0.1em, +1
line-height	Number and units	24pt, 20px
text-decoration	Value	underline, line-through, box, blink
text-transform	Value	capitalize, lowercase, uppercase, none
text-indent	Number and units or percentage	1in, 5%, 3em
vertical-align	Value or percentage	baseline, sup, sub, top, middle, 50%
text-align	Value	left, right, center, justify

Table A.2 shows the font style properties used to alter the font choice and appearance of text.

TABLE A.2 CSS Font Properties

Property	Value	Example(s)
font-family	Name of font	Helvetica, Serif, Symbol
font-size	Number/percentage	12pt, +1, 120%
font-weight	Number/strength	normal, bold, bolder, 100, 900
font-style	Name of style	italic, oblique, normal
font-variant	Name of style	normal, small-caps
font	Combination	12pt Serif medium small-caps
color	Word/hex number	Red, green, blue, #FF00FF

Table A.3 shows the background properties you can use to create boxes or blocks of patterns or colors.

TABLE A.3   CSS Background Properties

Property	Value	Example(s)
background-color	Color name of RGB value	white, #0000FF
background-image	url( )	url(image.gif),url(http://www.fakecorp.net/bgnd.jpg)
background-repeat	Word value	repeat, repeat-x, repeat-y, no-repeat
background-attachment	word value	scroll, fixed
background-position	Direction or percentage	top, left center, 20% 65%
background	Combination	white url (image.gif) repeat-x fixed

Table A.4 shows the block-level styles for altering block-level elements such as paragraphs.

TABLE A.4   CSS Block Appearance Properties

Property	Value	Example(s)
margin	Length or percentage	1in, 5% 10%, 12pt 10pt, 12pt 10pt
padding	Length or percentage	1in, 5% 10%, 12pt 10pt, 12pt 10pt
border	Width/style/color	Medium dashed red, 2in grooved, blue
width	Length/percentage	.5in, 10%
height	Length/percentage	10em, 12pt
float	Direction	left, right, none
clear	Direction	none, left, right, both

Table A.5 shows the pseudo classes for creating mouseover effects using CSS.

TABLE A.5   Pseudo Classes

Property	Explanation
:link	Properties of the hyperlink before it's clicked
:visited	Properties of the hyperlink after it's clicked
:hover	Properties of the link or object while the mouse pointer is over it

TABLE A.5   (continued)

Property	Explanation
:focus	Properties of the link or object while text is being entered or it's selected via the keyboard
:active	Properties of the link or object while it's being selected (that is, while the mouse button is down or the Enter key is pressed)

Table A.6 shows the aural properties of CSS, used to direct assistive browsers that speak the text of your site aloud.

TABLE A.6   CSS2 Aural Properties

Property	Values	Description
azimuth	left, center-left, center, center-right, right or an angle value (–360 to 360)	Enables you to specify the angle from which a sound seems to be coming
cue-after	url(sound_file_url)	Plays the sound file at the specified URL after reading the attached content (example: url(sound.af))
cue-before	url(sound_file_url)	Plays the specified sound file before reading the specified content
elevation	below, level, above, angle value (–90 to 90)	Enables you to specify the angle of a sound above or below the listener
pause-after	Seconds or milliseconds	Pauses for a certain number of seconds after the element is spoken
pause-before	Seconds or milliseconds	Pauses for a certain number of seconds before the element is spoken
pause	Seconds or milliseconds	Pauses before and after the element is spoken
pitch	low, medium, high, number (Hertz)	Chooses the pitch, or frequency, of the spoken text
pitch-range	0, 50 or any number	The inflection of the spoken text; 0 is monotone, 50 is normal
play-during	url(sound_file_url)	Plays a sound file while the text of the element is being read
speak	none, normal, spell-out	Sets how the element's text is spoken
speak-numeral	digits, continuous	Sets whether numbers are read as digits ("1-2-3-4") or words ("one thousand, two hundred and thirty four")

TABLE A.6   (continued)

Property	Values	Description
speak-punctuation	none, code	If it's "code", then punctuation is read aloud, as in "period" and "exclamation point"
speech-rate	slow, medium, fast, number	Sets how quickly text is read; if it's a number, the number represents words per minute
voice-family	male, female, child, Zervox	Specifies the name of the voice to be used for speech (similar to font families, the voice must be installed on the user's computer)
volume	silent, soft, medium, loud	Sets the volume of the spoken text

Index